Music Theory and Composition

Music Theory and Composition

A Practical Approach

STEPHEN C. STONE

ROWMAN & LITTLEFIELD

Lanham • Boulder • New York • London

Published by Rowman & Littlefield
A wholly owned subsidiary of The Rowman & Littlefield Publishing Group, Inc.
4501 Forbes Boulevard, Suite 200, Lanham, Maryland 20706
www.rowman.com

Unit A, Whitacre Mews, 26-34 Stannary Street, London SE11 4AB

British Library Cataloguing in Publication Information Available

Library of Congress Cataloging-in-Publication Data
Name: Stone, Stephen C., 1969–, author.
Title: Music theory and composition : a practical approach / Stephen C. Stone.
Description: Lanham : Rowman & Littlefield, [2018] | Includes index.
Identifiers: LCCN 2017034990 (print) | LCCN 2017035148 (ebook) |
    ISBN 9781538101247 (electronic) | ISBN 9781538101223 (hardcover :
    alk. paper) | ISBN 9781538101230 (pbk. : alk. paper)
Subjects: LCSH: Composition (Music) | Music theory. | Popular music—Writing
    and publishing.
Classification: LCC MT6.S7868 (ebook) | LCC MT6.S7868 M87 2018 (print) |
    DDC 781—dc23
LC record available at https://lccn.loc.gov/2017034990

Printed in the United States of America

CONTENTS

PART V: POPULAR MUSIC

APPENDIXES

THE BASIC PREMISE OF THIS BOOK

This book started from the same place that, I suspect, every music theory book begins: theory so often comes across as a set of rules, ones that seem irrelevant to the student's own performance or composition. When I was an undergraduate, music theory began with harmony, and the explanation for voice leading was, "Composers have avoided parallel fifths, so you should too."

In the years between my undergraduate and graduate programs, I worked my way through, among other books, J. Frederick Bridge's *Counterpoint*, which I found at a public library book sale. Although my goal was to practice and improve my composition, I was struck by something else: in doing the species counterpoint exercises, the rules of harmony and voice leading now made sense. Topics such as the role of perfect consonances or the instability of second-inversion chords had a context and reason. What had been missing in my earlier studies was the "why." Counterpoint provided it.

I was not alone in this epiphany. About a decade later, theory textbooks began to incorporate counterpoint. First, appendices appeared. Now many textbooks include a chapter before moving into harmony. In talking with grad students, I heard about numerous undergraduate curricula that focused on species counterpoint for the first semester and then harmony for the second. When I asked them what textbook they used, they always replied either, "We used two different ones," or "We used handouts from my professor for the species."

This book contains counterpoint and harmony together, both thoroughly covered. It begins with the most basic building block of a musical work, the melody, works through species counterpoint exercises, and then transitions into harmony. It provides a continuity in which the various elements build logically and in which later harmonic details can be fleshed out with their contrapuntal underpinning. As one of my students said, "Once you master the counterpoint, the harmony pops right out!"

In this way, I hope that students can appreciate both the big picture and the details of common-practice music theory. I have not managed to remove all rules

from the textbook. Every time I stipulate a theoretical restriction, however, I give an explanation for how it fits into the larger aesthetic ideal of the composers. It is not "a rule because that is what composers did"; rather, it is "a guideline because there are a few stylistic ideals, and it reinforces these ideals by doing this."

BUT THERE'S A HUGE POP SECTION

Although this book was first intended to serve as a text for classical music theory classes, approximately a fifth of it is on pop songs. I originally included the occasional pop example, like many authors do. Students may better understand a concept if they tie it to a piece of music they know well. Many of them have played Hoagy Carmichael's "Heart and Soul" as a duet, so why not use it to illustrate the submediant's role connecting tonic to pre-dominant?

I have reservations with this approach though. Courses called "Music Theory" generally mean "Classical Music Theory." When we use a pop example to illustrate classical theory, we are saying, "Here is a song that happens to follow classical norms." What we leave unsaid is that there are millions of pop songs that do not follow these conventions. Pop has its own, different set of stylistic traits. I remember sitting in my dorm room years ago, playing a pop song on the guitar, thinking, "He wrote a retrogression. He didn't know what he was doing." When I started teaching, students would say, "But the progression sounds fine; I don't know why you are saying it's wrong." Without an understanding that we are talking about a particular genre of music, the generalizations are meaningless, and we return to theory as a set of pointless rules.

I see two possible ways that simultaneously presenting multiple genres plays out. First is what usually happens. A textbook includes popular music examples, but teaches common-practice harmony and voice leading. I find this disingenuous, as well as patronizing to pop music. The other option is to give equal time to both genres, in which case the text will read, "A seventh will resolve down, but may not. You should avoid parallel fifths, but you don't have to. Pre-dominants lead to dominants, unless the dominant leads to the pre-dominant."

I agree that music programs need to be more inclusive, and I appreciate that many students are not versed in classical music. I decided to include an appendix on popular song. By separating it from classical music, it would clarify that conventions change with the genre. Through comparison and contrast, it would reinforce the general traits of each idiom. The appendix grew until I realized that I was treating pop the same way other authors were treating species. Why dedicate just a chapter to the subject? Go all the way.

The pop section now contains thirteen chapters. It assumes that the student has read the material on common-practice music since it presents pop through comparison with classical. It addresses harmonic function since that is the main focus of this textbook. I suspect that students will read these chapters on their own, but professors can also incorporate these chapters into their curriculum. Chapters 44 and 48 provide pop examples of common-practice functions. The section as a whole could serve as a final unit to a core undergraduate curriculum. Or with explanations about phrase structure, form, and lyrics, plus a few supplemental journal articles, this book could serve as the text for an upper-level elective on pop.

In the pop section, since the songs are still under copyright, I generally use short fragments, and I avoid lyrics. In the interest of variety and practicing different skills, I switch between lead sheet and piano notations. Since chord progressions are not eligible for copyright protection, when I wish to discuss the harmony in a longer passage, I revert to a grand staff with four voices, SATB.

HOW TO USE THIS TEXTBOOK

This book is flexible! I appreciate that different schools have different timelines, curricula, and students. I myself teach on two campuses within Johns Hopkins, and I do not teach the same way in both places. I have tried to make this book adaptable. I have made accommodations for what I think will be the most common variants of incorporating counterpoint into first- and second-year music theory. Sample curricula for these suggestions are included in the "Instructor's Manual," available from Rowman & Littlefield.

1. As written—This is the way I teach at the Peabody Conservatory. We work through all species in two and three voices. I let the students explore their own interval and chord choices before introducing figured bass and moving to functionality.

2. Skip three-voice counterpoint—This is the way I teach at the Arts and Sciences campus. We work through the two-voice exercises to establish the role of counterpoint. Then we move directly to four-voice realizations of figured bass, making the two-voice exercises the basis for the outer voices. To accommodate this approach, I have included "Chapter 12–15 Redux," a summary of the main points in Chapters 12–15, which cover three-voice counterpoint.

3. As written with figured bass—I have some colleagues who do not like species counterpoint since it allows the students to work with nonfunctional progressions. In order to address this concern, I am including figured basses with the cantus firmi in Appendix B. I personally would still teach two voices without it, focusing purely on intervals, and then teach Chapter 17 before Chapter 12, but some may choose otherwise.

4. With figured bass skipping three-voice counterpoint—Chapters 11 and 17 could be taught immediately following Chapter 4. Two-voice exercises could then be done by giving students a figured bass, over which they must write the best soprano melody that they can for each species. This could then be expanded to four voices, as in option 2 above. This is the way I teach my graduate review course.

5. Incorporate species counterpoint with fundamentals—Frequently, fundamentals are taught in a drill-intensive way, in order to produce the fluency necessary for later concepts. This book's chapters on melody and species incorporate many rudimentary concepts, not to teach them but to give them a musical context. Teachers can use these points of overlap to increase the musicianship of their fundamentals classes while simultaneously introducing voice leading earlier. After teaching scales and key signatures, the chapters on melody could be taught, and those compositional exercises incorporated into the class. Two-voice species would follow interval drills, and three-voice follows chords. The class culminates with figured bass and four-voice chorale style.

6. Do species exercises and compositions for a semester—This approach probably is not feasible in a college curriculum. It would, however, work well for students doing individual study or at a preparatory or a high school for the arts, where the curriculum can be paced more slowly. After a semester of fundamentals, students could have a semester of part writing, which would include four-voice species, chorale style, and figured bass without addressing harmonic function. Students would master voice leading completely, meaning that the units on harmony could move very quickly, focusing almost exclusively on function.

I appreciate that many people feel that species counterpoint is unmusical. To be honest, I do not disagree with that. Two factors, however, make me use it. First, it is a good tool for gradually introducing the concepts. Since each species focuses on one aesthetic principle—establishing voice-leading guidelines or handling a particular dissonance—it allows a systematic presentation of the musical ideas. Pedagogically, this is sound. Second, and related to the first, is that it provides a framework to help students with less experience. I have assisted in classes in which professors began with free counterpoint exercises. The students who had a significant amount of music theory before were fine, but those coming from a different genre quickly became overwhelmed. Their exercises were unstylistic because they had not worked enough in the idiom. The tighter constraints of species counterpoint provide the support these students need to acclimate to the different musical language. As for the stronger students, species can challenge at any level. I always tell the more experienced ones that they should make as musical an exercise as they can, despite the artificial limitations.

Because of its artificiality, though, species counterpoint can quickly revert to a bunch of rules. When colleagues start to use this book, I tell them two things. First, sing! To internalize the music principles, students must be vocalizing. For every exercise worked out on the board, the class should sing each melody, and then the group should be subdivided to sing the entire piece. Students need to feel that an interval is awkward, that a leading tone is left unresolved, or that a line feels natural. Professors should model how the students will approach their homework. Second, be up-front that species counterpoint is a tool, not an end goal. Just like we all take spelling tests and diagram sentences to help us learn how to write well, species counterpoint is a pedagogical approach to teach the concepts and aesthetic ideals of common-practice music. Once those are internalized and the students have a solid foundation, the training wheels can be removed.

ANCILLARY MATERIALS FOR STUDENTS AND INSTRUCTORS

Workbook Sections

The workbook sections at the end of each chapter may be downloaded as PDFs from textbooks.rowman.com. Students may print these PDFs as extra copies if they prefer not to tear out pages from their books.

Instructor's Manual

Access sample syllabi and handouts under the Resources tab at www.rowman.com/ISBN/9781538101230.

Answer Key and Tests

Instructors may request workbook section answers and sample test materials by emailing textbooks@rowman.com with the details of their course.

GROUND RULES FOR STUDYING INTRODUCTORY THEORY

When many students begin to study music theory, they are bewildered by the presence of so many "rules" of what is or is not allowed in music. Composers just write what they hear, don't they? Students also often do not understand why something sounds "bad" according to the teacher when, to them, it sounds fine or even interesting.

Three facts must be clarified at the beginning, and students should keep them in the back of their minds throughout the course.

1. The majority of this book, the first thirty-nine chapters, focuses on common-practice Western music. The common-practice period in music is the years 1600–1900. During this period, composers wrote functionally tonal music using the major and minor scales. The bulk of our classical concert music today was written in Western Europe during this time period, but note what a narrow category this is. This course is examining a particular style, written by composers from a handful of adjacent countries, over a three-hundred-year period. This reason is why a passage that sounds fine to you may not be appropriate to the music studied in this course. We are familiar with jazz, rock, world, and other types of music. These topics are outside of this genre. This is in no way a value judgment; it is about being able to make generalizations about the music. In the same way that baseball, basketball, and football are different games even though they all use balls, classical music, jazz, and rock are all different styles despite using the same basic keys and chords.

2. To emphasize this fact, and because I think it will be of general interest, the last 13 chapters discuss harmony in pop songs. By showing how pop differs from common practice, conventions in both genres will become clearer. My basic argument in the last section of the book is that pop music employs a variety of styles, some pulled from earlier styles and some unique to pop. Classical music is more narrowly defined and more codified than pop. As a result, the principles and progressions studied in the first section will still make sense in the second. (This explains why I can occasionally use a pop song to illustrate a common practice technique.) The reverse, however, is not true; rock and roll contains many idiomatic gestures that lie outside the classical style.

3. Music really does not have any "rules." When you talk about a style, however, certain tendencies must recur, otherwise people would not categorize the pieces under a single label. Also, composers do not work in a vacuum. They influence each other, and one generation passes techniques to the next. The "rules" of music theory describe those recurring traits that are most prevalent in Western common-practice music. For every "rule" in this book, you will be able to find exceptions in the classical literature. Statistically speaking, however, common-practice music follows the "rules" almost all of the time, so, in emulating this style, you should adhere to them.

Over time, you will gradually adapt the way you hear to adjust to different styles. It will no longer be a question of a musical gesture being right or wrong, but rather what, by then instinctively, sounds appropriate to a particular genre.

WORKBOOK SECTIONS

This text contains workbook sections at the end of chapters. These same sections are available for download at textbooks.rowman.com if you want to print extra copies.

ACKNOWLEDGMENTS

This book is the result of over a decade of work. My initial realization of the importance of counterpoint in explaining harmony goes back to the mid-1990s, truly twenty years ago. I began writing chapters in 2004, after completing my doctorate and getting a full-time job. Needless to say, after so much time, many people have given input and help on this book.

While a student at Peabody, I had two principal mentors, Eileen Soskin and Thomas Benjamin, who both taught me a great deal about music and teaching and who have been incredibly supportive over the years. The reorganization of the harmonic minor scale so that the tendency tones resolve (Chapter 3) comes from Eileen. Tom has also been incredibly supportive of this textbook, helping me navigate the publishing process, suggesting reviewers, and reading the proposal, despite the fact that it will be competition for his (and Horvit's and Nelson's) excellent book.

I owe a huge debt to Natalie Draper for her contribution to the Preludes section. Armed with a one-page outline, Natalie wrote the first draft of the section, including figures. If it were not for her efforts, the book release would have been delayed, and I am extremely appreciative of her help.

Over the years I have had a number of graduate assistants who have taught with me and given input on this book: Ben Quine, Mark Lackey, Sookkyung Cho, Josh Bornfield, Natalie Draper, and Trey Dayton. I apologize to any of you who may be looking through this book and thinking, "Wait, I wrote that figured bass!"

For the past three years, the professors at the Arts and Sciences campus have been teaching from this text and providing feedback. My thanks go to all of them for this help: Josh Bornfield, Faye Chiao, Sookkyung Cho, John Crouch, Natalie Draper, Travis Hardaway, Mark Janello, and Michael Rickelton. Special thanks go to Travis Hardaway, who suggested many substantial revisions, including reordering the chapters, clarifying the transitions between units, and making musical examples easier to play. Travis also showed me the diagram of summarizing functionality through motion by thirds (Chapter 24).

My Peabody colleagues have also provided support over the years. Mark Janello, continuo player extraordinaire, served as my consultant for all questions regarding the nuances of figured bass. Ian Sims answered my questions on jazz theory. David Smooke recommended the book for use at the Arts and Sciences campus, providing a new set of eyes to look at the text. Sharon Levy and Paul Mathews provided support and encouragement over the years. My office mate, Kip Wile, has endured many questions and conversations whenever I was stuck on a topic or searching for the perfect example. He also included this text in his pedagogy class's textbook review unit, providing critiques from impartial students.

Over the past twelve years, my students have had to work with the book in various stages of completion. My thanks go to them for their helpful comments on student evaluations, ranging from the early "This looks like a promising approach. I hope you write more and make a fantastic book," to the much more recent "Finish the damn book, Dr. Stone." The direction and tone of the book changed every year, as I saw how students reacted to and learned from it.

Finally, I want to thank my family, who was patient throughout the process, allowing me to disappear in the basement for many evenings and afternoons. Alex, although I did not use Offenbach's "Cancan" in here, I appreciate the suggestion. Chloe, "Long, Long Ago" did end up in here, so thank you for the help. Mary Margaret, you have seen the progress of this book from day one. Thank you for your support, faith, and love.

PERMISSIONS

Unless otherwise noted, musical excerpts were taken from public-domain sources. All efforts were made to verify adherence to fair use, and any oversights or errors will be corrected in future editions. Every effort was made to secure permissions for the following materials:

Joey Ramone, Dee Dee Ramone, and Jean Beauvoir, "My Head Is Hanging Upside Down (Bonzo Goes to Bitburg)," © Hal Leonard

David J. Matthews, "Ants Marching," © Hal Leonard

Billy Joel, "A Matter of Trust," © Hal Leonard

Cat Stevens and Rick Wakeman, "Morning Has Broken," © Hal Leonard

Sheldon Harnick and Jerry Bock, "If I Were a Rich Man" from *Fiddler on the Roof*, © Hal Leonard

John Lennon and Paul McCartney, "I'll Be Back" and "The Continuing Story of Bungalow Bill," © Hal Leonard

Frank Loesser, "Luck Be a Lady" from *Guys and Dolls*, © Hal Leonard

The following public-domain sources are used for counterpoint exercises:

Knud Jeppensen, *Counterpoint: The Polyphonic Style of the Sixteenth Century* (Mineola: Dover Publications, 1992) for figures 6.8, 7.10, 9.4, 12.5, and 13.4

J. Frederick Bridge, *Counterpoint* (Boston: Oliver Ditson, 1878) for figures 7.8, 7.9, 8.7, 13.4 and 14.8

Johann Joseph Fux, *Gradus as Parnassum* (Vienna: Johann Peter van Ghelen, 1725) for figures 7.7 and 12.6

RUDIMENTS

Before delving into a full study of music theory and composition in the common-practice period, it is important to have a solid background in the rudiments of music theory. This first section presents fundamental concepts along with a limited number of practice exercises. These drills are intended as a starting point for musical fluency. A list of supplemental websites and resources follows, and I hope that the dedicated student will spend the necessary time to become fluent in the fundamentals of music theory before approaching the later chapters of this text.

RESOURCES FOR MUSIC THEORY FUNDAMENTALS

Many excellent resources exist for teaching and drilling music theory fundamentals. Here are several that will provide many drills with answer keys.

Books

Harder, Paul O., and Greag A. Steinke. *Basic Materials in Music Theory: A Programmed Course with Audio CD.* Upper Saddle River, NJ: Pearson, 2009. ISBN: 0205633935.

Root, Jena. *Applied Music Fundamentals: Writing, Singing, and Listening.* Oxford: Oxford University Press, 2013. ISBN: 0199846774.

Soskin, Eileen. *Rudiments of Music for Music Majors.* Belmont, CA: Schirmer, 2004. ISBN: 0534638287.

Downloadable E-text

Sayrs, Elizabeth. *MFun.* https://www.macgamut.com/products/mfun/aboutMFun.asp.

Websites

Teoría: http://teoria.com/.

MusicTheory.net: https://www.musictheory.net/.

Notation of Sound

Sounds constantly surround us. Some of these sounds are unpitched, like the tapping of your fingertips on the surface of a wooden table or the crinkle of paper as you crumple it into a ball. We cannot match unpitched sounds with a tuned note. Certain unpitched sounds can evoke relative highness or lowness, called relative pitch. For instance, the sound produced by striking a small drum will sound higher than the sound produced by striking a large drum. Other sounds, like the whistle of a teakettle, a car horn, or the struck note of a piano, have a specific highness or lowness to them; these sounds are described as being pitched.

A *pitch* is a sound that has a distinct frequency. Frequency is the number of cycles per second, called hertz (Hz), produced by a resonating body. For example, the note A4, which is the A just above middle C on the piano, is 440 Hz. A tuning fork corresponding to this pitch vibrates back and forth 440 times each second, creating a sound wave with this same frequency. The higher the frequency is, the higher the pitch is. The note A3, which is the A just below middle C on the piano, has a frequency half that of A4—220 Hz.

Instead of using hertz for every pitch, musicians have developed a system called the *musical alphabet*, which uses letter names to represent distinct pitches. The musical alphabet spans only seven letters, A through G, before the letter names are reused. This system emphasizes *octave equivalence*, a particular relationship between the name and the frequency.

When we begin on a pitch and move up the scale eight letters, returning to the same name as the first pitch, the frequency doubles. For example, the notes labeled "A" have the following frequencies: A1 (55 Hz), A2 (110 Hz), A3 (220 Hz), A4 (440 Hz), A5 (880 Hz), A6 (1760 Hz), A7 (3520 Hz), and so on. Because of this relationship, we hear the second pitch as a higher version of the first. The two also blend together well when sounding simultaneously. All notes that share a letter name display octave equivalence and are said to be part of the same *pitch class*.

Musicians also developed a notational device called the *staff* that creates a visual depiction of the relative highness and lowness of sounds. The staff is made up of five lines, with each line and space representing a letter name in the musical alphabet. A *clef*, which is a symbol found at the very beginning of the staff, creates a specific point of reference for the pitches (figure P1.1). The *treble clef*, also sometimes called a G clef, has an inner spiral circling around the second line from the bottom of the staff; this line is G, which then determines all of the other pitches on that staff. For example, the space above the G line is A and the space below the G line is F. The letter names ascend up from G by following the musical alphabet (G, A, B, C, D, E, F, G, A, B, etc.). The *bass clef*, also referred to as an F clef, has two dots that surround the second line from the top of the staff, which is an F. The space above the F line is G and the space below the F line is E. The C clef has two curls which meet and point to middle C. Historically, all of these clefs could be moved vertically on the staff—for instance, a musician could decide which line of the staff was G and move the treble clef accordingly. Over time, however, the treble and bass clefs have settled into their typical formation, as explained above. Although the C clef still moves, the only two common positions for it today are the alto clef, where middle C corresponds to the middle line, and the tenor clef, where middle C is the second line from the top.

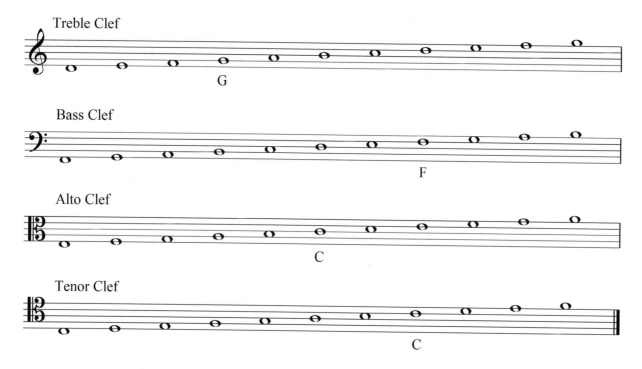

Figure P1.1 The common clefs

Often composers will present sounds on a *grand staff*, which is a formation that binds a treble clef staff to a bass clef staff. Grand staves are used to notate compositions requiring multiple voices or hands, such as piano music. They also make it easier to write simultaneous notes that differ significantly in pitch.

In figure P1.2, some of the notes go above or below the staff. These pitches use *ledger lines*, which extend the range of the staff upward or downward, as needed. The note one ledger line above the bass clef staff and the note one ledger line below the treble clef staff both correspond to middle C. In the first measure of the Boulanger *Improvisation*, middle C appears twice, once in the left hand and once in the right.

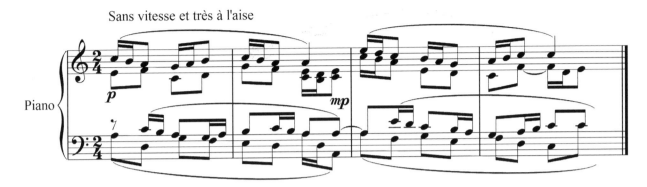

Figure P1.2 Boulanger, "Petit Canon" from *Troi Improvisations* ("Little Canon" from *Three Improvisations*)

In order to understand and to visualize pitch, it is helpful to become familiar with the piano keyboard (figure P1.3). The keyboard has 88 keys and a specific combination of white and black keys. The white keys on the piano represent the musical alphabet discussed above. After moving up eight white keys, we reach the octave and return to our first pitch's letter.

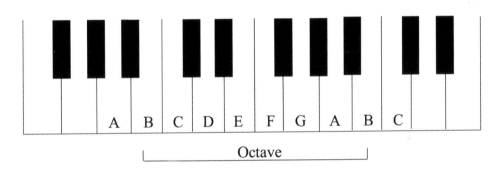

Figure P1.3 Piano keyboard

When the black keys are included, however, the octave divides into 12 equal *half steps*. Half steps are the smallest distance between two notes in common-practice music. They naturally occur between letter names B and C and between letter names E and F. Every other adjacent step between white keys is a *whole step*. In both whole- and half-step relationships, the two pitches sound like they are right next to each other, which is why each one is called a "step." Technically, however, a whole step is made up of two half steps and a half step carries more tension than a whole step. The black keys on the piano fill out the octave, allowing, along with the white keys, for these 12 equal steps and creating what is called the *chromatic scale*—a succession of pitches made up entirely of half-step relationships.

The specific names for the black keys on the piano are relative to their neighboring white keys. For example, the note between C and D can be referred to as either C♯ or D♭, depending on the context of the music. *Accidentals* are symbols that alter the sound of a letter-named pitch. A *sharp* symbol (♯) raises a pitch by a half step. A *flat* symbol (♭) lowers a pitch by a half step. A *natural* sign (♮) will lower a pitch that is already sharp or will raise a pitch that is already flat. For instance, an F-natural played after an F-sharp sounds a half step lower than that F-sharp. A B-natural, however, is a half step higher than a B-flat.

Music also makes use of *double sharps* (x), which raise a note by two half steps. Similarly, *double flats* (♭♭) lower a pitch by two half steps. Double sharps and flats may seem unnecessary at this stage, but they become important when we get to our discussion of keys, intervals, and chords.

Accidentals allow for a variety of ways to notate the same sound. Because C♯ sounds the same as D♭, these two written pitches are said to be *enharmonically* equivalent. See if you can come up with two alternate enharmonic spellings for each of the pitches in figure P1.4. (The first set of two pitches that sound like C is given as an example.)[1]

Figure P1.4 Enharmonic pitches

DURATION

At this point we know how to notate pitch. Another fundamental feature of sound is its *duration*. Some sound events are long; others are short. Musicians have established a notational system to represent the duration of both sound events (notes) and silence (rests). This system uses different representations of the *notehead, stem,* and *flags/beaming*.

This system builds upon successive 2:1 ratios. (See figure P1.5.) A *whole note* has no stem and is drawn as a hollow oval. A *half note* is half the duration of the whole note and is drawn as a hollow oval with a stem. A *quarter note*, which lasts for a quarter of the value of the whole note (or half the value of the half note), has a stem and a darkened oval. An *eighth note* is an eighth of a whole note (or half of a quarter note); an eighth note not only has a stem and a darkened oval, but it also has a flag. Flags may be beamed together when eighth notes appear in a group of two or more. (Beaming will be explained in more detail in Prelude 2). A *sixteenth note* looks similar to an eighth note but with two flags/beams, and it lasts half as long. This pattern continues indefinitely, adding another flag for each halving of the preceding value. There are equivalent symbols for rests of the same duration.

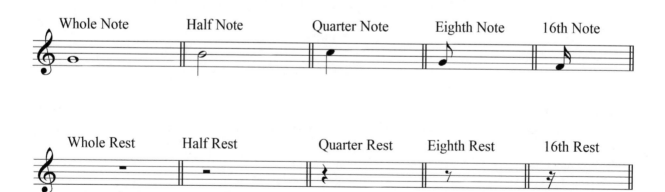

Figure P1.5 Durational notation

Ties and *dotted notes*, also shown in figure P1.5, allow for a wider range of note durations. A tie combines the duration of two note values. For instance, a whole note tied to a quarter note will last for 1.25 times the value of the whole note. A dot next to a notehead adds half the value of the note to its duration. In other words, a dotted quarter note will last for a duration equal to both a quarter note and an eighth note combined. You can have dotted rests, but you cannot have tied rests.

These values are all relative. The exact duration of a whole note will be determined by the tempo, or speed, of a piece. Meter, which is the way durations are organized in time, will be discussed in detail in Prelude 2.

At this point, it is helpful to offer a brief note about stem direction. For individual notes that are on the middle line of a staff, the stem always goes down and is on the left side of the notehead. Notes that appear anywhere above this line also have left-sided, downward facing stems (figure P1.6a). Notes that fall below the middle line have stems on the right side of the notehead, with the stem pointing up (figure P1.6b). The stem direction of groups of notes that are beamed together tends to adopt the rule of the majority of the notes. (figure P1.6c). Flags always appear to the right of the stem, regardless of if it points up or down (figure P1.6d).

Figure P1.6 Stem direction

SUMMARY

Terminology

Pitch. A tone with a distinct frequency.

Musical alphabet. The letters used as note names. Runs from A to G and then repeats.

Octave equivalence. Pitches an octave apart sound similar and behave the same way in tonal music.

Pitch class. The group of pitches that are the same when using octave equivalence. All pitches with the same note name, regardless of octave.

Staff. Five parallel lines used to indicate pitch.

Clef. A symbol used at the beginning of a staff to indicate the staff's location in pitch space. The clef indicates where a particular pitch is located on that staff.

Grand staff. A treble staff and bass staff joined together.

Ledger lines. Lines drawn through, above, or below notes that are above or below a staff. They extend the staff's range past the five lines.

Half step. The smallest distance between two notes in common-practice music.

Whole step. Made of two half steps. The second smallest interval in common-practice music; pitches separated by a whole step may still be perceived as adjacent.

Accidental. A symbol that changes a pitch, moving it up or down a half step (sharps, flats, and naturals) or a whole step (double flats and double sharps).

Enharmonic. Describes two notes that sound the same but have different spellings, e.g., C♯ and D♭.

Tie. A symbol that stretches between two notes, indicating that their durations are combined.

Dotted note. A note with 50 percent added to its durational value. A dotted note sustains 1.5 times the duration of the same note undotted.

Musical pitches are assigned letter names that run from A to G.

Pitches with the same note name sound similar to our ears and behave similarly in music, regardless of which octave they are in.

Pitches are represented on a five-line staff. Clefs indicate a reference pitch to orient the staff in pitch space.

The grand staff consists of a treble-clef staff and bass-clef staff joined together.

Although an octave contains seven different pitch name letters, it consists of twelve half steps. The five pitches that do not have unique letter names, those corresponding to the black keys on the piano, are named relative to their neighboring pitches, using flats and sharps.

A flat lowers a pitch a half step. A sharp raises it a half step.

Enharmonically equivalent pitches have different names but sound the same (E♭ and D♯).

Note durations are indicated through a system of hollow/filled noteheads, stems, and flags.

A tie combines two durations together.

A dot adds 50 percent to the duration of the dotted note.

NOTE

1. Answers: B♭, A♯, C♭♭; F♯, G♭, E♯♯; E, F♭, Dx

WORKBOOK

1. Label all of the pitches in figure P1.1, for all four clefs.

2. Label the following pitches by their letter name and accidental, if applicable. The first one is given as an example.

D♭

3. Find two different enharmonic spellings for each given pitch.

4. Assuming a quarter note gets one count, how many counts should each of the following sound/silence events get? Two are done for you as examples.

3.5 counts   .75 counts

5. Next to the whole note, write an eighth-note version of the pitch. Make sure to use proper stem and flag direction. The first two are done for you as examples.

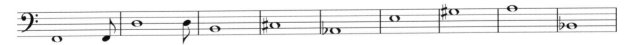

Meter

Broadly, *meter* is the way sound events are organized in time. When you listen to music, you can often discern the *beat*, which is a pulse in the music that recurs at a regular interval. Not all beats are necessarily created equal—it is typical for one beat in a series to be slightly stronger than the others. For example, the music might have an underpinning accent structure as follows:

> Strong Weak Weak Strong Weak Weak Strong Weak Weak Strong Weak Weak

In this example, all of the beats, both strong and weak, occur at a regular interval, with the strong ones recurring every three beats. In order to demonstrate this pattern and in order to make the music easier to read, musicians developed *measures* to separate these beat groupings in a pattern (figure P2.1).

Figure P2.1 Measures separate the units of the repeating accentuation pattern

Three main terms describe the number of beats heard in a measure. *Duple time* indicates that there are two beats per measure. *Triple time* indicates three beats per measure. *Quadruple time* indicates four beats per measure. As seen in figure P2.2, a measure always begins with the strongest beat of the pattern.

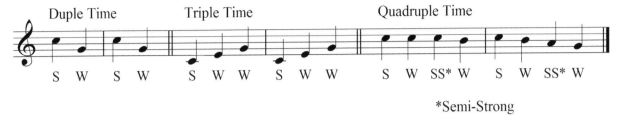

Figure P2.2 Duple, triple, and quadruple beat patterns

You can have more than four beats per measure, but typically the pattern will then be heard as containing subsets of the total number of beats. For example, five beats per measure will usually divide into either a 2 + 3 pattern or a 3 + 2 pattern.

So far we have discussed how multiple beats are grouped into a measure. Beats can also be subdivided in a variety of ways. If the beat is divided into groups of two or four equal-duration notes, the meter is said to be in *simple time*. In simple time, the beat is the *quarter note* (or any proportional equivalent) as it can be subdivided into groups of two eighth notes or four sixteenth notes (or any proportional equivalent). Subdivisions of the beat that are an eighth note or smaller are *beamed* together. Figure P2.3 shows how the beats are beamed into groups of two or four in simple times. When speaking, the + symbol is said as "and."

Figure P2.3 Beaming in simple time

If the beat subdivides into groups of three or six, the meter is said to be in *compound time*. In compound time, the beat is the *dotted quarter note* (or any proportional equivalent), as it can be subdivided into groups of three eighth notes or six sixteenth notes (or any proportional equivalent). Figure P2.4 shows how the beats are grouped into units of three in compound times.

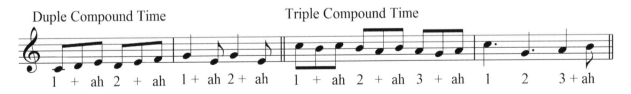

Figure P2.4 Beaming in compound time

A *time signature* is a symbol found at the start of a piece of music to indicate the meter. It includes two numbers stacked vertically. Time signatures indicate how much "temporal space" exists in a measure. For example, the time signature $\frac{4}{4}$ tells you that each measure has the equivalent value of four quarter notes ($4 \times \frac{1}{4}$).[1]

A time signature of $\frac{6}{8}$ tells you that each measure has the equivalent value of six eighth notes ($6 \times \frac{1}{8}$). Sometimes a C symbol will be used instead of two numbers. This C symbol indicates "common time," which is another way of saying $\frac{4}{4}$. If the C symbol has a slash through it, the time signature is "cut time," which is another way of indicating $\frac{2}{2}$ (two beats per measure; half note gets the beat). (See figure P2.5.)

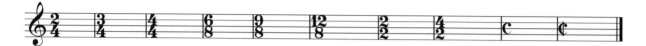

Figure P2.5 Time signatures

Examples of pieces written in the most common *simple* time signatures are featured in figure P2.6. See if you can write in the counts—at least one measure is done for you in each example.

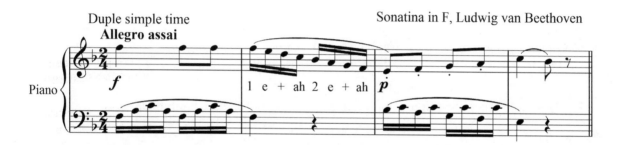

Figure P2.6 Pieces in simple meters

Compound time signatures are also frequently used in common-practice music. Examples of compound time signatures include ⅜, ⅝, and ¹²⁄₈. An example of ⅜ time appears in figure P2.7. While each measure contains six eighth notes in ⅜ time, the eighth notes are presented as two groups of three. In other words there are two beats, with each beat being subdivided into three equal parts: 1 + ah, 2 + ah. *The beat in ⅜ time is the dotted quarter note, not the eighth note.* Again, see if you can write in the counts—one measure is done for you as an example.

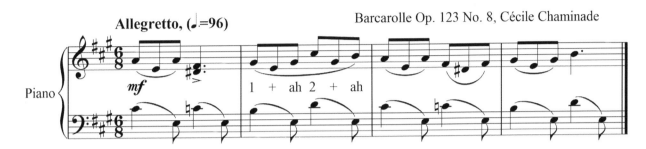

Figure P2.7 A piece in a compound meter

Some people learn that the bottom number of a time signature indicates which note value represents the beat and that the top number indicates the number of beats per measure. This way of reading a time signature only applies to simple time signatures, such as ²⁄₄, ³⁄₄, ⁴⁄₄, and ²⁄₂. Since the beat in ⅜ time is actually the dotted quarter note, interpreting ⅜ as having six beats per measure with the eighth note as the beat is incorrect. It is useful, however, to look to the top number in a time signature to determine the meter. If the top number is a multiple of three (6, 9, 12, etc.), the meter is in compound time, rather than simple time.

When listening to music, it is important to understand the strong and weak parts of musical patterns. The strongest beat occurs at the start of a measure and is called the *downbeat*. The last beat of the measure, a weak beat, is called the *upbeat*. (See figure P2.8.) Quadruple meters actually contain two strong beats (**1** 2 **3** 4), with the third beat being slightly less strong than the downbeat.

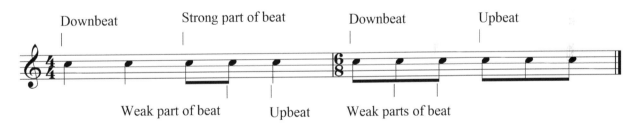

Figure P2.8 Downbeats, upbeats, and subdivisions of the beat

Subdivisions of the beat mirror the accent patterns found in measures, only on a smaller scale (figure P2.8 again). The subdivision that falls at the beginning of the beat is strong, and the rest of the subdivision is weak.

Sometimes music will begin with an incomplete measure—the notes that make up this incomplete measure are called the *pick-up* or the *anacrusis* (figure P2.9).

The same music can be written in any proportionally equivalent meter. For example, a melody that is in duple simple time could be written with the quarter note as the beat or with the eighth note as the beat. These two melodies will sound exactly the same, assuming that the beat occurs at the same *tempo*, or speed. In other words, in figure P2.10, if the first version with the quarter note as the beat has a tempo of 72 bpm (beats per minute) and the second version with the eighth note as the beat has a tempo of 72 bpm, the music will sound exactly the same.

Figure P2.9 Anacrusis (pick-up)

Figure P2.10 Proportionally equivalent meters

It is often the tendency to see smaller note values and assume a faster tempo; however, this is simply not the case. What determines the tempo of a piece is the rate at which the beats recur, not what note value gets the beat.

One final pitfall that often plagues students studying meter is the issue of *beaming*. Musicians beam shorter note values together in order to clarify the meter. Composers will beam a measure of six eighth notes differently if the music is in ¾ or ⅜ time. In ¾ time, the eighth notes will be beamed in pairs, emphasizing the fact that there are three beats per measure. In ⅜ time, the eighth notes will be beamed together in groups of three, emphasizing the fact that there are two beats per measure. (See figure P2.11.)

Figure P2.11 Beaming reflects the accentuation of the meter

Beaming should never obscure the strong beats, that is, carry over from a weak beat and continue through a strong beat. While it is acceptable to beam four eighth notes across the first two beats or the last two beats in quadruple simple time (see measure 2 of the first example in figure P2.10), it is not okay to beam four eighth notes across beats two and three. This incorrect manner of beaming fails to emphasize the metric importance of beat three as the second strongest beat in quadruple time.

SUMMARY

Terminology

Meter. The recurring accentuation pattern in the beats of a piece of music.

Beat. The underlying pulse of a piece of music.

Measure. A section of music that contains one unit of the recurring accentuation pattern of the meter. Every measure starts with the strongest beat of the pattern.

Duple time. A meter that contains two beats in every measure. It has an accentuation pattern of Strong–Weak.

Triple time. A meter that contains three beats in every measure. It has an accentuation pattern of Strong–Weak–Weak.

Quadruple time. A meter that contains four beats in every measure. It has a recurring accentuation pattern of Strong–Weak–Semi-Strong–Weak.

Simple time. A meter in which the beat subdivides into two or four smaller units.

Compound time. A meter in which the beat subdivides into three or six smaller units.

Time signature. A symbol that indicates the meter of a piece of music.

Downbeat. The first and strongest beat of a measure.

Upbeat. The last beat in a measure. It will be a weak beat that leads into the next measure.

Pick-up (anacrusis). An incomplete measure at the start of a piece, usually consisting of just the upbeat, that leads into the first full measure.

Tempo. The rate of the beats in a piece of music, measured in beats per minute (bpm).

The meter of music describes the repeating accentuation pattern of the beats.

Duple time contains two beats per measure. Triple time has three. Quadruple time has four.

In simple meters, the beat is subdivided into groups of two or four.

In compound meters, the beat is subdivided into groups of three or six.

Rhythmic durations are all relative. The actual pace of the music depends on the tempo.

The beaming of eighth notes, sixteenth notes, and shorter values should reflect the accentuation pattern of the meter.

NOTE

1. This is a mnemonic. These are time signatures, not fractions. And while on that subject, no line appears between the two numbers.

WORKBOOK

1. Write in the beats for the entire excerpt, including subdivisions. Note that this excerpt contains an anacrusis. Is this duple, triple, or quadruple time? Is this a simple or compound meter?

Chaminade, "Idylle," op. 126, no. 1

2. The following four measures are written in ⅔. Rewrite the music first in ⅝, then in ⅔. The first measure is given in each new time signature as a guide.

N. Draper

Scales and Key Signatures

Throughout history, many musicians composed music based on limited collections of pitches. A *scale* is a collection of pitches, presented theoretically as a stepwise succession of notes, usually ascending. A multitude of scales exist ranging from the *chromatic scale* (made up entirely of half steps) to the *church modes* of the Middle Ages and Renaissance (see Appendix C) to the octatonic scale, whole-tone scale, pentatonic scale, and blues scale. Those are just some of the ones in Western music; different cultures use still other scales. The two scales that were prevalent in the common-practice period, however, are the *major scale* and the *minor scale*. When identifying scales, it is important to label the type of scale and its starting pitch. For example, a major scale that starts on C will be identified as a C-major scale.

The *major scale* consists of a distinct pattern of whole and half steps (remember from Prelude 1, a whole step contains two half steps): W W H W W W H (figure P3.1). The standard example of a major scale is C-major, which is found by going from middle C up to the next C, using the white notes of the piano. A major scale does not have to start on C; it can be *transposed*, or moved, to start on any pitch, as long as the pattern of whole and half steps is maintained.

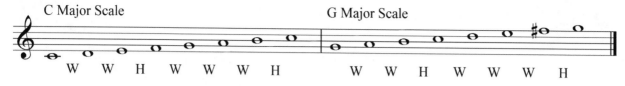

Figure P3.1 Major scales

The G-major scale contains an F♯ in order to maintain the pattern of whole and half steps. Also note that F♯ is used instead of G♭. In writing a major or minor scale, it is important to use only one instance of each letter name.

Certain pitches in the two keys behave similarly. The tension heard in going from B up to C in the C-major scale is equivalent to the tension heard in the sound going from F♯ up to G in the G-major scale. Similarly, the pitch C feels like "home," providing closure, in C-major, whereas the pitch G feels like "home" in G-major. These functional equivalencies are due to the identical pattern of whole and half steps found in any major scale. In order to discuss the roles of and the relationships between the different pitches in the major scale, we use *scale degrees*, which are numbers corresponding to each step in the scale. They are notated by Arabic numerals with carets above them (figure P3.2).

Figure P3.2 Scale degrees in major

Scale degree function (the role that each scale degree plays in the music) is one of the most important fundamentals to understand. The placement of the half steps in the major scale gives each pitch a distinct feeling or "function" in relation to the other pitches in the scale. Some scale degrees are strong and stable, such as 1̂, also known as the tonic. As just discussed, this pitch serves as home, providing stability and closure. Other scale degrees are weak and unstable, such as 7̂, called the *leading tone*. This note pulls to tonic, leading back home. Unstable scale degrees with a distinct pull and resolution, such as the leading tone, are called *tendency tones*. These two scale degrees, the tonic and the leading tone, define the two ends of the stable/unstable spectrum. The other scale degrees all fall somewhere between these two.

A full listing of the major scale degree functions is found in table P3.1. The names of the scale degrees should be memorized. The relative stabilities and resolutions illustrate the concept of functionality. You need not memorize them; they will become clearer as you work through the book.

TABLE P3.1	Scale Degree Stability and Function in Major Keys		
Scale degree	**Name**	**Function**	**Resolution**
1	Tonic	Home, Most Stable	
2	Supertonic	Middle of Scale	Often down to 1, or up to 3
3	Mediant	Relatively Stable	Various
4	Subdominant	Unstable	Down to 3 or up to 5
5	Dominant	Stable	Various
6	Submediant	Relatively Unstable	Often down to 5
7	Leading Tone	Tendency Tone, Least Stable	Up to 1

Major scales can be built on any pitch; however, the pattern of whole and half steps results in a variety of accidentals, depending on which pitch you start with. As mentioned above, starting the major scale on G will result in F♯ rather than F. If a composer wishes to write a piece in G-major, he or she typically will use a key signature. A *key signature* lists the accidentals in the key, setting them for the duration of the piece. It is placed after the clef on every staff and before the time signature at the start of the score. It is much easier for a composer to use a key signature that has an F♯ at the beginning, indicating that all Fs in this piece will be sharped, rather than going through the entire piece and sharping each individual F. (See figure P3.3.)

Without a key signature: With a key signature:

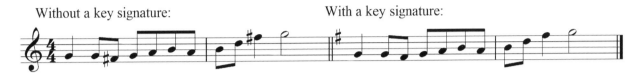

Figure P3.3 Key signatures simplify the notation

You should memorize the *circle of fifths*, which is a chart displaying the key signatures of each major key/scale (see figure P3.4). If you read the circle of fifths in a clockwise direction, you will notice that every time a major scale is transposed up five scale degrees (also known as a fifth), a sharp is added to the key signature. The sharp

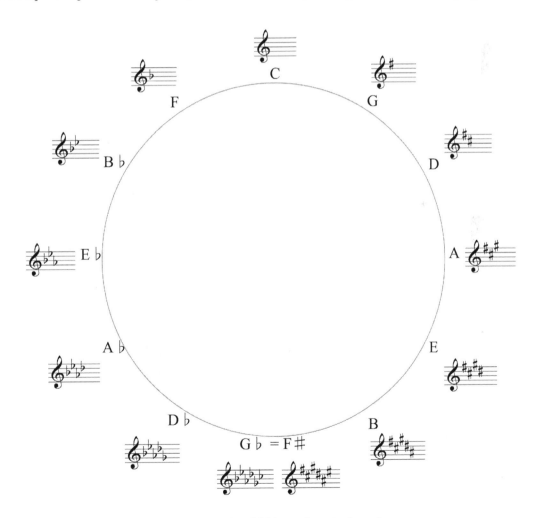

Figure P3.4 The circle of fifths with major key signatures

that gets added to each subsequent key signature is scale degree $\hat{7}$ in the new key. Conveniently, each added sharp is placed at the end of the key signature. This means that when you are looking at a sharp key signature you can identify the key by going to the last sharp and raising it a half step to scale degree $\hat{1}$, or the home note of your key. If you read the circle of fifths in a counterclockwise direction, you will see that every time a major scale is transposed down five scale degrees, a flat is added to the key signature. Specifically, the flat that gets added to each subsequent key signature is scale degree $\hat{4}$ in the new key. When looking at a flat key signature, the second-to-last flat will be the tonic note of your key. It is worth pointing out that adding a sharp is analogous to removing a flat. Also notice that the new alteration in each key signature follows the circle of fifths. Sharps are added in the order F, C, G, and so on. Flats are added in the reverse direction: B, E, A, and so on.

In the previous paragraph, the terms *key* and *scale* were used interchangeably. Key is a broader concept than scale. A scale is a specific abstraction, an ascending or descending stepwise collection of pitches that frequently occur in a key. A piece is in the *key* of C-major when it uses the notes in the C-major scale and the pitch C serves as its tonic.

The *minor scale* is also ubiquitous in common-practice music. Unlike the major scale, which only has one distinct pattern of whole and half steps, the minor scale has its main form, called *natural minor*, as well as two variants with small pitch alterations: *harmonic minor* and *melodic minor* (figure P3.5).

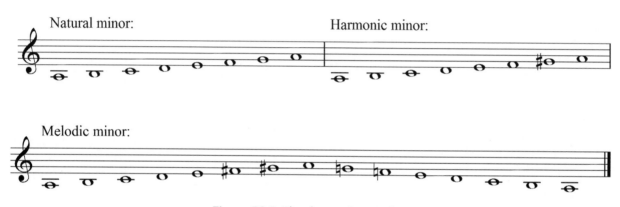

Figure P3.5 The three minor scales

The *natural minor scale* has the pattern W H W W H W W, and an example of it can be found by spanning an octave from A3 up to A4, using the white keys of the piano. Because the pattern of whole and half steps has been shifted from the major scale, the scale degree functions are slightly different in minor. The most important difference is the new tendency tone found on the *submediant*, scale degree $\hat{6}$, which has a strong pull toward scale degree $\hat{5}$, the *dominant*. Missing from the natural minor scale, however, is the tension created by the half-step pull of scale degree $\hat{7}$ up to $\hat{1}$, which was found in the major scale. In the natural minor, this "low" form of scale degree $\hat{7}$ is called the *subtonic* rather than the leading tone.

The *harmonic minor scale* follows the natural minor pattern, but it replaces the subtonic with the leading tone from the major scale. This alteration re-creates the tension found in the major scale between scale degrees $\hat{7}$ and $\hat{1}$. However, the altered scale degree $\hat{7}$ now is more than a whole step away from scale degree $\hat{6}$, creating an unusual interval known as an augmented second. The *melodic minor scale* covers this gap by raising *both* scale degrees $\hat{6}$ and $\hat{7}$ on the way up to $\hat{1}$, as if the pitches are leading to $\hat{1}$, and then lowering them both back to the natural minor scale on the descent, as if the pitches are leading to $\hat{5}$. Thus the melodic minor scale caters to the tendencies of both the leading tone and the minor submediant.

The three different minor scales are a theoretical construct. Pieces in *minor keys* incorporate pitches from all three variants. The key signature for a minor piece, however, will only show the pitches found in the natural minor scale. Any accidentals used to create the harmonic or melodic variants of the minor scale must be added within the body of the piece itself.

Every major key signature in the circle of fifths has a *relative minor* (figure P3.6). *Relative keys* share the same key signature. For example, C-major and A-minor share the same basic collection of pitches. C-major is A-minor's relative major and A-minor is C-major's relative minor. A is three half steps down from C. This relationship holds true for all relative keys. The starting note of the relative minor of a major key will always be three half steps down from the starting note of that major key. It is best to memorize the minor keys for the circle of fifths.

Figure P3.6 also shows a common and convenient notational shorthand. Capital letters indicate major keys, and lowercase letters signify minor keys. *A* refers to A-major, while *a* represents A-minor.

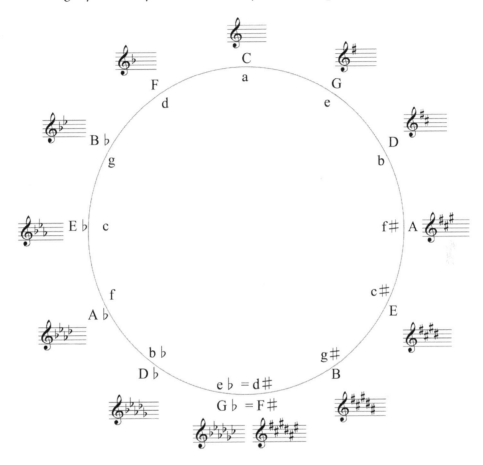

Figure P3.6 The circle of fifths including the minor keys

Another important key relationship is that of *parallel keys*. Parallel keys share the same tonic pitch. In order to derive the parallel minor from the major, you must lower scale degrees $\hat{3}$, $\hat{6}$, and $\hat{7}$ one half step (figure P3.7). To distinguish the alteration between the parallel modes, the scale degrees for these lowered forms are sometimes preceded with the letter L: L$\hat{3}$, L$\hat{6}$, L$\hat{7}$. (Traditionally, a flat symbol was used. For some keys, however, a sharp pitch is lowered to a natural. For example, compare A-major and A-minor. I prefer the L since it is more general.)

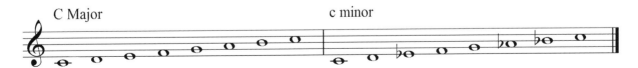

Figure P3.7 Parallel major and minor keys

Compositions do not always adhere completely to the pitches found in a key. For example, a composer could write a piece in C-major that occasionally incorporates a D♭ as well as D♮. In this piece, the D♭ would be described as a *chromatic* pitch—a pitch that is outside of the key. A pitch that is part of the key, such as D♮, is described as being *diatonic*.

SUMMARY

Terminology

Scale. A collection of pitches, presented as a stepwise succession of notes. Used to organize the pitches present in a key or section of music.

Major scale. A scale consisting of the interval pattern WWHWWWH.

Scale degree. The identification of a pitch and its melodic role through its position in the scale of the functioning key. Each scale degree has its own name and can be represented by an Arabic numeral with a caret above it.

Scale degree function. The amount of stability/instability in and the typical behavior of a pitch, based on where it falls in a scale.

Key signature. A listing of the accidentals in a key, placed at the start of the staff, to set the accidentals for the duration of the music.

Circle of fifths. An organizing of the keys and key signatures by ascending/descending perfect fifths around a circle, to show the gradual addition of accidentals to the key signatures. It also shows how closely related keys are to one another.

Natural minor scale. The minor scale that includes the pitches corresponding to the key signature.

Harmonic minor scale. The minor scale that uses the two tendency tones, L$\hat{6}$ and R$\hat{7}$; the pitches most frequently used in chords in minor.

Melodic minor scale. The minor scale that raises $\hat{6}$ and $\hat{7}$ when ascending (heading to tonic) and uses their lowered forms when descending (heading to $\hat{5}$).

Relative keys. The major and minor keys that share a key signature. The relative minor is located a minor third below its relative major.

Parallel keys. The major and minor scales that share a tonic pitch.

Chromatic pitches. Pitches from outside the scale of the functioning key.

Diatonic pitches. Pitches that fit within the scale of the functioning key.

The important pitch collections in the common-practice period were the major and minor scales.

The individual pitches in a key can be identified by their scale degree, which is the number corresponding to their location in the scale of the key.

Each scale degree indicates a particular role that that note plays within the key. Scale degrees function the same in every major or minor key, regardless of transposition.

When transposing to a new tonic, some pitches may need to be altered with accidentals in order to preserve the pattern of half and whole steps in a scale. These altered pitches can be listed at the beginning of the staff in a key signature.

The circle of fifths organizes the key signatures in order of increasing/decreasing number of accidentals. It also shows the order in which alterations are made to the key signature.

Relative major and minor keys share the same key signature. The tonic of the relative minor is three half steps below the tonic of its relative major.

The parallel major and minor share the same tonic pitch. They have different forms of scale degrees $\hat{3}$, $\hat{6}$, and $\hat{7}$.

WORKBOOK

1. Create the following ascending major scales.

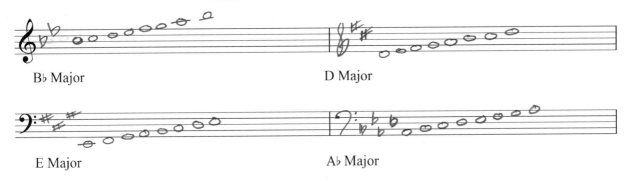

B♭ Major

D Major

E Major

A♭ Major

2. Create the following ascending minor scales.

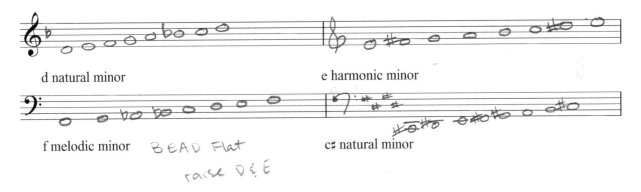

d natural minor

e harmonic minor

f melodic minor   BEAD Flat

raise D & E

c♯ natural minor

3. Identify each key signature by both its major and relative minor key.

E maj   G♭ maj   B♯ maj   G maj E♭ maj F maj A maj   D♭ maj

C♯ min   E♭ min   A min   E min C min D min F♯ min   B min

4. Draw the key signature on the staff for each given key.

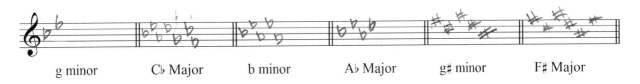

g minor   C♭ Major   b minor   A♭ Major   g♯ minor   F♯ Major

Intervals

Rarely do we hear a musical sound in isolation. A pitch gains meaning through its context with the notes that surround it. As you advance in your study of music theory, you will learn labels to describe various pitch relationships. The first such term is the interval.

An *interval* is the distance between two pitches. When the notes sound in succession, we have a *melodic interval*. Two pitches can also be heard simultaneously, in which case the interval is a *harmonic interval*.

The labels that identify intervals have two components: the generic interval (sometimes called the "size" or "number") and quality (or "type"). The *generic interval* describes the distance between the notes based solely on letter names; it is basically counting the lines and spaces that the interval spans. The two pitches in the interval are included in the count. For example, the interval C to E♭ contains three letter names—C, D, and E—so it is a third. The size is written as an Arabic numeral, so, in this example, it is 3.

Three aspects of the generic interval deserve emphasis. First, keep the notation clear. Intervals are indicated through Arabic numerals; scale degrees are indicated with Arabic numerals with carets above them. An interval, for example a 7, is a relationship between two pitches. A scale degree, for example $\hat{7}$, is a specific note.

Second, be sure to include the lowest note as your first count. A slightly confusing fact is that if you have the same pitch twice, the distance between them is a first, not zero. To avoid this terminology, musicians always refer to them as "unisons," but they still write them as the number 1.

Third, since we do not consider accidentals when calculating the size, different pitches can produce the same generic interval. C up to E♭ is a third, but so is C up to E, C♯ up to E, and C♯ up to E♭ (figure P4.1).

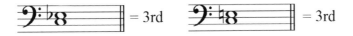

Figure P4.1 All are thirds

Obviously, C up to E does not sound the same as C up to E♭. The *quality* of the interval further refines the difference between sounds. There are five names that we use to describe the quality of an interval: perfect, major, minor, augmented, and diminished. When appended to the generic interval, they are abbreviated as P, M, m, A, and d. C to E is a major third, indicated M3, and C to E♭ is a minor third, represented as m3.

In determining the quality of an interval, the bottom note should always serve as your point of reference. If the higher note in an interval belongs to the major scale of the lower note, the interval will either be *perfect* or *major*. Put another way, all perfect and major intervals come from the major scale of the lowest note of the interval (figure P4.2).

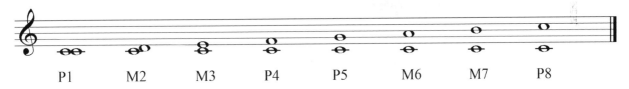

Figure P4.2 Perfect and major intervals can be derived from the major scale

The most hollow, open-sounding intervals are given the perfect label: the unison, fourth, fifth, and octave. Meanwhile, the richer-sounding intervals are described as major. For example, the interval from C up to D will be a major second (M2), whereas the interval from C up to F will be a perfect fourth (P4). As you can see, four size numbers from the major scale are designated as perfect, four as major.

Minor intervals are a half step smaller than their major equivalents. Just as there are no major unisons, fourths, fifths, and octaves, there are no minor versions of these intervals either. The four minor intervals that are possible above C are presented in figure P4.3.

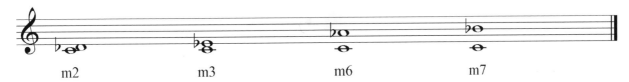

Figure P4.3 Minor intervals

The letter names in a minor interval do not change from their major counterparts. Instead, an accidental is used (or removed) to lower the top note down a half step. The M2 from C to D becomes a minor second (m2) when the D becomes D♭. The M2 from E to F♯ becomes a m2 when the F♯ becomes an F. Do not assume that minor intervals come from the minor scale. While the m3, m6, and m7 exist in the natural minor scale, the m2 does not.

Augmented intervals (figure P4.4) are a half step larger than their perfect and major equivalents. Again, the letter names do not change, as the size must stay constant, but the use of accidentals is altered.

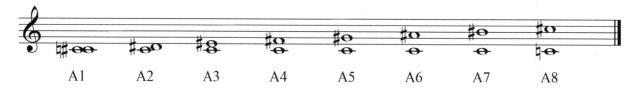

Figure P4.4 Augmented intervals

Diminished intervals are a half step smaller than their perfect and minor equivalents. There is no such thing as a diminished unison. As soon as you lower the unison pitch a half step, the lower note becomes the point of reference, making the interval an augmented unison, as shown in figure P4.5.

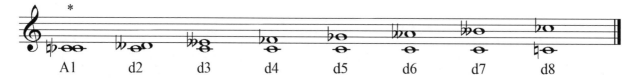

Figure P4.5 Diminished intervals

The sound that is produced by C and F♯ could also be written as C to G♭. However, the relationship between C and G♭ is that of a diminished fifth (d5), rather than an augmented fourth (A4). The A4 and the d5 above C are *enharmonically equivalent*, but they are written differently. Apart from the *tritone*, which is the interval described above (technically, a distance of three whole steps, forming an A4, but the term is also used for the d5), all augmented and diminished intervals can be enharmonically spelled as perfect, major, or minor intervals. Generally, augmented and diminished intervals appear in chromatic writing. For example, if a bass voice sings a C and a treble voice sings a chromatic ascent from G up to C above it, the music would be written as shown in figure P4.6. Because ascending chromatic pitches are typically written as sharped notes, augmented intervals result between the two voices in this passage.

Figure P4.6 Chromatic pitches creating augmented intervals

It is often easiest to determine the quality of an interval by considering the major scale or key of your lowest note. However, all of the intervals have their own unique number of half steps and can be memorized this way as well (see table P4.1).

TABLE P4.1	Calculating Intervals by Counting Half Steps											
Interval	P1	m2	M2	m3	M3	P4	TT	P5	m6	M6	m7	M7	P8
Half Steps	0	1	2	3	4	5	6	7	8	9	10	11	12

Simple intervals range in size from the unison (1) to the octave (8). Any interval spanning a distance larger than an octave is considered to be a *compound interval*. Typically, we reduce compound intervals to their equivalent simple name. For example, most theorists will describe a ninth as being a second, even though the pitches in a ninth are separated in register by more than an octave (figure P4.7). As the figure shows, removing an octave from an interval is the same as subtracting 7 from its size.

M9   M2   m10   m3   P11   P4

Figure P4.7 Compound and simple intervals

The size and quality of an interval are specific to the ordering of the notes in pitch space. G up to C (P4) is not the same interval as C up to G (P5), even though both intervals involve the same two letter names. Intervals that share the exact same pitches (including accidentals) but flip which pitch is on top and which is on bottom are said to be *inversions* of each other. (See figure P4.8)

P1   P8   m2   M7   M2   m7   m3   M6

M3   m6   P4   P5   A4   d5   P5   P4

m6   M3   M6   m3   m7   M2   M7   m2

Figure P4.8 Inverting intervals

It is fairly easy to calculate the new interval that results from inversion. First, the sizes of the original interval and its inversion always adds up to nine: a unison (1) inverts to an octave (8), a second (2) inverts to a seventh (7), a third (3) inverts to a sixth (6), and a fourth (4) inverts to a fifth (5). The qualities invert according to the following pattern: perfect intervals invert to perfect intervals, major and minor intervals exchange quality upon inversion, and augmented and diminished intervals flip quality upon inversion.

Quality	Size
P←→P	1←→8
M←→m	2←→7
A←→d	3←→6
	4←→5

SUMMARY

Terminology

Interval. The distance between two pitches.

Melodic interval. The distance between two adjacent notes in a melody, one heard immediately after the other. Contrasts with *harmonic interval*.

Harmonic interval. The distance between two intervals sounding simultaneously. Contrasts with *melodic interval*.

Generic interval. Also called *size*. The distance between two pitches, ignoring accidentals and counting only letter names.

Quality. Clarifies the difference in sound between ambiguous sonorities, such as intervals with the same generic size but different accidentals or chords with the same root but a different third or fifth.

Simple interval. An interval between and including a unison and an octave.

Compound interval. An interval that is larger than an octave.

An interval is the distance between two pitches. It is identified by two terms, its generic interval and quality.

The generic interval is the distance in terms of letter names or by counting lines and spaces on the staff.

The quality differentiates intervals accounting for their exact size, by considering factors such as accidentals.

The unison, fourth, fifth, and octave can be diminished, perfect, or augmented.

The second, third, sixth, and seventh can be diminished, minor, major, or augmented.

Simple intervals range from a unison to an octave. Compound intervals are larger than an octave, but people generally identify them by their simple interval name.

When inverting an interval: The original size plus the size of the inversion add to 9. Perfect remains perfect, but major turns into minor and vice versa, and augmented turns into diminished and vice versa.

WORKBOOK

1. Create the following intervals by adding a whole note next to or above the E♭.

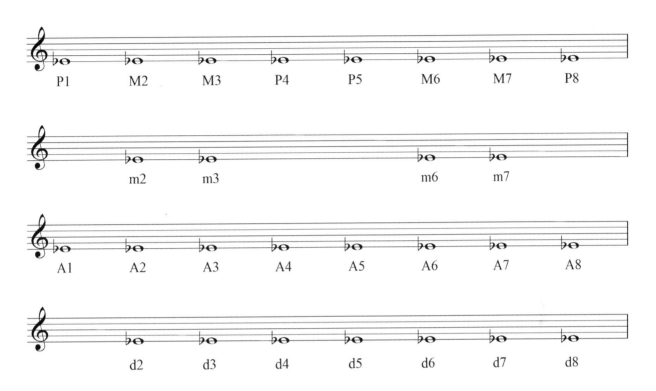

2. Identify the intervals by their size and quality.

3. On the staff, write the requested interval.

Write the Interval Above

P5   M3   m2   M6   A6   P4   d5   P1   A4   m7

Write the Interval Below

m3   M2   M2   M7   m2   A8   P4   m6   M3   m3

4. The following excerpt is from Certon's "Voyant Souffrier." Between the staves, every time a voice/melody moves, identify the quality and number of the resultant harmonic interval. The first few measures have been done for you.

P5 m6 m7 | m6 M6 M6 P5

5. Identify what interval will result from inverting the given interval. The first one has been done for you.

M3←→m6   P5←→   M6←→
A6←→   m7←→   P1←→
d7←→   m2←→   A4←→

Triads

A *chord* is any collection of more than two pitches that are grouped together in a meaningful way. Any chord that has three distinct pitches is described as a *trichord*. A *triad* is a trichord built from successive thirds. In the common-practice period, the triad is by far the most important harmonic sonority. Due to its prevalence, and despite the technical differences in the terms, people frequently use the words "chord" and "triad" interchangeably.

In its standard arrangement, a triad's thirds stack directly on top of each other. Like intervals, triads can be heard as melodic successions of pitches, called *arpeggios*, or as harmonic, *blocked* simultaneities (figure P5.1).

Figure P5.1 Arpeggios and block chords

Triads are identified with three labels: their root, quality, and inversion. The *root* is the lowest note when the triad is stacked in thirds, with the notes as close together as possible. All of the triads in figure P5.1 are in this stacked-third configuration. The root serves as our point of reference for a chord. The other pitches involved in the triad are called the *third* and the *fifth*, describing their relationship to the root. The name of the triad comes from the root. The chords in figure P5.1 are a C triad, an A triad, an F triad, and a G triad.

The *quality* of a triad is determined by examining the intervallic relationship between the root, third, and fifth of the chord (figure P5.2). A *major triad* features a M3 and a P5 above the root note. Triads can also be analyzed by their thirds—in a major triad, a M3 is on the bottom and a m3 is on the top. A *minor triad* features a m3 and a P5 above the root note. Minor triads involve a m3 on the bottom and a M3 on the top. An *augmented triad* features a M3 and an A5 above the root note, forming a stack of two major thirds. A *diminished triad* features a m3 and a d5 above the root note, forming a stack of two minor thirds.

Major triad   minor triad   Augmented triad   diminished triad

M3 + P5   m3 + P5   M3 + A5   m3 + d5

Figure P5.2 The four triad qualities

A shorthand notation for naming triads is to use a capital letter to indicate that the third of the chord forms a M3 with the root, and a lower case letter to show that the third is a m3. If the fifth is a P5, nothing else is necessary. If the fifth is an A5, then a plus sign is added to the triad's name. If the fifth is a d5, a small superscripted *o* is added. Thus, a major triad is indicated by a capital letter, a minor triad by a lowercase letter, an augmented triad by a capital letter followed by a +, and a diminished triad by a lowercase letter with a °. The triads in figure P5.2 are C, c, C+, and c°.

When the root is in the lowest voice, as it has been in all examples so far, the triad is in *root position*. Due to the presence of the P5, this configuration is the most stable one. Fortunately for the sake of musical interest, but perhaps unfortunately for the sake of labeling and analysis, triads do not always appear in root position. Triads can appear in two other formations, known as first and second inversion.

First inversion occurs when the third is in the bass (or is heard as the lowest note). *Second inversion* occurs when the fifth of the root-position chord is in the bass. *The root and quality of the triad do not change with inversion.* (This is different from the interval inversions discussed in the previous chapter.) For example, each triad in figure P5.3 is a C-major triad, despite the change in inversion. Do not confuse the *root* of the chord with the *bass* of the chord.

Root Position   First Inversion   Second Inversion

Figure P5.3 Triad inversions

Thus far, the examples of triads have been presented in *close spacing*, in which all the chord's pitches fit within an octave. Triads can, however, be spaced out in a variety of ways. Figure P5.4 demonstrates three different versions of root-position, first-inversion, and second-inversion C-major chords.

Root-Position Triads   First-Inversion Triads   Second-Inversion Triads

Figure P5.4 Different voicings for a C-major chord

Triads often appear in four voices; a string quartet has four unique players, a choir has four vocal sections (soprano, alto, tenor, and bass), and so on. If one of these groups wishes to create a triad, either one performer or section will have to be silent or a note must be doubled. Doubling a note does not change the fact that it is still heard as a triadic harmony.

Because four-voice writing is so prevalent, it is important to become fluent in identifying triads by their root, quality, and inversion in four-voice spacing. Until you recognize them immediately, try following these steps to identify the triads (figure P5.5):

1. Identify all the pitches involved in the harmony.

2. On a separate sheet of paper, restack these pitches until they form a root-position triad.

3. Identify the root and quality of your chord.

4. Go back to the original music and look at the pitch that is in the bass. Determine the inversion of the triad.

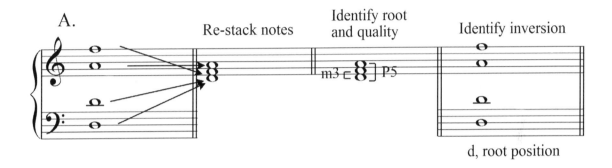

Figure P5.5 Identifying triads in chorale style

Imagine that you would like to compose a piece of music in C-major. Assuming that you never leave the key, you have only seven unique pitches available to you: C, D, E, F, G, A, and B. Writing solely in this key also means that you have only seven unique root-position triads available—the harmonies that are built on each scale degree. If we form triads on each scale degree of the C-major scale, each chord will have a specific quality, as shown in figure P5.6.

If we form triads on each scale degree of the D-major scale, using only the pitches available to us in D-major, the qualities of the triads match the equivalent scale degree qualities found in C-major. *The qualities of scale degree triads do not change from one major key to the next.* The tonic chord (the chord that has $\hat{1}$ as its root) will always be major; the supertonic chord ($\hat{2}$ as the root) will always be minor; and so on.

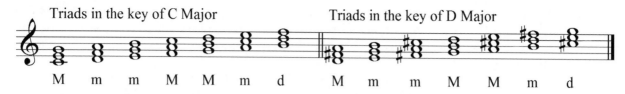

Figure P5.6 Triad qualities in major

If you wish to compose a piece in C-minor, technically you have more than seven pitches available for use, due to the variants of the minor scale. When writing in a minor key, however, composers typically limit themselves to constructing triads based on the pitches of the harmonic minor scale (which is why this scale was named "harmonic"). The one exception is the chord built on scale degree $\hat{3}$, which uses the subtonic rather than the leading tone, so as to avoid the unusual augmented sound. (See figure P5.7.)

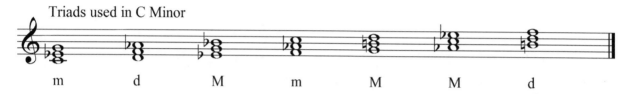

Figure P5.7 Triad qualities in minor

SUMMARY

Terminology

Chord. A harmonic sonority in which three or more notes sound simultaneously.
Trichord. Any three-note chord.
Triad. A three-note chord built from consecutive thirds.
Arpeggio. A melodic presentation of a chord. The melody skips through the pitches of the harmony.
Root. The bottom note in a chord stacked in thirds.
Major triad. A chord with a minor third on top of a major third. It contains a perfect fifth, and the third of the chord is a major third above the root.
Minor triad. A chord with a major third on top of a minor third. It contains a perfect fifth, and the third of the chord is a minor third above the root.
Augmented triad. A chord with two consecutive major thirds. It contains an augmented fifth.
Diminished triad. A chord with two consecutive minor thirds. It contains a diminished fifth.
Root position. Describes a chord with its root in the bass.
First inversion. Describes a chord with its third in the bass.
Second inversion. Describes a chord with its fifth in the bass.
Close spacing. A chord voicing in which the upper three voices are placed as closely together as possible. The three voices contain adjacent chord members. Contrasts with *open spacing*.

A triad is a chord made by stacking two successive thirds.
The four qualities of triads are major, minor, diminished, and augmented. These are determined by the intervallic relationships between the root, third, and fifth.
Root position, when the root is in the bass, is the most common and most stable inversion.
Triads may also appear in first inversion, with the third as the lowest note, or in second inversion, with the fifth in the bass.

WORKBOOK

1. Create the following root-position triads by stacking two whole notes above the given pitch.

Major   Aug.   minor   dim.   minor   Major

2. Create the first- and second-inversion triads based on the given root-position triad.

Root   1st inv.   2nd inv.   Root   1st inv.   2nd inv.

3. Identify the following triads by their root, quality, and inversion. The first one is given as an example.

d, 1st.

4. On the staff, write the requested chord. The first one is given as an example.

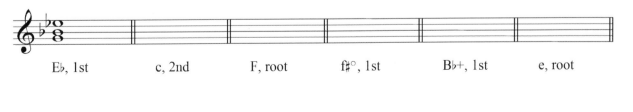

E♭, 1st   c, 2nd   F, root   f♯°, 1st   B♭+, 1st   e, root

A, 2nd   G♭, root   d♯, root   A♭, 1st   c♯°, 1st   g, 2nd

5. Identify the following triads, written in four voices, by their root, quality, and inversion. The first one is given as an example.

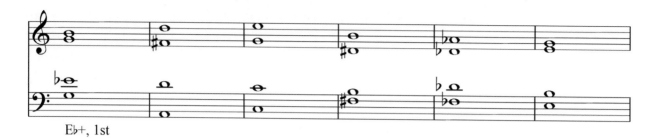

E♭+, 1st

Seventh Chords

A *seventh chord* is a specific third-based relationship between *four* distinct pitches. In its standard position, a seventh chord is built as a stack of three thirds, or a triad with the interval of a seventh on top (see figure P6.1). As with intervals and triads, seventh chords can be heard melodically or harmonically (blocked).

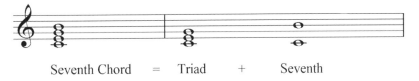

Seventh Chord   =   Triad   +   Seventh

Figure P6.1 A seventh chord

Just like triads, seventh chords are labeled in three ways—by their root, quality, and inversion. The *root* is the lowest note when the seventh chord is stacked in thirds. Also just like triads, the root serves as the reference point for the chord. The harmony in figure P6.1 is a C seventh chord. The other pitches involved in the seventh chord are described as the *third*, the *fifth*, and the *seventh* of the chord, based on the intervals they form with the root.

The *quality* of a seventh chord is determined by combining the qualities of the base triad and the seventh. Sixteen different combinations of triads and seventh qualities are possible; practically speaking, however, common-practice music uses only five types of seventh chords. A *major–major seventh chord* (MM), usually referred to as just a *major seventh chord* (M), has a major triad and a M7 above the root. A *major–minor seventh chord* (Mm) has a major triad and a m7 above the root. A *minor–minor seventh chord* (mm), usually shortened to a *minor seventh chord* (m), has a minor triad and a m7 above the root. A *half-diminished seventh chord* (ø) has a diminished triad and a m7 above the root. Technically, it is a dm7, but this name is not used. A *fully diminished seventh chord* (o) is the standard name for a dd7, which has a diminished triad and a d7 above the root. Usually it is simply called a *diminished seventh chord*. Figure P6.2 shows these five qualities.

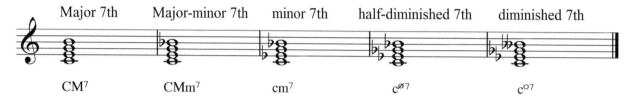

Figure P6.2 Seventh chord qualities

When the root is the lowest sounding note, the chord is in root position. Due to the presence of four unique pitches, seventh chords appear in three possible inversions in addition to the root-position formation (figure P6.3). *First inversion* occurs when the third of the chord is in the bass. *Second inversion* occurs when the fifth of the chord is in the bass. *Third inversion* occurs when the seventh of the chord is in the bass. *The root and quality of the seventh chord do not change upon inversion.*

Figure P6.3 Seventh chord inversions

Seventh chords can be found in a variety of spacings, and they often appear in a four-voice texture. The method for identifying and labeling a seventh chord in a wide four-voice spacing is the same as that of the triad. Until you recognize them immediately, try following these steps to identify the chords (figure P6.4):

1. Identify all the pitches involved in the harmony.

2. On a separate sheet of paper, restack these pitches until they form a root-position seventh chord.

3. Identify the root and quality of your seventh chord.

4. Go back to the original music and look at the pitch that is in the bass. Determine the inversion of the triad.

SUMMARY

Terminology

Seventh chord. A dissonant harmony in which a seventh has been added to the basic triad. Another third has been stacked on top of the fifth in the chord.

Major seventh chord. A seventh chord containing a major triad and a major seventh.

Major–minor seventh chord. A seventh chord consisting of a major triad and a minor seventh. In classical music, a major–minor seventh chord will function as a dominant. In popular music, the major–minor seventh is one of the most common sonorities and can appear on any scale degree.

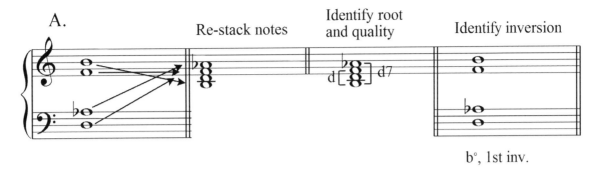

A. Re-stack notes | Identify root and quality | Identify inversion

b°, 1st inv.

B.

FMm7, 3rd inv.

Figure P6.4 Identifying seventh chords

Minor seventh chord. A seventh chord with a minor triad and a minor seventh.
Half-diminished seventh chord. A seventh chord with a diminished triad and a minor seventh.
Diminished seventh chord. A seventh chord containing a diminished triad and a diminished seventh. Also called a *fully diminished seventh chord.*
Root position. Describes a chord with its root in the bass.
First inversion. Describes a chord with its third in the bass.
Second inversion. Describes a chord with its fifth in the bass.
Third inversion. Describes a seventh chord with its seventh in the bass.

A seventh chord is formed by stacking an additional third on top of a root-position triad in close spacing. The new pitch forms a seventh with the root.
Five qualities of seventh chords appear regularly in common-practice music: major, major–minor, minor, half-diminished, and fully diminished.
Seventh chords can also appear in three inversions: first inversion has the third in the bass, second inversion has the fifth there, and third inversion has the seventh.

WORKBOOK

1. Create the following root-position seventh chords by stacking three whole notes above the given G.

Major   Major-minor   minor   half-dim.   diminished

2. Create first-, second-, and third-inversion seventh chords based on the given root-position chord.

Root   1st inv.   2nd inv.   3rd inv.   Root   1st inv.   2nd inv.   3rd inv.

3. Identify the following seventh chords by their root, quality, and inversion. The first one is given as an example.

dm7, 1st

4. On the staff, write the requested seventh chord. The first one is given as an example.

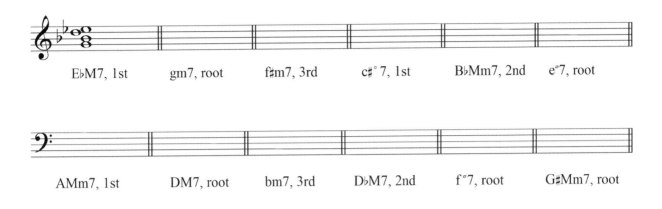

EbM7, 1st   gm7, root   f#m7, 3rd   c#°7, 1st   BbMm7, 2nd   e°7, root

AMm7, 1st   DM7, root   bm7, 3rd   DbM7, 2nd   f°7, root   G#Mm7, root

5. Identify the following seventh chords, in four-voice chorale style, by their root, quality, and inversion. The first one is given as an example.

cm7, 3rd

MELODY

Common-practice music grew from a vocal tradition. As such, we will begin by examining vocal melodies.

Note: Music theory explains why a composition sounds like it does. It focuses on what a listener hears as the music unfolds. Do not treat this material as a paper exercise. Always strive to write music. Sing the melodies. In the sections on scale degrees, do not merely memorize the functions of different scale degrees; work on feeling the tension and the way certain pitches pull toward others. The more quickly you internalize these traits, the easier and better your work will become.

I
PART

II
PART

III
PART

IV
PART

V
PART

Melodic Construction

CHAPTER LEARNING OBJECTIVES

This chapter:

- Explains five components that contribute to effective melodies

Figure 1.1

We start with two folk melodies. Some traits to notice:

1. The melodic lines contain predominantly *conjunct motion*, meaning that the motion from one note to the next is by step (whole or half). Since people find it easier to sing a note that is close than one

that is far away, most of the motion is by small intervals. The predominance of conjunct motion also helps the melody sound logical. A melody that contains predominantly leaps, called *disjunct motion*, can sound haphazard.

2. That is not to say that leaps do not appear in melodies, just that they are less common. Disjunct motion plays an important role because it is more distinctive than conjunct; the opening leaps in both of the folk songs stand out from the surrounding material. Leaps also involve a larger change in tension for a singer, so they impart more energy to the music than steps do. As a result, leaps are usually followed by stepwise motion in the opposite direction. This both serves to dissipate the energy created by the leap as well as to create a sense of balance in the melody. The larger the leap, the more important this balance becomes. A general guideline is that leaps of a fifth or larger should be followed by stepwise motion in the opposite direction. The counterbalancing may be delayed briefly, as in "Twinkle, Twinkle," but it will eventually arrive.

3. Rhythm is extremely important in music. The dotted eighth–sixteenth–eighth pattern in "My Bonnie" stands out and is as distinctive as the opening leap. Similarly, in "Twinkle, Twinkle," the repeated notes create more interest than a descending half-note scale would. Unfortunately, Western musicians have yet to develop a theory for rhythm as sophisticated as that for pitch. As a result, pitch will be emphasized over rhythm in this book. Do not let this deceive you, and do not ignore rhythmic issues. Rhythm is as important as pitch; we just lack the terminology to explain it as well.

4. Both of these melodies are internally *coherent*, meaning that the different parts sound like they belong together. A melody is not an amalgam of diverse musical patterns. Rather, composers choose a few patterns, called *motives*, and then reuse and vary them. In "My Bonnie," the pick-ups and downbeats in measures 1, 3, and 5 are identical. Measures 1 and 5 are completely identical. In "Twinkle, Twinkle," the opening four measures repeat at the end. The material between these two phrases consists of repetitions of measures 3 and 4, transposed up a step. The elements that make up a melody work together to create a single, logical idea.

The previous examples are folk songs, while this book is about common-practice music. Figure 1.2 gives a melody from the classical repertoire.

Figure 1.2 Verdi, "Questo o quella" from *Rigoletto* ("This Woman or That")

The same traits appear, although they are buried in more artifice. For example, a wider variety of rhythms appear here than in the previous two, but the longer melody allows for all of them to repeat and for the music to remain coherent. While no phrases repeat completely, subsections do, such as measures 1 and 2 reappearing in measures 9 and 10, also aiding coherence. The Verdi melody, however, contains an additional trait.

5. This melody has a sense of growth. It builds up to a climax and then pulls back from it. The individual phrases do this; the melody begins on A♭ and moves up to E♭ in the first measure, and the phrase then descends back down. (The F is much shorter and carries less weight than the E♭.) On the phrase level, this is also true about the folk songs; they open with leaps that are balanced by motion in the opposite direction. More important, though, is the overall climax of the melody. Verdi emphasizes the A♭ in measures 11 and 12 in many ways: It is the highest note. It is approached by leap. It is a sustained note. The melody gradually increases tension over several phrases, building to a single clear climax, and then releases the tension again. Just like with movies and novels, since the increase is more interesting than the release, the buildup lasts longer than the denouement. The climax often arrives between two-thirds and three-quarters of the entire length.

SUMMARY

Terminology

Conjunct motion. Melodic motion by step, whole or half.
Disjunct motion. Melodic motion by an interval greater than a second; motion by leap.
Motives. Short, distinctive melodic ideas that provide coherence to a melody and to an entire work. They may involve rhythm or rhythm and pitch.
Coherence. A melody or piece contains an internal consistency, resulting from the reuse of a limited set of ideas, rhythms, motives, or patterns.

Traits of a good classical melody:

1. Mostly conjunct motion

2. Distinctive leaps, balanced by motion in the opposite direction

3. Interesting rhythms

4. Internal coherence

5. Clear climaxes in each phrase and one principle climax within the overall melody

WORKBOOK

For these assignments, work away from an instrument. Double-check yourself afterward, but work on hearing the melodies in your head. The better you get at this skill, the more your musicianship will improve, and the easier these assignments will be.

1. Appendix A contains a dozen melodies from a variety of styles. Pick several and analyze them based on the five traits of a good classical melody. Do all of the parameters pertain? If not, do you think the differences result from stylistic issues or are they particular to this piece?

2. Find a melody you enjoy, from any genre of tonal music, and notate it below. Analyze it based on the five traits of a good classical melody. Do they all pertain? If you chose a piece that is not classical music, what characteristics are idiomatic to that style?

Major Key Functionality

CHAPTER LEARNING OBJECTIVES

This chapter:

- Defines functionality
- Explains the roles of scale degrees $\hat{1}$ and $\hat{7}$

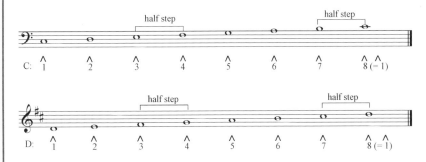

Figure 2.1 Two major scales

A way of organizing the pitches in a melody is to group them into a scale. Since the two scales in figure 2.1 come from different keys, they contain different pitches. The distances between successive pitches in both scales, however, are identical. A major scale consists of all whole steps, except for a half step between the third and fourth pitches and another half step between the last two pitches.

The fact that all major scales have the same structure is important. It means that, although specific pitches may vary from key to key, relationships between the notes will remain the same. *A scale is more than a listing of notes; it relates a hierarchy among the pitches.* Each note in the scale can be represented by its *scale degree*, that is, the number that corresponds to its location in the scale. For clarity of notation, scale degrees are represented by Arabic numerals with carets above them. (Arabic numerals without carets refer to intervals.) Each scale degree also has a name:

$\hat{1}$	Tonic	$\hat{5}$	Dominant
$\hat{2}$	Supertonic	$\hat{6}$	Submediant
$\hat{3}$	Mediant	$\hat{7}$	Leading Tone
$\hat{4}$	Subdominant	$\hat{8} = \hat{1}$	Tonic

These names are not merely labels. They explain relationships between the pitches. The term *functionality* expresses the idea that each scale degree serves a particular function in music. It is more informative to refer to pitches by their functional names (tonic, supertonic) than by their note names (C, D). The former conveys information about how much tension a pitch contains, where it wants to go, and how strongly it wants to get there.

By far, the most important scale degree is the tonic. The tonic serves as the point of rest and stability in a piece of music. Pieces end on the tonic, providing a sense of closure, and this is the name that is given to the key of a piece. Because of its importance, the tonic earns the number-one position in a scale.

The term *tonic* parallels the name of this particular hierarchical structure of music. Pieces written in either a major or minor key are referred to as *tonal*. Tonality is *the defining characteristic* of works from the common-practice period. Music written prior to 1600 was modal (for more details about modes, see Appendix C), and after 1900 a variety of styles developed.

If we organize the pitches of "My Bonnie" into a scale, with which note do we begin? Sing the melody in figure 2.2, and identify the tonic.

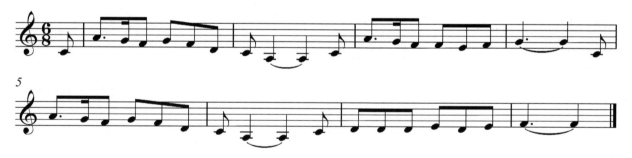

Figure 2.2 "My Bonnie" (Scottish traditional)

The tonic of the piece is F. This pitch provides a sense of closure and rest. F seals off the piece at the end, and we feel no need to continue.

Relying on key signature alone will not always work. It is not uncommon for the key, especially of an excerpt or in the middle of a piece, to differ from the key signature. The sound, not the notation, dictates the analysis. The subdominant does not appear in figure 2.2, so I was able to omit the key signature. Since we now know that the key of the melody is F-major, we also know that if the subdominant did appear, it would be a B♭, and that the key signature should contain this.

Here is an example of the strength of the tonic. In measure four, the melody pauses on the supertonic. The music still contains tension, though, and the listener knows that the piece is not done. By changing that single note to the tonic (see figure 2.3), the piece sounds finished. Listeners could leave the concert hall feeling satisfied.

Figure 2.3 First phrase of "My Bonnie" with the last note changed

The structure of "My Bonnie" is what is known as a *period*. The most typical structure for a period consists of two phrases. The first, called the *antecedent*, ends with a sense of incompletion, while the second, called the *consequent*, ends with a sense of finality. The sound of a period is often referred to as "call/response" or "question/answer." The scale degrees explain how this relationship works. The antecedent phrase ends on scale degree $\hat{2}$, so the listener knows that the music will continue. The second phrase ends on the tonic, providing the necessary closure.

The second most important scale degree in a melody is $\hat{7}$, the leading tone. Play an ascending scale starting on tonic and ending on the leading tone. Its function becomes apparent immediately—it contains a great deal of tension and wants to resolve up to the tonic. Its name corresponds to this function—it is leading home. Of course, the resolution does not have to be the very next note. In "My Bonnie," the leading tone is prolonged over the entire last beat of measure 7 by going down to the submediant and then back up. Once a prominent leading tone appears, however, it will almost always resolve in the near future. The one exception to this is in a descending scalar passage. In those cases the logic of the descending scale can counteract the leading tone's upward pull.

The following examples highlight the role of the leading tone in some melodies. When specifying scale degrees, and later when labeling chords, you should identify the key. The letters below the staff at the start of each example do this. Uppercase letters indicate major keys, and lowercase letters indicate minor keys.

In figure 2.4, the delayed resolution of the leading tone in measure 4 serves a purpose; when the G finally arrives in measure 5, it is the start of the second phrase, which begins identically to the first. The delay makes this arrival more pronounced.

Figure 2.4 Bach, "Jesus bleibet meine Freude" ("Jesu, Joy of Man's Desiring")

The Bach melody is a period. It is obscured slightly by the constant rhythmic motion, but the second phrase begins in measure 5 with the repetition of the opening material. The Schubert in figure 2.5, while a little too short to consider it a period, has a similar structure. The music pauses on $\hat{2}$ and closes on $\hat{1}$, exactly like "My Bonnie."

The Handel excerpt in figure 2.6 includes a leading tone in a descending passage, as well as a second one functioning more typically.

The leading tone is our first *tendency tone*. Tendency tones are scale degrees that contain tension and pull toward a particular resolution. They possess this trait because they are a half step away from another, significantly more stable scale degree. The tension of the leading tone reflects the strength of the tonic. The ear knows that the most stable pitch is only a half step away, so the listener feels a pull toward that pitch.

Figure 2.5 Schubert, Symphony no. 5, II

Figure 2.6 Handel/Watts, "Joy to the World"

The major scale also contains another half step between the mediant and subdominant. While it is true that $\hat{4}$ pulls toward $\hat{3}$, the strength of this attraction is weaker than that of the leading tone and also varies with context. The tension is more important in certain multiple-voice scenarios. As such, when thinking of melody alone, I do not consider the subdominant as a tendency tone.

(The two scale degrees are relatively close in stability. If the scale degrees were organized in order of decreasing stability, it would probably be: $\hat{1}$ $\hat{5}$ $\hat{3}$ $\hat{2}$ $\hat{4}$ $\hat{6}$ $\hat{7}$. While the subdominant is weaker than the mediant, it is not a large discrepancy.)

Spotlight On: ASYMMETRY AND THE TRITONE

Two elements contribute to the hierarchy established by the major scale: asymmetry and conditioning.

First, because of the two unequally spaced half steps, the major scale is not symmetrical. The most significant way to see this asymmetry is by comparing the various fifths contained in a scale.

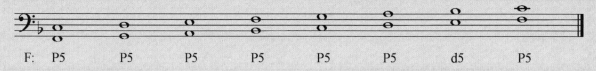

Figure 2.7 The fifths in a major scale

Every fifth within the scale is perfect except for the one between $\hat{4}$ and $\hat{7}$, which is diminished. It is the presence of this tritone that helps create the functional relationships. It is not coincidental that the two pitches involved in this interval are also our tendency tones. (When $\hat{4}$ and $\hat{7}$ are found side by side or, in multiple voices, simultaneously, thereby emphasizing this tritone, the subdominant becomes a tendency tone resolving to $\hat{3}$. This situation explains the "varies with context" comment in the penultimate paragraph of the preceding section.)

Second, comprehension of a style of music also comes from conditioning and familiarity. Once a listener hears a leading tone resolve to tonic in numerous pieces over many years, she will expect other pieces to do the same. Someone from another culture will not immediately appreciate the asymmetry in the scale and the hierarchy created by it. After hearing many pieces, however, he will begin to feel the pull of the tendency tones and the stability of the tonic.

SUMMARY

Terminology

Scale degree. The identification of a pitch and its melodic role through its position in the scale of the functioning key. Each scale degree has its own name and can be represented by an Arabic numeral with a caret above it.

Functionality. A system in which a musical element has a particular role. In common-practice tonality, the scale degrees and chords within a key serve characteristic functions.

Tonality. The functional system of common-practice music, that is, music written in the time period 1600–1900 and employing major and minor scales.

Tendency tones. Scale degrees that contain tension and pull to a particular resolution. They result when an unstable pitch is a half step away from a significantly more stable one.

Period. A frequent thematic structure in common-practice music, consisting of two phrases, the antecedent and consequent. The antecedent ends with a weaker cadence, while the consequent ends with a stronger one, creating an effect of a question and an answer.

Antecedent. The first phrase of a period, which ends in a weaker cadence, thereby creating a sense of incompletion. See also *period*.

Consequent. The second phrase in a period, ending in a stronger cadence, thereby providing a sense of closure. See also *period*.

The function of the tonic is the home pitch. It contains no tension and is stable.

The role of the leading tone is to create tension and resolve to the tonic.

WORKBOOK

For these assignments, work away from an instrument. Double-check yourself afterward, but work on hearing the melodies and the scale degree functions in your head. The better you get at this skill, the more your musicianship will improve, and the easier these assignments will be.

1. Choose two of the major melodies in Appendix A. Analyze each based on the five traits of a good classical melody. Do they all pertain? Analyze it in relation to scale degree functionality. Does it end on the tonic or another pitch? Does the leading tone appear, and if so, when does it resolve? Is the melody a period?

2. Find a major melody you enjoy, from any genre of tonal music, and notate it below. Analyze it based on the five traits of a good classical melody. Do they all pertain? Analyze it in relation to scale degree functionality. Does it end on the tonic or another pitch? Does the leading tone appear, and if so, when does it resolve? Is your melody a period?

3. Compose an eight-bar melody in any major key besides C-major. Do not use a time signature with 2 as the top number. You may do two four-bar phrases. It is better to think about the entire next measure rather than just the next pitch when deciding how to proceed. Once you are finished, analyze your melody, as in questions 1 and 2.

4. The following melodies are in a different key than the one implied by the key signature. Sing the melody, identify the tonic, and correct the key signature.

5. Transpose the following melodies three times. The first time, transpose up a perfect fifth, using accidentals instead of a key signature. The second time, transpose down a perfect fifth, again using accidentals rather than a key signature. Which scale degree is affected when you transpose it up a fifth? Which scale degree does it become? Which one is affected when you transpose it down? Which one does it become? For the third transposition, use a key signature and write the melody in the key of A-major. As you transpose each melody, think in terms of scale degrees, not by moving each pitch by a certain interval.

Minor Key Functionality

CHAPTER LEARNING OBJECTIVES

This chapter:

- Explains the role of scale degree L6̂

- Explains the choice of the form (raised or lowered) of scale degrees 6̂ and 7̂ in minor

Figure 3.1 Ciampi, "Nina"

The traits of a good melody as defined in the first chapter still apply here. How are they relevant to this song?

What is different here is the *mode*.[1] This song is in a minor key rather than a major one. Note: It is not in natural, harmonic, or melodic minor. We do not talk about a sonata in E harmonic minor. Common-practice pieces are in either major or minor. The idea of the natural, harmonic, and melodic minor is a purely theoretical construct that is not used in actual music. It is best to move beyond the idea of three different minor scales and realize that the minor scale contains all of the pitches shown in figure 3.2.

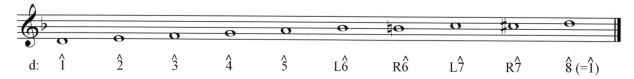

Figure 3.2 The complete minor scale

The scale degrees have the following names:[2]

$\hat{1}$	Tonic	L$\hat{6}$	Lowered Submediant
$\hat{2}$	Supertonic	R$\hat{6}$	Raised Submediant
$\hat{3}$	Mediant	L$\hat{7}$	Subtonic
$\hat{4}$	Subdominant	R$\hat{7}$	Leading Tone
$\hat{5}$	Dominant	$\hat{8}=\hat{1}$	Tonic

The reason for the different minor scales is that two different forms of a scale degree usually do not appear side by side in a scale. Theorists did not want L$\hat{6}$ and R$\hat{6}$, nor L$\hat{7}$ and R$\hat{7}$, to appear together. In trying to characterize the different situations for choosing between the two pitches, they came up with three different scales. In reality, all of the pitches above are usable, and two different "scales" may be implied on successive beats. Rather than thinking of three different collections, it is better to understand the contexts that require the particular scale degrees. I will refer to the three infamous scales to clarify why people use those terms, but after this chapter, they will not appear again.

The natural minor's name comes from the fact that the pitches occur naturally (i.e., without alteration) in the key signature.

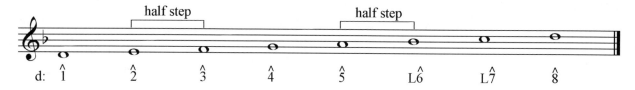

Figure 3.3 The "natural minor" scale

The half-step positions are different from the major scale. A new tendency tone emerges. The lowered submediant is a half step from the dominant, which is a strong pitch. As a result, L$\hat{6}$ is a tendency tone that pulls down to $\hat{5}$. The song "Nina" (figure 2.1) contains prominent use of L$\hat{6}$ in measures 1–3. This particular moment in the song creates a great sense of yearning as L$\hat{6}$ pulls toward $\hat{5}$, eventually resolving there.

Although the supertonic and mediant are a half step apart, they are close enough in relative strength to remain independent of each other. Neither behaves as a tendency tone.

The most important tendency tone, the leading tone, is missing in this scale. Notice that, while the two forms of the submediant both use the same name, modified by the word lowered or raised, scale degree $\hat{7}$ changes its name completely when altered. The leading tone is such an important scale degree, and the implication of its name is so important, that when the pitch is lowered, the name no longer makes sense. These names are not just labels; they describe particular functions. When $\hat{7}$ is a whole step away from the tonic, it loses its pull toward home.

Composers, however, wanted to continue using the leading tone, on account of its role in emphasizing and driving to tonic. So they altered the note. Whenever a melody is driving toward tonic, $\hat{7}$ is raised to give the leading tone. The crux of the minor-key situation rests on the two tendency tones, L$\hat{6}$ and R$\hat{7}$. When a melody is leading toward $\hat{5}$, composers employed the lowered submediant. When a melody is heading home, they used the leading tone.

When scale degree $\hat{7}$ is raised, the pitch collection results in the harmonic minor scale. It has this name because these pitches summarize the most common members of chords (as we will see later). It contains a problem, though. Playing only the top four notes of the scale produces something that sounds exotic—most Westerners describe it as Middle Eastern.

Figure 3.4 The "harmonic minor" scale

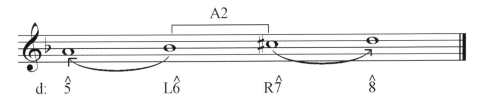

Figure 3.5 Augmented second in the harmonic minor scale

The interval created by L$\hat{6}$ and R$\hat{7}$ is an augmented second (A2). Clearly, this interval does not appear frequently in Western music; if it did, it would not sound foreign. Do not write augmented seconds in your assignments. Functionally, the problem with this interval is that one of the two tendency tones does not resolve. Going up, the pull of L$\hat{6}$ is ignored, and going down, the leading tone is thwarted. A better way to organize the harmonic minor scale is shown in figure 3.6. In this scale, all tendency tones resolve properly. It sounds more natural and less awkward.

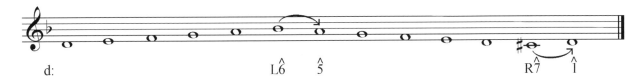

Figure 3.6 A functionally correct harmonic minor scale

What if scale degrees $\hat{6}$ and $\hat{7}$ appear next to each other in a melody? Rather than writing an augmented second, common-practice composers create a second alteration. They first decide which scale degree is the goal of the motion, tonic or dominant. They use the relevant tendency tone that leads to that scale degree, and then they adjust the other scale degree to remove its tension and pull, which then also avoids the augmented second. For example, if the goal of the passage is tonic, the music should contain a leading tone. Use R$\hat{7}$. In order to avoid the augmented second, employ R$\hat{6}$. When, however, the goal is the dominant, L$\hat{6}$ is the important tendency tone. Now the subtonic is necessary, lest you have an unresolved leading tone. The melodic minor scale summarizes the behavior of the pitches when $\hat{6}$ and $\hat{7}$ are side by side. The ascending motion has a goal of tonic, so the raised forms of both pitches are used. The descending scale has a goal of dominant, so the lowered scale degrees are used.

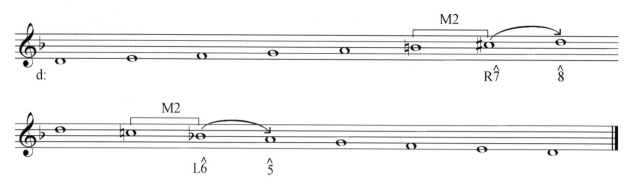

Figure 3.7 The "melodic minor" scale

The raised submediant and the subtonic both function to remove a tendency tone and to avoid the augmented second. It is only in this context that they should appear; neither of these scale degrees has any other significant function. Common-practice music does not use the subtonic to lead to the tonic; moving directly from L$\hat{7}$ to $\hat{1}$ sounds modal (as in the church modes), and passing through the leading tone (L$\hat{7}$ → R$\hat{7}$ → $\hat{1}$) is characteristic of jazz. Similarly, the raised submediant only occasionally leads to its lowered form.

The "three minor scales" serve a theoretical purpose: to summarize the behavior of the minor scale degrees in particular situations. Music, however, does not differentiate between them. Students should move beyond the idea of individual minor scales and toward the notion of a minor key with scale degrees that change based on their function (i.e., the need for a tendency tone). Several examples follow. In each example, the tendency tones are circled. As is always the case, the resolution may be delayed briefly; when this happens, an arrow shows the note of resolution. Sometimes, as a result of a delayed resolution, it may seem like the wrong accidental is used, but closer inspection will show when the true goal pitch arrives.

Figure 3.8 Beethoven, *Pathetique* Sonata, op. 13, III

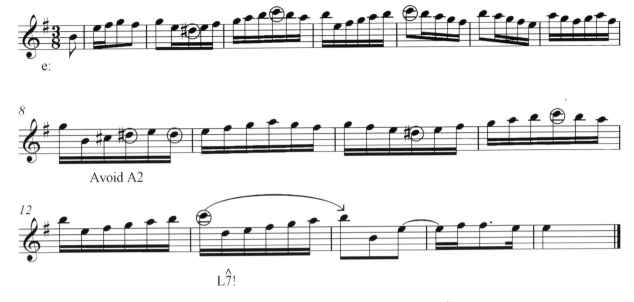

Figure 3.9 Bach, English Suite no. 5, "Passepied"

In measure 13 of the Bach "Passepied," the subtonic appears in a passage leading to the tonic—highly unusual. The important motion is from the C to the B, since these notes stand out both registerally (they are the highest notes) and metrically (they land on the downbeat of each measure). Bach could use either D or D♯ because, by jumping down, he avoids the augmented second. Even though he could use either, Bach chooses D, the subtonic, which is the usual partner to the lowered submediant. It looks unusual to have the subtonic in an ascending line, but it makes sense once the important tendency tone is determined.

Figure 3.10 Mendelssohn, Violin Concerto, I

In the Mendelssohn, although the Cs in measures 4 and 11 move back to E, there is no leading tone, so there is no danger of the augmented second. More importantly, the goal pitch is the B; it ends the phrase, a significant landing point. The C is the appropriate scale degree for pulling to B. In measure 8, although the D♯ moves to B, the pitch really connects with the tonic two measures earlier. Since measure 7 is an exact repetition of measure 5, the D♯ sounds like an answer to the E.

A common student error is forgetting the accidental that creates the leading tone. Be careful not to do this, as your music will sound modal rather than tonal. Play through all assignments once you complete them, and make sure that it sounds stylistically appropriate, not like medieval music.

SUMMARY

Terminology

Mode. In its broadest sense, any collection of pitches in a scale. In this book, it will usually mean the difference between a major and a minor key.

The lowered submediant is another tendency tone. It resolves down to the dominant.
In minor, alterations of scale degrees $\hat{6}$ and $\hat{7}$ depend on the goal of the motion.
If the tonic is the goal, use the leading tone.
If the dominant is the goal, use the lowered submediant.
If $\hat{6}$ and $\hat{7}$ appear next to each other in minor, use the appropriate tendency tone to pull to the goal pitch. Adjust the neighboring note to remove its tendency and to avoid an augmented second.

NOTES

1. *Mode* is a problematic term. Although it basically means a scalar organization of pitches, the implied scales change depending on the time period under discussion. Sometimes people use it to refer to the eight different scales employed in the Middle Ages and Renaissance. See Appendix C for more information about them. In the sentence above, mode implies major versus minor scales. Here, the mode is different because we were looking at major keys before and now we are discussing minor. Usually, context will clarify the implied definition.
2. Textbooks more commonly use the notation ♭$\hat{6}$ and ♭$\hat{7}$ for the lowered submediant and the subtonic. Sometimes, however, the lowered form may not be flatted but may actually be a natural. For example, in B-minor, the lowered submediant is G♮ and the subtonic is A♮. As a result, I prefer the more general notation.

WORKBOOK

Again, work away from an instrument. Work on hearing the melodies and the scale degree functions in your head.

1. Choose two of the minor melodies in Appendix A. Analyze each based on the five traits of a good classical melody and also on the role of tendency tones L$\hat{6}$ and R$\hat{7}$. Do all melodic traits and scale degree functions pertain? Is the melody a period? If the piece is not classical music, do you think any differences result from stylistic issues, or are they just particular to this piece?

2. Find a minor melody you enjoy, from any genre of tonal music, and notate it below. Analyze it based on the five traits of a good classical melody and also on the role of tendency tones L$\hat{6}$ and R$\hat{7}$. Do all melodic traits and scale degree functions pertain? Is your melody a period? If you chose a piece that is not classical music, what traits are characteristic to that style?

3. Compose an eight-bar melody in any minor key besides A-minor. Do not use a time signature with 2 as the top number. You may do two four-bar phrases. Remember, it is better to think about the entire next measure rather than just the next pitch when deciding how to proceed. Once you are finished, analyze your melody as in questions 1 and 2.

4. Transpose the following melodies twice, both up and down a perfect fifth. Use accidentals instead of a key signature. As you transpose each melody, think in terms of scale degrees, not by moving each pitch by a certain interval.

Chromaticism in Melodies

CHAPTER LEARNING OBJECTIVES

This chapter:

- Explains the role of chromatic pitches in a melody
- Explains the significance of and connection between notation and function

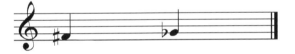

Figure 4.1

What is the difference between these two notes? F♯ and G♭ are *enharmonic*, which means that the two pitches are notated differently but sound the same. If played as written here, out of context, the pitches sound identical. If placed in the context of a particular key, however, the notes have different functions and therefore behave differently.

So far all the melodies studied have been *diatonic*, meaning that the pitches fit within a single scale. (In minor, both forms of scale degrees 6̂ and 7̂ are diatonic.) In classical music, accidentals often introduce *chromatic* pitches—pitches that do not belong to the tonic key. Chromaticism occurs on various levels in music. It can cause a piece to modulate, that is, it can change the tonic pitch. Modulation, however, is a topic for later. It requires longer pieces of music that have time to establish one key and then move to another. A single melody usually does not do this. (For example, in figure 2.2, the key signature does not match the key of the melody. The melody still is diatonic, however, just in F-major instead of C-major.) For now, therefore, we will focus on *local* effects, which affect only the altered note and its immediate neighbors. With local chromaticism, a listener hears the same tonic throughout.

Since a scale consists of all steps (whole or half), chromatic notes must be a half step from a diatonic pitch. Since the chromatically altered pitch is foreign to the key, it will be less stable than the neighboring scale degree. As a result, chromatically altered pitches function like tendency tones. They contain tension and pull toward the neighboring, stable scale degree. For this to be effective, the pitch of resolution should be stable. As a result, chromatic pitches do not resolve to tendency tones. For example, a chromatically altered $\hat{6}$ resolving to the leading tone does not occur.

Notation corresponds with function. Notes resolve to pitches with a different name. A♭ does not resolve to A♮. The natural undoes the chromaticism, rather than resolving it. A♭ will resolve down to G. If resolving to A♮, the altered pitch should be notated G♯. A rule of thumb that usually works is that chromatically raised pitches resolve up, while lowered pitches resolve down. In answer to the question posed at the beginning of the chapter, the difference between F♯ and G♭ is that usually the F♯ will resolve up to G, while the G♭ will resolve down to F.

Figure 4.2 The proper resolution of F♯ and G♭

Figure 4.3 shows the possible chromatic pitches in C-major and C-minor. Chromatic pitches can be labeled as raised and lowered variants of the normal scale degrees, so in the two scales in figure 4.3, D♭ is L$\hat{2}$ and F♯ is R$\hat{4}$. (As mentioned in the previous chapter, books more frequently refer to these scale degrees as ♭$\hat{2}$ and ♯$\hat{4}$, but I prefer the "lowered" and "raised" notation, since they are independent of the accidental used.) Figure 4.3 also contains two noteworthy reminders: (1) both forms of $\hat{6}$ and $\hat{7}$ are diatonic in minor, and (2) chromatic notes do not resolve to unstable pitches (tendency tones).

Figure 4.3 The chromatic pitches in C-major and C-minor

Deviations from the basic pattern usually are for ease of reading, for example, using E instead of F♭ or avoiding double flats or double sharps. These enharmonic equivalents are technically wrong but easier for the performer. Do not use them in a theory class.

The function of chromatic pitches is to add direction, emphasis, and color to a melody. Altered notes create direction by pulling toward another pitch; this drive results in additional emphasis on the note of resolution. The color added by chromaticism varies depending on its use. Several examples follow.

In figure 4.4, the melody is clearly still in D major, despite the presence of the chromatic pitch, so this note is a local effect. The chromatic addition helps create a lighthearted dance feeling.

Figure 4.4 Haydn, Symphony no. 104, III

In the Schumann example, on the other hand, the chromatic addition echoes the minor scale, creating a sad and pained feeling. The A♭ lands, appropriately enough, on the word "heart" in the phrase "even though my heart is breaking."

Figure 4.5 Schumann, "Ich grolle nicht" from *Dichterliebe* ("I Will Not Be Resentful" from *A Poet's Love*)

The Strauss piece is about a mischievous folklore character. Here the sustained chromatic pitches create a playful melody. By putting durational emphasis on a pitch that wants to resolve, Strauss creates an off-kilter melody. Also, although the piece is in 6, the pattern repeats every 7 eighth notes, shifting the accented, altered note within the meter, enhancing the mischievous feeling.

Figure 4.6 Strauss, *Till Eulenspiegels lustige Streiche*, op. 28 (*Till Eulenspiegel's Merry Pranks*)

Spotlight On: TEMPERED TUNING

Although we treat F♯ and G♭ as enharmonic, not every era has. As a matter of fact, in order to achieve this enharmonicity, most notes in our scale are slightly out of tune.

If a musician tunes an instrument by beginning with C, then tunes G a perfect fifth above and F a perfect fifth below, and continues around the circle of fifths in both directions, the two will not meet again at F♯ and G♭. There will be a slight difference between the two pitches, known as the comma. This system is called "natural tuning," as noted in the Beatles' song, "Baby, You're a Rich Man": "How does it feel to be one of the beautiful people, tuned to a natural E?"

During the seventeenth century, musicians realized that by slightly adjusting each pitch, the difference could be averaged out. For the first few pitches, such as the G and F, the deviation is negligible. As the pitches move farther from C, however, the adjustments get larger. In the end, all half steps lie equidistant from each other. This system is known as even-tempered tuning.

The result of this tuning is that all keys become accessible. Prior to its development, composers rarely used keys that contained more than three sharps or flats. These more remote keys sounded out of tune and were not practical. With even-tempered instruments, all keys sound equally in tune. Bach wrote *The Well-Tempered Clavier*, a collection of preludes and fugues in every single key, to showcase the new system.

Although tempered tuning is now the norm, some people lament its presence. Some argue that the sound of natural tuning conveys more emotion and power. Others argue that having all scales sound equally in tune is detrimental to the listening experience. In the past, keys sounded different because they varied in intonation. Now, unless a person has perfect pitch, all keys sound essentially the same.

SUMMARY

Terminology

Enharmonic. Describes two notes that sound the same but have different spellings, for example, C♯ and D♭.
Diatonic. All pitches in the music fit within the scale of a single key.
Chromatic. The music contains pitches from outside the scale of the functioning key.
Local chromaticism. A chromatic note that has implications only for itself and the next note. Contrasts with *long-range chromaticism*.

Chromatic pitches function like tendency tones and resolve to the nearest diatonic pitch (a half step away) with a different note name. Alterations that raise a diatonic pitch usually resolve up. Lowered notes generally resolve down.

WORKBOOK

1. Look at the melodies in Appendix A that contain chromatic notes. Do they resolve correctly? What scale degrees do they resolve to and thereby emphasize?

2. Look for examples of local chromatic pitches in some of the pieces you are currently playing. Notate the examples below. Do they resolve correctly? What scale degrees do they resolve to and thereby emphasize?

SPECIES COUNTERPOINT TO CHORALE STYLE

In 1725, the composer Johann Joseph Fux (1660–1741) published the book *Gradus ad Parnassum* (Steps to Parnassus), a treatise on how to compose music. The book was immensely successful, and most of the great musicians of the common-practice era studied it.

The book used species counterpoint to teach composition in the style of Giovanni Pierluigi da Palestrina (c. 1525–1594), whom Fux considered the greatest composer. Species counterpoint is a pedagogical tool that, while in some ways unmusical, can be a useful structure for the gradual introduction of various issues in composing. Although it is a teaching method, be musical in your assignments. Try to write the best melodies you can. Try to hear in your head what you are writing. Always double-check an assignment by singing it with a friend or playing it on the piano.

Since species exercises emulate a pre-common-practice style, the present textbook will deviate from tradition in several ways. The most notable difference is the use of tonal, rather than modal, cantus firmi.

I — PART

II — PART

III — PART

IV — PART

V — PART

CHAPTER — 5

Background for Species Counterpoint

CHAPTER LEARNING OBJECTIVES

This chapter:

• Defines the terminology for counterpoint

Figure 5.1 shows a piece of contrapuntal music. The goal of *counterpoint* is to combine independent melodies into a satisfying whole. Looking at the individual parts, is any voice more important than another? Is any melody more engaging than another? When you listen to the piece, what is the overall effect?

Counterpoint underlies all common-practice music. Although the Baroque is the only common-practice era that is predominantly contrapuntal, the later, more *homophonic* (melody with accompaniment) eras still followed the principles of counterpoint. As it underlies all of the music we will study, we must understand it.

Species counterpoint is a useful pedagogical tool to introduce the basics of contrapuntal writing. In these exercises, an existing melody, called the *cantus firmus* (fixed song) is given. To the cantus, the student adds a new melody. Five species exist. Each of the first four introduces a new musical concept. They do this by limiting the rhythmic values of the notes. Each species has a particular ratio between the rhythms of the cantus firmus and of the new melody. The fifth freely uses the rhythms and techniques from the previous four.

Before starting on exercises, however, we must establish the conventions used in theory assignments and some guidelines for creating effective counterpoint. As in the previous section on melody, this work emulates a vocal tradition. Melodies are written for one of the standard voice types: soprano, alto, tenor, or bass. The clefs and ranges for each of these voices are given in figure 5.2. In actual scores, tenor parts are not usually written in bass clef (see the Palestrina example), but for our purposes, it works better.[1] Also, we assume a basic church choir, so these ranges are not typical for professional singers. As a memory aid, all of the ranges begin and end on C or G, aside from the lowest note of the bass.

Figure 5.1 Palestrina, "Sanctus" from *Missa Aeterna Christi Munera*

Soprano   Alto   Tenor   Bass

Figure 5.2 Vocal ranges for theory exercises

Melodies in the exercises should be easy to sing; the goal is smooth, natural lines. The melodies should not contain awkward intervals. In Chapter 3, augmented seconds were forbidden because they were out of the common-practice style. Now the prohibition extends to all awkward intervals, including augmented seconds, tritones, sevenths, and ninths (figure 5.3). Leaps of these sizes are not common in the style because musicians viewed them as either difficult to sing or unduly harsh. In addition, awkward composite leaps—two or more leaps adding up to one of these intervals—are also out of the style (figure 5.3d). Another way to view this is that multiple leaps in the same direction should be members of a triad. (Although this book has not yet introduced triads, it assumes knowledge of the fundamentals.)

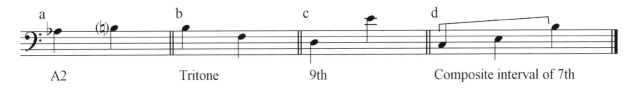

A2   Tritone   9th   Composite interval of 7th

Figure 5.3 Awkward vocal leaps

Avoid having two voices cross or overlap (figure 5.4). A *voice crossing* occurs when a lower voice moves above a higher one. A *voice overlap* occurs when a voice crosses beyond where the neighboring voice was one beat before. Overlaps and crossings confuse the ear as to which voice has which melody. They were permitted in the Renaissance, but by the common-practice period, they were mostly gone. For our purposes, they should be avoided. It is acceptable for two voices to meet on the same pitch.

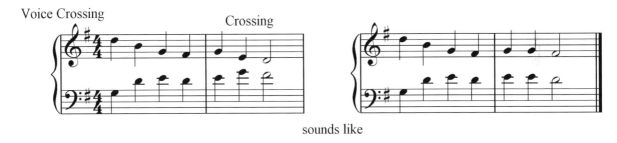

Voice Crossing   Crossing

sounds like

Voice Overlap

Overlap   Unison - fine

Figure 5.4 Voice crossing and voice overlap

Avoid cross-relations. *Cross-relations* (figure 5.5) result when one form of a pitch, for example F♮, appears in one voice, and on the next beat another form, for example F♯, appears in a different voice. They sound harsh and give the impression that one of the voices made a mistake. If at least one beat separates the clash, it becomes acceptable. A chromatic line in a single voice is also fine.

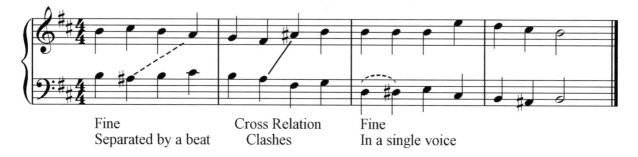

Fine
Separated by a beat

Cross Relation
Clashes

Fine
In a single voice

Figure 5.5 Cross-relation

As the melodies move, the relationship between the two voices changes in one of four possible ways. These are called the four types of motion and are shown in figure 5.6. They are:

- Parallel: voices move in the same direction from one interval to an identical generic interval (same number, but quality may be different)
- Similar: voices move in the same direction from one interval to a different interval
- Contrary: voices move in opposite directions
- Oblique: one voice moves and the other does not

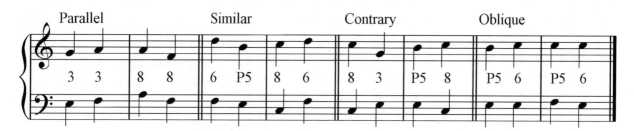

Parallel   Similar   Contrary   Oblique

Figure 5.6 Types of motion

The list of the types of motion is organized from the least useful to the most useful for counterpoint. If two melodies are always the same interval apart (parallel motion), then they are identical. Oblique motion provides the most independence, especially if the stationary voice sustains, providing rhythmic independence.

Finally, an important component of counterpoint is to understand which harmonic intervals sound best. A *harmonic interval* is the distance between two voices sounding simultaneously. (A melodic interval, on the other hand, is the distance between two adjacent notes within the same melody.) *Consonances* sound pleasant together, while *dissonances* clash. Consonances can be divided into two smaller categories, making three types of intervals:

- Perfect consonances—P1, P8, P5
- Imperfect consonance—m3, M3, m6, M6
- Dissonances—everything else (includes m2, M2, P4, m7, M7, and all diminished and augmented intervals)

The difference between the perfect and imperfect consonances is the amount of stability. Perfect consonances are extremely consonant (what could be more consonant than a unison?) and therefore very stable. They also sound more "hollow" (again, a unison has no "depth" to it; it is a single pitch). The imperfect consonances are stable, but less so, and they contain more "depth" or "warmth." The dissonances, since they clash with one another, have no stability at all.

The perfect fourth is a dissonance. This fact confuses many students, because it is the least harsh of all the dissonances and its name includes the word *perfect*.

Although the definitions of the consonances and dissonances include the quality of the intervals, these are not typically included in analyses of counterpoint. As long as the music is diatonic, all thirds and sixths will be major or minor and therefore imperfect consonances; all seconds, sevenths, and fourths are dissonant regardless of quality. The one interval that causes problems is the fifth. Most fifths will be perfect, but certain scale degrees lead to a diminished fifth. Students think that they are writing a consonance, but instead they are actually using a dissonance. The fifth is the one interval for which I ask that students include the quality. See figure 5.6 for an example.

Spotlight On: PERFECT AND IMPERFECT CONSONANCES

The descriptive terms to differentiate perfect and imperfect consonances—"hollow," "depth," and "warmth"—are vague, but they are the ones that musicians have used for ages. Physical/acoustical reasons exists for the difference. First, you can look at it in terms of overtones. All of the overtones in a pitch in one octave are also in the overtone structure of the pitch an octave below it. Figure 5.7 shows three fundamental pitches, A2, A3, and C#3, and their first three overtones. The composite overtone structure of the octave contains only six pitches (and although not shown, the two top two are already part of A2's overtones). The composite overtone structure of the M3 contains eight pitches.

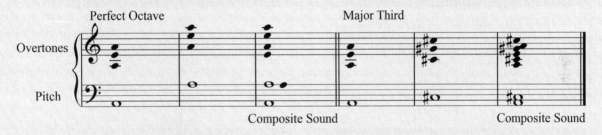

Figure 5.7 The overtone structures of a P8 and a M3

There is also an acoustic phenomenon called sum and difference tones, in which, due to interference between the two sound waves, we will hear new pitches equal to the sum and difference of the frequencies of the original tones. The ratio of the frequencies for perfect octaves and fifths are whole numbers. (For example, the frequency of a pitch an octave above another is exactly twice the lower pitch's frequency. The common tuning pitch is A = 440 Hz. The octave above is 880 Hz, and the octave below is 220 Hz.) Because of these even ratios, the sum and difference tones of an octave reproduce already-sounding frequencies. For other intervals, new pitches appear. If the sum and difference frequencies were included in figure 5.7, the perfect octave would still have only six pitches sounding, while the major third would increase to ten. We hear this more complicated overtone structure as richer and less hollow.

SUMMARY

Terminology

Counterpoint. Combining two or more independent melodies in a way to make a satisfying whole.

Homophony. A style of music characterized by melody with an accompaniment.

Species counterpoint. A pedagogical tool for teaching the basics of composition, specifically focusing on voice leading and dissonance control.

Cantus firmus. "Fixed song"; the given melody in a species counterpoint exercise, to which a newly composed melody is added.

Voice crossing. A lower voice sounds above a higher voice and vice-versa.

Voice overlap. A higher voice moves below the position of a lower voice on the preceding beat or vice-versa.

Cross-relation. Two forms of the same pitch, for example D♮ and D♭, appear on adjacent chords in different voices.

Parallel motion. Voices move in the same direction, maintaining the same generic interval.

Similar motion. Voices move in the same direction from one interval to a different interval.

Contrary motion. Voices move in opposite directions.

Oblique motion. One voice moves and the other does not.

Harmonic interval. The distance between two intervals sounding simultaneously. Contrasts with *melodic interval*.

Perfect consonance. A consonance in which the two pitches are so complementary that they sound extremely stable and somewhat "hollow." Intervals in this category are the P1, P8, and P5.

Imperfect consonance. A consonance in which the two pitches are less stable and have a fuller sound than the perfect consonances. Intervals in this category are the m3, M3, m6, and M6.

Dissonance. Two pitches that clash with each other, sounding unstable and pulling toward a resolution. Any intervals not listed in the consonances are dissonances.

In order to emulate the common-practice style of music, adhere to the following:

1. Keep voices within their ranges.

2. Avoid awkward leaps.

3. Avoid voice crossings and voice overlaps.

4. Avoid cross-relations.

NOTE

1. The clef in the Palestrina excerpt is the standard one used by tenors today. It transposes an octave down, which is an unnecessary additional step for us; by using the bass clef we can see the pitch where it sounds.

WORKBOOK

1. Analysis: Analyze the intervals in the two excerpts given.

- Between the staves, identify the interval that occurs every time a voice moves. You may use simple intervals, and you do not need to label the quality, just the number, except for the P5 (to distinguish it, a consonance, from the d5, a dissonance).

- Count the occurrence of each interval and complete the tables that follow the examples. What do you notice about the intervals, with regard to either their frequency or how they are used?

A. Morley, "Fantasia: The Shepherd's Pipe"

TABLE 5.1	Interval Count							
Interval	1 (and 8)	2	3	4	d5	P5	6	7
Occurrences								

B. Guami, Ricercare 16

TABLE 5.2	Interval Count							
Interval	1 (and 8)	2	3	4	d5	P5	6	7
Occurrences								

First Species in Two Voices (Note against Note)

CHAPTER LEARNING OBJECTIVES

This chapter:

- Explains the role of perfect and imperfect consonances in a two-voice passage

- Explains the prohibition of parallel perfect consonances to ensure independence between the melodies

- Explains how to clarify the key at the beginning of a passage

- Explains how to provide closure at the end of a passage

In first species, the new melody contains one note for every note in the cantus firmus, and the two voices move at the same time, hence the name "note against note." The new voice may be added above or below the given melody. The duration of the notes does not matter. Traditional species exercises use whole notes in the cantus firmus, but this book employs a variety of durations to emphasize that the important parameter is the ratio between the voices, not the absolute duration. The repercussions of this fact are more significant in later species.

Each species employs only a few rules. Although the rules are extremely limiting, at the same time, they allow for an enormous number of possible melodies. The rules for first species are the following:

1. All harmonic intervals must be consonant.

2. The exercise begins and ends with perfect consonances that clarify tonic.

3. Avoid parallel and direct perfect consonances.

The first rule teaches the consonances. It is one of the main lessons of first species exercises. Consonances provide the support for all later uses of dissonances, so it is important to establish them at the beginning.

The second rule concerns the key and scale degree functions. A cantus firmus begins and ends on the tonic, since this structure is the most common for melodies. Octaves and unisons are the most common opening and closing sonorities. Opening on a doubled tonic quickly establishes the tonality (key), and ending on a doubled tonic provides a sense of closure to the exercise. You may open on a perfect fifth, but note that it must be the tonic and the dominant. The ear hears a fifth as reinforcing the bottom note. A fifth using $\hat{1}$ and $\hat{5}$ still states the tonality. Opening with a fifth below the tonic, however, emphasizes the subdominant and obscures the key (see figure 6.1).

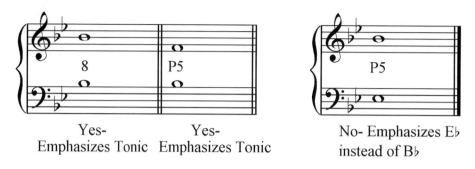

Yes-   Yes-
Emphasizes Tonic   Emphasizes Tonic

No- Emphasizes E♭
instead of B♭

Figure 6.1 Suitable opening sonorities

The last rule encourages independence of the melodies, a crucial aspect of counterpoint and the second important lesson of first species. When a family sings "Happy Birthday," individual members will use different octaves. No one would say that they are singing different melodies; a listener essentially hears a single line. The danger with parallel perfect consonances is that they minimize the independence of the lines. Taking the extreme case, if a unison immediately follows another unison, the melodies clearly lose their independence for those two beats. Parallel octaves and fifths have the same basic effect (figure 6.2a).

Stylistically Inappropriate

Stylistically Acceptable

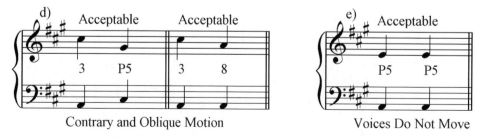

Contrary and Oblique Motion   Voices Do Not Move

Figure 6.2 Common-practice handling of perfect consonances

Direct perfect consonances result from the two voices moving by similar motion to a perfect consonance (figure 6.2b). Although not as problematic as parallel perfect consonances, the effect is still poor according to the common-practice period's musical ideals. The voices should approach perfect consonances by contrary motion (figure 6.2d).

Two clarifications: First, moving from a perfect consonance to the same perfect consonance through contrary motion, while not technically a bad parallel, remains weak and is a cheap way around the problem (figure 6.2c). Second, repeated notes do not constitute parallel motion. The voices have to move to create bad parallels (figure 6.2e).

One exception exists to the prohibition against direct perfect consonances. Common-practice composers use them if the top voice moves by step. The smooth melodic motion softens the impact. A leap in the top voice draws too much attention to the perfect consonance, no matter what the bottom voice does (see figure 6.3).

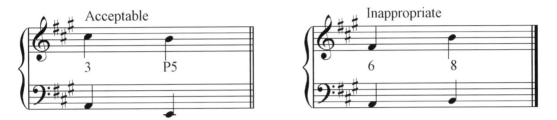

Figure 6.3 Exception to the prohibition against direct perfect consonances

Rule number three describes *voice leading*, that is, the relationship between voices as they move. Any topic regarding the motion and interplay of voices falls under this category. Voice crossings, voice overlaps, cross-relations, parallel perfect consonances, and direct perfect consonances are all voice-leading issues.

Those three rules are all that are necessary to practice first species exercises. Before beginning, here are some aesthetic issues to keep in mind.

Aside from the opening and closing, use perfect consonances sparingly. Because of their stability and hollowness, perfect consonances interrupt the flow of the music and make it sound less full. Imperfect consonances, on the other hand, have more warmth and are not completely stable, so they propel the music forward. Avoiding perfect consonances will also minimize the chances of writing bad parallels.

Similar and parallel thirds and sixths can be a nice effect, but use them in moderation, no more than three or four in a row. Too much similar motion undermines the independence of the melodies, and your exercises will be more in the style of a campfire sing-along than a classical piece.

A *cadence* is an arrival in a piece of music. It is a landing point where a musical thought has been completed. Composers can use them to delineate sections of the music, ranging from the ending of a phrase to the close of the entire piece. Different cadences exist for different effects; some pause but maintain tension, while others dissipate energy, creating a sense of finality. Cadences often use standard gestures, so that the endings are clear and readily understood.

Species exercises are microcosms of pieces of music. They are short, complete works that typify the basics of larger compositions. Cantus firmi do this by beginning and ending on the tonic pitch, capturing the overall motion from rest to tension and back to rest. From this perspective, we need a strong sense of closure at the end. The cadence is one of finality. Cantus firmi usually end with the pattern $\hat{2} \rightarrow \hat{1}$, because this is a common melodic gesture at the end of a tune. For the strongest sense of closure, the new melody should also end on the tonic. Since melodies usually move by stepwise motion, the most likely conclusion for the newly composed line is $\hat{7} \rightarrow \hat{1}$. The basic cadential gesture for these exercises is shown in figure 6.4, where C.F. indicates the cantus firmus. When we look at two-voice compositions, we will see that this is the actual cadence composers used. (Look at the two excerpts for the workbook in Chapter 5. How do they end?) Students should use this standard cadence in their exercises.

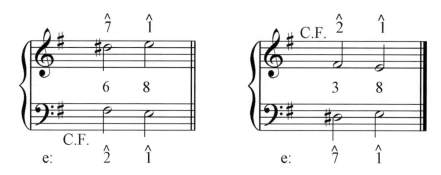

Figure 6.4 Possible cadences

Finally, sing through the exercises. Begin by singing through the cantus firmus. Look for interesting moments, such as distinctive leaps or significant repetitions. Sing the new melody as you compose it. Feel the tendency tones. Try to craft an interesting and engaging tune. (This is difficult, especially for first species exercises.) Imagine what the two melodies will sound like before playing them on the piano.

Figure 6.5 gives a suggestion of how to limit your options to help you begin working. You already know that, when composing a new melody above, your opening interval should be a perfect fifth or octave. You also know what the standard cadence is. For the measures in between, I have identified the consonant pitches for each note in the cantus. The top two pitches are the imperfect consonances. The bottom two are the perfect ones.

Figure 6.5 The possible consonances for each note of the cantus firmus

Once all of the options are laid out, it becomes a mix of artistry, logic, and experimentation. There is no single correct answer. Figure 6.6 gives four options for the first four notes of the new melody, and many more possible solutions exist. You have to try different possibilities, crafting the best melody you can, while avoiding unstylistic traits, such as too many perfect consonances and inappropriate parallels.

This chapter and the following ones will contain examples of species exercises taken from various authors (Bridge, Fux, Jeppeson, Schenker, or Stone). Figure 6.7 shows two first species exercises using the same major-key cantus firmus. One melody is written above the cantus firmus and the other is added below. Between the two staves are numbers identifying the intervals between the voices. The letters above the top staff and below the bottom staff describe the type of motion between the two voices. This analysis highlights the emphasis on imperfect consonances and contrary and oblique motion. The two minor-key exercises in figure 6.8 are left unanalyzed, in order to be done in the workbook section.

Figure 6.6 Four possible openings for the new melody

Figure 6.7 Two major-key exercises

Above

Jeppesen

Below

Stone
(C.F. by Jeppesen)

Figure 6.8 Two minor-key exercises

SUMMARY

Terminology

Parallel perfect consonances. Two of the same perfect consonances occurring in the same two voices on adjacent harmonies. The voices must move to constitute parallel perfect consonances; repeated notes do not count.

Direct perfect consonances. Two voices moving to a perfect consonance by similar motion.

Voice leading. The relationship between voices as they move in music. Topics such as types of motion, voice crossings, voice overlaps, parallel perfect consonances, and direct perfect consonances are all voice-leading issues.

Cadence. An arrival in music, indicating the completion of a thought. Cadences can end a phrase, a section, or an entire piece. Cadences of varying strengths are used for different effects.

First species counterpoint involves one note in the new melody for each note in the cantus firmus.

Rules:

- All harmonic intervals must be consonant.
- Open and close with perfect consonances.
- Avoid parallel and direct perfect consonances.

Use perfect consonances sparingly mid-exercise.
Use parallel and similar thirds and sixths in moderation.
Use the standard cadence at the end of the exercise.

WORKBOOK

1. Analysis: Analyze the minor-key exercises in figure 6.8.
   - Below each system, identify the key of the exercise.
   - Between the staves, identify the interval that occurs every time a voice moves. You may use simple intervals, and you do not need to label the quality, just the number, except for the P5.
   - Outside the system, identify the type of motion between the two voices.

2. Counterpoint: Using some of the cantus firmi at the end of the book, write two-voice first species exercises above and below. For variety, vary the key and register of the cantus firmi. Provide an analysis of your exercise:
   - Below each system, identify the key of the exercise.
   - Between the staves, identify the interval that occurs every time a voice moves. You may use simple intervals, and you do not need to label the quality, just the number, except for the P5, in order to ensure that you do not use a tritone.
   - Outside the system, identify the type of motion between the two voices.

Second and Third Species in Two Voices (Two and Four Notes to One)

CHAPTER LEARNING OBJECTIVES

This chapter:

- Explains rhythmic accentuation and its role in using dissonances
- Defines and explains the handling of passing tones and neighbor tones

In second species, the new melody contains two notes for each note in the cantus firmus, while in third species, four notes occur for each note in the cantus. The notes in the new melody are always of equal durations. Traditionally, these species are presented separately. The important concepts in each of them are the same, however, so this book combines them.

The rules for these species are:

1. The voice-leading issues from first species (no parallel or direct perfect consonances) still hold.

2. The harmonic intervals on strong beats or strong parts of beats must be consonant.

3. The harmonic intervals on weak beats or parts of beats may be consonant or dissonant. If dissonant, they must be approached and left by step. If consonant, they may be approached and left in any fashion.

These rules emphasize two important concepts. First, a measure or beat subdivides into strong and weak beats. This principle is true whenever any unit is divided into smaller parts. This book uses different durational values in the cantus firmi to highlight this fact. Many people know that in a common-time measure, the first beat is strongest, the third beat is next strongest, and the second and fourth beats are weak. An analogous accentuation pattern occurs when a quarter note is divided into four sixteenth notes. In general, when a value is split into two, the first subdivision is strong while the second is weak. If these two are further split into four, the aforementioned strongest–weak–strong–weak pattern results. Everything is relative to the smallest subdivision—the pattern continues indefinitely (figure 7.1).

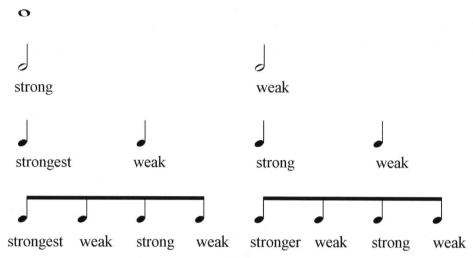

Figure 7.1 Accentuation of subdivisions

Second, these species introduce the role of dissonances. Since dissonances clash, they create tension and instability. They want to move to a stable (consonant) pitch, which gives the music direction and forward drive. In common-practice music, dissonances do not exist without connecting to a stable pitch. This connection helps propel the music.

These two species introduce the two most common dissonances, the passing tone and neighbor tone (figure 7.2). The *passing tone* is by far the most common dissonance. It occurs on a weak subdivision and connects two consonances a third apart. It is approached by step and left by step in the same direction. The *neighbor tone* also occurs on a weak subdivision, and it is approached by step and left by step in the opposite direction.

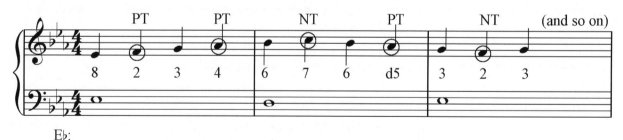

Figure 7.2 Passing tones and neighbor tones

These two concepts, accentuation and dissonance, complement each other. Stable consonances occur on strong subdivisions so that they are emphasized. The first note in each grouping, the strongest, must be consonant. Unstable dissonances, on the other hand, occur in weak positions, where they can be more subtle. In third species, the third note of each group of four is strong, but not as strong as the first. Accordingly, it usually is consonant, but may be dissonant. For these exercises, the size of the smallest rhythmic value and the ratio between the cantus firmus and the new melody take precedence over metrical issues. For examples, if the new melody moves in sixteenth notes, all downbeats, regardless of their position in the measure, must be consonant (figure 7.3). Beat 2 may be metrically weak, but relative to the other three sixteenth notes on that beat, the downbeat is strong.

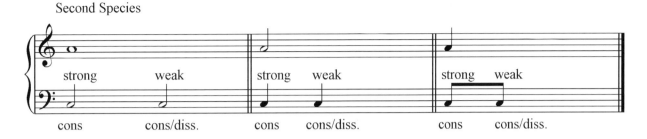

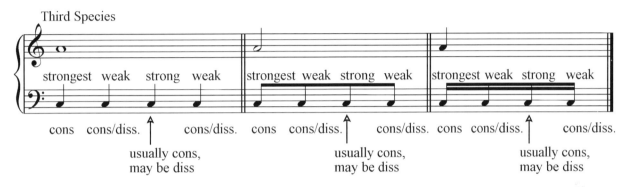

Figure 7.3 Accentuation and dissonance in species exercises

Consonances provide a stable underpinning for the music. The dissonances move over this stable structure, connecting the consonances. Dissonances are less fundamental to the structure than consonances. As a result, dissonances cannot break up unstylistic parallels (figure 7.4a). In order to break up problematic voice leading, the melody must move to a new consonance. Although nothing is technically wrong with having perfect consonances on successive strong beats if interrupted by another consonance, the music sounds hollow because of the emphasis on the perfect consonances (figure 7.4b). It is better to avoid this pattern, especially in two voices. Placing perfect consonances on successive weak beats is fine (figure7.4c).

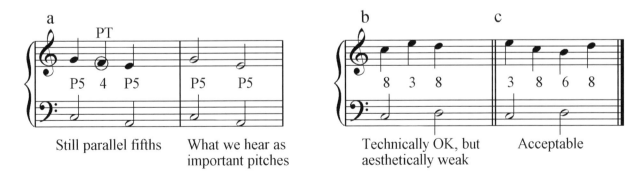

Figure 7.4 Dissonances do not fix voice-leading issues, but consonances can

As if life were not unfair enough, while dissonances cannot fix bad voice leading, they can cause it. Although more problematic with three or more voices, it can happen with two.

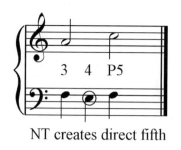

NT creates direct fifth

Figure 7.5 Dissonances can cause unstylistic voice leading

A few last thoughts. These exercises may open with a rest. The first note must still be a perfect consonance that reinforces the tonic, but it may begin on the offbeat.

Cadences occur in metrically strong positions. This placement aids the finality of the sound. In light of this fact, the last note of the new melody is not subdivided. Both voices end with the same durational value.

Do not immediately repeat notes in second and third species. It is not musically wrong, but it defeats the purpose of the exercise. In second species, repeating a pitch against the same note in the cantus firmus reduces to first species. Repeating a note across two notes in the cantus (from weak to strong) relates to fourth species. For third species, the problems are similar (reducing to second species, in the first case). Octave leaps are an acceptable way around this problem, but they can make the melody disjointed and awkward to sing.

As before with cadences, the new melody moves from $\hat{7}$ to $\hat{1}$ for its final two notes. Second species has a typical cadence above and below (figure 7.6), although others are possible. For third species, with four notes in the new melody moving against scale degree $\hat{2}$ in the cantus firmus, a variety of patterns exist.

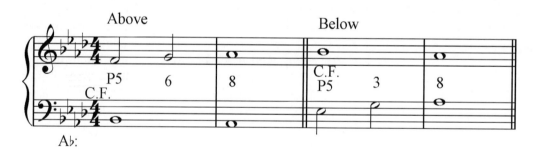

Figure 7.6 Common second species cadences

It is also possible to do these exercises in triple meters. When the new melody contains three pitches for each note in the cantus, the first note is strong while the other two are weak. Accordingly, the first beat must be consonant, while either or both of the other two may be dissonant. If dissonant, approach and leave by step.

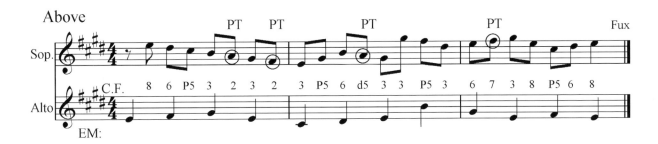

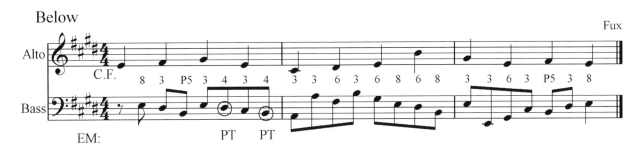

Figure 7.7 Two major-key second species exercises

Figure 7.8 Two minor-key second species exercises

Figure 7.9a Two major-key third species exercises

Figure 7.9b

Figure 7.10 Two minor-key third species exercises

SUMMARY

Terminology

Passing tone. A weak dissonance approached by step and left by step in the same direction.
Neighbor tone. A weak dissonance approached by step and left by step in the opposite direction.

Second species has two equal-duration notes for each note in the cantus firmus.
Third species has four equal-duration notes for each note in the cantus firmus.

Rules:

- Voice leading from first species still holds.
- Strong beats must be consonant.
- Weak beats may be consonant or dissonant.
  o Dissonances must be approached and left by step.

Dissonances do not break up parallel perfect consonances, but they may create them.
Avoid the immediate repetition of a note.

WORKBOOK

1. Analysis: Analyze the minor-key exercises in figures 7.8 and 7.10.
   - Below each system, identify the key of the exercise.
   - Between the staves, identify the interval that occurs every time a voice moves. You may use simple intervals, and you do not need to label the quality, just the number, except for the P5.
   - Circle and label any dissonances.

2. Counterpoint: Using some of the cantus firmi at the end of the book, write two-voice, second- and third-species exercises above and below. Provide an analysis of your exercise:
   - Below each system, identify the key of the exercise.
   - Between the staves, identify the interval that occurs every time a voice moves. You may use simple intervals, and you do not need to label the quality, just the number, except for the P5, in order to ensure that you do not use a tritone.
   - Circle and label any dissonances.

Fourth Species in Two Voices (Syncopations and Suspensions)

CHAPTER LEARNING OBJECTIVES

This chapter:

- Explains how to handle dissonances in accented positions
- Defines suspensions

In fourth species, the new melody contains two notes for each pitch in the cantus firmus, but the first note is tied to the preceding pitch and the second note is tied to the following pitch (figure 8.1). In essence, this species is like first species, but the new melody is syncopated relative to the cantus. As with second and third species, the exercise may begin with a rest.

Figure 8.1 Rhythmic pattern for fourth species

The rules for this species are the following:

1. The weak beat or weak part of the beat (i.e., the second note) must be consonant.

2. The strong beat or part of the beat (i.e., the first note) may be consonant or dissonant, but if it is dissonant, it must resolve down by step to a consonance. If it is consonant, it can move anywhere.

This species emphasizes dissonance. The dissonances appear on accented locations, drawing attention to the clash and savoring the tension produced by it. Because the dissonance is in a prominent position, composers handle it carefully. It is approached by common tone and resolved by step down. This type of dissonance is called a *suspension*.

Downward motion dissipates the tension more efficiently than upward, so composers usually resolve all strong dissonances down by step. The one exception is the leading tone. In order to satisfy the upward pull, leading tones may resolve up to the tonic when suspended. Any pitches that have a tendency to resolve upward (the other case is chromatically raised pitches) may do so when suspended. This sentence says "may." Even leading tones usually resolve down in suspensions, showing just how important a downward resolution is for a strong dissonance.

Although any dissonance to consonance is possible, resolutions into imperfect consonances are preferable to those into perfect consonances, for the reasons presented in previous chapters. Figure 8.2 shows examples of possible suspensions; the name of a suspension corresponds to the intervals involved. For the most part, simple intervals are used, but people differentiate between the 9–8 and 2–1 suspensions. The 2–1 is extremely rare because, on account of the unison, the resolution is lost. Rather than hearing a suspension and resolution, the dissonance just seems to disappear. Also, a 7–8 suspension below the cantus does not occur. When a composer has a dissonance of a seventh, they resolve the top voice to a sixth, an imperfect consonance, rather than the bottom voice to an octave, a perfect consonance. In addition, since 7–6 suspensions are so common, people expect the top voice of a seventh, instead of the bottom, to move down.

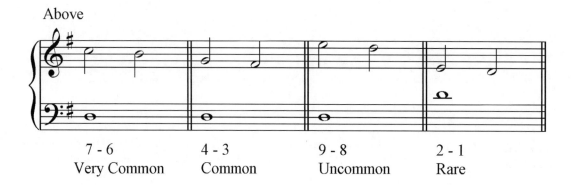

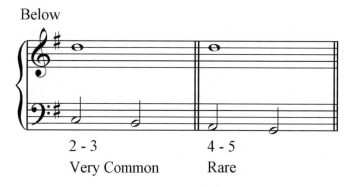

Figure 8.2 Possible suspensions

Later, in a functional harmonic context, a 6–5 suspension is possible. For now, since both intervals are consonant, a 6–5 is not a suspension.

As mentioned with passing tones and neighbor tones, dissonances cannot fix voice-leading problems. The consonances provide the fundamental structure, so check for unstylistic parallels by examining the intervals on the second note of each pair (figure 8.3). If the first note is consonant and not a suspension, then both notes are considered part of the underlying structure.

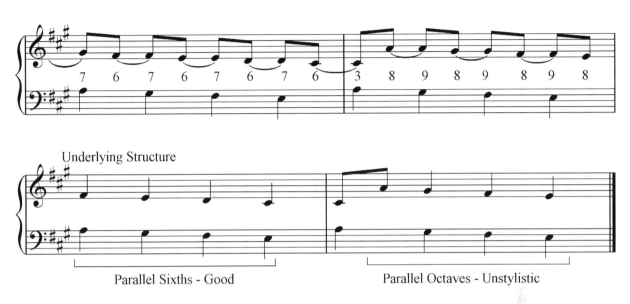

Figure 8.3 Underlying consonant structure and voice-leading issues

The standard cadences for this species involve suspending the tonic over the supertonic. $\hat{1}$ resolves into $\hat{7}$, which then returns to $\hat{1}$ at the cadence (figure 8.4).

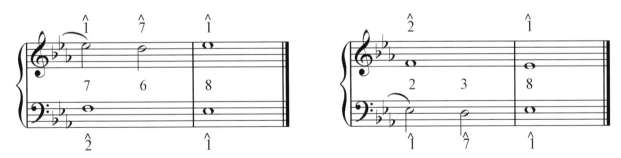

Figure 8.4 Standard cadences

A few final words of advice: When the cantus contains a descending scalar passage, a *chain of suspensions* is an effective device (figure 8.5). In a chain, the two voices move downward alternately, creating a suspension on every strong beat (or part thereof). This pattern will not work with a suspension that resolves to a perfect consonance (see figure 8.3).

If necessary, you may use second species briefly, in order to set up more suspensions. Because these exercises are for practice, try to syncopate as many notes and suspend as many dissonances as possible. Although the new line should be easy to sing, it is almost impossible to write a truly engaging melody for a fourth species exercise.

Figure 8.5 Chain of suspensions

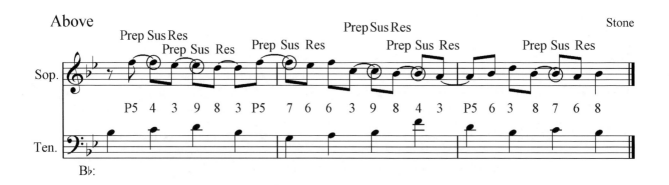

Figure 8.6 Two major-key fourth species exercises

Above

Below

Bridge

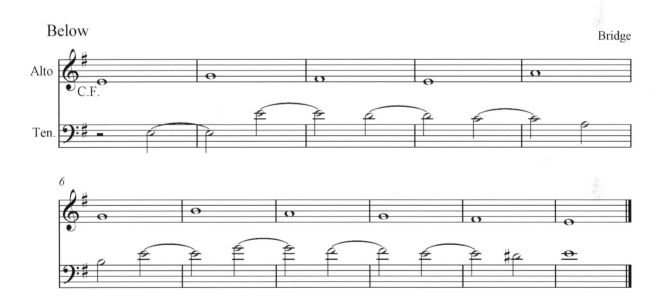

Figure 8.7 Two minor-key fourth species exercises

SUMMARY

Terminology

Suspension. A strong dissonance, approached by common tone and resolved by step down.
Chain of suspensions. A pattern in which the resolution of one suspension serves as the preparation for the next.

Fourth species has two notes in the new melody for each note in the cantus firmus, but the first is tied to the previous note and the second is tied to the following note, creating a syncopated melody.

Rules:

- The second note of each pair must be consonant.
- The first note may be consonant or dissonant.
  - Dissonances must resolve down by step.

Suspensions do not fix voice-leading problems.

WORKBOOK

1. Analysis: Analyze the minor-key exercises in figure 8.7.
   - Below each system, identify the key of the exercise.
   - Between the staves, identify the interval that occurs every time a voice moves. You may use simple intervals, and you do not need to label the quality, just the number, except for the P5.
   - Circle and label any dissonances. Also label the consonant preparation and resolution of each suspension.

2. Counterpoint: Using some of the cantus firmi at the end of the book, write two-voice fourth species exercises above and below. Provide an analysis of your exercise:
   - Below each system, identify the key of the exercise.
   - Between the staves, identify the interval that occurs every time a voice moves. You may use simple intervals, and you do not need to label the quality, just the number, except for the P5, in order to ensure that you do not use a tritone.
   - Circle and label any dissonances. Also label the consonant preparation and resolution of each suspension.

Fifth Species (Florid Counterpoint) in Two Voices

CHAPTER LEARNING OBJECTIVES

This chapter:

- Explains fifth species, which combines the preceding four species

- Explains some idiomatic rhythmic patterns and ornamental gestures in common-practice music

The first four species introduce some fundamental principles of music composition. First species focuses on the dominance of consonance and the basics of voice leading. Second and third species present the strong and weak subdivisions of a beat as well as the use of common weak dissonances. Fourth species teaches accented dissonances.

Fifth species freely employs all of these concepts. Anything from the previous four species can now be used in order to create a well-crafted, engaging melody. As with the previous species, these exercises should begin with a perfect consonance that establishes the key, and should end on an octave. Like the second through fourth species, a melody may begin on an upbeat.

Since the goal is the creation of an engaging melody, keep in mind the characteristics presented in the first section of this book. Make sure that the melody is singable, has direction and growth, and is balanced. Coherence is crucially important and useful because, as with composing free melodies, once you have a good opening, the rest falls into place. Look for places in the cantus firmus where you can reuse the opening pattern, providing coherence and saving time.

The freedom of fifth species introduces a few new issues. First, rhythmic values usually reinforce the strong and weak subdivisions of beats. Longer notes often fall on accented beats or subdivisions, while shorter notes commonly fall in weak positions. Basically, rhythms should drive forward, toward the next strong beat. Contradicting this tendency produces a syncopated or even jerky feeling. While it is not wrong to use a *backward rhythm*, be aware that, unless handled carefully, it will make a piece sound less classical and may make it sound awkward. *Forward rhythms* are more common.

Figure 9.1 Forward and backward rhythms

Along related lines, forward and backward ties exist. In a *forward tie*, a longer note precedes a shorter one. In a *backward tie*, the reverse is true. Backward ties are much less common than backward rhythms in common-practice music, so generally avoid them.

Figure 9.2 Forward and backward ties

The resolutions of suspensions may be ornamented. Some common ornaments include a fast neighbor motion, a leap to a consonance preceding the note of resolution, and an anticipation of the note. Examples of these ornaments appear in figure 9.3. Whatever ornament a composer opts to use, the note of resolution still occurs in its typical position. Even if the notes appears earlier in the ornamentation, the true resolution arrives at its normal location.

Figure 9.3 Ornaments on suspensions

Finally, although cadences from any of the preceding species are possible, the suspended tonic gesture from the fourth species is most common.

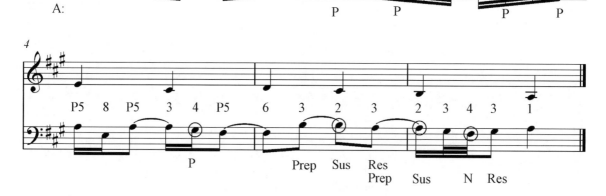

Figure 9.4 Two major-key fifth species exercises

Figure 9.5 Two minor-key fifth species exercises

SUMMARY

Terminology

Forward rhythm. A rhythmic pattern in which the shorter durations fall in weaker positions, driving into the next strong beat.

Backward rhythm. A rhythmic pattern in which the shorter durations land in stronger positions, leading to a syncopated effect.

Forward tie. A tie in which a longer duration is tied to an equal or shorter one.

Backward tie. A tie in which a shorter duration is tied to a longer one.

Fifth species freely employs all of the preceding four species.

Craft a good melody, being aware of steps and leaps, contour and growth, and coherence.

Be aware of backward rhythms.

Avoid backward ties.

WORKBOOK

1. Analysis: Analyze the minor-key exercises in figure 9.5.
   - Below each system, identify the key of the exercise.
   - Between the staves, identify the interval that occurs every time a voice moves. You may use simple intervals, and you do not need to label the quality, just the number, except for the P5.
   - Circle and label any dissonances. For suspensions, also label the preparation and the resolution.

2. Find the Errors: The two fifth species exercises given here contain numerous stylistic errors. Circle and identify the mistakes.

3. Counterpoint: Using some of the cantus firmi at the end of the book, write two-voice fifth species exercises above and below. Provide an analysis of your exercise:

- Below each system, identify the key of the exercise.
- Between the staves, identify the interval that occurs every time a voice moves. You may use simple intervals, and you do not need to label the quality, just the number, except for the P5, in order to ensure that you do not use a tritone.
- Circle and label any dissonances. For suspensions, also label the preparation and the resolution.

Two-Voice Counterpoint

CHAPTER LEARNING OBJECTIVES

This chapter:

- Explains the connection between the preceding exercises and actual two-voice contrapuntal compositions

We can now move beyond species counterpoint exercises into the realm of actual pieces. The current examples will be Renaissance pieces, because later works will contain other dissonances. These other dissonances will be explained in Chapter 18. For now, we are focusing the basics of voice leading and the most common dissonances.

Although some composers and styles incorporated a cantus firmus, many pieces did not. Often the two voices move at approximately the same rate. In such instances, either voice can contain dissonances. Regardless of which voice contains the dissonance, however, it is still handled in the same fashion: the music does not leap to or from a dissonance, and accented dissonances resolve down.

The one dissonance resolution that may look different is the suspension. In species exercises, the suspension always resolves while the other voice sustains its note. When the two voices move at approximately the same rate, it is possible for the nonsuspended voice to move while the suspension resolves. The suspension still has to resolve down into a consonance. In the example in figure 10.1, the music may leap from the E in the bass since that is a consonant note. The note it goes to, however, is still consonant with the resolution of the suspension.

Cadences will usually be the suspension gesture from fourth (and fifth) species. As mentioned in Chapter 6, different strength cadences exist to demarcate different sections of a piece. The cadences in our exercises always mirror a final, closing cadence. In actual music, a phrase can cadence on any pitch, not just the tonic. This provides variety and helps

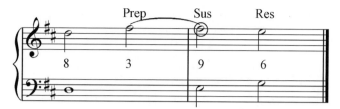

Figure 10.1 A possible suspension resolution

the music flow. If a composer repeatedly cadences on the tonic, the piece sounds sectional, as if continually coming to a conclusion and then restarting. Of course, the final cadence will be on the tonic and will be what we use in our exercises.

As you look at scores and listen to pieces, think about all of the musical parameters involved. What keeps the melodies independent? What creates coherence within a single voice? What creates coherence between the two voices? Where are cadences and what pitches do they emphasize? Is there a climax in each voice? Is there one overall climax?

Figure 10.2 shows a two-voice canzonet by Thomas Morley. The score includes labels on the dissonances.

First, a few comments on the voice leading and dissonance control. In measure 7, beat 4, the tenor's B is the dissonance. It looks odd because we usually see the dissonance in the faster-moving voice; passing tones are usually on the offbeat on the eighth-note level. The leap between the G and E, however, indicates that they are both consonances. The implied consonance is with the C that has been present in the tenor for the first three beats. The B is a passing tone, approached and left by step, falling on the metrically weak fourth beat.

In measures 10 and 11, the fifths are broken up by consonances, so they are not parallel fifths. If this same passage were written with suspensions instead of consonances, parallel fifths would be present. Dissonances cannot fix problematic voice leading; consonances can.

Measure 11 also contains an example of an ornamented resolution of a suspension.

In measures 48 and 61, the tenor moves one note out of our ranges. All of the "rules" we study are generalizations. Occasionally, composers will break them, always for musical reasons. For theory classes, demonstrate comprehension by following the generalizations.

Notice the presence of accidentals. Since species exercises are short, chromatic pitches rarely appear in them. In a larger work, they provide variety. Chapter 4 explained that chromatic pitches behave like tendency tones. A raised pitch usually resolves up by half step while a lowered pitch resolves down. All of the chromatic pitches in this piece resolve as expected, except for the B♭ in measure 21. Arrows show the usual resolution.

Finally, all cadences use the most common pattern—the fourth species suspension gesture.

Now consider the piece overall. What makes it work as a piece of music? First, look at the cadences. As mentioned previously, not all phrases end on the tonic. Once the music establishes the tonic, any strong cadence on 1̂ will sound like the end, either of the piece or of a significant section. Because of this fact, Morley avoids cadencing on the tonic until the end. The first time he arrives on the tonic, he resolves to a third rather than a unison. This voicing makes the cadence sound less final and allows the music to continue with the repetition. For the last phrase, even though cadencing on the unison would sound more final, Morley opts to repeat the third.

The two voices are coherent in the sense that they work together as counterpoint. For that reason alone they do not sound unrelated. Morley heightens the connection between them even more by writing a canon. A canon is a technique where one voice imitates the other by following some rule. For example, for the first line the rule is "repeat the melody transposed up a fifth." Morley also keeps the work coherent overall by repeating sections. Measures 55 to the end are a repetition of measures 42 to 54. In these ways, Morley creates an internally consistent work that holds together well.

This analysis scratches the surface because it states facts. An analysis should delve into the realm of interpretation. Where is the climax of the work? Should a performer vary the material on a repetition? Is it a good piece of music? Why or why not? Rather than pushing my opinions, I leave those questions for class discussion.

In Nets of Golden Wyers

Thomas Morley
(1557-1603)

Figure 10.2a

Figure 10.2b

Figure 10.2c

SUMMARY

Many two-voice compositions do not use a cantus firmus.
Either voice may use dissonance; the dissonances will be treated in the normal fashion.

WORKBOOK

1. Analysis: Analyze the two motets "Motet" by Banchieri and "Justi Tulerunt Spolia" by Lassus.

- From the beginning to the downbeat of measure 17, identify the harmonic intervals every time a voice moves. (Place them between the staves.)

- Throughout the entire score, circle and label all dissonances. If the dissonance is a suspension, identify the consonant preparation, the resolution, and the intervals involved.

- Throughout the entire score, at each cadence, place a bracket above the cadential gesture and write, "Cadence on _____," where the blank is the pitch on which the phrase closes.

Motet
from *The Cartella Musicale*

Adriano Banchieri
(1568-1634)

Justi Tulerunt Spolia

Orlande de Lassus
(1532-1594)

2. Composition: Write a twelve-measure, two-voice canon at the octave (the second voice imitating the first one octave up). You may break off the imitation a few measures before the cadence in order to create a convincing conclusion. Work away from an instrument, and double-check by singing it with a friend or playing it on the piano. You may use one of the beginnings provided, or you may write your own piece altogether. Analyze your composition. Identify the key, label all intervals between the staves, and circle and label the dissonances.

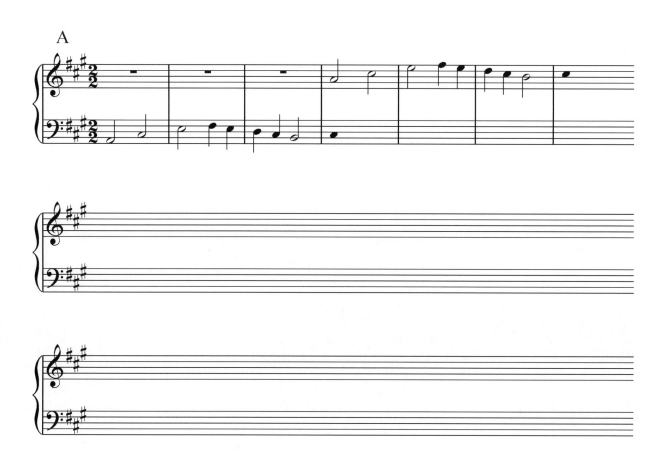

B

Three Voices and Chords

The addition of a third voice presents a new issue. What are the basic consonant harmonic sonorities (sounds)?

The three-voice stable sonorities result from combining consonant intervals. Composers viewed the bass as supporting the pitches in the upper voices. For a combination of notes to be stable, all intervals must be consonant with the bass. The upper voices should also be consonant with each other, although the weak dissonances of the perfect fourth and the tritone can appear. Following these guidelines, two stable diatonic combinations exist for a given bass note (figure 11.1).

Figure 11.1 Stable three-voice sonorities

The first harmony in figure 11.1 is more stable than the second because every voice is consonant with every other voice and because it contains a perfect consonance. This structure is also known as a root-position triad.

TRIADS

A *triad* consists of three notes stacked in successive thirds. The bottom note is called the *root*, and the upper two notes are named the *third* and *fifth*, according to their distance from the root.

Combining major and minor thirds produces four possible sonorities. *Major* and *minor triads* both contain perfect fifths; the quality of the chord corresponds to the quality of the interval between the root and third. *Diminished triads* contain a diminished fifth, while *augmented triads* contain an augmented fifth.

The name of the chord[1] is the name of the root plus the quality (see figure 11.2). The root does not always have to be in the bass. When it is, the chord is said to be in *root position*. If the third is in the bass, the chord is in *first inversion*. A *second-inversion* chord has the fifth as its lowest note.

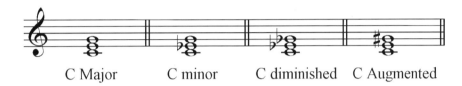

Figure 11.2 Possible triads with C as the root

IMPORTANT POINTS

As shown above, root position is most stable. First-inversion chords are also stable but less so due to the fourth between the upper voices and the lack of perfect consonance. In common-practice music, second-inversion triads are not stable because they contain a fourth, a dissonance, with the bass. Second-inversion chords cannot be used freely; the dissonance requires resolution.

The only stable inversion for diminished and augmented triads, however, is first inversion. In root position, the fifth is dissonant with the bass, creating an unstable voicing; only in first inversion are both upper voices consonant with the bass. As a result, these triads appear in first inversion.

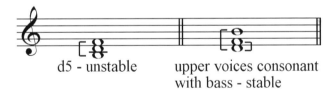

Figure 11.3 Diminished triads are stable in first inversion

SUMMARY

Terminology

Triad. A three-note, tertian chord.

Chord. A harmonic sonority in which three or more notes sound simultaneously.

Root. The bottom note in a chord stacked in thirds.

Third. The chord member that is a third above the root when the triad is in root position.

Fifth. The chord member that is a fifth above the root when the triad is in root position.

Major triad. A chord with a minor third on top of a major third. It contains a perfect fifth, and the third of the chord is a major third above the root.

Minor triad. A chord with a major third on top of a minor third. It contains a perfect fifth, and the third of the chord is a minor third above the root.

Diminished triad. A chord with two consecutive minor thirds. It contains a diminished fifth.
Augmented triad. A chord with two consecutive major thirds. It contains an augmented fifth.
Root position. Describes a chord with its root in the bass.
First inversion. Describes a chord with its third in the bass.
Second inversion. Describes a chord with its fifth in the bass.

The stable sonorities in three voices are root-position and first-inversion triads.
Root position is more stable than first inversion.
Second inversion is unstable and requires particular resolutions.
Augmented and diminished triads are relatively stable only in first inversion.

NOTE

1. A *chord* is a general term for any harmonic sonority. It includes triads, seventh chords, added-note harmonies, and clusters. A triad is specifically a three-note, tertian (built on thirds) chord. In common language, though, the word *chord* is used more frequently than *triad*. Usually, it is qualified to clarify the harmony being discussed, such as "a C-major chord" versus "a C-seven chord."

WORKBOOK

1. Write out the triads possible in F-major and G-major. Identify them by name and quality. Do the same for their relative minors. When working in minor, use the tendency tone forms of $\hat{6}$ and $\hat{7}$. The other forms appear in music, but the tendency tones are more common.

First Species in Three Voices (Note against Note)

CHAPTER LEARNING OBJECTIVES

This chapter:

- Explains the role of triads and their inversions in three-voice counterpoint
- Explains the loosening of some voice-leading rules in three voices
- Explains the standard cadences in three voices

Species exercises in three voices are conceptually similar to those in two. Now two voices are added to the cantus firmus instead of one, but the basic principles of each species remain the same. As before, in first species, every pitch in the cantus firmus is matched with an equal-duration note in the other two voices. Pedagogically, it again establishes consonances and voice leading. The rules for this species are the following:

1. All harmonic sonorities must be stable.

2. Use proper voice leading.

The realization of these principles, however, is different. Now the stable harmonic sonority is the triad. The pitches added to the cantus firmus must create a stable root-position or first-inversion chord. (While intervals still have relevance, it is better to think about the triads that can harmonize the cantus firmus.) In your exercises, try to use complete chords as much as possible. Melody is important, however, so if you must choose between a complete triad or smooth voice leading, choose the smooth voice leading.

The opening and closing chords should be root-position tonic triads, in order to shape the phrase from rest to tension and back. Either of the upper voices may open or close with the third. The opening and closing chords also may be an open perfect consonance—a bare fifth or a tripled tonic, containing no third or sixth with the bass.

Within the phrase, avoid open octaves and fifths. When using an incomplete triad, write a third or a sixth. The surrounding complete chords further accentuate the contrast in fullness, making the open perfect consonance sound even more hollow and static than in two voices. These stable sonorities may appear only as the first or last chord, where complete stasis is appropriate.

Incomplete chords require two notes on the same pitch. Always double stable pitches. For the exercises at hand, this statement translates to "never double tendency tones." Doubling a tendency tone places emphasis on an unstable pitch, which is out of the common-practice style. Also, these pitches have specific functions. When doubled, either both will resolve and parallel octaves will result, or one of them will be left unresolved.

Lastly, with regard to rule 1, the upper two voices should be within an octave of each other. Composers found that if the upper voices get too far apart, the ear no longer hears them as blending together. They sound too independent. The bass voice, however, which serves a support function, may be more than an octave away from the next voice up.

With regard to voice leading, the presence of the third voice allows the rules to relax slightly. The reason is because we do not hear all three voices equally. The top voice stands out more clearly than the other two, the bass is then the next most prominent, and the middle voice is the least clear. As a result, all voice-leading principles from two-voice counterpoint must be followed between the outer voices. Whenever the middle voice is involved, however, direct perfect consonances and cross-relations are allowed. Although they are permissible, use them sparingly. (Some musicians forbid direct perfect consonances in all voices.) Parallel perfect consonances are never stylistically appropriate. Voice crossings and overlaps should also be avoided in all voices.

Understanding this hierarchy of voices can help determine how to "break the rules." The violation is less offensive if the irregularity is in an inner voice. For example, if you want to move a tendency tone in an atypical fashion, place it in the alto or tenor. Although composers do break the rules, they usually do so in a musical fashion, considering factors such as this.

For cadences, two of the voices will function the same way as in two-voice exercises. The cantus moves $\hat{2} \rightarrow \hat{1}$, and another voice will move $\hat{7} \rightarrow \hat{8}$. That leaves two options for the penultimate chord, adding either $\hat{5}$ and making a triad on the dominant, or adding $\hat{4}$ and creating the triad built on the leading tone (see figure 12.1).

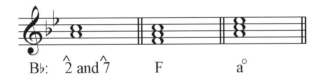

Bb: $\hat{2}$ and $\hat{7}$ F   a°

Figure 12.1 The two options for the penultimate chord

The choice of chord depends on if the cantus firmus appears in the bass or not (see figure 12.2).

1. If the upper two voices have the typical cadence and the bass is the last note to add, it has to be $\hat{5}$, and the chord is the dominant chord. Adding $\hat{4}$ would create a dissonance of a tritone between the bass and another voice. All intervals must be consonant with the bass.

2. If the $\hat{7} \rightarrow \hat{8}$ appears in the bass, then the third note must also be $\hat{5}$ because, again, adding $\hat{4}$ would create a tritone with the bass, making an unstable sonority.

3. When the cantus appears in the bass, however, the last note cannot be $\hat{5}$, because it would form a P4 with the bass, and that would result in an unstable sonority. Now the third voice must contain $\hat{4}$, and the penultimate chord is built on the leading tone. In this scenario, the leading tone chord is diminished and appears in first inversion, as all good diminished chords do.

Figure 12.2 The choices for the penultimate triad

Figure 12.3 shows the most typical cadences. $\hat{2}$ and $\hat{7}$ resolve as before. In the first cadence, the bass has to go to B♭, or else it will not sound final. (Open and close on root-position triads.) In the second and third examples, other resolutions are possible in the middle voice, but most composers would use a third rather than an open octave or fifth.

Figure 12.3 Typical three-voice cadences

A final thought: When writing a contrapuntal piece, all three voices should be equally independent and melodically interesting. The goal of this text, however, is to work toward understanding traditional harmonic progressions and part writing. In this light, it is appropriate to write "boring" inner voices; in fact, it is encouraged. While using many repeated notes and common tones in the outer voices leads to a dull exercise, using them in the inner voice is wise. If the inner voice does not move, it cannot create voice-leading problems. The middle voice is the hardest to hear clearly, so the use of common tones here does not distract from the overall effect. I usually leave the inner voice for last, and then write the smoothest line possible. (The assumption of this approach in figure 12.3 is clear. The "main" new melody, which usually ends with $\hat{7} \rightarrow \hat{8}$, always appears in an outer voice.) Also, if all three voices move in the same direction, double-check the voice leading. This situation often results in unstylistic parallels.

Of course, it is possible to write the first new melody in the inner voice; in the upcoming major example, Jeppesen does just that. Figure 12.4 shows the setup for Jeppesen's exercise. Once the cantus firmus is in the soprano, and once you have sung through it to get a sense of what it contains, you can start composing. First, you know that you have to start on a root-position tonic chord, and you know the standard cadence. Then you have to consider what chords are possible to harmonize each note in the cantus. This will, in turn, give you the possible pitches for your new melody. Then the process of trial and error, combined with artistry and logic, begins.

Figure 12.4 Possible chords to harmonize each note
in the cantus firmus and possible notes for the middle voice

When working on the bass melody, fewer pitches are available since second-inversion chords are not stable. The note at the bottom of each list of possible pitches will not work in the bass voice; it will form a fourth with the cantus. If you were to start this exercise by first composing the main melody in the bass voice, then you would only have the top four pitches from which to choose. The two notes in the middle row may or may not work in the bass; it will depend upon the harmony used. For example, on the second note in the cantus, the E, the bass could have a G if an E-minor chord is used. If a C chord is chosen (for example, if while writing the middle voice first, you put a C on the second beat), then the G is not available.

Figures 12.5 and 12.6 show two examples of first species counterpoint in three voices. The chords are labeled in the major-key exercise. Since figured bass has not been introduced yet, inversion figures are omitted. As the book assumes familiarity with fundamentals, add in inversion symbols, if desired. When only two notes are present, the ear usually hears them as the root and third of the chord. Some exceptions can exist, but those will be addressed in the chapters on functional harmony.

As with all examples in this book, work through them by both singing each line and playing the composite at the piano. As you sing a line, feel the tension in the tendency tones and see how they resolve. As you play at the piano, identify the chords' roots, qualities, and inversions.

Jeppesen

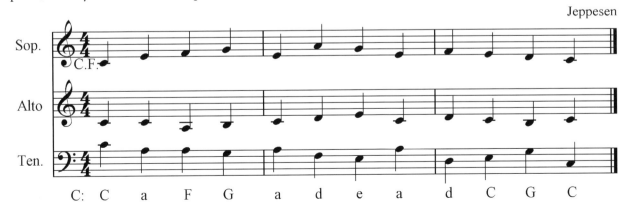

Figure 12.5 Major-key example

Figure 12.6 Minor-key example

SUMMARY

The rules of this species are analogous to those in two voices:

- All harmonic sonorities must be stable (i.e., root-position or first-inversion triads).
- Use proper voice leading.

Use complete triads when possible, but you may omit pitches to achieve better melodies.
Avoid open octaves or fifths (those lacking an imperfect consonance).
The outer voices should form proper two-voice counterpoint.
Direct perfect consonances and cross-relations are permitted if the middle voice is involved.

WORKBOOK

1. Analysis: Analyze the minor-key exercise in figure 12.6.

   - Below the system, identify the key of the exercise.
   - Label the chords by identifying the root and quality. Use an uppercase letter for major, lowercase for minor, and lowercase with a small circle for diminished. You can follow the examples in the chapter for guidance. If instructed by your teacher, include inversion by labeling first-inversion chords with a superscript 6.
   - To aid you in your own counterpoint exercises, note how many chords are incomplete versus complete.

2. Counterpoint: Using some of the cantus firmi at the end of the book, write first species exercises in three voices. Provide an analysis of your exercise:

   - Below each system, identify the key of the exercise.
   - Label the chord by identifying its root and quality.

Second and Third Species in Three Voices (Two and Four Notes to One)

CHAPTER LEARNING OBJECTIVES

This chapter:

- Explains the roles of passing tones and neighbor tones in three voices

As before, in second species one of the new melodies has two equal-value notes for each note in the cantus firmus. In third species, one of the new melodies has four equal-value notes against each note in the cantus firmus. In both cases, the third voice moves at the same rate as the cantus firmus (i.e., as in first species). Since cadences will occur in strong locations, the final note is not subdivided; the same duration occurs in all three voices.

These species reinforce the most common weak-beat dissonances, the passing tone and the neighbor tone. The rules for these species are basically the same as for two voices:

1. Use proper voice leading.

2. The strong part of the beat must be stable—a root-position or first-inversion triad.

3. The weak part of the beat may be consonant or dissonant with the chord. If it is dissonant, the note must be approached and left by step.

In three voices, dissonances are also called *nonchord tones* or *nonharmonic tones*. Since a triad defines the stable sonority, a pitch is categorized as dissonances based on whether or not it is a member of the chord. Although the three terms are not identical, they are close and will be used interchangeably.

Review figures 7.1 and 7.3. Figure 7.1 explains the accentuation pattern of subdivided notes. Essentially, any subdivision into two results in a strong beat followed by a weak beat. Further subdivision results in a hierarchy of more strong and less strong beats with weak beats interspersed between them. For example division into four, such as in third species, results in strongest–weak–strong–weak. As a result, the third beat, which is strong, is usually consonant, but since a stronger beat exists, it may occasionally be dissonant. Figure 7.3 summarizes how accentuation pairs with dissonance control.

Dissonances clash with the surrounding harmony and pull toward consonance. Through this creation of tension and resolution, they give direction to the music. Placing them in weak positions enables them to work in a subtle way.

Another ramification of the strong/weak dichotomy is that typical doublings and chord voicings are more important in accented positions. The downbeat should be a complete triad or at least contain an imperfect consonance. If the moving line then creates an incomplete triad or an open fifth on the weak subdivision, that is acceptable.

One ambiguous situation exists for nonchord tones. Usually, there is a single chord on a beat. If the moving voice has a fifth and a sixth above the bass, it may be viewed as a change in harmony, meaning two triads within that beat (see figure 13.1). If the pitches are approached and left by step, either analysis (one chord with a PT/NT or two different chords) is correct (figure 13.1a). Viewed as a chord change, both pitches are consonant, and composers may leap to or from both (figure 13.1b). Later, once functional harmonic progressions are introduced, the context will often, but not always, clarify the harmony.

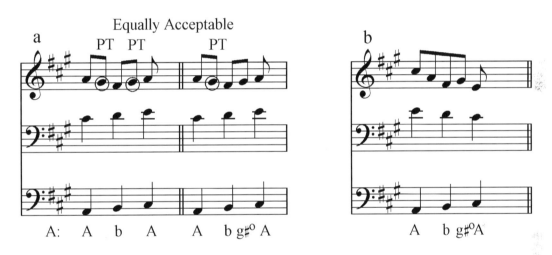

Figure 13.1 Ambiguous situation for nonchord tones

For second species, a problem arises at the cadence. Usually, the faster-moving melody, the "main" melody, ends with $\hat{7} \rightarrow \hat{8}$. Since we are not supposed to repeat notes, if we put the leading tone in that voice on the downbeat, we cannot have it on the second half of the beat (figure 13.2a). If we put it on the second half of the beat, where it should be, we have an open fifth on the downbeat (figure 13.2b). Since $\hat{7}$ is an unstable tendency tone, it should never be doubled. How can the leading tone appear either (1) on both subdivisions of the beat without being doubled or (2) on the second half of the beat without having an open fifth in the strong position?

One solution is to put the leading tone in the slower-moving voice (figure 13.3a). This arrangement is acceptable. Placing the important leading tone in the more prominent, faster-moving voice is more typical though, so a more common solution is to use a suspension (figure 13.3b). By suspending the tonic and letting it resolve to the leading tone, the fifth on the first half contains a dissonance that gives it more depth. On the second half, the leading tone appears when appropriate. The use of the suspension also makes sense because, as mentioned in two-voice fifth species and as seen in the Morley canzonet, the suspension is the most common cadential gesture in Renaissance music. Because more notes are available before the last beat, third species does not have this problem. There are a variety of cadences for it.

Figure 13.2 Problem with second species cadences

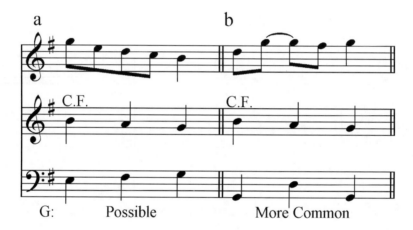

Figure 13.3 Possible cadences in second species

As in two voices, the moving melody may begin on an upbeat.

These exercises can also be done in compound meters. Then the accentuation pattern is strong–weak–weak, and the dissonance control should correspond with it.

For an extra challenge, the two species may be combined, where one voice is moving two-to-one with the cantus firmus while the other is moving four-to-one.

In the second measure of the major-key exercise in figure 13.5, two nonchord tones appear in succession. As long as neither dissonance lands on the strong beat, this is possible.

In measure 3 of the minor-key exercise in figure 13.5, having G♮ and F♮ as the first two notes of beats one and three would also be appropriate. The most immediate goal is the dominant, E. The G♯ and F♯ also work, however, because the goal of the entire beat is the A on the ensuing downbeat.

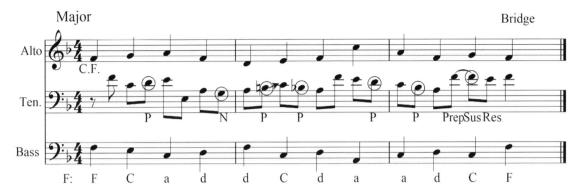

Figure 13.4 Second species examples

Figure 13.5 Third species examples

SUMMARY

Terminology

Nonchord tone. Another term for a dissonance in the context of chords. Synonymous with *nonharmonic tone*.
Nonharmonic tone. Another term for a dissonance in the context of chords. Synonymous with *nonchord tone*.

In second species, one voice has two notes for each note in the cantus firmus.
In third species, one voice has four notes for each note in the cantus firmus.
Second and third species counterpoint reinforce the passing tone and the neighbor tone.

Rules:

- Use proper voice leading.
- Strong beats must be stable root-position or first-inversion triads.
- Weak beats may be consonant (a member of the chord) or dissonant (not a member of the chord).
  - Nonchord tones must be approached and left by step.

WORKBOOK

1. Analysis: Analyze the minor-key exercises in figures 13.4 and 13.5.
   - Below the system, identify the key of the exercise.
   - Label the chords by identifying the root and quality. If instructed by your teacher, include inversion labels.
   - Circle and label the nonchord tones.

2. Counterpoint: Using some of the cantus firmi at the end of the book, write second and third species exercises in three voices. Provide an analysis of your exercise:
   - Below each system, identify the key of the exercise.
   - Label the chord by identifying its root and quality.
   - Circle and label the dissonances.

14

Fourth Species in Three Voices (Syncopations and Suspensions)

CHAPTER LEARNING OBJECTIVES

This chapter:

- Explains the handling of suspensions in three voices

In fourth species, two melodies are newly composed, with one moving in a two-to-one ratio and the other in a one-to-one ratio with the cantus firmus. The two-to-one voice has its notes tied across the beat, syncopating the line against the cantus. The rules for this species are basically the same as for two voices:

1. Use proper voice leading.
2. The weak part of the beat must be a stable chord.
3. On the strong part of the beat, the moving voice may be consonant or dissonant. If it contains a nonchord tone, the note must resolve by a step down.

Once again, fourth species exercises drill syncopations and suspensions. Certain aspects are completely analogous to fourth species in two voices. Suspensions are wonderfully expressive since they are prominent, strong dissonances. Since the dissonances are strong, however, composers handled them more carefully than passing tones and neighbor tones. They are prepared by common tone and resolved by a step down.

The addition of a third voice requires a new consideration: the note of resolution should not appear in either of the other voices (figure 14.1). A suspension is a delay of the chord tone. Much of its expressive power comes from the ear knowing which pitch should be there and hearing that that pitch is missing. To include the pitch at the same time as the suspension ruins the effect. Rather than sounding like a suspension, it sounds like a mistake; the complete harmony is already there, and an extra note has been added to it. The only exception to this is the 9–8 suspension, which, by definition, must have the note of resolution sounding below it, specifically in the bass.

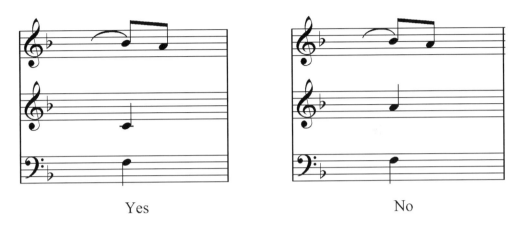

Yes   No

Figure 14.1 The note of resolution should not sound during a suspension

Another consideration in three voices is doubling. If using an incomplete triad, you have to double one of the two pitches. The basic rule is to double the most stable pitch. The suspension, a dissonance, is completely unstable. Also, it has a particular resolution. Doubling it both emphasizes the instability and leads either to parallel octaves, if both suspensions resolve, or to an unresolved dissonance. When a suspension occurs over an incomplete triad, double the cantus firmus, not the nonharmonic tone.

Since the bass is the most important voice for harmonic support, suspensions are identified by their intervallic relationship to the bass. These names are the same as in two voices.

The most common suspension in one of the upper voices is the 7–6. Since the sixth must be a consonant resolution, the suspension must resolve into a first-inversion chord. Therefore, the third voice, if using a complete triad, must be a third (figure 14.2).

Figure 14.2 7–6 suspension

The next most common upper-voice suspension is a 4–3. This suspension could resolve into either a root-position or first-inversion chord. It more commonly resolves into a root-position triad. The clash of the fifth above the bass with the suspended fourth provides more bite and makes the missing note all the more obvious (figure 14.3).

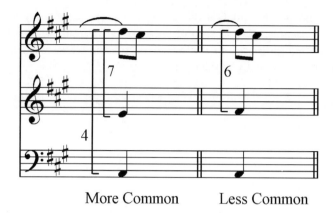

More Common   Less Common

Figure 14.3 4–3 suspension

Finally, the least common upper-voice suspension, the 9–8, resolves into an incomplete chord. It may be accompanied by a third or sixth, although the third is more common. Imperfect consonances are preferred in this style, so do not resolve it into an open fifth (figure 14.4).

Good   Good   Unstylistic
                                          Open Fifth

Figure 14.4 9–8 suspension

In three voices, there is only one possible suspension in the bottom voice, the 2–3, now called a bass suspension. It can be part of either a root-position or first-inversion chord, and both happen regularly. The 4–5 suspension, a distinct and separate suspension in two voices, now becomes subsumed into the bass suspension, resolving to a root-position triad (figure 14.5).

Good   Good

Figure 14.5 Bass suspension

In chains of suspensions, inappropriate parallel consonances become apparent by examining the voice leading of the consonances. Suspensions that resolve into perfect consonances will cause unstylistic parallels. The fifths that appear on the downbeats in a chain of 7–6 suspensions are not a problem. They are purely a product of the dissonance and have no bearing on the underlying harmonic structure, which is a succession of first-inversion chords (figure 14.6).

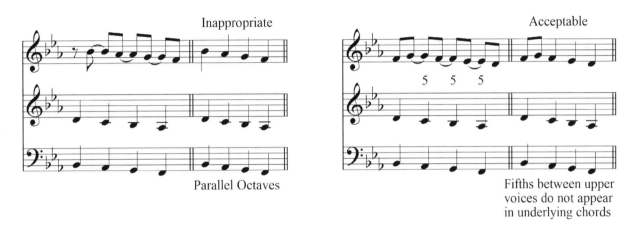

Figure 14.6 Parallel perfect consonances depend on underlying harmonies

Once again, the typical cadential gesture is the suspended tonic resolving to the leading tone. Which type of suspension this is will depend on the melody in the bass. Other cadences are possible if the leading tone is placed in another voice (figure 14.7).

Figure 14.7 Cadences

Finally, you may break off the syncopation and briefly use second species in order to set up more suspensions.

Figure 14.8 shows two fourth species exercises. The major-key example contains yet another way to get to the leading tone for the cadence.

Figure 14.8 Fourth species exercises

SUMMARY

In fourth species, one voice has two notes for each note in the cantus firmus, tied across the beat. The third voice moves with the cantus firmus.

Rules:

- Use proper voice leading.
- Weak beats must be consonant, that is, chord tones.
- Strong beats may be consonant or dissonant.
  - ○ Nonchord tones must be approached by common tone and left by step down.

Do not sound the note of resolution simultaneously with the suspension.
Do not double the suspension.
Suspensions are still named by the interval formed with the bass.

WORKBOOK

1. Analysis: Analyze the minor-key exercise in figure 14.8.
   - Below the system, identify the key of the exercise.
   - Label the chords by identifying the root and quality. If instructed by your teacher, include inversion.
   - Circle and label the nonchord tones. For suspensions, label the consonant preparation, circle and label the suspension itself, and label the resolution.

2. Counterpoint: Using some of the cantus firmi at the end of the book, write fourth species exercises in three voices. Provide an analysis of your exercise:
   - Identify the key of the exercise.
   - Label the chord by identifying its root and quality.
   - Circle and label your nonharmonic tones. For suspensions, also label the preparation and resolution.

Fifth Species (Florid Counterpoint) in Three Voices and Three-Voice Counterpoint

CHAPTER LEARNING OBJECTIVES

This chapter:

- Explains the combination of the preceding species into fifth species exercises

- Explains the connection between fifth species and actual three-voice compositions

FIFTH SPECIES

As with two voices, florid counterpoint in three voices employs all previous species. The increased freedom can lead to better melodies. The issues put forth in Chapter 9 still hold here. Forward rhythms and ties are more common that backward ones. The resolution of suspensions may be ornamented.

As you work, consider the characteristics of a good melody as presented in the first section of this book. Write an engaging melody that is singable, well shaped, and coherent. Think about growth and balance as the melody progresses.

In three voices, one voice moves in fifth species while the other moves with the cantus firmus. Both newly composed voices may also use fifth species; if you do this, have the voices complement each other rhythmically. When one moves quickly, the other should be slower. This structure gives greater freedom to the lines, since oblique motion is the most independent type of motion. It also keeps the music from sounding too busy.

Figures 15.1 and 15.2 show examples of fifth species exercises. The example in figure 15.1 uses the melody from the hymn "A Mighty Fortress" as the cantus firmus. The last chord in measure 2 is incomplete, so it is ambiguous. I labeled it as D, even though there is no root to the chord. f♯° might make more sense, given that two notes generally imply root and third. Diminished chords do not usually appear in root position, though, so I decided to label it as a first-inversion D triad. Throughout the exercise, when there are ambiguous harmonies that could be labeled as passing tones or chord changes, I labeled fewer harmonies and more dissonances. The one exception to this is at the cadence. The leading tone to the tonic gesture is so important that I felt it deserved its own chord.

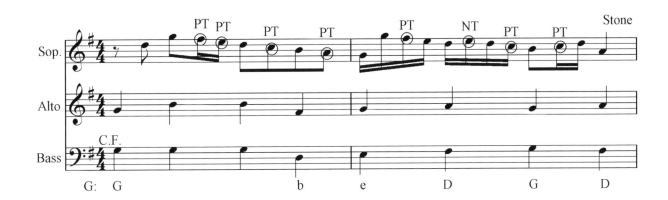

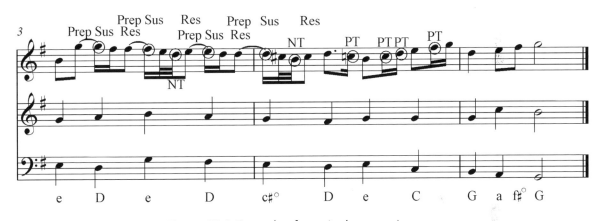

Figure 15.1 Example of a major-key exercise

Figure 15.2 Example of a minor-key exercise

In figure 15.3, two melodies in fifth species are added to the cantus firmus. Their rhythms complement one another.

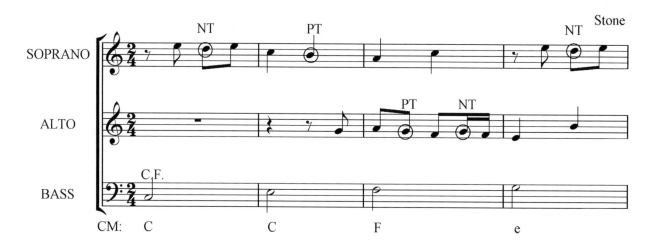

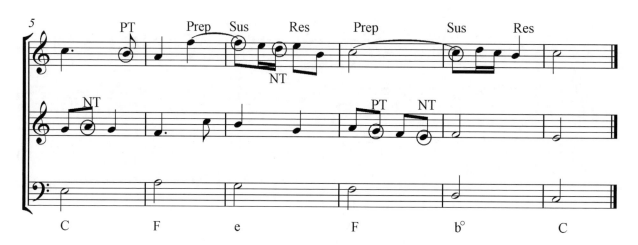

Figure 15.3 Example with two moving voices

THREE-VOICE MUSIC

The connection between three-voice exercises and actual pieces is analogous to that in two voices. Many pieces do not include a cantus firmus. In these pieces, any melody may contain a dissonance. Nonharmonic tones will still follow the basic guidelines. Passing tones and neighbor tones will be in weak positions and approached and left by step. Suspensions will be prepared by common tone and resolved by step down.

Figures 15.4 and 15.5 show two examples. Figure 15.4 is a madrigal by Weelkes. Madrigals were secular songs, written for amateur entertainment at home. Rhythmically, they tend to be straightforward, with the voices moving together, much like first species. (Metrically, though, this work has some interesting time-signature changes.) Figure 15.5 is from a mass by Palestrina. In this one, the voices have rhythmic independence, characteristic of the more contrapuntal sacred music of the Renaissance. It ends with an inconclusive cadence because the music continues but with four voices.

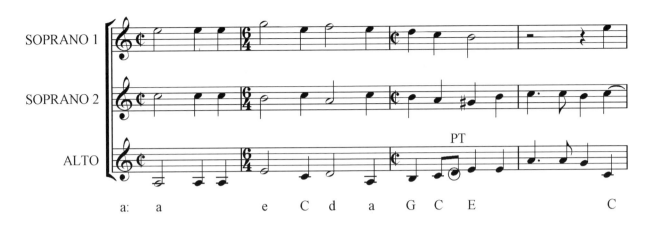

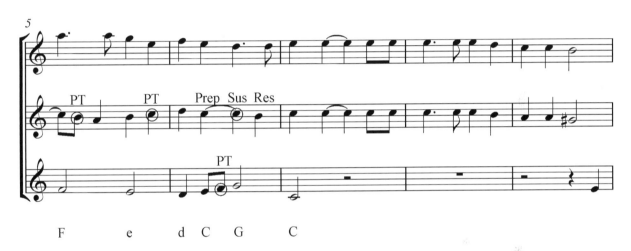

Figure 15.4a Weelkes, "The Ape, the Monkey, and Baboon"

Figure 15.4b Weelkes, continued

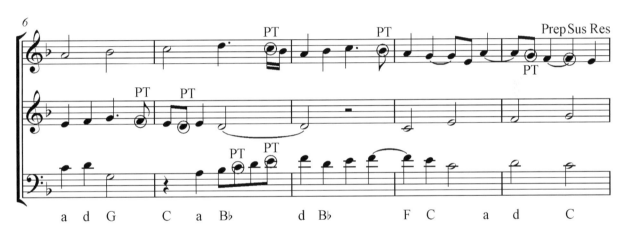

Figure 15.5a Palestrina, "Benedictus" from *Missa Aeterna Christus Munera*

Figure 15.5b Palestrina, continued

Figure 15.5c Palestrina, continued

Lyrics were removed to leave space for the analysis. When only two voices are singing, the implied harmony is not labeled, since the vertical sonority is viewed in terms of intervals, not chords. When three voices are singing, incomplete chords are assigned implied harmonies, in light of the surrounding context. Both examples have brief voice crossings, which occasionally happened in the Renaissance era but were rare in common-practice works. They should be avoided in theory classes.

SUMMARY

Fifth species freely uses all four other species.
When adding two voices in fifth species counterpoint to the cantus firmus, complementary rhythms are useful.

WORKBOOK

1. Analysis: Analyze the minor-key exercise in figure 15.2.
   - Below the system, identify the key.
   - Label the chords by identifying the root and quality. If instructed by your teacher, include inversion.
   - Circle and label dissonances. For suspensions, also label the preparation and the resolution.

2. Find the Errors: The two fifth-species exercises given here contain numerous stylistic errors. Circle and identify the mistakes.

3. Counterpoint: Using some of the cantus firmi at the end of the book, write fifth species exercises in three voices. Provide an analysis of your exercise:

- Below each system, identify the key of the exercise.
- Label each chord by identifying its root and quality (and inversion if so instructed).
- Circle and label dissonances. For suspensions, also label the preparation and resolution.

4. Three-Voice Music Analysis: Complete the analyses of the pieces in figures 15.4 and 15.5. Continue by analyzing the chords and the nonchord tones.

Chapters 12–15 Redux

CHAPTER LEARNING
OBJECTIVES

This chapter:

- Provides a brief overview of three-voice counterpoint

In the interest of time, some courses move directly from two voices to four. This chapter serves to highlight the important concepts in three voices, to smooth the transition if skipping Chapters 12–15.

The basic harmonic consonance is now a root-position or first-inversion chord. The term *consonance* now refers to a chord member within this triad. Dissonance is defined by if a pitch is or is not a member of the chord. *Nonchord tone* and *nonharmonic tone* are other terms for dissonance in three or more voices.

Composers use complete triads as much as possible. In order to write a good melody, however, they will sometimes use an incomplete chord. In three and more voices, common-practice composers did not use open perfect consonances (lacking an imperfect consonance). The surrounding complete chords further accentuate the contrast, making the open perfect consonance sound even more hollow and static than in two voices. When using an incomplete triad, double a stable pitch. Do not double tendency tones or nonchord tones.

The upper two voices should stay within an octave of each other. If they get too far apart, the ear no longer hears them as blending together. (While counterpoint uses independent melodies, they still need to work together to create the overall sound.) The bottom voice, which serves as support for the upper voices, does not have this limitation. It can be any distance from the next voice up.

A hierarchy develops among the voices because of how our ears work. We hear the top voice the clearest, followed by the bottom voice. The inner voice is the least distinct. As a result, some voice-leading rules are relaxed for the inner voice. The outer voices follow the rules of two-voice counterpoint. Direct perfect consonances and cross-relations become acceptable when the inner voice is one of the lines involved. Parallel perfect consonances are always inappropriate in the common-practice style, and voice crossings and voice overlaps should still be avoided in all voices.

A contrapuntal work should contain three equally independent and interesting melodies. As this book is working toward harmony and part writing, however, it is acceptable to write a "boring" inner voice. The inner voice is less distinct, so a flat melody with many repeated pitches will not distract from the overall effect like it would in an outer voice. The sound will be fuller, while being kinder to the singers. Less motion will also lead to fewer unstylistic parallels.

Cadences still involve the leading tone and supertonic resolving to tonic. The third voice will have either $\hat{4}$ or $\hat{5}$, depending on which pitch creates a stable triad. Chapter 12 explains cadences in more detail.

Finally, for nonchord tones, passing tones and neighbor tones behave in the same way as in two voices. Suspensions are named after the interval formed with the bass, except when the suspension is in the bass, in which case it is called a bass suspension. The pitch of resolution should not sound during a suspension. The delayed note needs to leave a hole in the chord, which is then filled upon resolution. The one exception to this is the 9–8 suspension, which by definition includes the note of resolution.

SUMMARY

Terminology

Nonchord tone. Another term for a dissonance in the context of chords. Synonymous with *nonharmonic tone*.
Nonharmonic tone. Another term for a dissonance in the context of chords. Synonymous with *nonchord tone*.

Stable harmonic sonorities are root-position and first-inversion triads
Use complete triads when possible, but you may omit pitches to achieve better melodies.
Avoid open octaves or fifths (those lacking an imperfect consonance).
Double stable pitches.
The outer voices should form proper two-voice counterpoint.
Direct perfect consonances and cross relations are permitted if the middle voice is involved.
Do not sound the note of resolution simultaneously with a suspension.
Suspensions are named by the interval formed with the bass.

Four-Voice Counterpoint and Chorale Style

CHAPTER LEARNING OBJECTIVES

This chapter:

- Explains the expansion from three- to four-voice counterpoint, which primarily concerns the doubling in the triad

- Explains the change from species counterpoint to chorale style, the common format used in theory classes to study chord progressions

FOUR-VOICE COUNTERPOINT

Three voices provide harmonic clarity, and much music is based on this texture. During the common-practice era, however, use of four voices— soprano, alto, tenor, and bass (SATB)—was standard. The preference for four voices results from two factors. First, this grouping provides a slightly fuller sound than three voices. Second, with four voices, complete triads are almost always possible. The occasional third or sixth that occurs in three voices can be kept as a full chord in four.

Four-voice counterpoint is merely an extension of three-voice counterpoint. The rules and concepts are all the same. The basic harmonic sonority is still the triad. The soprano and bass follow the rules of two-voice counterpoint. The inner voices may contain direct perfect consonances and cross-relations. Passing tones and neighbor tones occur on weak beats or weak parts of beats. Suspensions are prepared by common tone and left by step down. The note of resolution should not sound during the suspension.

The spacing of the voices is essentially the same. As mentioned before, if adjacent voices get more than an octave apart, they stop blending and sound too independent. As a result, adjacent voices should stay within an octave of each other: the soprano and alto should stay within an octave of each other, and the alto and tenor should be within an octave of each other. Due to its role as the foundation of the harmony, the bass can be as far away from the tenor as necessary.[1]

Close spacing and open spacing describe the voicing of the soprano, alto, and tenor. *Close spacing* means that no chord tones can fit between the upper three voices; *open spacing* means that a chord member has been skipped over. Figure 16.1 shows the difference between the two. In the first triad, each note of the chord is stacked upon the previous. In the open spacing, a B♭ could be inserted between the soprano and alto and an E♭ could be inserted between the alto and tenor. Close spacing has a fuller sound, while open spacing has a more expansive, dramatic sound. The spacing does not affect voice leading.

Figure 16.1 Close versus open spacing

The only new parameter in four voices is doubling. A triad consists of three unique notes, so one voice must double the pitch of another. The general rule, as introduced in Chapter 12, is to double a stable pitch. In three voices, that means never double tendency tones or strong dissonances, which still holds true in four.

In four voices, however, doubling becomes an issue in *every* triad. In order to maintain the balance of the harmony, the general rule is to double the most stable pitch. For a basic triad, the pitches in order of decreasing stability are the root, then the fifth, and then the third. Accordingly, composers double the root most frequently, the fifth next most, and the third infrequently. I had an office mate who describes the third of a chord like salt when making soup. A third must be present. An open fifth sounds empty and hollow, and the third fills in the sound. The third also clarifies the quality of the chord. Due to its distinctive flavor, however, too much third spoils the broth, so to speak.

This doubling rule has one exception. Diminished and augmented chords have a dissonance between the root and fifth. The third is the only pitch not involved in a dissonance, and is therefore the most stable note. For diminished and augmented triads, the third should be doubled. This reason is also why these chords usually appear in first inversion (see Chapter 11). Figure 16.2 shows an excerpt with typical doublings.

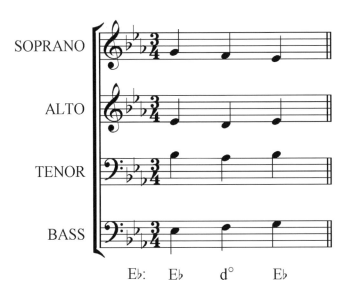

Figure 16.2 A progression with typical doublings

Although infrequent, incomplete chords occur. The root is essential to hear what chord it is. The third is necessary to avoid the hollow sound of the open fifth and to clarify the quality. When an incomplete chord is necessary, the fifth is omitted. The root is tripled rather than putting emphasis on the less stable third.

These doubling rules are guidelines. Strong melodies are an important issue, so it is acceptable to use an atypical doubling in order to have a more convincing melody. Too many deviations from the norm, however, will make it sound uncharacteristic of the common-practice era. Stravinsky often used unstylistic doublings as part of his twentieth-century sound.

A word of advice—write the main melody first, as before; then work on the remaining two voices simultaneously. Writing the third voice in its entirety can force the fourth voice into some difficult passages. Writing the complete third-voice melody is fine, as long as you are willing to change it (or another voice) to accommodate the final line.

Figure 16.3 shows two examples of four-voice species exercises. Both are written with the same cantus firmus. The first is in first species, the second is in fifth. Students should be able to write four-voice exercises in any

First Species

Fifth Species

Figure 16.3 Four-voice species exercises

species. Analysis will show that these examples closely parallel assignments in three voices. The doubling is the only new issue, and that is somewhat flexible.

CHORALE STYLE

At this point, the student should practice four-voice exercises for all of the species. It is excellent experience. This book, however, has chorale style and harmonic analysis as its goal, and it is now time to turn toward that.

Chorale style gets its name from exactly what it sounds like: an emulation of the way chorales are written. Chorales are harmonizations of hymns for use in churches. For ease of reading, these arrangements are written on the grand staff. Voices are indicated by the staff it is on and the stem direction. Sopranos are on the treble staff with the stem pointing up. Altos are also on the treble staff, but with the stem pointing down. Tenors are on the bass staff with stems up, and basses are on the bass staff with stems down. (See figure 16.4a.) When two notes share a pitch and are on the same staff, they share a notehead. Note that the alto and tenor are always associated with their staff, even if they require ledger lines. They never share noteheads, and they never jump onto the other staff. Because of this fact, it is easy to miss voice crossings between the alto and tenor voices (figure 16.4b).

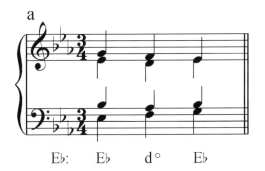
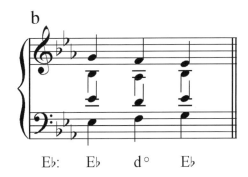

Beware of voice crossings that may not be immediately apparent.

Figure 16.4 Figure 16.2 rewritten on the grand staff

Figure 16.5 shows an excerpt from a chorale arrangement by Bach. Bach's chorales serve as the models for theory classes, and they define the rules and guidelines. For example, Bach doubles the expected way in 13 of the 17 triads. Although Bach occasionally deviates from the standard doublings in the interest of creating convincing melodies, the basic guideline is good. And it should be; it was developed based upon these chorales.

Some ambiguity exists in the analysis. In measure 1, the B could be a chord tone in an E-minor chord. In measure 2, the second beat could be a B chord or a D chord. These ambiguities will be addressed in the third section of the book, which is on harmony.

Although chorale style may appear as a new topic, it is not. A large part of the change from species counterpoint to chorale style is formatting. Figure 16.6 shows the two species exercises in figure 16.3 rewritten on the grand staff. They look a lot like a chorale.

The substantive difference between the two is that in species, only one voice has rhythmic freedom, while in chorale style, all voices can be embellished with nonchord tones and leaps within the chord. Granting this freedom to the species exercises can smooth the lines and provide more rhythmic interest (figure 16.7). It can also fix some voice-leading problems. On the second and third beats of the second measure of the fifth species exercise, there is a voice overlap between the soprano and alto. The new rhythmic freedom allows the alto to move and revoice the chord, thereby avoiding the overlap.

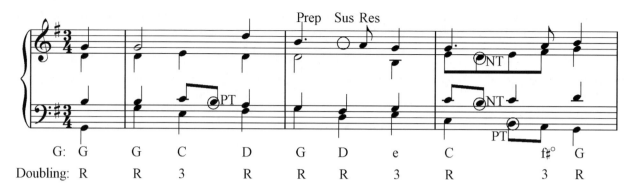

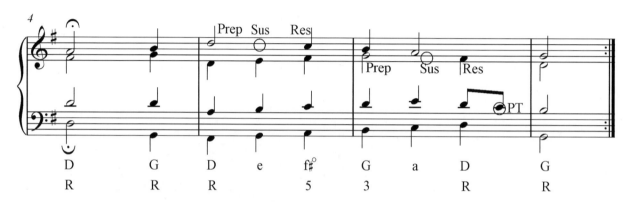

Figure 16.5 Bach, "Aus meines Herzens Grunde" ("From the Depths of My Heart")

First Species

Fifth Species

Figure 16.6 The exercises in figure 16.3 rewritten on the grand staff

Formerly First Species

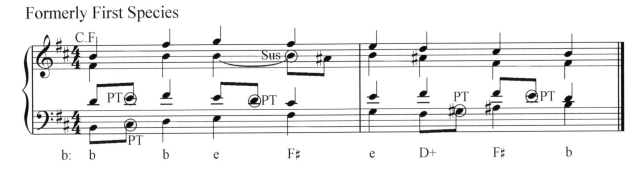

Formerly Fifth Species

Figure 16.7 The exercises in figure 16.3 with rhythmic freedom in all four voices

Chorale style is more homorhythmic (the voices move with the same or similar rhythms) than counterpoint. This trait results from practical considerations. Chorales are sung by the congregation in a church; the homorhythmic setting both allows the words to be heard more clearly and also makes the music easier for the untrained singers. Both of the exercises in figure 16.7 are in chorale style, but the "formerly first species" is aesthetically closer to what we normally mean when speaking of chorales.

That is the crux of this chapter. In theory classes, it is completely appropriate to treat chorale style as first species in four voices. Adding in a few dissonances and chordal leaps can make assignments more musical and create smoother lines, but it is not required. When adding nonchord tones, remember that the basic pulse is the quarter note; dissonance control is now defined relative to whether it is on the beat or off the beat. This is analogous to having a cantus firmus in quarter notes.

As this book shifts focus to chorale style and harmony, never forget that counterpoint lies at the heart of common-practice music. Despite the more homorhythmic structure, the music is still rooted in melody. Sing each line in the Bach chorale. Even the inner voices, which are less distinctly heard, are decent melodies. Examine the two outer voices and see how they work together in nice two-voice counterpoint (figure 16.8).

Figure 16.8 The outer voices of Bach's "Aus meines Herzens Grunde"

Spotlight On: DOUBLING IN TRIADS

Several systems for doubling exist, but they all reduce to the same basic principles. Three common ones are the following:

1. Double in the order root, fifth, third.

2. Double by inversion: double the bass, except in first inversion, where you double the soprano.

3. Double scale degrees $\hat{1}$, $\hat{2}$, $\hat{4}$, and $\hat{5}$ (the stable ones that do not change with mode) and avoid doubling $\hat{3}$, $\hat{6}$, and $\hat{7}$ (the modal ones that change in switching between major and minor).

Model 2 clearly is similar to model 1. If you double the bass in a root-position chord, you are doubling the root. By doubling the soprano of a first-inversion chord, you are avoiding doubling the bass, that is, the third, so again, it is saying to double the root or fifth rather than the third.

Model 3 seems different, doubling scale degrees rather than chord members, but it also boils down to the same thing. Figure 16.9 identifies the chord tones that could be doubled using the scale degree method. For three of the seven chords, F, B♭, and C, the doubling is again root or fifth. For the G chord, you can double the root, as expected, or the third, which is less likely, but these are guidelines. The same is true for the E diminished chord. You may double the third, as would be expected for the quality of the chord, or the fifth, which is less likely. The only chords that truly deviate from the other two models are the A-minor and D-minor chords. As will be seen in the section on harmony, these chords appear infrequently. Also, for the D chord, as will be explained in Chapter 24, doubling the third is common in some uses of this triad.

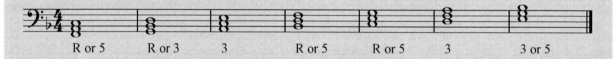

Figure 16.9 Chord members doubled using the scale degree guidelines

The idea of doubling the most stable pitch in the chord makes musical sense and provides consistency with facts such as diminished chords appearing in first inversion. If, however, you learned another model in another class, or if your teacher requests one of these other models, feel free to use it. In the end, they are all essentially the same.

SUMMARY

Terminology

SATB. Indicates a chorale style setting using soprano, alto, tenor, and bass.

Open spacing. A chord voicing in which the upper three voices are placed so that at least one chord member is missing between two adjacent voices. Contrasts with *close spacing*.

Close spacing. A chord voicing in which the upper three voices are placed as closely together as possible. The three voices contain adjacent chord members. Contrasts with *open spacing*.

Chorale style. An arrangement emulating church hymns, with four voices moving in a relatively homorhythmic pattern.

In four voices, double in the order root, fifth, third. In general, avoid doubling the third.

The exception to the doubling rule is for diminished and augmented triads, in which the third should be doubled.

NOTE

1. Some professors limit the bass and tenor separation to a twelfth (an octave and a fifth), others say two octaves, and still others place no limit on it. The only way the two voices can be more than two octaves apart is if the bass is on its lowest note (E2) while the tenor is on its highest note (G4). This occurrence is too rare to require its own rule. If your teacher prefers the limit of the twelfth, of course follow his or her instructions.

WORKBOOK

1. Species Counterpoint Analysis: Analyze the fifth species exercise in four voices in figure 16.3.
   - Below the system, identify the key of the exercise.
   - Label the chords by identifying the root and quality. If instructed by your teacher, include inversion.
   - To aid you in your own counterpoint exercises, note the doublings in the triads.

2. Counterpoint: Using some of the cantus firmi at the end of the book, write species exercises in four voices. Use a variety of species, and put the cantus in different voices. Provide an analysis of your exercise:
   - Identify the key of the exercise.
   - Label the chords with their roots, qualities, and, if requested, inversions.
   - Circle and label nonchord tones. For suspensions, also identify the preparation and resolution.

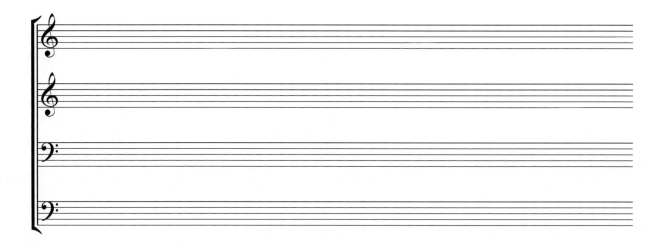

3. Species and Chorale Style:

   - Analyze the chorale-style arrangement of the fifth species exercise in figure 16.7. Identify the key, the chords, and the nonharmonic tones. What has changed from species counterpoint?

   - Reduce the first phrase (up to the fermata in measure 4) of the Bach chorale in figure 16.5 to first species. This will involve removing the dissonances and presenting only the underlying harmonies. Analyze the key and chords. How has it changed from chorale style?

4. Chorale-Style Counterpoint: Using cantus firmi at the end of the book, create four-voice chorale-style exercises. Vary the location of the cantus firmus, placing it in different voices. Provide an analysis:

   - Identify the key of the exercise.

   - Label the chords with their roots, qualities, and, if requested, inversions.

   - Circle and label nonchord tones. For suspensions, also identify the preparation and resolution.

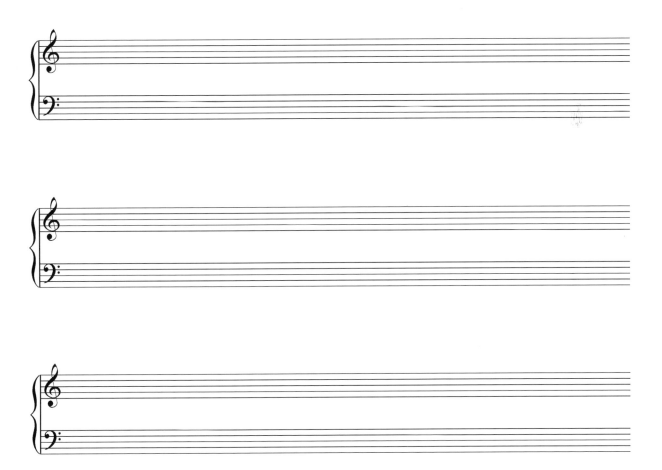

Figured Bass

CHAPTER LEARNING OBJECTIVES

This chapter:

• Explains figured bass, the Baroque shorthand notation for chords

A piano player in a bar gets a request for a song. How does he figure out the music? In popular styles, performers often use a "fake book." A fake book uses a shorthand known as lead sheet or chart notation. The melody is written out on a single staff, and above the staff is the chord that harmonizes the melody at that point. The pianist then "fakes" an arrangement of it.

Baroque composers developed a shorthand for their improvisation needs too. Since they viewed the bass as the support for the harmony, their system is relative to the bass note. In *figured bass*, the bass melody is given and the intervals of the pitches above the bass note are written below the staff (see figure 17.1). The numbers under the bass are called *figures*, hence the name *figured bass*. *Realizing* a figured bass means writing it or performing it in four parts (or however many voices will be playing).

The two stable sonorities in common-practice music are the root-position and first-inversion triads. The root-position chord contains a third and a fifth above the bass. The first-inversion chord contains a third and a sixth above the bass. Figured bass is shorthand, so the music must be kept clear and uncluttered. Since a third is common to both chords, it was left off. Similarly, since the root position chord is the more stable and more fundamental sonority, the five was also left off. So a bass note with nothing below it has an implied third and fifth above it. A note with a sixth below it contains a third and a sixth above the bass. (See figure 17.2.)

Figure 17.1 An example of figured bass: Bach, "Herr, Nicht Schicke Deine Rache" ("Lord, Do Not Send Your Revenge")

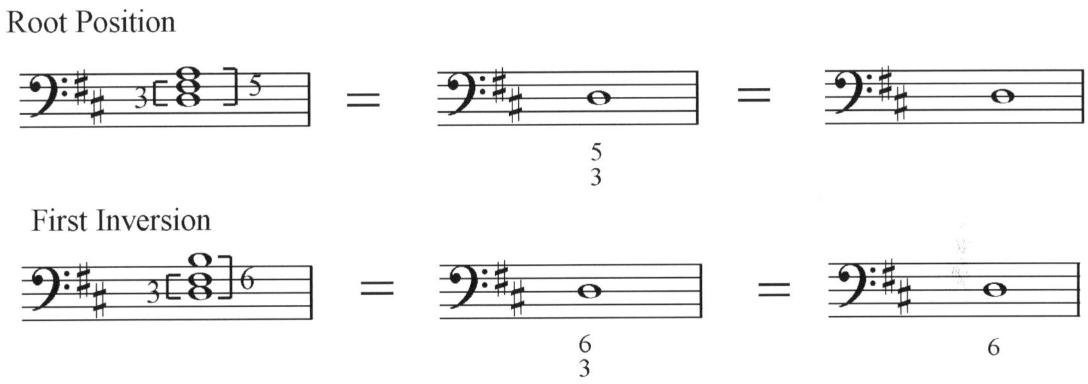

Figure 17.2 The stable triads in figured bass notation

Figures only tell which pitches are present. They do not differentiate between simple and compound intervals, so those pitches can appear in any octave. Figures go up to about 9, because there is a 9–8 suspension but not a 2–1, as was seen in Chapter 8. A six could mean a sixth, a thirteenth, a twentieth (a sixth plus two octaves), or higher. Figures say nothing about the location of the pitches or the order of voices; the numbers are ordered in decreasing value. The sixth could be in any of the other three voices, as could the third. Figures usually do not specify doubling, although every now and then one clarifies an unusual doubling. Figure 17.3 shows a basic root-position triad and lists a variety of ways it can be voiced. Many other voicings are possible.

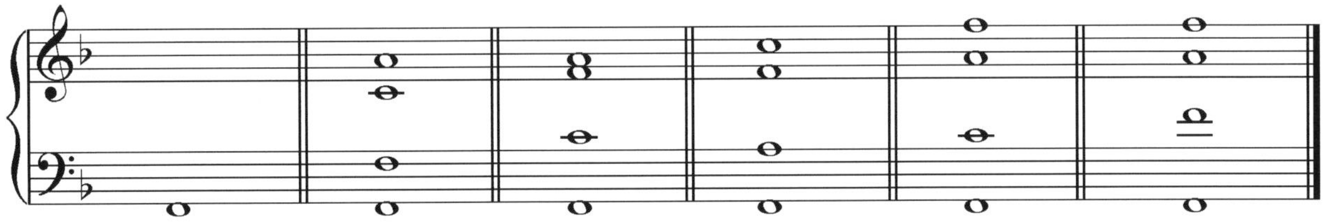

Figure 17.3 All valid ways to voice the first measure

Because of this freedom, no one solution exists for a figured bass. Lines may be moved to different voices, as with figures 17.4a and 17.4b, or they may have completely different melodies in them, as in 17.4c. As long as the counterpoint works, the realization is correct.

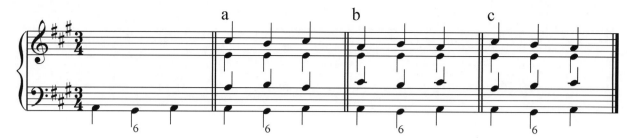

Figure 17.4 Different realizations of a passage

Since figures indicate intervals above the bass, any sonority can be represented with them. Second-inversion chords contain a dissonance and are unstable, but the intervals above the bass are a sixth and a fourth (figure 17.5).

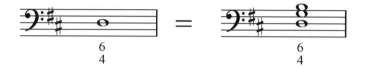

Figure 17.5 A second-inversion triad

Seventh chords add a seventh above the root. This addition is a dissonance, and now three numbers are needed since the chord contains four unique notes. Seventh chords, however, also have implied figures. For example, a seventh chord in root position is represented by just a seven; the fifth and a third are implied, just like in the root-position chord. A first-inversion seventh chord contains a sixth, fifth, and third, but again, the third is left off, just like the first-inversion triad. (The fifth must be included to differentiate the seventh chord from a basic triad.) A second-inversion seventh chord has an implied sixth, and a third-inversion seventh chord has an implied sixth and sometimes even an implied fourth. Although it can be confusing since numbers are omitted, the few chords just listed are the most common ones, and it is best to memorize the handful of implied intervals. Figure 17.6 summarizes this.

Figures assume that the key signature is in effect. For example, in a piece in D-major, if an A has a six written below it, that means that there is an F♯ in the chord. In D-minor, the same notation would imply an F♮. To notate a chromatic pitch, the figure has an accidental beside it. An accidental with no number affects the implied third. Raising a pitch is more common than lowering because in minor you have to raise the leading tone. As a result, there is even shorthand for this chromatic alteration. A slash through a figure means to raise that pitch by a half step. (See figure 17.7.)

Performers may add weak dissonances to the music when realizing a figured bass. During a strong-beat dissonance, such as a suspension, the note of resolution should not sound. Because of this, composers included strong dissonance in the figures. To help differentiate them from chord tones, the resolution is usually indicated. A line between two numbers shows the actual voice leading. In the example in figure 17.8, the line says that the seventh resolves to the sixth in the same voice. Without this notation, or at least without the second number, the figure would look like a seventh chord in root position.

Figures are often attached to chord names to indicate inversion. See figures 17.10 and 17.11 for examples of this notation. As a result, many people think of figures in terms of inversions. They see a six, think first inversion, and then figure out the pitches in the chord. This system works much of the time, but it can fail when the harmony gets complicated. One of the strengths of figured bass is that it can represent any combination of tones. It shows much more than just inversion. The cluster in figure 17.9 would not happen in common-practice music,

Root Position

First Inversion

Second Inversion

Third Inversion

Figure 17.6 Seventh chords in figured bass notation

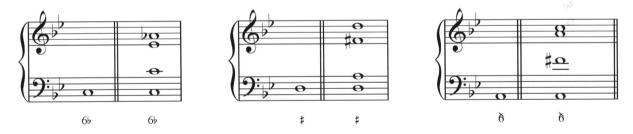

Figure 17.7 Chromatic pitches in figured bass

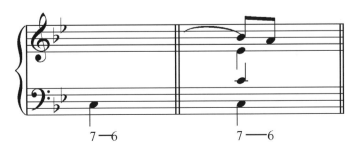

Figure 17.8 The notation of a suspension

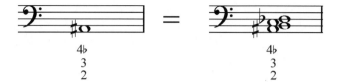

Figure 17.9 A cluster in figured bass notation

but figured bass can still notate it. When figures get messy, it is best to write the notes by calculating intervals; then unravel the harmony.

In Baroque music, the soprano and bass lines are usually given, as in figure 17.1. In theory classes, only the bass is given so that the student has complete control of the counterpoint above it. Since the goal is always to have strong melodies, it is preferable to write the soprano line first and complete the inner voices second. Figure 17.1 also shows that sometimes the bass includes weak dissonances that the figures do not indicate. Bach trusted musicians' knowledge to know that the A and C in measure 1 are passing tones.

Figures 17.10 and 17.11 show two figured basses and their realizations. The first, in major, is relatively straightforward. The second, in minor, includes many accented dissonances. To simplify that one, a melody has

Identify the harmonies and write a melody.

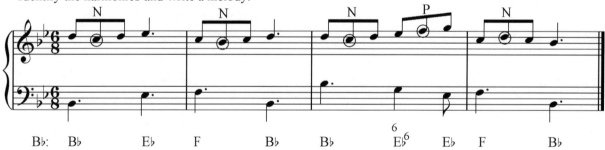

Add inner voices.

Figure 17.10 A major-key figured bass and its realization

been provided. Figures are included in the harmonic analyses to indicate inversions. Also, in the second example, the third and fourth beats of the second measure include accented passing tones, a dissonance that we have not encountered yet. (We will in the next chapter.) The figures indicate exactly how to handle them, so not knowing their name should not affect the realization.

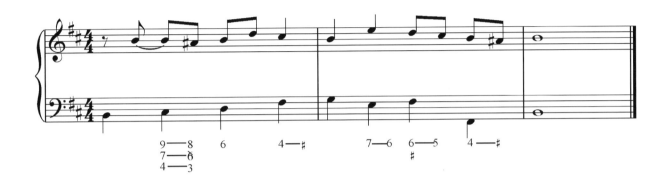

Figure 17.11 A minor-key figured bass and its realization

Spotlight On: VARIATIONS IN FIGURED BASS NOTATION

Figured bass has several variations that are stylistic choices of the publisher and have no larger meaning. For example, in representing a chromatic alteration, some editors prefer to put an accidental in front of the number rather than after it. Whether it is ♭6 or 6♭ has no significance; both say to flat the pitch that is a sixth above the bass note.

Slashes perhaps have the largest variety. The slash may lean forward or backward (compare the slashes through the 6 and the 5 in figure 17.11 above). Sometimes they go through the entire number, and sometime just the edge. Again, these variations are stylistic and still mean the same thing: raise the pitch a half step.

SUMMARY

Terminology

Figured bass. A Baroque shorthand for harmony, in which chords are represented by a bass notes with numbers below them. See also *figure*.

Figure. In figured bass, the number below the bass note, indicating the intervals present above that pitch.

Realization. In figured bass, the writing/completion of all voices.

Figured bass is shorthand for identifying the chords in a progression.

The figures indicate intervals above the bass note.

The figures indicate the pitches present but not their locations.

Accidentals are added to figures to indicate chromatic pitches.

A line between two figures indicates actual melodic motion within a single voice.

WORKBOOK

1. Notation Drill: Realize the following chords in a four-voice chorale style (SATB). Make sure to use proper spacing, staff affiliation, and stem orientation.

2. Find the Errors: The figured bass realization given here, intended to emulate common-practice ideals, contains numerous stylistic errors. Identify the mistakes. Given the space limitations, number the mistakes on the score and write an explanation of each below or on a separate piece of paper. The first has been done for you.

1. Doubled Third

3. Choose several of the figured basses from the back of the book and realize them in a four-voice chorale style (SATB). Circle and label any weak dissonances you add in. Below the system:

- identify the key
- label the chords, identifying the root, quality, and inversion

Other Dissonances

CHAPTER LEARNING OBJECTIVES

This chapter:

- Defines the common-practice dissonances that do not appear in species

Species counterpoint introduces the three most common dissonances: passing tones, neighbor tones, and suspensions. During the Renaissance, the era emulated by species, composers primarily used these dissonances. Throughout the common-practice period, however, each successive generation treated dissonances more freely.

As musical styles became more homophonic than contrapuntal, the more clearly defined harmonies allowed for less limited dissonance control. During the Baroque era (1600–1750), it was unusual to leap to or from a nonchord tone. During the Classical era (1750–1827), composers began treating the dissonance more freely. During the Romantic era (1828–1900), it became common to approach or leave a nonharmonic tone by leap. Composers did not approach *and* leave by leap. To do that would undermine the point of the dissonance, which is to propel the music by connecting to a consonance.

This chapter introduces the other possible nonchord tones in common-practice music. The first group is approached and left by common tone or step. These dissonances were common throughout the common-practice era.

Chromatic passing tones and *chromatic neighbor tones* are a variation of the passing tone and neighbor tone. They are weak dissonances that move between two pitches or neighbor a single pitch, but now they are chromatically altered and not diatonic. A chromatic passing tone connects two pitches a major second apart, while a normal passing tone fills in a third. Note in figure 18.1 that the notation (G♯ versus A♭) corresponds to the melodic function and resolution.

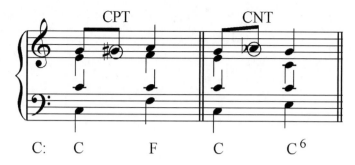

Figure 18.1 Chromatic passing tone and chromatic neighbor tone

As stated in the name, *accented passing tones* and *accented neighbor tones* are passing and neighbor tones that fall in accented positions. As we saw with the suspension, because of their prominent placement, accented nonchord tones tend to resolve down. Although accented passing and neighbor tones do not have to resolve down, they often do. The exception to this rule, as with suspensions, is pitches that have a particular resolution. For example, if a chromatically raised pitch falls in an accented position, it will resolve up, in its usual direction. Also, the note of resolution should not sound during these dissonances. Since these dissonances are strong, they are included in the figures in a figured bass. As shown in figure 18.2, the figure may be appended to the harmonic analysis to show the nonchord tone. If the note itself is circled and labeled, the redundant figure is optional, and vice-versa.

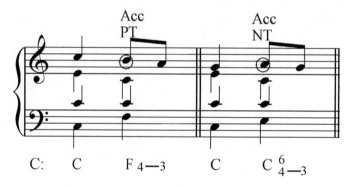

Figure 18.2 Accented passing tone and accented neighbor tone

Double neighbor tones are weak dissonances that give the upper and lower neighbor of a pitch side by side. Although there is a leap between the two notes, composers still viewed them as neighbor tones; it is two neighbors together.

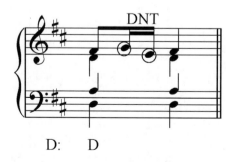

Figure 18.3 Double neighbor

Anticipations are exactly what they sound like; the pitch arrives a moment early, sounding shortly before the beat on which its chord arrives. They are usually approached by step since melodies usually move conjunctly. They are resolved by common tone. Anticipations appear frequently throughout the common-practice era, often at cadences.

Figure 18.4 Anticipation

Pedal points are sustained pitches. They start consonant, and when the other voices move, changing the harmony, they become dissonant. Eventually, the other voices become consonant with it again, at which point that voice can move freely. Pedals are not really strong or weak. They are approached and left by common tone. (See figure 18.5a.) Pedal points were common throughout the common-practice era. They are usually in the bass but sometimes appear in other voices. As seen in figure 18.5, when a pedal is in the bass, inversions are not relevant in an analysis. Also, although they are usually sustained pitches, they can occur as repeated notes (figure 18.5b). They most commonly sustain scale degrees $\hat{1}$ or $\hat{5}$. Pedal points get their name from the pedals on the organ; musicians held down the pedal with their foot while changing the chords above.

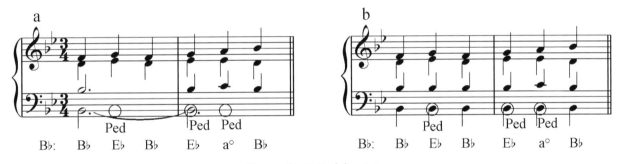

Figure 18.5 Pedal point

Retardations have already been introduced, although they were not given that name. A retardation is a suspension that resolves upward. They are rare throughout the common-practice era; composers preferred resolving strong dissonances down. When they happen, it is usually because the suspended pitch has a clear upward pull, for example, a leading tone at the final cadence (figure 18.6) or a chromatically raised pitch. I do not think of them as a separate category from suspensions. Some musicians prefer to differentiate between the two.

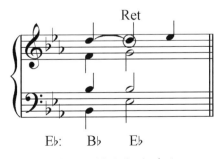

Figure 18.6 Retardation

The next group is called incomplete neighbors. *Incomplete neighbors* are nonharmonic tones that are either approached or left by leap. This name indicates that they connect with a pitch like neighbor tones do, but they are incomplete because they connect only on one side. These are the dissonances that are not common until the Romantic era. The most frequent incomplete neighbors are the appoggiatura and the escape tone.

An *appoggiatura* is an accented nonchord tone that is approached by leap and resolved by step in the opposite direction. As with all accented dissonances, appoggiaturas usually resolve down. Essentially, they are unprepared suspensions. The fact that the music leaps into an appoggiatura makes it all the more striking and poignant. The leap to an appoggiatura is usually in the opposite direction of the resolution, so it is most common to leap up, and then resolve down by step. Of course, composers also can leap down to the leading tone or to a chromatically raised pitch that will then resolve up. Once again, the pitch of resolution should be absent while the dissonance is sounding. (The 9–8 is the one exception, exactly like in suspensions.) Since appoggiaturas are accented, figures may be included in the harmonic analysis.

Figure 18.7 Appoggiatura

An *escape tone* is a weak beat event that is approached by step and resolved by leap in the opposite direction. Resolution by leap is not much of a resolution, so escape tones usually ornament a clear melodic line, such as a descending scale.

Figure 18.8 Escape tone

Other combinations of leaps and steps are possible, but none of them happen with any frequency. Rather than have unique names for uncommon dissonances, I leave them with their general title—incomplete neighbors.

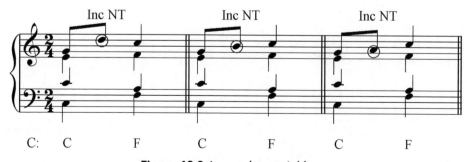

Figure 18.9 Incomplete neighbors

Theorists categorize nonharmonic tones by three parameters: if they are strong or weak, how they are approached, and how they are resolved. Table 18.1 defines all of the nonchord tones in this way.

TABLE 18.1 | Nonchord Tones Defined by the Three Parameters

Type of Dissonance	Strong/Weak	Approach	Resolution
Passing Tone	Weak	Step	Step in same direction
Neighbor Tone	Weak	Step	Step in opposite direction
Suspension	Strong	Common Tone	Step down
Pedal	N/A	Common Tone	Common Tone
Anticipation	Weak	Step	Common Tone
Chromatic Passing Tone	Weak	Step	Step in same direction
Chromatic Neighbor Tone	Weak	Step	Step in opposite direction
Double Neighbor	Weak	Step	Step (leap in middle)
Accented Passing Tone	Strong	Step	Step in same direction
Accented Neighbor Tone	Strong	Step	Step in opposite direction
Escape Tone	Weak	Step	Leap in opposite direction
Appoggiatura	Strong	Leap	Step in opposite direction (usually down)
Incomplete Neighbor	Catchall for other nonchord tones: varies		

Although this chapter introduces many new nonchord tones, most are variations on the three basic ones. Chromatic and accented passing tones and neighbor tones are almost identical to regular passing tones and neighbor tones. The double neighbor is a clear variant. Appoggiaturas are unprepared suspensions. Pedal points, anticipations, and escape tones are really the only dissonances with a new handling.

Dissonances cannot fix unstylistic voice leading or break up inappropriate parallels. They can create these problems though.

The pieces in figures 18.10 and 18.11 display a variety of these other nonchord tones. The Brahms excerpt shows the Romantic predilection for accented dissonances, containing both an appoggiatura and two accented passing tones. These beautifully complement the direction of the line, which leaps up at the beginning and gradually works back down, with the accented dissonances giving extra intensity to the descent. The chromatic F♮ in the second to last measure continues and strengthens the downward pull of the melody. The Mozart excerpt contains different dissonances from the Brahms, including double neighbors and chromatic passing and neighbor tones. In measure 3, there are accented dissonances that resolve up. The pitches are chromatically raised, which means that they have an upward pull. Placing the dissonance in a strong position accentuates their instability and direction, and the ascending resolution is appropriate. Also in measure 3, beats 2 and 4 are repetitions of beats 1 and 3. I analyzed the nonharmonic tones the same way both times, although the approach to the dissonance is different. I hear repetition as what is happening, not the reuse of an idea in a new context. Comparing the first beat of measures 1 and 3 shows a reuse in a different context. The two moments share the same melodic gesture, yet they have completely opposite dissonance analyses.

Figure 18.10 Brahms, "Wie Melodien zieht es mir," op. 105, no. 1
("Like Melodies, It Moves through My Mind")

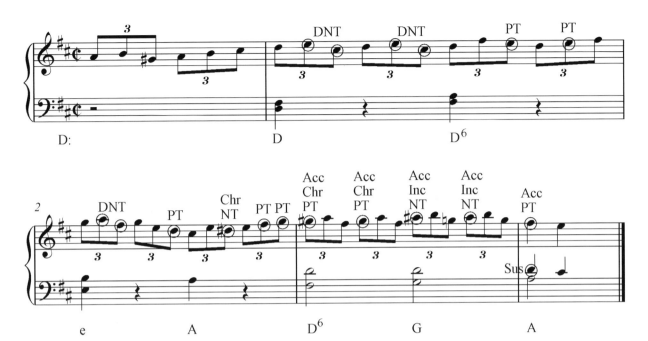

Figure 18.11 Mozart, Piano Sonata, K. 284, III, Theme

Spotlight On: DISSONANCE AND MUSICAL ERAS

Dissonances are frequently underappreciated in theory classes. Music theory tends to focus on harmony, and the nonchord tones are not part of the chord, so they are discarded almost immediately in many analyses. Dissonance, however, plays a huge role in the actual sound of the music. The music of various eras sounds different partly because of the way the composers treated the nonharmonic tones. Baroque composers handled them carefully, using the three basic dissonances more than anything else. As a result, their music seems smooth and refined. Romantic composers enjoyed using incomplete neighbors, especially appoggiaturas. Not only that, but they often sustained the nonchord tones for a long time, drawing out the yearning feeling and helping give Romantic music its dramatic sound.

To be fair to each era, I should qualify this statement. My description of nonchord tones and the sound of each period is relative only to the other common-practice eras. At the time, compared to the Renaissance, Baroque composers were seen as being free with their dissonances. Considering jazz and rock, Romantic composers seem tame. In the same way that Elvis once seemed wild, or the Ramones are now mainstream, what is new and garish eventually becomes old and classic.

SUMMARY

Terminology

Chromatic passing tone. A weak nondiatonic dissonance approached by half step and left by half step in the same direction.

Chromatic neighbor tone. A weak nondiatonic dissonance approached by half step and left by half step in the opposite direction.

Accented passing tone. A strong dissonance approached by step and left by step in the same direction.

Accented neighbor tone. A strong dissonance approached by step and left by step in the opposite direction.

Double neighbor tone. A dissonance in which both the upper and lower neighbor tones are given in succession with a leap of a third between them.

Anticipation. A weak dissonance, approached by step and resolved by common tone.

Pedal point. A nonchord tone approached and left by common tone. The pedal point sustains while the harmony changes.

Appoggiatura. A strong dissonance approached by leap and left by step in the opposite direction. Usually approached by leap up and resolved by step down.

Escape tone. A weak dissonance approached by step and left by leap in the opposite direction.

Incomplete neighbor. A dissonance that is approached or left by leap.

Species counterpoint teaches the three most common nonchord tones. Others occur frequently in common-practice music. Many are variations of the basic passing and neighbor tones.

Nonchord tones are defined by if the occur in weak or strong positions, how they are approached, and how they are resolved.

WORKBOOK

1. Analysis: Analyze the following excerpts. Do the following:

- Below the system, identify the key of the excerpt.
- Label the chords with their root, quality, and inversion.
- Circle and label nonchord tones.

In the last example (Mozart, K. 533), measure 5 may be tricky. Look at measure 7 for clarification.

A. Mozart, Piano Sonata, K. 333, I

B. Beethoven, *Variations on a Theme by Paisiello*, Variation I

C. Mussorgsky, "Limoges. Le marché" from *Tableaux d'une exposition*
("The Marketplace at Limoges" from *Pictures at an Exhibition*)

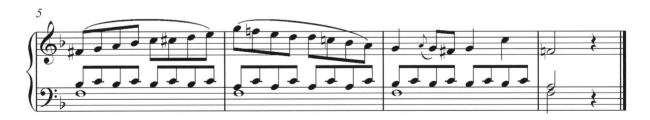

D. Mozart, Piano Sonata, K. 533, I

The Purpose of Chorale Style

CHAPTER LEARNING OBJECTIVES

This chapter:

- Explains the reduction of common-practice pieces to chorale style
- Explains the use of chorale style in theory classes to see the voice leading and harmonic progression more clearly

This book dedicated 18 chapters to arriving at chorale style. Why is this idiom the ultimate goal?

The usefulness of chorale style in music theory is that the chord changes every beat, with minimal ornamentation. It is an excellent way to see how the voices move in a given harmonic progression. In many pieces, chords last longer than a beat, the melody is heavily embellished with dissonances, and the rhythm is complicated. Regardless of these complexities, the basic voice leading of a progression remains the same. The shorter, even rhythmic durations and the clean melodic lines of chorale style allow this voice leading to be more apparent. The following examples show how pieces can be reduced to chorale style to see the progression and voice leading more clearly.

Figure 19.1 shows the slow movement of Beethoven's *Pathetique* Sonata. It appears to have three voices, two outer ones moving more slowly and a middle one moving in sixteenth notes. This interpretation, however, is wrong. Arpeggios, especially in voices other than the main melody, often move between two voices. The arpeggiation provides energy and motion. This particular movement is slow. If it moved in quarter notes the entire time, it would drag. By having sixteenth notes alternating between the alto and tenor, Beethoven moves the music forward.

The chorale-style arrangement of this excerpt would look like figure 19.2. In this reduction, it is easier to see the musical aspects this book has discussed, such as the counterpoint between the outer voices and the smooth inner voices. In the last two measures, the bass has a wonderful descent from A♭ down to E♭. It jumps up an octave, but once a performer sees that, she can articulate it in performance

Figure 19.1 Beethoven, Piano Sonata no. 8, op. 13, II

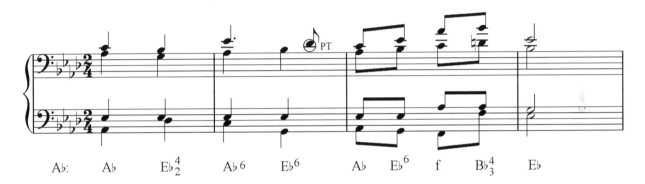

Figure 19.2 Beethoven, Piano Sonata no. 8, op. 13, II, in chorale style

The Bach excerpt in figure 19.3 involves a similar situation. It appears to be three voices, with the bottom two sustaining and the top one playing arpeggios. As with the Beethoven example, the arpeggios imply different voices. This piece is actually written in five lines. In figure 19.3a, which shows the score, each voice is numbered the first time it appears. Figure 19.3b compresses these into block chords by removing the rhythmic ornamentation. Figure 19.3c shortens the rhythmic values to make it look exactly like chorale style.

Two systems of music now fit into one measure. Viewing the passage this way, it is much easier to see what is happening. Basically, the two outer voices do a neighbor gesture (not dissonances, but the analogous gesture) in contrary motion around a C chord. When performing this, it should not be about playing the arpeggios; rather, the pianist needs to bring out the E moving up to F and back while C moves down to B and back up. Notice, too, that the C in measure 2 is a bass suspension; the idea of tension in that voice releasing into measure 3 should be brought out.

Finally, the reduction clarifies the larger picture too. This excerpt is the opening of the piece. At the end of the first four measures, the music is exactly where it began. This passage establishes the tonic by taking a single chord and stretching it out with neighbors. On the surface level, the running sixteenth notes continue throughout the entire piece. As a result, it is not clear where subsections of the piece are and where the cadences lie. Looking at it in chorale style, however, makes it clear that measure 4 is an appropriate place to hold back and breathe before moving forward again. It is a single complete thought and musical unit in the larger work.

Reducing a passage or piece to chorale style involves two steps. First, identify which pitches belong to each voice. This can be tricky. Sometimes arpeggios indicate different voices; sometimes they are single lines. Composers sometimes add voices briefly for a fuller sound and then drop them again. Generally, the accompaniment is less embellished and ornate than the melody, so it is a good place to start. Look at the lowest notes on each beat or in each measure and see if they work together melodically. Look for patterns in the accompaniment and if a certain position in the pattern corresponds to a single voice. Once the voices are identified, the passage can be written as block chords. The second step involves removing the dissonances, if there are a lot of them.

Figure 19.3 Bach, Prelude no. 1 from *Das Wohltemperirte Clavier I* (*The Well-Tempered Clavier Book I*)

(C♯ connects with next phrase)

Figure 19.4 Mozart, Piano Sonata, K. 545, II, mm. 17–20

Figure 19.4 shows an excerpt from a Mozart piano sonata. The arpeggiated pattern in the left hand is known as an *Alberti bass*, which, just like with the Beethoven excerpt, provides rhythmic motion to propel the music forward. The left-hand pattern is consistent, allowing the voices to be distinguished relatively easily. The downbeat is always the lowest note, so it is probably the bass line. The second and fourth sixteenth notes keep a common tone throughout the passage. The third sixteenth notes, taken together, give a smooth, slow-moving line. Separating the voices gives figure 19.5. (This is also a nice example for nonchord tones.)

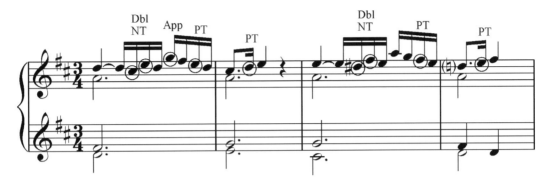

Figure 19.5 Mozart, Piano Sonata, K. 545, II, mm. 17–20, accompaniment reduced

The reduction clarifies the voice leading, such as the revoicing in the fourth measure to avoid a doubled third. While this level of reduction is enough to see the harmonies and the melodic lines, removing the dissonances will clarify the underlying structure even more (figure 19.6). Playing through figure 19.6, you will still recognize the piece. The basic structure is present and identifiable.

Figure 19.6 Mozart, Piano Sonata, K. 545, II, mm. 17–20, melody reduced

It is still possible to go one step further. The F♯ in measure 1 and the G in measure 3, although chord tones, are clearly ornamentation of the D and the E. In measure 2, the C♯ is the third of the chord, so I am going to give it priority over the E. Since measure 4 parallels measure 2 musically, I will do the same thing there. Now everything is block chords and can be written in quarter notes, best showing the underlying contrapuntal interplay of the voices.

Figure 19.7 Mozart, Piano Sonata, K. 545, II, mm. 17–20, fully reduced

Figure 19.7 parallels the Bach nicely. The two outer voices move in a double neighbor gesture in contrary motion, embellishing a single chord.

The final example (figure 19.8) is from a Chopin mazurka. This piece is a dance. The left hand provides the oompah-pah so common to dance pieces. (In the second measure, he disturbs the rhythm by jumping back to the bottom note, and in the third measure he writes a rest. Throughout the rest of the passage, the oompah-pah continues uninterrupted.) Clearly, this music is about block chords accompanying a melody.

Figure 19.8 Chopin, Mazurka, op. 7, no. 1

Despite the fact that the accompaniment is so harmonically oriented, it is still dependent on counterpoint. Once it is written in chorale style, it becomes clear that the chords are not independent blocks but contrapuntal lines (figure 19.9). The bass is oompah-pahing, but the inner voices are smooth melodies. The nonchord tones in the melody have been removed too in this reduction. The F in parentheses at the end is because its presence is implied by the nonchord tone at that moment.

Figure 19.9 Chopin, Mazurka, op. 7, no. 1, reduced

In chorale style, it becomes clear why Chopin threw off his accompaniment rhythm in measures 2 and 3. The soprano and tenor contain parallel octaves in moving from measure 2 to measure 3. Chopin wrote a passage with bad voice leading; he changed the pattern to hide it! He ensures that neither the two Fs nor the two Gs sound at the same time, thereby weakening the effect of the parallels. In measure 3, the last pitch we hear in the left hand is the G in the tenor. This could create an effect of contrary octaves with the melody when moving into measure 4. Technically, these would have been fine, since they are in different voices, but they would be audible. Had Chopin used the same bass-note pattern as in measure 2, the direct octaves between the outer voices would have been apparent. Rather than write either of these, he just put in a rest. Clearly, Chopin thought about his counterpoint.

Reducing an excerpt to chorale style can be carried out to different extremes. I usually leave the melody intact and simplify the accompaniment, basically giving the appearance of a fifth species exercise. As seen in the previous examples, it is possible to reduce pieces to essentially a first species exercise in four voices.

SUMMARY

Terminology

Alberti bass. An accompaniment pattern that involves a repeating arpeggiation of a chord in order to provide rhythmic energy and motion.

Chorale style enables a more direct and clearer view of harmonic progressions and their voice leading.

WORKBOOK

1. Reduction: Reduce the following excerpts to chorale style. You may preserve the durations of the chords or reduce all harmonies to a quarter-note duration.

   All three pieces can be reduced to four voices, although Waldteufel occasionally adds in a fifth voice for fullness. Beethoven and Mendelssohn both have some voices doubled in octaves, for example, the bass line. Composers do this to make a voice more prominent or to give the music more fullness. It does not affect the underlying voice leading. You can use either octave in the reduction, and you need only one of them. In both the Beethoven and Mendelssohn, when the melody enters, it is doubling an inner voice in octaves. Choose the more important octave and drop the other.

A. Waldteufel, *Les Sirènes* (*The Sirens*)

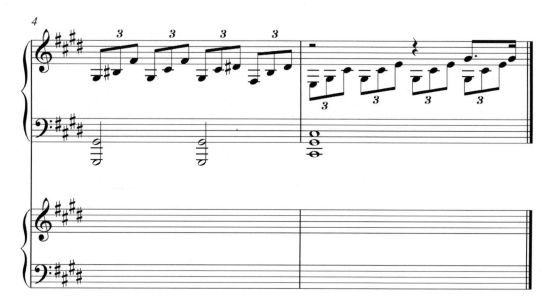

B. Beethoven, Piano Sonata no. 14, op. 27, no. 2 ("Moonlight"), I

C. Mendelssohn, "Venezianisches Gondellied" from *Lieder ohne Wörter*, op. 19, no. 6
("Venetian Boat Song" from *Songs without Words*)

DIATONIC HARMONY TO FORM

In 1722, three years before *Gradus ad Parnassum* appeared, the composer Jean-Philippe Rameau published the book *Traité de l'harmonie* (Treatise on Harmony), an exploration of how chords connect to one another and the order in which they appear. Rameau changed the way musicians think, shifting the emphasis from counterpoint to harmony. He introduced the concept of inversions (prior musicians named the chord after the bass note), introduced the idea of seventh chords, and named the scale degrees and chords (tonic, supertonic, etc.). Although the focus of this book will now move to chords, all voice-leading issues of the previous chapters hold true. Counterpoint underpins all harmonic motion.

I

PART

II

PART

III

PART

IV

PART

V

PART

Harmonic Progressions

This chapter:

- Defines Roman numerals as a way to present harmonic function
- Explains the impact of chord inversions on harmonic function

Have you ever noticed how many popular songs sound similar? Many are built from just three chords, and even though they are in different keys, the chord patterns sound the same. A common pattern in the 1950s consisted of four chords; "Stand By Me," "Duke of Earl," and "Heart and Soul" all share the same pattern.

Although more chords are involved, the same principle holds true with common-practice music. (And to show that patterns even cross genres, Pachelbel's Canon in D has the same pattern as Green Day's "Basket Case," although Green Day's song is in E♭.) The reason is that, in a single key, we have only seven chords to choose from. A limited number of combinations exist for these chords. Considering that chords sometimes have to contain particular pitches, such as at a cadence where the leading tone must be supported, the possible combinations are further limited.

Like scale degrees, chords also have functionality; in context, they play a particular role. As discussed in Chapter 2, to describe a chord by its root's name, "C-major," does not explain any sort of function; it merely tells you the notes in the chord. To show function, chords must be named relative to the tonic, just as was done with scale degrees. For example, if the chords to Pachelbel's Canon and "Basket Case" are written side by side with root names, they appear completely different (D–A–b–f♯–G versus E♭–B♭–c–g–A♭). Change to functional labels, and they will be identical (I–V–vi–iii–IV).

For chords, functional labels are written as Roman numerals. Uppercase Roman numerals represent major triads while lowercase ones represent minor. Diminished quality is shown by adding a ° symbol to a lowercase Roman numeral, and augmented by adding a + to an uppercase one. The seven possible chords and their qualities in both modes appear below. In minor, although both 6̂ and 7̂ have two possible forms, the important forms are the tendency tones, L6̂ and R7̂. R6̂ and L7̂ exist only to remove the pull of an unnecessary tendency tone and to avoid the melodic augmented second. The one exception is the III chord, which usually appears as major rather than augmented.

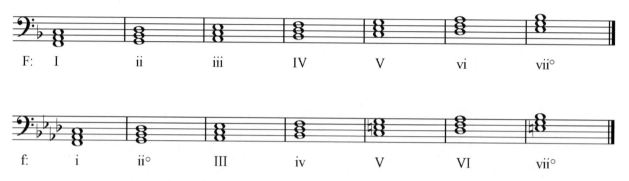

Figure 20.1 The possible functional chords in each mode

Notice that only the V and vii° chords are the same in both modes. A convenient aspect of harmonic function is that, even though chord quality changes between the modes, the function does not. A iv chord in minor functions the same as a IV chord in major. (Note, however, that a IV chord in *minor* probably indicates that the functionality is changing.)

Inversion also does not affect function. *Harmonic motion is defined by root motion, not bass motion.* Inversions result from the melody in the bass, not a change in the chord's role in the music. Sometimes composers will use an inversion for a less stable sound too, for example, to avoid a cadence. Since root-position and first-inversion chords function the same way, this book will not treat inversions separately.

The one exception to this statement is second-inversion chords. Second-inversion chords contain a dissonance (P4 with the bass), and by definition, a dissonance is not part of a chord. For example, suspensions do not count as chord tones; their resolution gives you the actual triad member. The same concept holds with second-inversion chords: although they look like they can stack up into thirds, in reality the nonchord tone has to resolve to give you the true structure. So second-inversions chords do not really violate functional principles; rather, the dissonance disguises the functioning chord, making it look like another one.

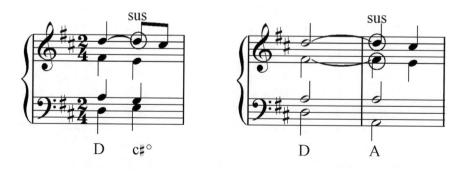

Figure 20.2 Dissonances must resolve to see the true chord structure

The following chapters are organized from the most important to least important chords. As the chords drop in importance, their roles are less clearly defined, and they function in more ways. The first two harmonic levels, tonic and dominant, each have one unique role. Pre-dominants have two roles. We end with the mediant, which has no clearly defined role in basic progressions.

As a final reminder that Roman numerals are not mere labels, but actually describe levels of musical tension, I will paraphrase the composer Arnold Schoenberg: we use the term *harmonic progression* because that is what it is—not a succession, but a *progression.*[1]

SUMMARY

Roman numerals show harmonic function.
Harmonic function is the same for both major and minor modes.
Harmonic function is not affected by inversion (not including second-inversion chords, which are unstable).
Harmonic motion is always defined by root motion, not bass motion.

NOTE

1. See Arnold Schoenberg, *Structural Functions of Harmony* (New York: W. W. Norton, 1969), 1.

Tonic and Dominant
The Fundamental Relationship

**CHAPTER LEARNING
OBJECTIVES**

This chapter:

- Explains the relationship
  between tonic and dominant,
  the defining trait of common-
  practice functionality

- Explains voice-leading issues
  when moving between tonic
  and dominant

- Defines the three most
  common cadences in
  common-practice music

- Explains the harmonic and
  cadential patterns in periods

The function of chords parallels, but does not mirror, the function of scale degrees. Of course the most important chord is the *tonic*. Just like $\hat{1}$, the tonic chord is the point of rest in a key. It is home, and it is the goal of a piece of music on every level, be it the phrase or the entire work. A root-position tonic chord is at rest, and it gives a sense of finality to the passage or piece.

The second most important chord also makes sense in light of the scale degree functions. It is easiest to see this in the structure of the typical contrapuntal cadences. In the various species chapters, a standard cadential figure was given, not to make life easier, but because that is the way most common-practice music ends.

Cadences always include the resolution of the leading tone. They also include the supertonic moving to tonic. When beginning three voices, we saw that only two chords can complete this gesture. Either we add the dominant below ($\hat{5}$, $\hat{7}$, and $\hat{2}$) or we add the subdominant above ($\hat{7}$, $\hat{2}$, and $\hat{4}$). The choice of chord (V or vii°) depends on the bass note. If the supertonic is in the bass, vii° is used. Otherwise, V is used. See Chapter 12 for a more detailed explanation of this subject. Figures 12.1 and 12.2 are reproduced as figures 21.1 and 21.2 for convenience.

These two chords make up the next most important functional level, called *dominant*. The function of these chords is identical to that of the scale degree they support ($\hat{7}$); they contain tension and pull to the tonic.

Although both chords function the same way, V is "stronger" and more important than vii°. V is a stable major triad rather than an unstable

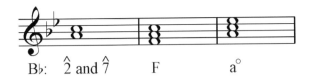

Figure 21.1 The possibilities for the penultimate chord

Figure 21.2 The choices for completing the penultimate triad

diminished triad. It also can appear in more inversions and work with a wider variety of basslines. Most importantly, composers just preferred its sound and, as a result, used V much more than viiº. For this reason, the functional level takes its name from the dominant chord and not the leading-tone chord.

These two functional levels, tonic and dominant, create *the fundamental relationship* in tonal music: V →
I (or V → i). (I am using V to denote the dominant functional level. It could be viiº, but it usually is a V chord anyway.) All pieces have a dramatic arc leading from the tonic to the tension of the dominant and back to tonic. All tonal music, spanning from a phrase to an entire work, is underpinned by the basic structure I–V–I (or i–V–i). Since the fundamental relationship is V → i, the dominant chord is always major. It has to support the leading tone in order to pull back to tonic.

When resolving V or viiº to tonic, the only pitch that needs to resolve is the leading tone. All of the other pitches will move as either dictated by the melody or by the smoothest line. As discussed in the previous chapter, the inversion does not affect a chord's function or resolution.

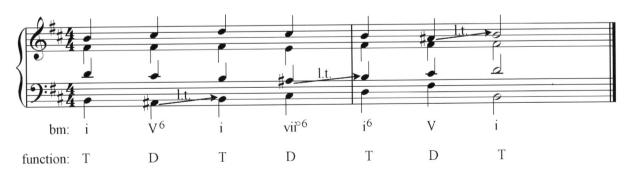

Figure 21.3 Resolution of dominant chords in context

As mentioned above, the dominant–tonic relationship plays an important role at cadences. Three basic cadences use these two chords.

Authentic cadences move harmonically from V to I. Since they end on the tonic chord, the dominant resolves and these cadences have a feeling of release and rest. They can be divided into two subcategories based on how stable the final chord is. A *perfect authentic cadence* (PAC) is defined by two criteria: the outer voices both end on $\hat{1}$, and the bass moves from $\hat{5}$ to $\hat{1}$. The first criterion provides melodic closure. Both soprano and bass melodies have a strong sense of completion due to ending on the tonic. The second aspect, bass motion from $\hat{5}$ to $\hat{1}$, creates very clear harmonic motion, making the cadence obvious and harmonically strong. As a result of the harmonic clarity and the melodic finality, PACs are extremely stable. They often finish significant sections or entire pieces. *Imperfect authentic cadences* (IACs) are cadences in which the soprano ends on a note other than tonic (either $\hat{3}$ or $\hat{5}$), the dominant is inverted, or a vii° is used in place of V. (See the spotlight section for a discussion of competing definitions of the IAC.) For the same reasons as before—either the less clear harmonic motion or the lack of closure in the soprano melody—this cadence contains slightly more tension than a PAC and therefore sounds less final. It is useful for internal cadences in a piece.

On the score, cadences are marked by placing a half bracket (like a first and second ending mark) over the two chords involved. Figure 21.4 shows the notation as well as the difference between the two types of authentic

Figure 21.4 Leopold Mozart, Variation 6 from *Nannerl Notenbuch (Nannerl's Music Book)*

cadences. Having PACs at both repeat signs would make the piece sound sectional, but placing an imperfect cadence in the middle (counting the da capo) leaves some tension and provides continuity. The imperfect cadence is created both by the choice of dominant chord (a vii° instead of V) and by the scale degree in the soprano. The PAC at the fine is perfect (pun intended) for closing the variation.

Sometimes the chords are hard to determine in two-voice works. Remember to look for arpeggios and the implication of multiple voices, as in the bass above, and to group as many beats as possible. Notice that, even though the melody in figure 21.4 is heavily ornamented, all of the nonchord tones are the basic passing tones, neighbor tones, and suspensions. Seventh chords, as in measure 2, will be discussed in Chapter 23. Inversion changes are not labeled if the harmony does not change. I usually label the lowest note, but some prefer labeling the strongest beat. Following the latter convention, the third measure in figure 21.4 would begin with a root-position tonic chord. Either analysis works. Finally, not every V–I motion is a cadence. Remember that a cadence is an arrival at the end of a musical thought; it is the pause at the end of a phrase. V–I can occur within the phrase and just be part of the progression, not a cadence.

Half cadences (HCs) conclude on a dominant chord. They will involve a root-position V chord (not a vii°) because a stable chord is necessary to halt the musical flow. Since the V contains tension, half cadences do not feel restful; although there is a pause, the music wants to continue on.

Cadences contribute to the common phrase relationship called a *period*. As explained in Chapter 2, a period consists of two phrases, the *antecedent* and *consequent*, also often referred to as the question and answer. The antecedent phrase ends with a weaker cadence, usually a half cadence. Because of the lack of resolution at the end, it sounds like a question. The consequent, on the other hand, ends with a stronger cadence, usually a perfect authentic cadence, providing a strong conclusion, which sounds like an answer. Many classical melodies, and even nonclassical ones such as "My Bonnie" at the start of the book, use this structure.

While it is possible for a period to have a HC–IAC or an IAC–PAC relationship between the two phrases, the example here, with a HC and PAC, is by far the most common.

Figure 21.5 Beethoven, "An die Freude" from Symphony no. 9, IV, mm. 164–171 ("Ode to Joy"), a period

Spotlight On: THE DEFINITION OF CADENCE

The definition of a cadence has changed over the past twenty years. When I was a student, it was "the chord/progression at the end of a phrase." An important use of cadences, though, is understanding the larger structure of a work—how the different sections relate to one another. The definition is shifting to their significance as arrivals; they mark the end of a passage or idea.

The biggest change for the definitions in this book, where we are only briefly looking at the big picture of entire movements or pieces, is for the imperfect authentic cadence. On one end of the spectrum, some professors define it as the soprano ending on $\hat{3}$ or $\hat{5}$, or any chords, dominant or tonic, being inverted. At the other end of the spectrum is the new definition, where all cadences involve root-position chords, and authentic cadences are always V–I. The only difference between the IAC and the PAC is the note in the soprano voice. This is a narrower definition. Using it, there are phrases that just end and do not have a cadence.

My definition falls in the middle. I include vii° and V⁶ as possibilities in an IAC. I do not include inverted tonics. I have yet to find a passage where an inverted tonic sounds like closure and not like avoiding the cadence. There is too much instability.

I have no qualms with the new definition, provided it has the same qualifier that everything in this book has had: there are exceptions. As stated in the Student's Introduction (at the start of this book), music theory is about the common patterns. Yes, 95 percent (a made-up number, but probably not far off) of IACs have V–I with the soprano on a pitch other than tonic. But it seems odd to say that measure 8 of the Leopold Mozart piece (figure 21.4) does not have a significant arrival or closure to it.

SUMMARY

Terminology

Tonic. The most important scale degree and chord in a key, being the point of rest and ultimate stability.

Dominant. The second most important harmonic functional level in a key, consisting of the V and vii° chords. The role of these chords is to provide the most tension of any harmonies and to pull back to tonic.

Perfect authentic cadence. A cadence ending with V–I, in which the soprano line ends on tonic. Since there is both harmonic and melodic closure, a PAC is the most final sounding cadence.

Imperfect authentic cadence. A cadence ending with dominant moving to tonic, in which the soprano ends on $\hat{3}$ or $\hat{5}$, the V is in inversion of, or a vii° appears instead of a V.

Half cadence. A cadence ending on V, containing tension and requiring the music to continue.

Period (in terms of harmony now). A frequent thematic structure in common-practice music, consisting of two phrases, the antecedent and consequent. The antecedent ends with a weaker cadence, while the consequent ends with a stronger one, creating an effect like a question and an answer.

Antecedent phrase. The first phrase of a period, which ends in a weaker cadence, thereby creating a sense of incompletion. See also *period*.

Consequent phrase. The second phrase in a period, ending in a stronger cadence, thereby providing a sense of closure. See also *period*.

The fundamental relationship in functionally tonal music is the dominant moving to the tonic.
V and vii° function as dominants.
When resolving a dominant chord, the leading tone should resolve to tonic.

WORKBOOK

1. Analysis: Analyze the following excerpts. Below the first system, identify the key of the piece. Then provide a functional Roman numeral analysis, including figures for inversions. Below the analysis, identify the functional level of each chord (D or T). Circle and label all nonchord tones, and bracket and label all cadences. Show the resolution of the leading tone with an arrow. If a harmony sustains over a measure or two, the voices may exchange pitches. The leading tone should resolve in the voice it last appears. Reducing the passage to chorale style may help clarify the voice leading.

   If a chord other than tonic or dominant appears, label it with the appropriate Roman numeral. Also, although we have not discussed sevenths, if a chord contains one, include it in the figures in the analysis. It will not affect the function of the chord.

A. Schubert, "Das Wandern" from *Die schöne Müllerin* ("Wandering" from *The Beautiful Miller Woman*)

B. Haydn, Sonatina 4, Scherzo

C. Beethoven, Ecossaise

2. **Figured Bass with Two Voices Given:** Realize the following figured basses by adding the alto and tenor voices. Follow the conventions of common-practice voice leading. You may add weak-beat dissonances if you like, but circle and label any that you use. Below the system, identify the key of the exercise and perform a functional (Roman numeral) harmonic analysis. Below each Roman numeral, identify its functional level (T or D).

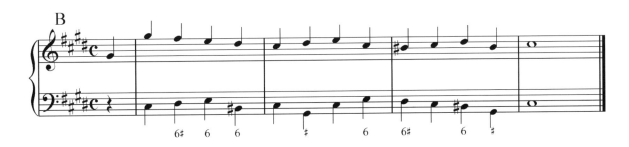

3. **Figured Bass:** Realize the following figured basses in a four-voice chorale style (SATB), following the conventions of common-practice voice leading. You may add unaccented dissonances as you like, but circle and label any that you use. Below the system, identify the key of the exercise and perform a functional (Roman numeral) harmonic analysis. Below each Roman numeral, identify its functional level (T or D). Bracket and label cadences.

Pre-dominant
The Basic Progression

The third most important category of chords is *pre-dominant*. This functional level includes ii and IV (ii° and iv in minor, but the fact that the quality changes with mode does not affect the function). As mentioned in Chapter 20, as the functional levels become less important, they broaden to include multiple uses. The pre-dominant chords can serve two different purposes:

1. Precede and connect to a dominant-level chord.
2. Return to tonic harmony.

PRECEDING DOMINANTS

Clearly, given the name *pre-dominant*, the first function, connecting to dominant chords, is more important than the second. The inclusion of pre-dominants creates the *basic functional progression*: T → PD → D → T.

Some noteworthy aspects of this basic progression: (1) Although tonic and dominant are functionally the most important chords, building a piece exclusively from them can lead to an unclear tonic. For example, in C-major, I and V are C and G. But these could also function as IV and I in G-major. The appearance of a pre-dominant, F or d, solidifies the tonal center. In terms of scale degrees, $\hat{4}$ clarifies the key. In this example, you need the pitch F to differentiate between C-major and G-major.[1] The pre-dominant chords support $\hat{4}$. (2) The basic progression reflects the importance of motion by descending fifth. IV is a fifth below tonic; ii is a fifth above V. (Root motion, not the bass note, defines harmonic motion. Even though the ii chord is in inversion, the motion is still by fifth down.)

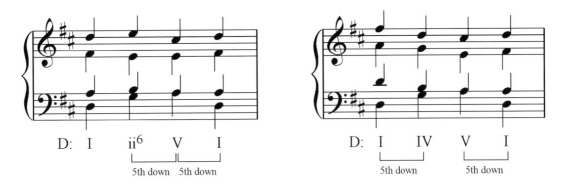

Figure 22.1 Fifth relationships in the basic progression

The pre-dominant chords provide a segue from tonic to dominant. Tension builds over a phrase to its highest point, and then it is released through the resolution to the tonic. Although the next statement sounds obvious, it causes confusion: pre-dominant chords do not follow dominant chords. A dominant followed by a pre-dominant is called a *retrogression*, because the harmony is moving backward, toward less tension, rather than forward, toward resolution. They undermine the whole purpose of the dominant and the leading tone. The prohibition against retrogressions causes confusion, however, because they regularly occur in pop music; our twenty-first-century ears are well acclimated to them. The most basic blues progression, the 12-bar blues, prominently features a retrogression (see figure 22.2). In the common-practice style, however, they do not happen.

Figure 22.2 The 12-bar blues contains a retrogression

Of the two pre-dominant chords, the ii occurs more frequently than the IV. (The opposite is true for pop music.) As we saw with the dominant chords, the chord that is a third lower (here ii, there V) is stronger than the higher one (IV and vii°). If pre-dominant harmony is sustained over two different chords, the progression is much more likely to move IV–ii than ii–IV.

One reason for the strength of ii is that it moves to V by descending fifth, which is a strong harmonic motion. Another reason, however, is voice leading. Moving from IV to V often creates parallel perfect consonances. Any time the harmony moves by step without changing inversion, parallels tend to result because the smoothest voice leading moves all voices by step. The way to avoid parallels is to have the three upper voices move contrary to the bass. Of course, even easier is to use ii instead of IV. Hence the supertonic is the more common pre-dominant chord when moving to the dominant.

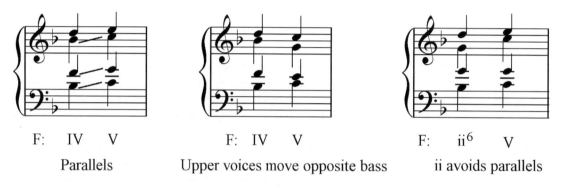

F: IV   V   F: IV   V   F: ii⁶   V

Parallels   Upper voices move opposite bass   ii avoids parallels

Figure 22.3 Voice leading when the root moves by step and inversion does not change

We can now incorporate pre-dominants into our standard cadences. The most common authentic cadence contains the pattern ii⁶–V–I. Harmonically, this uses the most common chords for each functional level. Melodically, in the bass, the dominant is approached by step, but then the $\hat{5}$–$\hat{1}$ gives the clear harmonic motion of a cadence. A way to find some cadences is to look for $\hat{4}$–$\hat{5}$–$\hat{1}$ in the bass. The standard half cadence stops on the dominant, giving ii⁶–V.

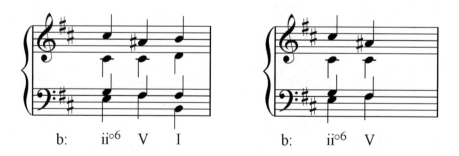

b: ii°⁶ V I   b: ii°⁶ V

Figure 22.4 The standard authentic and half cadences

A *Phrygian cadence* occurs when the harmony moves iv⁶ → V. The name comes from the bass motion of L$\hat{6}$ → $\hat{5}$. This sound reminds musicians of cadences in the Phrygian mode, where $\hat{2}$ is only a half step from $\hat{1}$. (See Appendix C for more information on the modes.) Sometimes, however, terms that are too specific can create more confusion rather than clarity. Although the name describes the colorful sound of it, a Phrygian cadence is a half cadence. While the term has merit, *half cadence* works just as well.

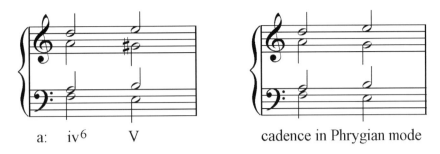

Figure 22.5 The namesake and the original Phrygian cadence

RETURNING TO TONIC HARMONY

Pre-dominants can also return to tonic. Moving from pre-dominant back to tonic does not constitute a retrogression; no leading tone is undermined and no particular resolution is thwarted.

A particular use of IV → I is to prolong tonic harmony. *Prolongation* is the expansion of a harmony or functional level through other chords. For example, I–IV–I prolongs the tonic harmony by inserting a subdominant chord between the two tonics. The IV is seen as embellishing the I; the harmony moves away and then returns. Prolongation will be discussed in more detail in Chapter 32. For now, it is important to know that IV is often used in a I–IV–I pattern. Although the secondary function of pre-dominant chords is subordinate to the primary one (moving to dominant), prolongation of tonic happens with great frequency.

IV → I also occurs at cadences and is called a *plagal cadence* (PC). The plagal cadence is final sounding, since it ends on tonic, but weak, since it avoids the tension of the dominant and the leading tone. It is most familiar as the "Great Amen" appended to the end of hymns in Christian churches. In this context, it follows a strong, key-affirming, authentic cadence. Plagal cadences can end phrases on their own, but due to their softness, they are uncommon. In the following excerpt, the plagal cadence creates the calm feeling Debussy requests much more than an authentic cadence would (see figure 22.6).

Figure 22.6 Debussy, "La fille aux cheveaux de lin," *Preludes*, no. 8 ("The Girl with Flaxen Hair")

It is possible for the supertonic to prolong the tonic or to create a plagal cadence, but as explained earlier, harmonic motion by step without changing inversion encourages stylistically inappropriate parallels. As a result, ii usually moves to dominant, while IV more commonly returns to tonic. These pairings also employ the common harmonic motion by descending fifth.

An analysis of a portion of a Bach minuet follows. The functional levels are labeled below the Roman numerals to emphasize where the chords fit in the hierarchy. All basic roles appear. The excerpt also displays a period structure.

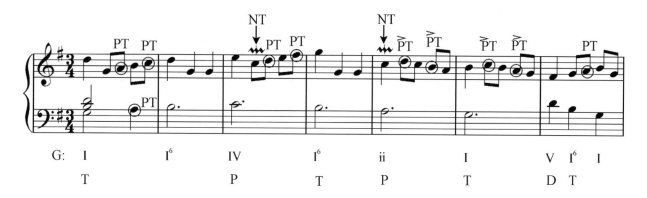

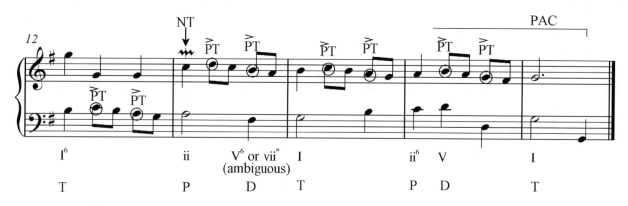

Figure 22.7 Bach, Minuet, from *Notenbüchlein für Anna Magdalena Bach*, mm. 1–16
(*Notebook for Anna Magdalena Bach*)

SUMMARY

Terminology

Pre-dominant. The third most important functional level, consisting of the ii and IV (ii° and iv) chords. These chords serve two functions, either leading to dominant or returning to tonic.

Retrogression. Harmonic motion from dominant to pre-dominant, which is not appropriate in the common-practice style.

Phrygian cadence. A half cadence in minor, in which iv⁶ moves to V.

Prolongation. The expansion and elaboration of a main harmony or functional level through other chords.

Plagal cadence. A cadence with a pre-dominant, usually IV, moving to I.

The pre-dominant level's main function is to lead to dominant.
The most basic harmonic progression is T–PD–D–T.
Pre-dominant harmony may also return to tonic.

NOTE

1. This explanation is an oversimplification. As seen in the previous chapter, there are ways to clarify your key with just tonic and dominant. Metric placement, duration, and repetition can all help. But the essence of the statement still holds true. $\hat{4}$ defines the tritone in the scale, thereby solidifying the tonic.

WORKBOOK

1. Analysis: Many composers have written piano primers, which in the nineteenth century were often called "Album for the Young." The following analyses are from such books by Schumann and Tchaikovsky. The Tchaikovsky is a complete piece from the book. Analyze the following pieces.

- Below the first system, identify the key of the piece.
- Provide a functional Roman numeral analysis.
- Below the analysis, identify the functional level of each chord (P, D, or T).
- Circle and label all nonchord tones
- Bracket and label cadences.

   Although we have not discussed sevenths, if a chord contains one, include it in the Roman numeral. It will not affect the function of the chord. Also, for now, treat chromatic pitches (the A♯s in both Schumann pieces) as chromatic nonchord tones. Finally, second-inversion chords are not stable. When you encounter one, figure out what the dissonance is and label it.

A. Schumann, "Erster Verlust" ("First Loss")

B. Schumann, "Ländliches Lied" ("Rustic Song")

C. Tchaikovsky, "Melodie antique francaise" ("Old French Song")

2. Figured Bass: Realize the following figured basses in a four-voice chorale style (SATB). You may add unaccented dissonances as you like, but circle and label any that you use.

- Below each system, identify the key of the exercise
- Perform a functional (Roman numeral) harmonic analysis.
- Below each Roman numeral, identify its functional level (T, P, or D).
- Bracket and label cadences.

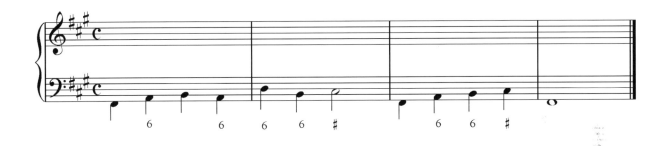

23

CHAPTER

Intensifying the Motion
Adding Dissonance

CHAPTER LEARNING OBJECTIVES

This chapter:

- Explains how dissonances can color and intensify a progression

- Explains how sevenths can be added to dominant and pre-dominant chords and the stylistically appropriate resolution for these harmonies

- Explains how second-inversion chords can embellish the dominant at cadences and the stylistically appropriate resolution for these harmonies

After first species, which establishes consonant sonorities, the ensuing species add in dissonances, which serve to smooth the lines and to propel the music forward through tension and its release. An analogous situation exists in harmony. The basic progression is T–PD–D–T. By adding harmonic dissonances, the progression can be intensified, pushing it forward and enhancing the dramatic arc.

The two most common harmonic dissonances result from the addition of a seventh to the basic triad and from the use of second-inversion chords. Both sonorities have pitches that pull toward a particular resolution, thereby intensifying the progression to the next harmony.

SEVENTH CHORDS

Seventh chords are created by adding another third on top of a triad. This new note forms a seventh with the root, hence the name.

Figure 23.1 A seventh chord

Being a dissonant interval, this seventh makes the harmony inherently unstable. The seventh itself is the dissonance, and it is strong since it is part of the chord and usually present for the harmony's entire duration. As a result, the seventh must resolve down by step, just like other strong dissonances, such as suspensions and appoggiaturas. Sevenths actually started as suspensions, as shown in figure 23.2. Although ambiguity can exist between a suspension/appoggiatura and a seventh, a general rule of thumb is that, while nonchord tones usually resolve within a single chord, a seventh resolves into the next harmony.

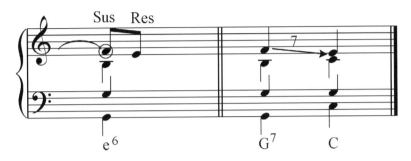

Figure 23.2 A suspension and a seventh

Seventh chords can appear in any inversion. The root and seventh always form the interval of either a seventh or second, depending on which is on top. (This is analogous to a 7–6 suspension turning into a 2–3 suspension when the voices flip.) Basically said, regardless of inversion, the seventh of the chord is dissonant and must resolve down by step.

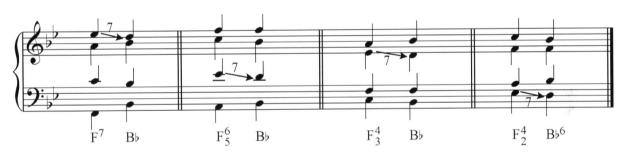

Figure 23.3 Regardless of inversion or which voice contains it, the seventh must resolve down by step

Since seventh chords contain four pitches, each voice usually gets one of them. If a note is omitted, it should be the fifth. The root and third are still required, the same as with regular triads, and the seventh is necessary to hear the dissonance. When the fifth is omitted, the most stable pitch should be doubled, which is the root. Never double the seventh. It is active (unstable) and has a particular resolution, just like a tendency tone. See figure 23.2 for an example of an incomplete seventh chord.

V⁷

V^7 is by far the most frequent seventh chord. If any motion should be intensified, the fundamental harmonic relationship is the one; it is the obvious choice.

A dominant seventh chord contains two pitches that must resolve. The first is the leading tone, which resolves up to the tonic. The other is the seventh of the chord, which resolves down by step.

Figure 23.4 The two pitches that must resolve in a V⁷

There is another way to view this resolution. The two pitches involved are $\hat{7}$ and $\hat{4}$, which form a tritone. (Note: Keep intervals and scale degrees straight. The seventh of the chord is $\hat{4}$. The leading tone is $\hat{7}$. Scale degrees are written with carets; intervals are not.) Since the tritone is a dissonant interval, it should resolve. The way to resolve intervals is similar to the resolution of chromatic pitches. For chromatic pitches, the general rule is that a lowered pitch wants to continue moving lower (G♭ goes to F) while a raised pitch wants to continue ascending (F♯ goes to G). For intervals, if it is diminished, that is smaller than a stable interval, it wants to keep shrinking, and both voices resolve inward. If it is an augmented interval, larger than a stable interval, it continues expanding, and both voices resolve outward. The resolution of the tritone is either inward or outward, depending on if it is written as a d5 or A4.

Figure 23.5 The resolution of the tritone

In either viewpoint, the same voices move the same way: $\hat{7} \rightarrow \hat{8}$ and $\hat{4} \rightarrow \hat{3}$.

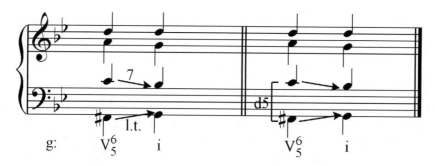

Figure 23.6 The resolution of V⁷ from different viewpoints

These scale degrees resolve the same way regardless of inversion. The other two pitches in the seventh chord can move anywhere, and their motion will depend on context and counterpoint.

In root position, a complete V⁷ leads to an incomplete tonic triad. If the leading tone is in an inner voice, composers sometimes leave it unresolved and jump to $\hat{5}$ instead. This is fine, even in a regular dominant chord without the seventh added. Since the leading tone is in an inner voice, it does not sound like it is left hanging. The leading tone must be in an inner voice to do this. Never thwart a tendency tone in one of the outer voices.

Figure 23.7 Thwarting the leading tone to get a complete tonic triad

Dominant seventh chords do not appear at half cadences. The seventh weakens the stability of the chord too much to support a convincing pause in the music.

Pre-dominant Seventh Chords

The second most common seventh chord is ii⁷, which makes sense since ii is the next most common and important chord. The seventh intensifies the harmonic motion and pushes ii forward to the V. In major, the only pitch that requires resolution in ii⁷ is the seventh. In minor, two pitches require resolution: the seventh and L6̂.

IV⁷ can also have a seventh added to it. The only pitch that needs to resolve in major is again the seventh. In minor, L6̂ appears and should be resolved too. With IV⁷, the third of the chord (6̂) and the seventh (3̂) risk forming parallel fifths. In major, 6̂ is not a tendency tone, so it can move anywhere, provided it does not violate the basic voice-leading principles. In minor, L6̂ has to resolve down, so the two active tones need to be voiced as fourths and not as fifths. (This solution also works in major.) Or just use ii.

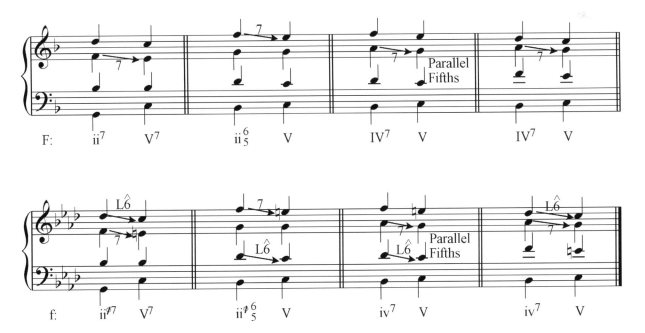

Figure 23.8 Pre-dominant seventh chords

Leading-Tone Seventh Chords

For the leading-tone seventh chord, the quality change between the modes leads to conceptual differences in the resolutions. The actual voice-leading patterns are the same though.

In major, the chord is half-diminished. There are three pitches that resolve. The leading tone still resolves up. The seventh still resolves down. Although it is no longer the seventh of the chord, like in V^7, $\hat{4}$ still forms a tritone with $\hat{7}$ and should resolve accordingly, down by step to $\hat{3}$. Only the third of the chord, scale degree $\hat{2}$, can resolve freely. When $\hat{2}$ is below the seventh ($\hat{6}$), parallel fifths will result if both move down by step. In this case, $\hat{2}$ usually resolves up, resulting in a doubled third. It can also leap away, if desired.

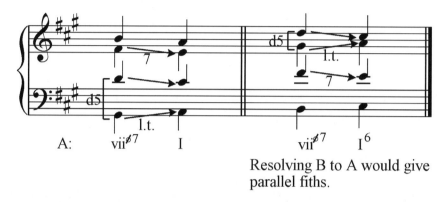

Resolving B to A would give
parallel fiths.

Figure 23.9 The resolution of the half-diminished leading-tone seventh chord

In minor, the leading-tone seventh chord is fully diminished. This chord has a tense sound because it contains two tritones: $\hat{7}/\hat{4}$ and $\hat{2}/L\hat{6}$. (Hence its use in *The Perils of Pauline* when Pauline is tied to the railroad tracks and the train is approaching.) These two tritones mean, however, that all four pitches have particular resolutions. The leading tone resolves up, the seventh resolves down, and $\hat{4}$ resolves to $\hat{3}$, the same as before. Now, though, $\hat{2}$ should resolve up to $\hat{3}$ too. This voice leading resolves all of the dissonances contained in the chord.

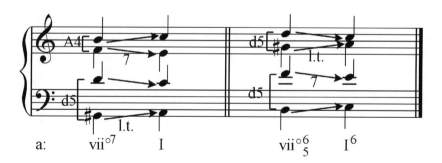

Figure 23.10 The resolution of vii°⁷

This voice leading also leads to a doubled third. In order to avoid the doubling, composers often ignore the tritone between $\hat{2}$ and $L\hat{6}$ and resolve the supertonic to tonic. (Not all tritones are created equal. The tritone between $\hat{2}$ and $L\hat{6}$ is often left unresolved, such as when ii° moves to V. The tritone between $\hat{7}$ and $\hat{4}$ usually demands resolution.) As with all irregular resolutions, the thwarted tendency is best softened or hidden. It is better when the tritone and its irregular resolution are similar fourths rather than similar fifths. Similar fifths are softened if in the inner voices. The weakest case is similar fifths with the irregular resolution in the bass. Some teachers forbid the second example below, while others allow it. Either way, it is weak.

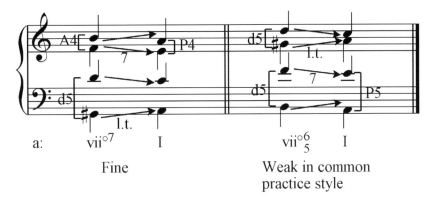

Figure 23.11 Acceptable resolutions of the vii°⁷

For all practical purposes, the resolutions of two leading-tone chords are the same. The only scale degree with flexibility in its resolution is $\hat{2}$. It will sometimes resolve up, giving a doubled third, in order to avoid parallel fifths or to resolve a tritone.

The fully diminished vii°⁷ also commonly appears in major. Composers often prefer the darker sound of this chord to that of the naturally occurring half-diminished harmony. The technique of using a pitch or chord from the parallel mode is called "modal borrowing" or "modal mixture." In this case, the composer "borrows" L$\hat{6}$ from the parallel minor in order to get the fully diminished sound. Mixture has no effect on the resolution of the chord.

This chapter has contained a lot of specifics about which scale degree has to move where. Do not lose the big picture for all of these details. The new concepts here are that sevenths resolve down by step, and that $\hat{7}$ and $\hat{4}$ form a tritone that should resolve. Whenever you encounter a seventh chord, resolve the tendency tones, the seventh, and relevant tritones. Watch out for voice-leading errors.

Finally, I⁷ chords do not exist in common-practice music. Tonic implies stability and rest, while a seventh means tension and pushing forward; the two are incompatible. A tonic chord with a seventh on it means one of two things: (1) the seventh is actually a nonchord tone, or (2) the chord is no longer functioning as tonic. (They are common in jazz and pop though. For example, one appears at the end of "Twist and Shout" as well as in the 12-bar blues [figure 22.2].)

CADENTIAL SIX–FOURS

Although second-inversion chords are unstable, two appear in the example in figure 23.12. Beethoven is exploiting that very instability to enhance the basic tonal relationship. In common-practice music, it is not that unstable harmonies are not allowed; it is that the dissonances must be handled and resolved properly.

Figure 23.12 Beethoven, Piano Sonata, op. 2, no. 1, II

To begin with, second-inversion chords are optical illusions. The fourth in the chord is a dissonance, not a chord tone. When a suspension sounds, it is not considered part of the chord. We disregard the dissonance and talk about the chord underneath it. Similarly, the fourth should not be considered a chord tone in the harmony above. Once the dissonance resolves, we will know what the true chord is. Being a prominent nonharmonic tone, the fourth must resolve down by step, just like a seventh. In the example above, the sixth also moves down to a fifth. The resulting chord is a dominant. Note that, although the rhythm is slower in the second example in figure 23.13 (and that is why this chord is given its own name), the concept is the same.

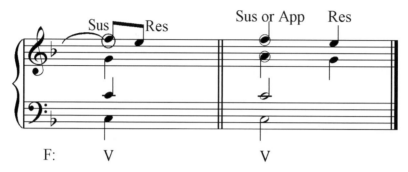

Figure 23.13 Dissonances are not considered part of the chord

The *cadential six–four*, so named because it occurs at cadences, is not a tonic chord at all, even though stacking up the pitches makes it look like one. It is an intensification of the V chord by putting two nonchord tones above it. This gesture grew from cadences in Renaissance counterpoint. The standard cadence in counterpoint was to suspend the tonic and let it resolve into the leading tone. The first half of figure 23.13 is analogous to this cadence (compare it with the suspended tonic cadences in figure 14.7, especially the 4–3 suspension). The gesture carried on for hundreds of years more, through the entire common-practice period, written as a sixth and a fourth (the suspended tonic pitch). Beethoven uses suspensions in both cases above (note the preparations) even though by this point in time the nonchord tones could have been appoggiaturas. Although the sixth is not technically a dissonant *interval*, it does not fit into the *harmony*, so it usually resolves too. Composers are freer with it than they are with the fourth, but for the most part, it also moves down by step.

Since both upper voices are nonchord tones, the only stable pitch is the dominant in the bass. Therefore, the appropriate doubling is the bass note. Technically, this is doubling the root of the chord, so it is the best choice.

The notation for the cadential six–four is a subject of much debate. The chord looks like a I, but a tonic chord is about stability while a second-inversion triad is about instability. Just like a I^7, this combination of terms makes no sense. Roman numerals are about function, not about a label, so there should be a better way. This book will label it as a V chord with a suspension over it. That is how it functions. Some people find this confusing, however, since the notes do not stack up to make a dominant chord. To avoid this confusion, people leave off the Roman numeral or write CAD in place of V. Several options are given in figure 23.14.

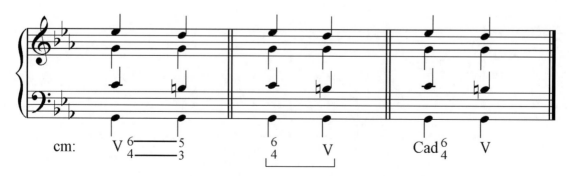

Figure 23.14 Some possible notations for the cadential six–four

The cadential six–four is a metrically strong event; it occurs on beats 1 or 3. This placement results from its association with cadences. Cadences occur on strong beats since they are significant arrivals. The cadential six–four is the arrival of the V chord, so for a half cadence it makes sense that it is metrically accented. For an authentic cadence, the cadential six–four also occurs on a strong beat, the unveiling of the underlying dominant chord occurs on the weak beat, and then the tonic lands on the next strong beat. This positioning also accentuates the dissonances contained in the chord.

Other second-inversion chords appear in music. The cadential six–four is the most significant one because it is a common way to indicate and emphasize a cadence. It appears frequently, and people recognize and understand the sound immediately. The other second-inversion chords will be discussed in Chapter 28.

Figure 23.15 shows the same progression realized in two ways—the first without dissonances and the second with them. The dissonances impact the progression in several ways. One is that the passage sounds fuller with the additional pitches. Secondly, the dissonances help smooth some lines. Note that the leap in the tenor at the end of the first measure is gone in the second version. Just like passing tones can fill in leaps in a melody, chordal dissonances provide additional notes to choose from, allowing for smoother lines. Thirdly, the dissonances drive the music forward. Try stopping on the downbeat of the second measure. In the second harmonization, the cadential six–four pulls forward. Even though the second one has a flatter melody, the whole is relatively engaging because of this pull.

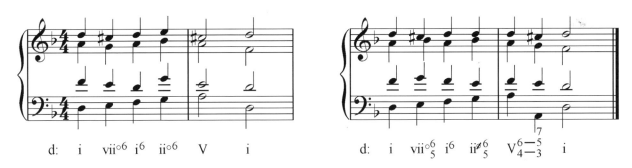

Figure 23.15 The addition of dissonances to a progression

Two more observations regarding voice leading: The resolution of a dissonance can be delayed. In the second progression, the seventh of the predominant turns into the fourth of the cadential six–four. It eventually resolves the way it should; it turns into another dissonance first and then reaches its goal pitch. Also, notice that all of the chordal dissonances can be thought of as passing tones, neighbor tones, or suspensions. This fact belies their origins, but by the common-practice era, it was not required to handle them this carefully.

SUMMARY

Terminology

Seventh chord. A dissonant harmony in which a seventh has been added to the basic triad. Another third has been stacked on top of the fifth in the chord.

Cadential six–four. A dissonant harmony in which the dominant chord at a cadence is embellished by what appears to be a second-inversion tonic chord but is actually a collection of nonchord tones.

The basic progression of T–PD–D–T is commonly intensified through two techniques.

1. The addition of a seventh to the dominant or pre-dominant chords
2. The use of a cadential six–four

Chordal dissonances are strong and resolve down by step into the next chord.

1. Sevenths resolve down by step.
2. Both the fourth and the sixth in a cadential six–four resolve down by step.

Dissonant intervals resolve in two ways:

1. By expanding if it is an augmented interval
2. By contracting if it is a diminished interval

WORKBOOK

1. Analysis: Analyze the following pieces. Be sure to include the following.
   - Below each system, identify the key of the piece.
   - Provide a functional Roman numeral analysis.
   - Below the analysis, identify the functional level of each chord (P, D, or T).
   - Circle and label all nonchord tones.
   - Bracket and label all cadences.
   - If the chord has a seventh or a cadential six–four, use an arrow to show the resolution of the dissonance.

Reduce the passage to chorale style if that will help you. Remember, especially on the Schumann, to think about which pitch is the bass note.

A. Beethoven, Piano Sonata, op. 2, no. 1, II

B. Mozart, Piano Sonata, K.570, I

C. Schumann, "Die alten, bösen Lieder" from *Dichterliebe* ("The Old, Evil Songs" from *A Poet's Love*)

D. Beethoven, Piano Sonata, op. 31, no. 1, II

2. Resolution Drill: You are given a chord and a key. Identify what the chord is and resolve it properly to the chord to which it leads. Label both chords with Roman numerals.

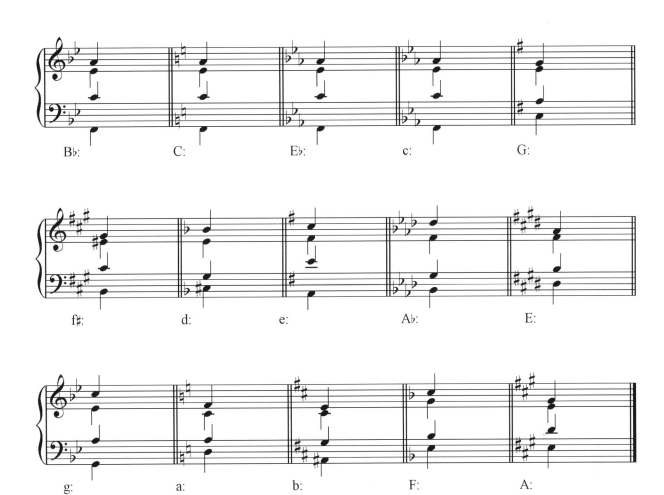

Bb: C: Eb: c: G:

f#:   d: e: Ab: E:

g: a: b: F: A:

3. Figured Bass: Realize the following figured basses in a four-voice chorale style (SATB). You may add unaccented dissonances as you like, but circle and label any that you use.

- Below each system, identify the key of the exercise.
- Perform a functional (Roman numeral) harmonic analysis.
- Below each Roman numeral, identify its functional level (T, P, or D).
- Bracket and label cadences.

A

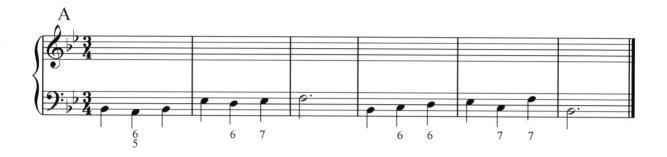

B

Submediant

**CHAPTER LEARNING
OBJECTIVES**

This chapter:

- Explains the three functions of
the submediant chord
- Defines deceptive motion and
the deceptive cadence

As chords become less important functionally, they both appear less in actual music and begin to have less defined functions. Tonic and dominant have one clearly defined function. Pre-dominants are still common but have two possible functions. The submediant chord appears much less than any of the previously discussed harmonies. It also has three possible functions in music.

Figure 24.1 shows what is arguably the most famous use of the vi chord: "Heart and Soul" by Hoagy Carmichael. This first role of the sub-mediant chord is to lead to pre-dominant chords. It can connect to either form of pre-dominant. I hear different students play different versions, I–vi–IV–V or I–vi–ii–V, when I ask them to play "Heart and Soul." (I hear the IV chord more frequently, but the ii chord is what Carmichael originally wrote.)

In this role, vi usually follows I. Leading from the tonic to the sub-dominant chord works well because of the repetition of the harmonic motion by third down. Motion by descending third creates particularly smooth voice leading since two notes stay as common tones, yet the new root in the bass clarifies the harmonic change and propels the music forward. In moving to the supertonic chord, the motion vi–ii is by fifth down, so of course it sounds good.

Figure 24.1 Carmichael, "Heart and Soul" (familiar duet fashion)

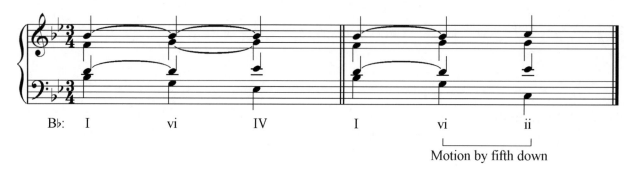

Figure 24.2 Submediant connecting tonic to pre-dominant harmonies

The second use of the vi chord is to substitute for tonic after a dominant chord. Just as vii° and V share the dominant function, and IV and ii share a pre-dominant function, vi has the ability to replace I. In this case, however, unlike the dominant and pre-dominant chords, the function is very different. Motion to vi from a dominant chord is a surprise, from both the unexpected harmony as well as the unexpected quality (minor in major and major in minor), so it creates an increase in tension rather than a release. This type of progression is called *deceptive motion*. When it occurs at a cadence, it is called a *deceptive cadence* (DC). This type of harmonic motion often appears toward the end of a larger section as a way to stretch out the tension. Deceptive motion can also harmonize a melody with a metrically strong $\hat{1}$ in order to keep the music from sounding too final. For example, in figure 2.3, "My Bonnie" was changed to end early through the placement of a metrically strong tonic note. The use of the submediant chord to harmonize that moment would keep the music from sounding conclusive.

When a dominant chord resolves deceptively, the typical voice leading must be followed; the leading tone should resolve up, and a seventh, if present, should resolve down (see figure 24.3). As is always the case, harmonic motion by step without a change in inversion lends itself to parallel perfect consonances. As a result, and also since the vi is substituting for I, the tonic pitch is usually doubled, giving the chord a doubled third. This doubling is completely acceptable.

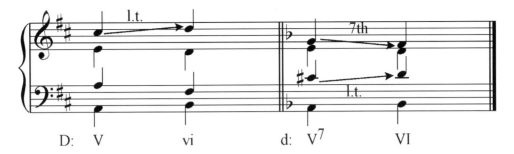

Figure 24.3 Deceptive motion

The final use of this chord is motion to the dominant. This progression is much less common than the preceding two but is still significant. Again, harmonic motion by step without a change in inversion can lead to bad parallels. The upper voices move opposite to the bass, as recommended in Chapter 22, figure 22.3. If the submediant chord has a doubled third, as when approached by deceptive motion, the voice leading is less problematic (see figure 24.4).

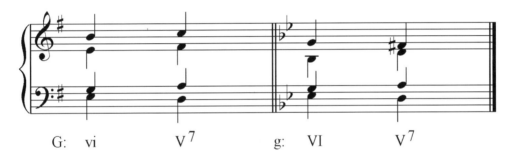

Figure 24.4 Motion from vi to V

Although it is acceptable to move between the submediant and either dominant-function chord, V or vii°, the motion usually involves V. Composers preferred the strength and harmonic clarity of V over vii°. The vi chord is not very common; vi and vii° paired together is rarer still.

The infrequency of the submediant chord and its lack of a unique function lead to two other traits. First, the vi⁷ chord is uncommon. The purpose of a seventh is to intensify the forward motion of a chord. Since the submediant function is not well defined, its intensification is less effective than that of pre-dominants and dominants. Second, vi almost always appears in root position. If it appears in first inversion, it often sounds like the more common and clearly defined tonic. For example, in a melodically ascending passage, scale degree $\hat{6}$ sounds more like a nonchord tone than the root (figure 24.5a). When used deceptively, $\hat{6}$ again sounds like a nonchord tone waiting to resolve (figure 24.5b). Placing the root in the bass clarifies the change of harmony. Neither of these situations is conceptually problematic or strictly forbidden; the problem lies in the lack of clear function plus the weaker inverted position. Our ears interpret music according to the most familiar patterns; since vi is not that common, tonic in the bass sounds like tonic harmony.

It is now possible to have a 6-5 suspension or appoggiatura. When working exclusively intervallically, as in two-voice species, or without regard to harmonic progression, as in three-voice species, both the sixth and the fifth are stable. When functionality is considered, it is possible to have a particular chord implied, such as tonic following dominant. In figure 24.5b, this situation happens. Because of the V preceding it and the tonic pitch in the bass, the listener hears a tonic harmony with a nonchord-tone sixth over it.

236 \ Chapter 24

Figure 24.5 In root position, vi sounds stronger than in inversion

As harmonic function becomes less defined, rather than trying to remember all the different progressions, it may be easier to remember what can approach a chord and where that chord leads. One can approach vi by tonic or dominant harmony (usually V). It may lead to pre-dominant or, less commonly, dominant (again, usually V). Any combination that follows these two paths will work.

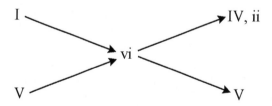

Figure 24.6 Possible chords leading to and away from vi

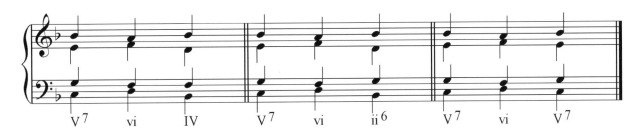

Figure 24.7 Some possible progressions involving vi

Figure 24.8 Mozart, Piano Sonata, K. 284, III

Figure 24.9 Schumann, "Volksliedchen" from *Album für die Jugend* ("Folksong" from *Album for the Young*)

Spotlight On: DESCENDING THIRDS

As seen in figure 24.2, motion by descending third creates smooth voice leading and clear harmonic direction. Motion by third down between most chords is strong. Examples are vii° moving to V and IV moving to ii. Motion by ascending third, however, is weak. Because the root of the second chord is already present in the first harmony, the new pitch sounds like the addition of a seventh rather than a new chord. The reverse of the two motions just mentioned will probably sound like a root-position V to a first-inversion V⁷ and a root-position ii to a first-inversion ii⁷. Moving down, however, provides a new pitch that cannot belong to the previous chord, creating a clear harmonic change.

Putting all of the chords thus far together in motion by thirds produces a chart that is another way to summarize functionality. The diagram groups the pre-dominant and dominant chords together, simplifying to the familiar PD–D–T pattern. The submediant falls between tonic and pre-dominant, which corresponds to its function in different cases (substituting for tonic in deceptive motion and substituting for pre-dominant when moving to dominant). Moving from left to right in this chart, whether skipping over chords or not, will create a functional progression. Tonic can move to vi, IV, ii, vii°, or V. Subdominant can lead to ii, vii°, V, or I. Dominant pulls to tonic. The only motion that is not included is deceptive.

Figure 24.10 Motion by thirds

Moving from right to left, however, produces nonfunctional progressions. Motion from dominant to pre-dominant is a retrogression. Motion by ascending third is weak. The only time it happens is between V and vii°; ii rarely if ever moves to IV. IV definitely does not move to vi, and vi definitely does not move to I (classically speaking).

SUMMARY

Terminology

Submediant. The chord built upon the sixth scale degree, vi (VI in minor).
Deceptive motion. Motion from a dominant-function chord to a harmony other than tonic, usually the submediant.
Deceptive cadence. Motion from dominant harmony to a chord other than tonic, usually the submediant, creating a surprising effect and an increase in tension.

The vi chord has three typical functions.

1. vi–PD, frequently I–vi–PD
2. Deceptive Motion: V–vi
3. vi–V (less common)

The submediant may be approached from tonic or dominant harmony. It may move to pre-dominant or dominant.

WORKBOOK

1. Analysis: Analyze the following pieces. Be sure to include the following.

- Below each system, identify the key of the piece.
- Provide a functional Roman numeral analysis.
- Below the analysis, identify the functional level of each chord (P, D, or T). The submediant does not need a functional label other than its Roman numeral.
- Circle and label all nonchord tones.
- Bracket and label all cadences.

Reduce the passage to chorale style if that will help you.

A. Mozart, Piano Sonata no. 2, K. 280, II

B. Schumann, "Hör ich das Liedchen klingen" from *Dichterliebe* ("When I Hear the Song" from *A Poet's Love*)

2. Figured Bass Realization: Realize the following figured bass in a four-voice chorale style (SATB). You may add any weak-beat dissonances you like, but circle and label any that you use.

- Bracket and label cadences.
- Below the system, identify the key of the exercise.
- Perform a functional (Roman numeral) harmonic analysis.

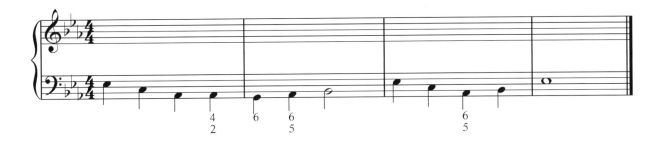

3. Outer Voices Given: You have the outer voices for two pieces of music. Determine the harmonies and complete the passage in a four-voice chorale style (SATB), following common-practice conventions. For the first one, the nonchord tones are identified. For the second one, you will have to determine what to include in the harmony.

- Below the system, identify the key of the exercise.
- Provide a functional (Roman numeral) analysis.
- Label cadences.
- Circle and label nonchord tones.

Mediant

This chapter:

- Explains that the mediant
  chord rarely appears in
  common-practice music
- Explains that the mediant
  lacks a clear function

If the submediant's function is not well defined, that of our final chord,
the mediant, is completely vague. The iii chord rarely appears, especially
in major. Textbooks usually list several different functions (I have seen as
many as eight). Here are six:

1. The mediant can move to the submediant chord. Motion by
   descending fifth is strong and works from any chord, such as I–IV
   or vi–ii–V–I; iii–vi is another option (see figure 25.1).

2. Due to the presence of a perfect fifth below scale degree $\hat{7}$, the iii
   chord can stabilize a leading tone so that it is not forced to resolve.
   In a melodically descending passage, it may be preferable to harmonize $\hat{7}$ with a iii rather than either of the dominant-function
   chords. This enables the harmony to move onto IV without a retrogression (see figure 25.2). Although this seems useful, it actually
   does not occur much. The $\hat{7}$ can more simply function as a passing
   tone instead (see figure 25.3).

3. The mediant can substitute for tonic, in place of a I^6. In the chorale
   at the opening of the *1812 Overture* (figure 25.4), Tchaikovsky uses
   a tonic chord to harmonize the G in measure 15. In measure 21,
   however, he uses a III. He also uses a chromatic chord in order to
   make the moment more striking.

Figure 25.1 Bourgeois, harmonization of hymn tune "Old Hundredth"

Figure 25.2 Schumann, "Die Rose, die Lilie, die Taube" from *Dichterliebe*
("The Rose, Lily, Dove, and Sun" from *A Poet's Love*)

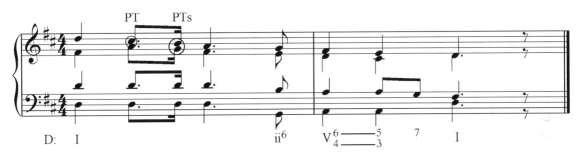

Figure 25.3 Handel/Watts, "Joy to the World"

Figure 25.4 Tchaikovsky, *1812 Overture*, mm. 14–24

4. In minor, III chords often appear midphrase. While this is true, this is not a function. These midphrase III's are approached and left in a variety of ways. These situations involve a brief pull toward the relative major. Notice how the Schumann piece in figure 25.5 brightens as it gets to the mediant harmony. The brightening is the result of a brief implication of a major key. More on this and the V/III notation in Chapter 30.

Figure 25.5 Schumann, "Armes Waisenkind" from *Album für die Jugend*
("The Poor Orphan Child" from *Album for the Young*)

5. The mediant can lead to dominant harmony. Yes, sometimes. The iii⁶, however, is almost always a V with a nonchord tone on it. The nonchord tone usually resolves, meaning that the chord should be labeled as a dominant chord not a mediant. In figure 25.6, the motion into the second full measure sounds deceptive, implying that the previous chord (the last chord in the first complete measure) is a dominant. Here is another case where harmonic motion, in this case PD → D, makes a sixth into a dissonance, resolving into a fifth, as discussed in Chapter 24.

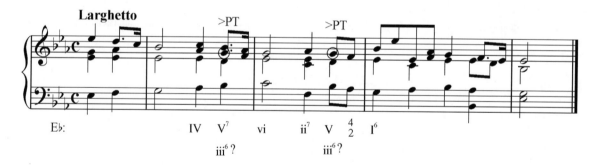

Figure 25.6 Giordani, "Caro mio ben"

6. In minor, the III+⁶ can substitute for V. This situation is similar to the preceding discussion, and the chord is essentially a dominant chord with a nonchord tone. Figure 25.7 is analogous to figure 25.6, but here the nonchord tone, F, does not resolve into the E. If the underlying V never sounds on its own, the harmony has a distinctive sound and can be labeled III+⁶.

d: ii°$_5^6$ III+^{6} i

Figure 25.7 Schumann, "Volksliedchen" from *Album für die Jugend* ("Folksong" from *Album for the Young*)

The take-home message is that the mediant appears infrequently and does not have a clear function. If it can substitute both for the tonic (function 3) and for the dominant (function 6), how can a function be assigned? In the examples in this chapter, iii was approached by I, ii, V, vi, and maybe IV (if you count the iii⁶ as a chord). The iii moved to I, ii, IV, V, and vi. Almost every chord can lead to it, and it can lead to almost any chord.

As mentioned at the start of the chapter, the mediant chord rarely occurs in common-practice music. If you analyze a chord as iii, double-check to make sure it is not something else with nonchord tones confusing the harmony. When writing a iii chord, make sure that the part writing is correct and that the chord does not sound abrupt approaching or leaving. When tempted to use a mediant chord, think about your future (since you have that fast metabolism now): when you are forty, how often should you have a bag of chips and a soda? That is how often you should use a mediant chord.

SUMMARY

Terminology

Mediant. The chord built upon the third scale degree, iii (III in minor).

The iii chord has no clear function. It appears infrequently in minor. It rarely appears in major.

WORKBOOK

1. Analysis: Analyze the following Bach chorales. Be sure to include the following:

   - Below each system, identify the key of the piece.
   - Provide a functional Roman numeral analysis. You do not need to add functional levels.
   - Circle and label all nonchord tones.
   - Bracket and label all cadences.

The second one is the complete chorale. One chromatic chord has been labeled for you since secondary dominants are still several chapters away. Treat the other chromatic pitches as nonchord tones.

A. Bach, "Nun lob', mein Seel', den Herren" ("Now Praise the Lord, My Soul")

B. Bach, "Lobt Gott, ihr Christen, allzugleich" ("Praise God, All Together, You Christians")

2. Figured Bass Realization: Realize the following short and sweet figured basses in a four-voice chorale style (SATB). You may add any weak-beat dissonances you like, but circle and label any that you use.

- Bracket and label cadences.
- Below the system, identify the key of the exercise.
- Perform a functional (Roman numeral) harmonic analysis.

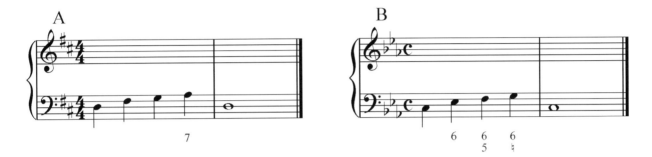

3. Composition: Compose a period. Choose a key other than C-major or a minor. The period should be eight measures, with a 4+4 phrase structure, or sixteen measures with an 8+8 structure. Even though this chapter is on the mediant, you do not have to use a iii chord. All diatonic harmonies have been covered; use the ones you want. Be musical with this. Include tempo, dynamic, and expression markings. Include an analysis with your piece. Identify the key, chords (Roman numerals), nonchord tones, and cadences. Also label the antecedent and consequent phrases.

Harmonic Rhythm

CHAPTER LEARNING OBJECTIVES

This chapter:

- Explains how chord changes complement and contribute to the meter of a piece
- Defines harmonic rhythm

An important part of the rock-and-roll style is syncopation. The basic backbeat involves the drummer hitting a snare drum hard on beats 2 and 4, accenting the offbeats. If they hit these beats so hard, why do we not feel them as downbeats? What in the music tells us where the metrical accents (beats 1 and 3) are? How do we know that the drummer is syncopating against them?

Several components of the music influence this. For example, phrase beginnings usually land on strong beats, as do cadences. Another significant factor is the chord changes.

Changing the harmony is a more significant event than remaining on the same chord. The ear notices there is something new, so when it occurs, it creates an accent. This change in harmony helps define the meter. The fact that chord changes usually happen on beat 1 of the measure tells the listener that the strong beat is there and that the drum is syncopating. Looking at it in reverse, the harmonic changes should not contradict the meter's accentuation pattern. The relationship between harmonic change and meter is a bit of the chicken-and-egg question. Does the change in harmony follow the meter or does it help create it? Yes.

Harmonic rhythm is the rate of change of the harmony, defined by a change in the root of the chord (i.e., the Roman numeral has to change). The common metric for it is in terms of how many beats a chord lasts (i.e., "The harmonic rhythm is every two beats," which means that in the piece under discussion, the harmony generally changes that frequently). Some observations about harmonic rhythm:

1. Once a harmonic rhythm is established, it usually continues at that basic rate or some logical ratio of it.

2. The harmonic rhythm often increases as the phrase ends, driving the music into the cadence. The cadence itself, however, sits on a single chord.

3. When harmony changes, it is usually on a strong beat. The reverse is not true; a strong beat does not require a change of chord.

4. Harmony does not begin on a weaker beat and carry over to a stronger one. Beginning a chord on beat 4 and continuing it on beat 1 contradicts the meter.

The Mozart theme in figure 26.1 has a harmonic rhythm of a chord per beat (note the cut time meter). Chord changes occur on the beat; they are not syncopated. The rate of a chord per beat is consistent over the entire phrase, until the half cadence, where the music remains on the dominant chord for the entire measure. This pause in the harmonic rhythm contributes to the feeling of repose at the cadence.

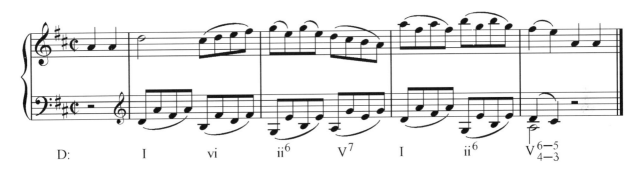

Figure 26.1 Mozart, Sonata in D, K. 284, III, Theme

In the second Mozart example, the harmonic rhythm contributes significantly to the shaping of the phrase. Once again, the basic harmonic rhythm is a chord every half note (which again is a beat). In the third measure, as the cadence approaches, the harmonic rhythm increases to a chord every quarter note. The tension rises in this bar, both through the ascending melodic line and through the increased pace of the harmonic rhythm. At the cadence, the harmonic rhythm slows to a chord for the entire measure, again providing the rest that a cadence requires.

In the first and fifth measure, the harmony changes to a vi chord on the fourth quarter note instead of the third. While this change is not typical, it also is not forbidden. The harmony changes again on the very next quarter note, which it should do, since it should not continue from a weaker to a stronger beat. If the submediant harmony continued across the barline, the music would feel wrong. It is possible, too, that the third beats in measures 1 and 5 are part of the vi chord, but since there is no root present, it is impossible to hear them as such. Interestingly, when the Alberti bass is added in measures 8–16, the vi chord arrives on the third quarter note, as expected.

The Beethoven excerpt in figure 26.3 shows more flexibility in harmonic rhythm than the preceding two examples. The harmonic rhythm fluctuates between a chord every beat (measures 1 and 3) and a chord every measure (all other measures). Three observations about this passage: (1) The change of inversion in measure 5 does not constitute a change of chord since the root does not change. (2) The fluctuations in harmonic rhythm do not contradict the metrical accentuation pattern. (3) The downbeat of the last measure of the excerpt looks like a dominant chord since the majority of the notes create a V^7. This interpretation is incorrect. The harmony arrives on the strong beat. The bass is the only note that is "correct." The other three voices contain suspensions that resolve properly on the next beat. We hear it this way because our ears know what chord will follow the dominant, and the bass, the note that provides the foundation for the chord above it, arrives on time, according to the pattern of the harmonic rhythm. As a result, the other three voices sound like (and are) dissonances that need to resolve.

Figure 26.2 Mozart, Sonata in B♭, K. 333, III

Figure 26.3 Beethoven, Piano Sonata 5, op. 10, no. 1, II

Figure 26.4 Analysis of the last measure of the Beethoven excerpt

Spotlight On: THE ALBERTI BASS

Harmonic rhythm slowed down over the course of the common-practice period. During the Baroque, the harmonic rhythm was faster, usually lasting for one beat. During the Classical era, the harmonic rhythm changed to one to two chords per measure. As a result, composers began using the Alberti bass, as seen in the two Mozart examples. The Alberti bass is a way to keep the music moving, even though a single chord is being sustained. As explained in Chapter 19, the Alberti bass is actually the alternation of three voices, not one single voice arpeggiating. In this way, the composer gives the music more energy than sitting on a block chord for what would feel like a long time.

SUMMARY

Terminology

Harmonic rhythm. The rate of change of the harmony.

The harmonic rhythm is the rate of change of the harmony, as defined by a change in the Roman numeral (root) of the chord.
Chords usually change on strong beats.
The harmony should not change on a weaker beat and carry over to a stronger one.
Harmonic rhythm often moves at a consistent rate. It may speed up as the phrase approaches the cadence and then slow down upon reaching the cadence.

WORKBOOK

1. Look at the pieces used in figures and analysis assignments in the previous chapters, beginning with Chapter 21. Describe the harmonic rhythm. Does it change on every strong beat? Does it speed up at cadences? Does it ever contradict the meter? If it contradicts the meter, starting on a weak beat and continuing through the next strong one, does it make musical sense in some way? (For an example of this contradiction of the meter, look at the Schubert "Das Wandern" workbook analysis in Chapter 21.)

Harmonizations

CHAPTER LEARNING OBJECTIVES

This chapter:

- Explains strategies for adding a functional harmonic progression to a melody

All of the assignments thus far have given the harmonies, to which the student adds a melody. Now that we have all diatonic functions at our disposal, we can begin from the melody and work out a harmonic progression.

The steps to harmonizing a melody are the following:

1. Identify important structural points. Music usually begins on the tonic chord. Cadences are usually dominants or tonics. Look at these important structural points and figure out what harmony is appropriate in these locations.

2. List all possible chords to harmonize the melody. Go through the melody and write down every chord that can harmonize each moment. Be aware that notes in the melody, even accented notes, may be nonchord tones. Remember that any note that you decide should be a nonchord tone should resolve properly. Seventh chords are an option, too, although a seventh in the melody must resolve down by step.

    Keep in mind harmonic rhythm. Theory class assignments typically use a chorale-style setting, so the harmonic rhythm is often a chord per beat. In most musical styles, however, a slower harmonic rhythm is preferable. It sounds more characteristic (unless setting a chorale), it gives you fewer chords, and that in turn leads to fewer places for mistakes. Think about what the music implies and what you want to do, then choose an appropriate harmonic rhythm.

3. At this point, two options exist:
   a. List the possible bass notes and construct a bassline in counterpoint with the melody. Once you have a nice line, determine what harmonies it implies.
   b. Choose a harmonic progression. Then construct a bassline.

We return briefly to two-voice counterpoint, with the goal of creating a nice line to go with the melody. While basslines usually are not as independent as the top line, they still need a nice sense of flow and direction. If you choose to emphasize the counterpoint (option 3a), then on the second part, when determining the chords, you may need to adjust your bass melody in order to create a functional progression.

In reality, these two steps are not mutually exclusive. Ideally, you will switch between the two methods in order to create the most interesting line and progression.

4. Complete the inner voices. As with earlier counterpoint and figured bass assignments, the inner voices are subordinate to the two outer voices.

5. Embellish to make it as interesting as possible. Use rhythm to free up the music and make it more engaging. The addition of nonchord tones can also help.

As an example, I will harmonize the melody in figure 27.1 several times.

Figure 27.1 The melody to harmonize

First, identify the salient features of the melody and its important structural points. The piece is in A-major. It has two phrases, both ending on authentic cadences. Both phrases begin similarly. Since the quarter notes in most measures can be passing tones, especially the E♭ in measure 6, which would be a chromatic passing tone, a harmonic rhythm of one chord per measure will suffice. The exceptions are in measures 3 and 7, where the leaps of a third define changing chords on each beat. As we are heading into cadences at both of these moments, the increase in harmonic rhythm makes sense. (It would also be perfectly acceptable to harmonize this in a chorale style, in which case every note or beat could be given its own harmony.) Figure 27.2 presents the information we know at this point. The lines indicate chord changes.

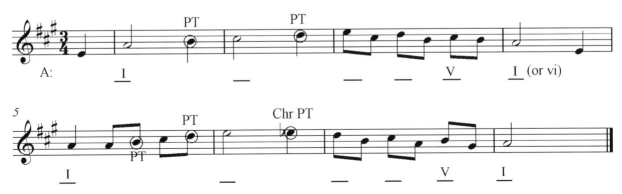

Figure 27.2 The salient features of the melody

Now we list all possible chords that could harmonize the rest of this melody (figure 27.3). I am listing function only. Inversions, sevenths, and other details can be added later. Whenever I include a seventh in figure 27.3, it implies that the note in the melody is the seventh.

Figure 27.3 Possible chords

I will begin by emphasizing counterpoint and writing a bassline without worrying about the progression (option 3a). I begin by listing all possible notes for the bass melody (figure 27.4).

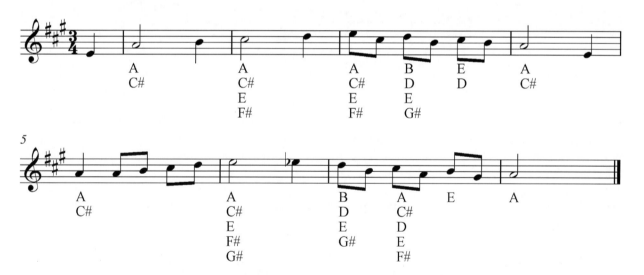

Figure 27.4 Possible notes for the bass

A few details in figure 27.4 merit discussion. First, sevenths can be added to chords if desired. In the cadence leading into measure 4, a V^7 is possible, even though I did not list the seventh explicitly before. I did, however, include D in my list of possible notes for the bass melody at that point. Also, I included a cadential six–four (the pitch E) at measure 7, beat 2, even though by the rules of species exercises this option would not exist. Working out the chords before writing the bassline will give you more options than using only the intervals available in two-voice counterpoint. Finally, I decided to end with $\hat{5} \rightarrow \hat{1}$ in the bass since that is the standard final cadence. Figure 27.5 shows the two outer voices for my harmonization.

Figure 27.5 Two-voice counterpoint

From here, I determine the implied progression, making sure that it works functionally (see figure 27.6).[1]

Figure 27.6 The implied progression

I then fill in the inner voices (figure 27.7) and enliven the rhythm for interest (figure 27.8).

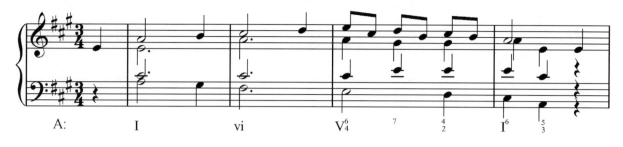

Figure 27.7 The four-voice realization

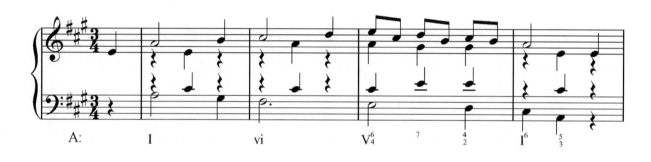

Figure 27.8 Rhythmic interest

Now I will take the approach of step 3b. Once I have my options of chords, I choose a harmonic progression I like. After I choose a progression, the number of options for bass pitches becomes small, and I write the best melody I can. In this case, I chose a simple progression (figure 27.10). The melody itself implies a certain simplicity, so I feel it is appropriate to use basic tonic, dominant, and pre-dominant harmonies. Other options are, of course, possible, depending on the desired sound.

Once I have a progression, I am limited to the root or third of each chord in the bass, unless it is a seventh chord, in which all inversions are allowed. The bassline writing goes faster than in the previous harmonization (figure 27.11).

Figure 27.9 Possible chords (same as figure 27.3)

Figure 27.10 The functional progression chosen

Figure 27.11 The bassline from the functional progression

Finally, I fill in the inner voices. In this case, I am opting to leave the arrangement in more of a chorale style (figure 27.12).

Figure 27.12 Final arrangement by determining harmonic progression first

I add a few passing tones, but nothing else. I introduced a seventh on the pre-dominant chord in measure 3 to avoid parallel fifths between the alto and tenor. I also used a seventh in the penultimate measure. Once the seventh is introduced, I want to hear the resolution in some voice, so I transferred it to the alto rather than allowing it to disappear. Finally, the sustained chords at the beginning of the phrases are a little long; the introduction of some rhythmic variation would help.

As mentioned above, the two approaches are not mutually exclusive. I find that students like working out the progression first because it gives a more defined framework. With experience, you can be more flexible, having an idea of what will work harmonically but being open to other options if an inspired bassline comes to you.

Figure 27.13 gives an example in which a few mistakes have made their way into the harmonization. In measures 2–3, a vi chord moves to I, a nonfunctional progression. (It also creates parallel fifths between the soprano and bass.) In measures 3–4, the harmonic rhythm is wrong, with the tonic harmony arriving on a weak beat and carrying over to a strong one. In measures 6–7, a retrogression occurs. Finally, although not wrong, ending a piece with a perfect authentic cadence, with $\hat{5} \rightarrow \hat{1}$ in the bass, is more typical.

Figure 27.13 Harmonization with unstylistic traits

SUMMARY

To harmonize a melody:

1. Analyze the melody for its salient features, including important structural moments, the locations of clearly defined harmonies, and the implied harmonic rhythm.

2. List all possible chords that can harmonize the melody.

3. Write a bassline and progression that works with the melody. You may want to start with a bassline and determine the harmonies, or you may want to determine the harmonies first and then compose the bass. To be most effective, you have to balance the two.

4. Fill in the inner voices.

5. Adjust the rhythm of the new voices and add dissonances to them to complement the feeling of the melody.

NOTE

1. The floating figures indicate changes in inversion without a change in the harmony. This notational convention emphasizes chord changes (harmonic rhythm) and keeps the score a little cleaner.

WORKBOOK

1. Find the Errors: The following harmonization has several errors according to the common-practice style. Identify the errors.

2. Harmonization: Harmonize the given melodies in four voices, following the stylistic features of common-practice music. The first two were written to be harmonized in chorale style; the second two were designed for a slower harmonic rhythm and a sense of melody with accompaniment. Of course, other options are possible.

- Below the harmonization, identify the key.
- Provide a Roman numeral analysis.
- Circle and label nonchord tones.
- Identify cadences.

Linear Chords

CHAPTER LEARNING OBJECTIVES

This chapter:

- Defines linear chords
- Explains the four types of second-inversion chords

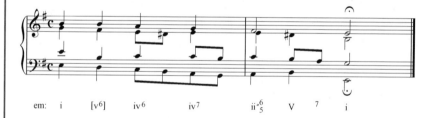

Figure 28.1 Bach, "Jesu, meine Freude" ("Jesus, My Joy")

The second chord of Bach's harmonization of "Jesu, meine Freude" is odd. It looks like a dominant chord, but it does not use the leading tone, violating a basic tenet of functional harmony. The reason for this deviation is the melody in the bass voice. The descending scalar line works well as a melody, but in order to avoid the augmented second and an unresolved leading tone, Bach must use the subtonic. Since the line is not returning to the tonic pitch, this is fine melodically, but it creates an atypical harmony.

Linear chords are harmonic sonorities that result from melodic rather than harmonic concerns. Rather than working together, the counterpoint takes over briefly and determines the harmony. Although linear chords look like basic triads or seventh chords, they are not. They do not have typical or expected functions. The chord above is not a dominant; it does not contain a leading tone, and it does not resolve to tonic. It is incorrect to label a linear chord with a Roman numeral; one of the hallmarks of linear chords is their functionally odd Roman numerals. Rather than leave the chord unlabeled, however, theorists write the Roman numeral that the chord looks like and place it in brackets. The brackets identify the numeral as a mere label, not a function.

Sometimes the linear chord results from nonchord tones. Although it looks like one chord, a different harmony truly functions, with the nonchord tones hiding it. A cadential six–four exemplifies this; it is actually a dominant, but it looks like a tonic. In cases like this, it is best to label the chord that is functioning and identify the dissonance.

Although uncommon, linear chords are not rare. They happen in many contexts. This chapter will focus on the most common diatonic ones: second-inversion chords. Others exist, as seen in the Bach chorale above; melodic lines and dissonances can create linear chords in a wide variety of ways.

SECOND-INVERSION CHORDS

As discussed in Chapter 11, second-inversion chords are not stable sonorities because of the interval of the fourth between the bass and another voice. The fourth is a dissonance and must resolve, although the resolution depends on the particular type of dissonance creating the fourth. Second-inversion chords are categorized by the type of dissonance involved.

Accented

Accented six–four chords involve a suspension or an appoggiatura over the bass. Cadential six–fours belong to this category. Figure 28.2 shows a noncadential example from Chopin. Notice how Chopin plays with the listener's expectations. Most pieces begin with tonic harmony. This piece does too, but it is disguised with an accented second-inversion chord. (Although the interval of a sixth is not a dissonance in itself, in the context it is heard as a downward-pulling nonchord tone. The fact that it is L6̂ adds to the pull.) The appoggiatura and neighbor tone resolve down by step as they should. The two notational options are compared here too. Note how the reduction not only shows the true function of the first chord but also illuminates the parallel structure between measures 1–2 and 3–4 and the analogous dissonance control.

Figure 28.2 Chopin, Mazurka in A-Minor, op. 7, no. 2

Passing

Passing six–four chords result from a passing tone in the bass. There are two common gestures for this. The first is when the bass moves as a passing tone and the other two pitches hold as common tones. This frequently happens in popular music, such as in the beginning of the Beatles' "A Day in the Life" and Billy Joel's "Piano Man" (figure 28.3). In the pop world, where second-inversion chords are considered stable, those chords are viewed as second-inversion iii chords. In the classical world, they are tonic chords with a passing tone in the bass. A classical example of this type of passing six–four is in Chapter 10. Measure 7 of Morley's "In Nets of Golden Wyres" implies a C-major chord, and on the last beat the bass moves as a passing tone. The soprano leap to the E confirms that E is still a consonance and that the bass must contain the dissonance.

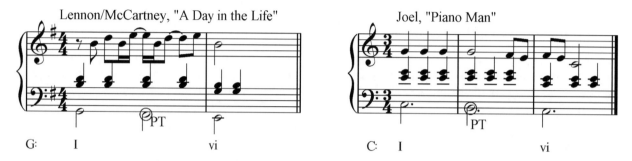

Figure 28.3 Passing six–fours in pop music with classical labels

The second context for passing six–fours, which is more common in classical music, is the voice exchange. A *voice exchange* is a short chord progression in which two voices trade pitches. Usually, the first and last chords in the voice exchange are the same function; it is a contrapuntal way to revoice the chord. In measure 3 of figure 28.4, the alto and bass undergo a voice exchange, swapping the pitches G and B♭. The first and last notes of the voice exchange are consonances, both times part of a supertonic chord. The middle pitch, A, is a passing tone. The F in the tenor is a neighbor tone. When the bass is involved in a voice exchange, the second beat often uses a passing six–four chord. Passing six–fours are common enough that they can be labeled with a *P*, as shown in figure 28.4. (Functional chords are also possible for a voice exchange. For example, when the voices exchange pitches across a tonic harmony, vii°⁶ sometimes appears in the middle.)

Figure 28.4 Beethoven, Piano Sonata, op. 28, II

Pedal or Neighbor

The name of this linear chord is ambiguous. It either involves a change of chord with a pedal point in the bass, or it is a sustained chord with neighbor tones above it. The resulting chord looks the same, and some textbooks prefer one name over the other. I choose the name that best describes what is happening in the music. In the first line of the song "Nina" (figure 28.5), three second-inversion chords occur. All look like second-inversion iv chords. Based on duration, contour, and metrical placement, however, I hear the first two as neighbor six–fours, with a sustaining chord and neighbor tones in the melody, and the third as a pedal six–four, with a change of chord and a pedal in the bass. In all three cases, the dissonances resolve as they should.

Figure 28.5 Ciampi, "Nina"

Arpeggiated (Consonant)

This second-inversion triad is stable and not linear. It happens when the bass arpeggiates the sounding chord. The motion through the second-inversion is not considered significant, since the other inversions establish a stable harmony. The melodic motion in the bass serves merely to enliven the texture, not to affect harmonic stability. These six–fours do not need to be notated. Figures 28.6 shows a common example—the bass to a waltz. The basslines in marches often behave similarly. Figure 28.7 shows an example where the main melody to the piece is in the bass.

Figure 28.6 Waldteufel, Estudiantina Waltz, mm. 13–28

Figure 28.7 Chopin, Prelude in B-Minor, op. 28, no. 6

SUMMARY

Terminology

Linear chord. A harmony that is created and driven by melodic issues rather than harmonic function.

Accented six–four. A linear chord that falls in a strong metrical position and appears as a second-inversion triad. The functioning harmony is revealed when the dissonances creating the apparent six–four resolve.

Passing six–four. A linear second-inversion chord built upon a passing tone in the bass. Frequently occurs in conjunction with a voice exchange.

Pedal six–four. A linear second-inversion chord that results from a pedal point in the bass.

Neighbor six–four. A linear second-inversion chord that results from neighbor tones in the upper voices.

Consonant six–four. A second-inversion chord that expands a more stable inversion through melodic motion or an arpeggio in the bass.

Voice exchange. A contrapuntal pattern in which two voices swap pitches, frequently through scalar melodies in contrary motion.

A linear chord is a harmonic sonority that is determined by contrapuntal concerns rather than harmonic considerations. They result from melodic motion or from the presence of dissonances. When possible, it is best to indicate the chord actually functioning and to label the nonchord tones. If this is not possible, the Roman numeral should be enclosed in brackets to indicate that it is a label, not a function.

WORKBOOK

1. Analysis: Analyze the following excerpts. Be sure to include the following:

- Below each system, identify the key of the piece.
- Provide a functional Roman numeral analysis.
- Circle and label all nonchord tones.
- Bracket and label all cadences.
- Identify second-inversion chords according to their functions (how the dissonances are behaving)—accented, cadential, passing, neighbor, pedal, or arpeggiated.
- Identify voice exchanges

The first excerpt was already analyzed as an assignment in Chapter 22, but it is a nice example of that type of second-inversion chord.

A. Tchaikovsky, "Melodie antique francaise" from *Album pour la jeunesse*
("Old French Song" from *Album for the Young*)

B. Bach, "Jesu, nun sei gepreiset" ("Jesus, Now Be Praised)

C. Haydn, Piano Sonata 50, III

D. Schumann, "Wild Reiter" from *Album für die Jugend*, mm. 1–8 ("Wild Rider" from *Album for the Young*)

E. Schumann, "Wild Reiter" from *Album für die Jugend*, mm. 9–16 ("Wild Rider" from *Album for the Young*)

2. Figured Bass Realization: Realize the following figured basses in a four-voice chorale style (SATB), following the conventions of the common-practice period. You may add any weak-beat dissonances you like, but circle and label those that you use.

- Below the system, identify the key of the exercise.
- Perform a functional (Roman numeral) harmonic analysis. If using a Roman numeral for a linear chord, enclose it in brackets.
- Bracket and label cadences.
- Identify second-inversion chords by their functions—accented, cadential, passing, neighbor, pedal, or arpeggiated.
- Identify voice exchanges.

A

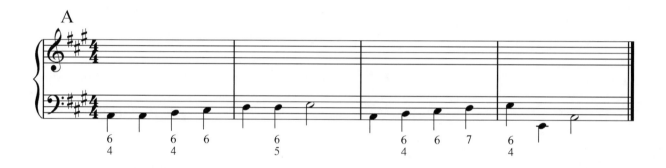

B

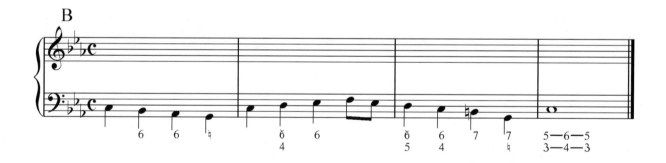

29

CHAPTER

Sequences

CHAPTER LEARNING OBJECTIVES

This chapter:

- Defines sequences
- Defines the common motion and nomenclature for sequences
- Explains voice leading in sequences

Figure 29.1 Vivaldi, *Le quattro stagioni*, "La primavera," III, mm. 17–22 (*The Four Seasons*, "Spring")

The progression in the Vivaldi excerpt in figure 29.1 has many peculiarities. There is a ♭VII, a major IV, a minor v, and a retrogression.[1] Just like linear chords in the last chapter, something other than harmony is propelling this passage.

This passage is a sequence. A *sequence* is the repetition of a musical pattern at successively higher or lower pitch levels. The interval of change is the same for each repetition, allowing for deviations between half steps and whole steps in the scale. The sequence above begins in the second half of the first measure and continues to the end of the third measure. The pattern is two beats long. Each statement is a step lower than the preceding one.

Sequences usually contain three repetitions of the pattern and break during the third. Two full statements of the pattern establish that a sequence is happening. The third satisfies the expectation of another repetition, but to go on much longer would become trite. The Vivaldi example contains five statements, which is atypical, but at least it is a short idea and the tempo is fast.

The driving force behind a sequence is the repetition. The pattern gives the passage coherence and logic and propels it forward. As a result, the harmony does not have to be functional, as seen above. Oftentimes it is functional, but that is not a requirement. Chords such as ♭VII, v, or ♯vi may occur; retrogressions may appear. Similarly, odd voice leading can result. Sequences may contain doubled leading tones or root-position diminished chords. These anomalies make sense to the listener's ears since they are dictated by the repeating pattern.

Since the progression need not be functional, Roman numerals are not relevant. The first chord must be functional since it connects with the preceding material, as does the last chord, which leads to the ensuing music. Label these two. Identify the sequence by describing the direction and interval of the repetition (e.g., "sequence by descending second" in the Vivaldi above). The next section discusses the types of sequential motions possible.

The first and last chords of a sequence may have any relationship. The sequence may begin and end on the same harmony. It may connect two different triads, such as in this example, which begins on tonic and ends on subdominant. Or it may modulate, beginning in one key and ending in another.

Sequences are common and important to common-practice music. They show up most frequently in modulatory and developmental passages, but they can, and do, occur anywhere.

TYPES OF SEQUENCES

Theorists categorize sequences by the direction and interval of the repetition in the harmonic motion. The fact that sequences take their names from how the harmony repeats is important. Although the melody and harmony often repeat together, they do not have to. The pattern in the *chords* defines the sequence. Remember, too, that changes in harmony are defined by the change in the root; inversions do not affect the type of sequence.

Since the direction—ascending and descending—can be specified, there are only three intervals of sequential motion: second, third, and fifth. A descending second is identical to the ascending seventh; the third inverts to a sixth. Given the importance of fifths in harmonic progressions, most theorists refer to sequences by fifth rather than sequences by fourth.

The way to identify the sequence is to label the chords by name, not Roman numeral. Really, all that is required is the name of the root. Examine the intervals of root motion and look for a pattern. Once the repeating pattern is identified, look for the interval at which the sequential unit repeats.

Motion by Fifth

Motion by fifth is by far the most common and most important sequential motion. It almost always occurs in the descending direction since motion by fifth down is strong. Figure 29.2 shows the standard motion by fifth and how to derive its name.

If labeled with Roman numerals, the sequence by descending fifth will make functional sense since functional progressions rely extensively on this motion (e.g., iii–vi–ii–V–I is all functional). Deviations in the part writing, however, still occur.

Not every fifth in figure 29.3 is perfect. The use of the diminished fifth between the second and third chord allows the sequence to remain diatonic. If perfect fifths are used throughout, the sequence will modulate, which is fine if that is what the composer wants to do.

Sequences by fifth may be tricky to identify since the melodic line often moves by second (figure 29.4). The sequence takes its name from the *harmonic* motion.

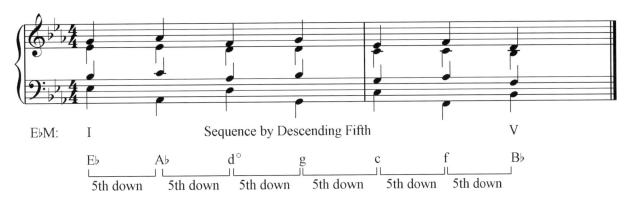

Figure 29.2 Sequence by descending fifth

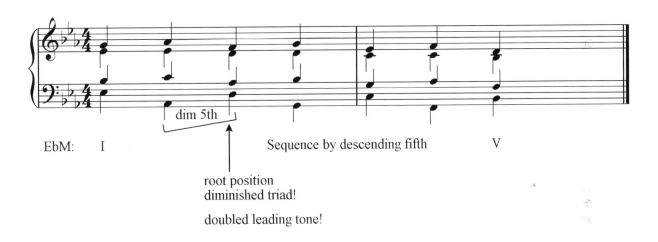

Figure 29.3 Deviations in part writing

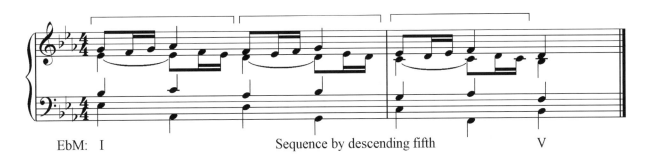

Figure 29.4 The melody in a sequence by fifth may move by second

Given the motion by descending fifth, seventh chords work well with this sequence (figure 29.5).

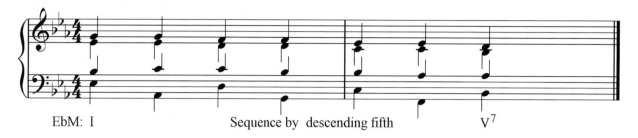

Figure 29.5 Using seventh chords in the sequence by descending fifth

Finally, since root motion determines the name, inversions do not affect it. Figure 29.6 shows an example from the literature that employs inversions.

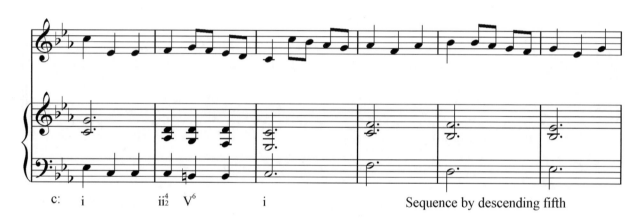

Figure 29.6 Durante, "Danza, danza, fanciulla gentile," mm. 51–62 ("Dance, Dance, Gentle Girl")

Motion by Second

Two types of patterns are common for motion by second. The first is the use of parallel first-inversion chords (figure 29.7). The pattern can asecend or descend.

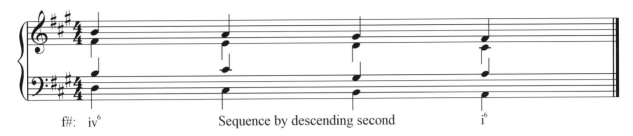

Figure 29.7 Sequence by second with parallel first-inversion chords

Another common pattern involves two chords (figure 29.8). Naming the sequence requires a larger sequential unit than in the previous examples; the pattern repeats every two harmonies rather than every chord. The name of the sequence is taken from the interval at which the entire unit repeats.

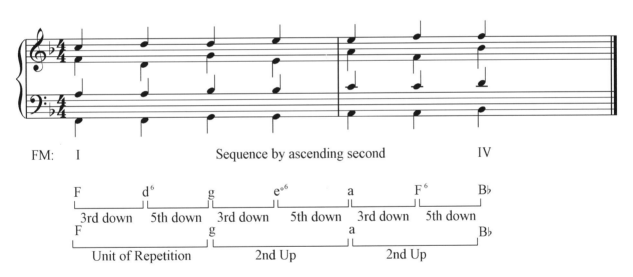

Figure 29.8 Another sequence by second

The motion in this sequence basically staggers the voices that form a fifth in order to avoid parallel perfect consonances. In moving from the first chord to the second, the C moves to D, giving a first-inversion chord. Then the bass moves from F to G. The parallel fifths that would result between the bass and soprano are staggered. This perspective also explains why this sequence is a two-step process.

This sequence usually happens ascending. If reversed, it contains motion by third up, which is weak. Of course, there are always exceptions. The Vivaldi excerpt in figure 29.1 is exactly this. Figure 29.9 shows what the keyboardist would play when realizing the continuo. The pattern is the exact reversal of figure 29.8, leading to a sequence by descending second.

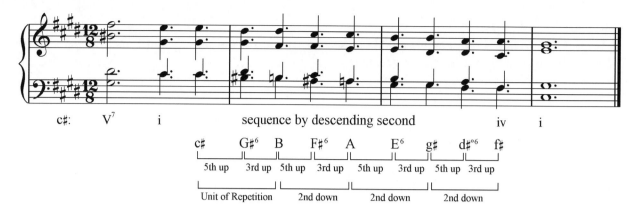

Figure 29.9 Vivaldi sequence realized in four voices

Motion by Third

Sequences by third are almost always descending. Figure 29.10 shows a common one. The name again comes from a two-chord unit of repetition. This pattern also appears frequently with all chords in root position. Figure 29.11 shows an example of the root-position variant in what is the most famous example of a sequence by descending thirds.

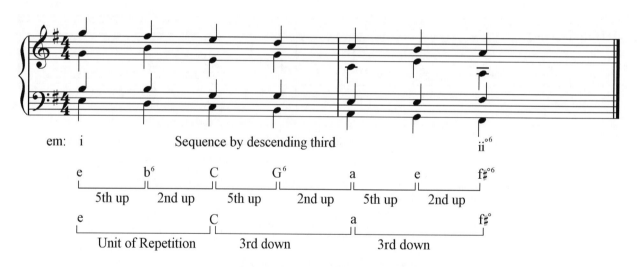

Figure 29.10 Sequence by third

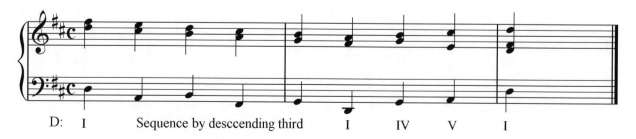

Figure 29.11 Pachelbel, Canon in D, mm. 5–6

Spotlight On: SEQUENCES AND TONALITY

As mentioned at the start of the chapter, sequences occur frequently in common-practice music. They are musically effective because the pattern changes its position within the scale; the shift in whole steps and half steps creates interest and tension. The common-practice era is the only era in which they were common. In the Middle Ages and the Renaissance, the shift in scale degree would be heard instead as an abrupt change of mode, which was not idiomatic. In the twentieth century, atonal composers were aware of the sequence's dependence on scale degree and its role in common-practice music, so they consciously avoided sequential passages in their music. In the late twentieth century and early twenty-first century, many composers returned to more tonal idioms. Sequences may enter the vocabulary again.

SUMMARY

Terminology

Sequence. The repetition of a musical pattern at successively higher or lower pitches, each time moving by the same interval.

A sequence is the repetition of a musical pattern at successively higher or lower pitch levels. Sequences usually contain three statements of the pattern, breaking off during the third. The repetition propels the music, and the chords within may or may not be functional. The voice leading within a sequence may also be irregular. It is best to label the first and last chords with Roman numerals and label the rest by identifying the interval and direction of the sequence. The intervallic pattern made by the roots of the chords determines the name of the sequence. Sequences may connect a chord to any other chord, and they can modulate.

NOTE

1. Two important clarifications about notation. First, as discussed in the note 2 in Chapter 3, many textbooks use a flat to represent the lowered form of scale degrees and chords. I prefer the more general L for scale degrees. When it comes to chords, however, I use the flat. L is the number 50 in Roman numerals, and it looks confusing to me to see a chord labeled 57. Second, a flat, natural, or sharp in front of a Roman numeral indicates that the root of the chord has been altered from what naturally occurs in the key. For example, in C-major, III is the E-major triad, while ♭III is the E♭-major triad.

WORKBOOK

1. Analysis: Analyze the following excerpt.

- Identify the key and provide Roman numerals where functional harmony is relevant.
- Identify the first and last chord of each sequence with Roman numerals.
- Identify the other chords in chart notation (e.g, ♯).
- Name the sequence by identifying the interval of harmonic motion (e.g., "Sequence by X," where *X* is the interval by which the root moves).

Bach, Prelude, English Suite no. 3

2. Part Writing: You are given the first statement of the cell of a sequence. Continue it, remaining diatonic and ending in a cadence, either half or authentic. Remember that sequences usually break off during the third statement.

- Label the first and last chords of the sequences with Roman numerals.
- Label the other chords with chart symbols (e.g, ♯).
- Identify the interval of motion in the sequence (e.g., "Sequence by X," where X is the interval by which the root moves).
- Bracket and label the cadence.

A

B

C

Tonicization

CHAPTER LEARNING OBJECTIVES

This chapter:

- Defines tonicization and secondary dominants

- Explains the resolution of applied V and vii° chords

- Explains the role of secondary dominants in sequences

- Explains some common apparent secondary dominants that are linear chords

The third chord in the first measure of figure 30.1 contains a chromatic pitch. The music is still in F; all the other chords make functional sense, and the passage ends with a clear imperfect authentic candence. The E♭ in the bass could be analyzed as a passing tone (albeit chromatically altered), but it also makes harmonic sense. The four pitches form a seventh chord: F–A–C–E♭. The tritone between the A and E♭, in conjunction with F♮ rather than F♯, indicates that this chord functions in B♭. In B♭, this harmony would function as V^7 and want to resolve to I, a B♭ chord. In the Bach passage, the chord after this chromatic chord is a B♭ chord.

Tonizcization is briefly implying a harmonic center other than tonic. It usually lasts for only one or two chords, and we never lose our sense of the true key. The easiest way to imply another key is through the dominant–tonic relationship, the basis of all tonal music. Preceding a chord with its dominant intensifies the motion to the goal chord and emphasizes its arrival.

A *secondary* (or *applied*) *dominant* is a chromatic chord that has a dominant function in another key. Secondary harmonies may be applied to any major or minor chord. A diminished chord cannot have an applied dominant; diminished keys do not exist, so it is impossible to tonicize one. Since the purpose of a secondary dominant is to emphasize the chord of resolution, it is not surprising that the most common goal chord is V.

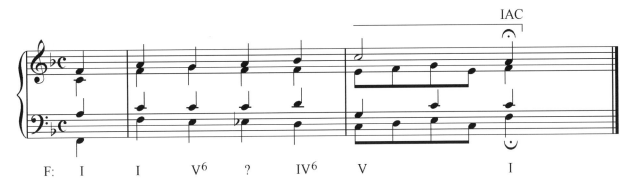

Figure 30.1 Bach, "Christus, der ist mein Leben" ("Christ, He Is My Life")

The secondary dominant tonicizes its goal harmony. Although the key never truly changes, for that brief moment, the music functions as if it had. The applied dominant resolves exactly as it would in its own key. The local leading tone still goes up, and the seventh of the chord resolves down (figure 30.2). Any dominant-function chord may be used as an secondary dominant—V, V^7, vii^o, vii^{o7}, and $vii^{o/7}$—and they may appear in any typical inversion. In all of these cases, the chords resolve as they would in their briefly implied key.

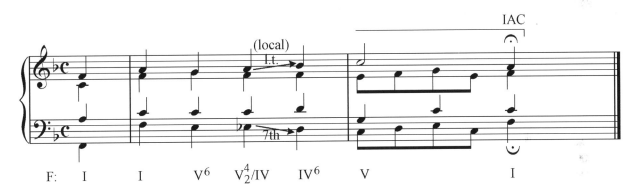

Figure 30.2 Bach, "Christus, der is mein Leben," showing notation and resolution

As shown in figure 30.2, the notation for a secondary dominant is V/(Goal Chord). Another, less common notation is to use a curved arrow pointing from the applied dominant to its goal chord. Figures 30.3 and 30.4 show two applied dominants and the two different options for their notation. Note the resolutions of the chords in each.

As discussed in Chapter 23, vii^{o7} can have two different resolutions, one in which both tritones resolve, resulting in a doubled third, or one in which the third of the chord resolves down rather than up, leaving a tritone unresolved but giving the more typical doubled root. These hold for secondary dominants too. But vii^{o7}/V must use the latter resolution, since the third of the goal chord is the leading tone in the actual key. In the excerpt in figure 30.5, every time Beethoven uses a vii^{o7}/V, he avoids the doubled leading tone by moving A down to G. (In measure 1, if the texture did not reduce to three voices, the motion would be clearer, but this is the underlying voice leading. The A moves to the G in the left hand.) In measure 4, Beethoven resolves the local leading tone irregularly, jumping to the fifth of the chord, as is allowed when $\hat{7}$ is in an inner voice. All principles and guidelines regarding the resolution of dominant chords still apply for secondary dominants.

g:

V$_5^6$/V   V$_4^6$——5——3

Figure 30.3 Schubert, "Erlkönig" ("The Elf-King")

a:

V   III

Figure 30.4 Schumann, "Armes Waisenkind" from *Album für die Jugend*
("The Poor Orphan Child" from *Album for the Young*)

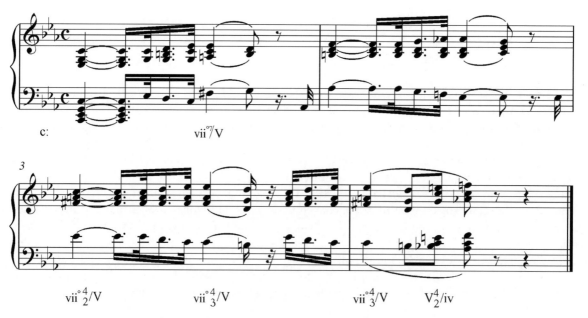

c: vii°⁷/V

vii°$_2^4$/V   vii°$_3^4$/V   vii°$_3^4$/V   V$_2^4$/iv

Figure 30.5 Beethoven, Piano Sonata no. 8 (*Pathetique*), op. 13, I

The approach to a secondary dominant requires nothing special, as long as the voice leading works. Any diatonic chord can lead to an applied dominant (figure 30.6). The chromaticism provides a clear chord change, and since the harmony is not diatonic, it also increases the tension, regardless of what chord preceded it. The main voice-leading issue is cross-relations. As discussed in Chapter 5, a cross-relation is when two different forms of the same pitch, such as F♮ and F♯, appear in different voices on adjacent chords. As discussed in Chapter 12, in three or more voices, these should not be written between the outer two. They are acceptable if at least one of the voices involved is an inner voice. The best voice leading involves the chromatic alteration of the pitch in the same voice (figure 30.6b). This produces a smooth, convincing chromatic line. Figure 30.6d has a cross-relation between the outer voices, but the smooth chromatic line in the soprano provides strong motion that justifies it. Had the soprano not had the F on the first beat but the cross-relation was still present between the soprano and bass, it would be poor writing in the common-practice style.

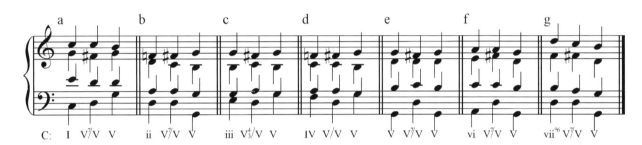

Figure 30.6 Possible approaches to V/V

The previous examples show a variety of approaches to the applied dominants. In the Bach excerpt in figure 30.1, the V⁷/IV is approached the same way its analogous diatonic chord is approached. The diatonic analog is tonic, so it is approached by V. It can also be thought of as reinterpreting the tonic chord, turning it into a V⁷/IV. Interestingly, Bach does not resolve the leading tone in the bass; he resolves it down into the seventh of the secondary dominant. This is fine. The logic of the descending chromatic line is clear. In the example in figure 30.3, Schubert chromatically alters the analogous diatonic chord. He arrives on the ii chord in a typical fashion, and then he turns ii into V⁷/V through chromatic alteration. In figure 30.4, Schumann approaches the secondary dominant from a tonic chord.

Misidentifying secondary dominants and notating them as diatonic chords leads to unusual Roman numerals. Some older books use II instead of V/V. This notation is antiquated. It does not show the functional relationship, which is the point of Roman numerals. As mentioned in Chapter 23, I⁷ does not exist, but V⁷/IV does. In popular music, ♭VII appears (such as in the vamp at the end of the Beatles' "Hey Jude"), but it does not appear in common-practice classical music. Most likely, ♭VII is V/III in minor. If you find yourself writing an unusual Roman numeral, one that has an unusual quality or that does not fit in with the functions as explained in the diatonic chapters, look for another explanation.

Chromatic alterations from secondary dominants still follow the basic guideline presented in Chapter 4: chromatically lowered notes resolve down and chromatically raised notes resolve up. Raised pitches usually function as the leading tone in the tonicized key and therefore resolve up. Chromatically lowered pitches usually function as the sevenths of applied dominants, so they need to resolve down (figure 30.7). The functional implications of chromatic pitches make sense on both the melodic (scale-degree) and harmonic (chordal) level.

Figure 30.7 shows that almost every chromatic pitch must resolve according to the melodic rule of thumb. The only exceptions are these:

1. R4̂ in V⁷/iii and vii°⁷/iii in major (in figure 30.7, the G♯ in the third measure of the first two lines). It may resolve up, as expected, or down to avoid a doubled third. Since iii is an uncommon chord, so is an applied dominant to it.

2. R$\hat{6}$ in V^7/V and vii^{o7}/V in minor (in figure 30.7, the B♮ in the fifth measure of the third and fourth lines). This scale degree will resolve down, contrary to expectation, in order to avoid the doubled leading tone.

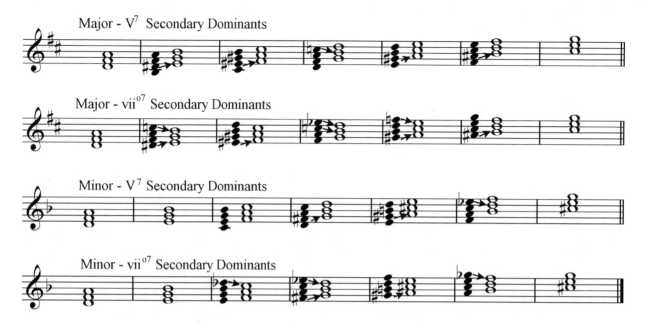

Figure 30.7 Resolution of chromatically altered pitches in secondary dominants

Practically speaking, as long as you remember not to double the leading tone, the only true exception to the guideline will fall into place. Otherwise, chromatically raised pitches resolve up and chromatically lowered pitches resolve down.

SEQUENCES AND SECONDARY DOMINANTS

Any sequence containing a descending fifth unit or subunit can be made chromatic through the use of secondary dominants. The most obvious choice is the common descending-fifth sequence (figure 30.8). The one moment that moves by diminished fifth, here the A♭ chord that moves to D, cannot support an applied dominant, but all of the other harmonies can. When dominant seventh chords are used, the leading tones can resolve down chromatically to produce the seventh of the next chord. As with the Bach example (figure 30.1), the smooth line with the clear downward direction justifies the irregular motion of the leading tone. Both of these sequences remain diatonic overall, ending on the dominant in the original key, but they sound full of instability because of the extensive chromaticism.

The two-step sequence by ascending second also contains motion by fifth. Those moments also can be turned into secondary dominants (figure 30.9). Like the sequence by fifth, this progression is overall diatonic, but the secondary dominants add color and drive.

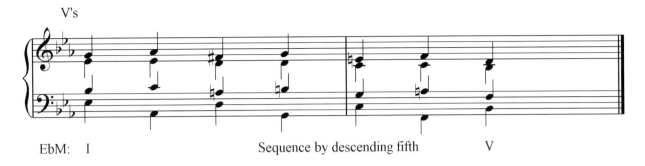

V's

EbM: I   Sequence by descending fifth   V

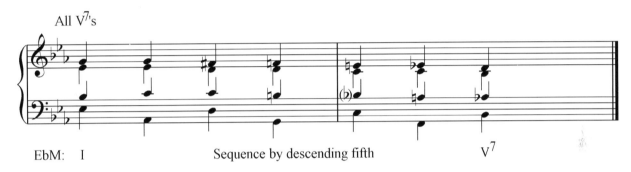

All V⁷'s

EbM: I   Sequence by descending fifth   V⁷

Figure 30.8 Sequences by descending fifths with secondary dominants

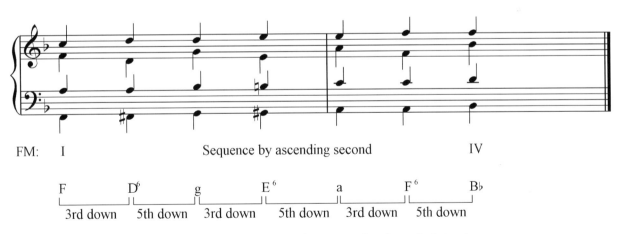

FM: I   Sequence by ascending second   IV

F   D⁶   g   E⁶   a   F⁶   B♭
3rd down   5th down   3rd down   5th down   3rd down   5th down

Figure 30.9 Sequence by ascending second with applied dominants

SECONDARY DOMINANTS AND LINEAR CHORDS

Sometimes the Roman numerals for linear chords appear as secondary dominants. Being linear chords, they will not function as expected and will not resolve to the goal chord. As discussed in Chapter 28, the use of Roman numerals should be limited to harmonically functional passages. If there is no better way to label a linear chord, use the Roman numeral but enclose it in braces. If it is possible to label the functioning harmony and identify the dissonance obscuring it, do that.

In figure 30.10, two analyses of a passage are compared. The labels in the first analysis are clearly nonfunctional—applied dominants that do not resolve where they should. The second analysis, a voice exchange with three passing tones in the alto and bass, makes more musical sense. The chromaticism in this passage is all contrapuntal, with no harmonic implications. It is a single chord with melodic dissonances.

Measure 5-6, Reduced Two Different Ways

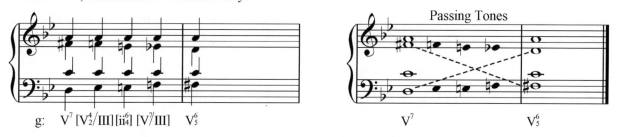

Figure 30.10 Ciampi, "Nina," mm. 4–6

Common-Tone Diminished Seventh

Although not frequently occurring, the common-tone diminished seventh is a linear chord that has managed to earn its own name. It looks like an applied vii°⁷. In a functional vii°⁷, all pitches move during resolution. In a common-tone diminished seventh, one pitch remains as a common tone, hence the name. This chord is also a collection of melodic dissonances; the only pitch that is a chord member is the root, which serves as the common tone. The other voices resolve appropriately, depending on what type of dissonance they are. In the example in figure 30.11, the entire phrase is tonic harmony. The E♭ is the common tone in the linear chord; the other voices are all neighbor tones. For all of the nonharmonic tones to resolve, the chord of resolution usually has a doubled fifth, as happens here.

Figure 30.11 Tchaikovsky, "Valse" from *Album pour la jeunesse* ("Waltz" from *Album for the Young*)

As in Chapter 28, the chords mentioned here are not exhaustive. Linear chords happen in a variety of contexts.

SUMMARY

Terminology

Tonicization. Briefly implying a different key, other than the main one that is functioning.

Secondary (applied) dominant. A chromatic chord that has a dominant function in a key other than the main one that is functioning. A secondary dominant places emphasis on the following harmony by exploiting the dominant–tonic relationship in that key. *Secondary dominant* and *applied dominant* are synonymous.

A tonicization is briefly treating another key as the tonal center. The tonic does not really change.

Secondary dominants resolve exactly as they do in their implied keys.

The secondary dominant vii°7/V must resolve with the doubled root since the doubled third resolution leads to a doubled leading tone.

Unusual Roman numerals, whether because of function or quality, usually result from misidentified secondary dominants.

WORKBOOK

1. Analysis: Analyze the following excerpts. Be sure to include the following:

- Below each system, identify the key of the piece.
- Provide a functional Roman numeral analysis.
- Circle and label all nonchord tones.
- Bracket and label all cadences.
- When you encounter a secondary dominant, indicate the resolutions of the leading tone and seventh with arrows.

Bach's entire Prelude 1 from the *Well-Tempered Clavier Book I* is also an excellent exercise.

A. Schubert, Waltz

B. Mozart, Piano Sonata, K. 457, III

C. Beethoven, Piano Sonata no. 8, op. 13 (*Pathetique*), II

D. Mendelssohn, *Lied ohne Wörter*, op. 38, no. 2 (*Song without Words*)

2. Drills: Identify and resolve the secondary dominant chords. In the first half, you are given the chord on the staff. Identify the secondary dominant, resolve it, and label both it and its goal chord with functional (Roman numeral) labels. The quality of the chord will let you know if it is a V or a vii°. In the second half, you are given the Roman numeral, and you must write and resolve the chord on the staff. Identify the chord of resolution. The example shows how your answer should look in both types of drill.

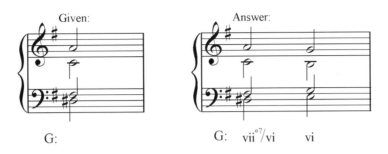

G: G: vii°⁷/vi   vi

C: d: A: c: D:

Ab: V⁷/V   b: V⁶₅/V   Bb: vii°⁷/iii   e: vii°⁷/VI   Eb: V⁷/ii

3. Figured Bass Realization: Realize the following figured basses in a four-voice chorale style (SATB), following the conventions of the common-practice style. You may add any weak-beat dissonances you like, but circle and label any that you use.

- Below the system, identify the key of the exercise.
- Perform a functional (Roman numeral) harmonic analysis.
- Bracket and label cadences.

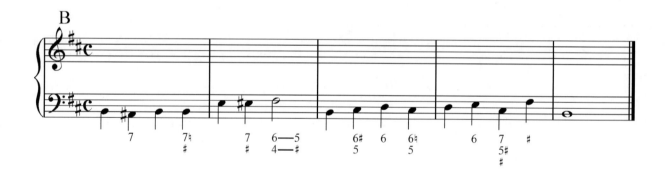

4. Outer Voices Given: You have the outer voices for a piece of music. Determine the harmonies and complete the passage in a four-voice chorale style (SATB), following common-practice conventions. If the note has an asterisk, harmonize it with a secondary dominant. One has been marked with a diminished seventh chord for variety.

- Below the system, identify the key of the exercise.
- Provide a functional (Roman numeral) analysis.
- Label cadences.
- Circle and label nonchord tones.

5. Harmonization: Harmonize the given melody in four voices, following the stylistic features of common-practice music. If the note has an asterisk, harmonize it with a secondary dominant.

- Below the harmonization, identify the key.
- Provide a Roman numeral analysis.
- Circle and label nonchord tones.
- Identify cadences.

Modulation

CHAPTER LEARNING OBJECTIVES

This chapter:

- Defines modulation, pivot chord, and closely related keys
- Explains the four ways to modulate
- Explains the connection between modulation and larger formal structures

This book has covered all diatonic harmony, explaining the basic functions of chords in a given key. All chromaticism thus far has been short, local effects. The larger structures of classical music, however, hinge on an important concept: modulation. *Modulation* is when music moves to a new key. It is an actual change in the harmonic center; the listener hears a new tonic pitch.

As mentioned in Chapter 20, the power of scale degrees and Roman numerals for harmonic analysis is that they separate function from a specific note. The tonic pitch and chord in one key behave exactly like the tonic pitch and chord in another key, so "1̂" and "I" represent both well. Modulation itself involves no new concepts of functionality; the only new detail is to indicate the change of key. This book uses the actual key name, notated exactly as the key has been indicated all along, plus, below that in parentheses, the Roman numeral relationship to the original tonic of the piece. The reason for the Roman numeral will become clear soon. Figure 31.1 shows the notation as well as the fact that there are no new scale-degree or chord functions to learn. Music still moves through a PD–D–T progression. The leading tone (of the new key) should resolve up. Sevenths are prominent dissonances and must resolve down by step. All that we have learned still applies; it just has shifted to a new tonal center.

Figure 31.1 Giordani, "Caro mio ben," mm. 15–18 ("My Dear Beloved")

Several aids to identifying modulations and the new key exist. First, look for cadences. They will help clarify the home key. Cadential six–fours resolving into dominants are particularly key-defining gestures. Second, look for chords that function definitively in one key. Seventh chords are especially useful for this. Figure 31.2 compares all possible diatonic seventh chords and shows that certain qualities are unique to particular functions. V^7s are major–minor seventh chords, regardless of the mode. More importantly, the major–minor seventh sound is unique to V^7s. The instant a listener hears a major–minor seventh sonority, she instantly hears a dominant harmony and knows what the tonic is. The same is true for a fully diminished chord; it has to function as a vii^{o7}. (Fully diminished chords often appear for vii^{o7} in major too, as mentioned in Chapter 23.) Since major–minor seventh and fully diminished seventh chords function only one way, they can identify the key.

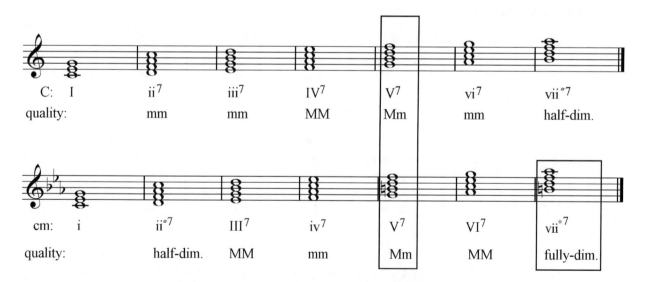

Figure 31.2 Seventh chord qualities on each scale degree

This fact also explains why secondary dominants, even though they may last for one brief chord, are so effective. As soon as the listener hears a major–minor seventh or a fully diminished sonority, he instantly knows the implied key and goal chord.

METHODS OF MODULATING

The new concept with modulations is how the modulation occurs. Four methods exist:

1. Pivot Chord
2. Direct (Chromatic)
3. Sectional
4. Sequence

Pivot Chord Modulations

Pivot chord modulations are by far the most common type. In this method, the *pivot chord*, a chord that is diatonic in both keys, simultaneously functions differently in each. The progression up to and including that chord makes sense in the old key; the progression including and following that chord makes sense in the new key. The pivot chord smooths the transition, working as a common point between the two keys, a seam holding them together. The pivot must be diatonic in both keys; it must create a logical progression both moving into the chord and moving away from the chord.

The notation for the pivot chord shows its analysis in both keys. The function in the new key sits below the function in the old key. A backward Z-shaped line separates the two keys and shows where the new tonal center replaces the previous one. Figure 31.3 gives an example.

Figure 31.3 Mozart, Piano Sonata in D, K. 284, III, Theme

The easiest way to find a pivot chord is to find the first occurrence of a chord clearly in the new key, then move back one chord. For example, the V^7 in measure 6 of figure 31.3 is clearly in A-major. Backing up one harmony gives a chord that functions diatonically in both D and A. That is the pivot.

Pivot chords usually function as pre-dominants in the new key. This makes sense, since the best way to clarify a new key is through its dominant. If the first chord clearly in the new key is the dominant, then the preceding chord—the pivot—is usually a pre-dominant. Composers also often cadence shortly after pivoting to solidify the new key in the listener's ear.

Figure 31.4 shows a modulation in minor. Just like the Mozart example, the first phrase defines the home key and the second quickly modulates. Although Bach's pivot chord functions as a submediant chord in the new key, it behaves similarly to a pre-dominant, leading to a V chord.

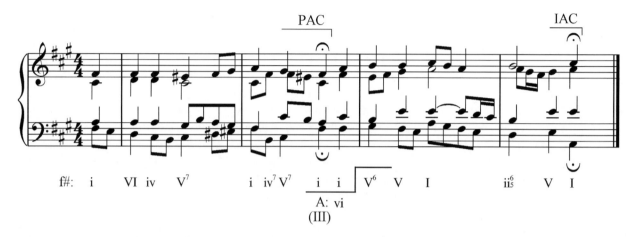

Figure 31.4 Bach, "Verleih' uns Frieden gnädiglich" ("Grant Us Merciful Peace")

Direct (Chromatic) Modulation

Sometimes composers modulate without a pivot chord. When the modulation happens midphrase, through the chromatic alteration of a chord, it is called a *direct* or *chromatic modulation*.

In figure 31.5, measures 61 and 62 contain the key change. The key of B♭ does not contain an F♯, so the chord in measure 62 cannot be analyzed in B♭. While the chord in measure 61 could be considered a III in g, this chord is not that common, and in addition the motion of the F to F♯ implies an abrupt change of focus. The best way to analyze this passage is with a change of key simultaneous with the chromatic alteration of the F. (The augmented sixth chord in measure 63 will be discussed later, in Chapter 36.)

The power of a pivot chord resides in its ability to function diatonically in two keys simultaneously. With a direct modulation, there is no seam but rather an immediate change of center. As a result, direct modulation sounds slightly more abrupt than that with a pivot chord (see figure 31.6).

Sectional Modulation

The easiest type of modulation to identify is sectional. In this method, a phrase or section of music ends in one key, and the next begins in another (see figure 31.7).

Sequence

A sequence is another common way to modulate. As discussed in Chapter 29, the first and last chords of a sequence may have any relationship. They can be the same chord, different chords in the same key, or function in different keys. Figure 31.8 shows an example of a sequence that modulates. No precise moment of switching from C-minor to G-minor exists; over the course of the sequence, the motion by fifth gradually works itself into the new key. In measure 8, the music is still solidly in C-minor, with the B♮ and a clear V → i. In measure 9, the A♮ is introduced and briefly implies B♭, but the sequence keeps moving forward. In measure 11 the F♯ appears, shifting into G-minor.

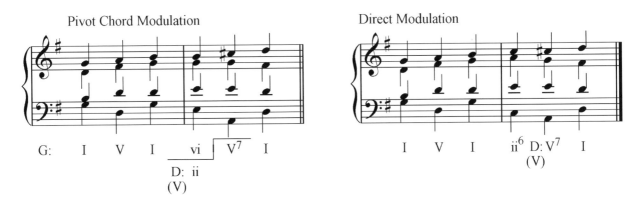

Figure 31.5 Mozart, Piano Sonata in B♭, K. 333, III, mm. 56–68

Figure 31.6 Comparison of a pivot chord modulation and a direct modulation

Figure 31.7 Strauss, *Emperor Waltz*, mm. 59–74

MODULATION, FORM, AND CLOSELY RELATED KEYS

As mentioned at the start of this chapter, larger musical structures and forms rely on modulation. Just as the tonic pitch and tonic chord serve as melodic and harmonic goals in a key, common-practice composers used the initial key as the tonic to entire works. Modulating away from this home key creates tension that is resolved only upon return to it. In this way, composers create large-scale movements that can last ten to twenty minutes or even longer; a key is defined, the music moves away and then must find its way home again.

During much of the common-practice era, composers limited themselves to closely related keys. A *closely related key* is one that differs from the home key by 0–1 accidentals. There are several ways to think about them.

1. Think about key signatures. B♭ has two flats. G-minor also has two flats. F-major and D-minor have one flat. E♭-major and C-minor have three flats. The keys closely related to B♭ are G-minor, F-major, D-minor, E♭-major, and C-minor.

2. Create a grid with two rows and three columns, as shown in table 31.1. Assuming tonic is major, put the home key in the middle of the top row. To its left is the key a perfect fifth down (i.e., adding a flat or removing a sharp). To its right is the key a perfect fifth up (i.e., removing a flat or adding a sharp). The lower row contains the relative minors of the keys on top. In minor, the home key goes in the middle of the bottom row.

Figure 31.8 Durante, "Danza, danza, fanciulla gentile," mm. 5–14 ("Dance, Dance, Gentile Girl")

TABLE 31.1	General Closely Related Keys Grid		
P5 Down	Home Key (or Rel. Major)	P5 Up
Rel. Minor of P5 Down	Rel. Minor (or Home Key)	Rel. Minor of P5 Up

TABLE 31.2	Closely Related Keys Grid for B♭		
E♭	B♭	F
c	g	g

What this grid represents is a straightened-out section of the circle of fifths. In the course of a piece, composers explore the tonal space that surrounds a given key—that is, the part of the tonal universe (the circle of fifths) that neighbors that key.

3. The closely related keys also connect with the diatonic chords in a key. The possible chords in B♭-major are shown in figure 31.9. The diatonic chords of a key and its closely related keys match, both in terms of tonal center and quality/mode; vii° does not match with any closely related key, but diminished keys do not exist, so that makes sense.

Figure 31.9 Chords possible in B♭

In minor, the lowered submediant and subtonic are used (i.e., the natural minor is used) because we are interested in key signatures (see figure 31.10 and table 31.3). Since we usually see the leading tone in minor, theorists emphasize the atypical root of the subtonic key area by including a flat sign—♭VII. The normal Roman numeral is fine for VI since the key area corresponds to the chord that we call VI in minor.

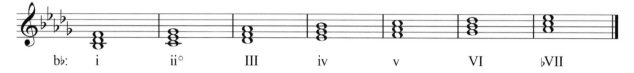

Figure 31.10 Chords possible in b♭

TABLE 31.3	Closely Related Key Grid for b♭	
G♭	D♭	A♭
e♭	b♭	f

The third method above explains why Roman numeral relationships are included in identifying the key of a modulation. Closely related keys can be represented with a simple Roman numeral that correspond to a typical functional label. (The two exceptions to this are v and ♭VII in minor, which are not functional as chords.) *Distantly related keys* (or *foreign keys*)—those that are not closely related—require alterations of the Roman numerals. The Roman numerals show how far the piece has strayed from home and help demonstrate its harmonic boldness. The harmonic boldness can indicate the time period of the piece. Composers generally limited themselves to closely related keys for the first 200 years of the common-practice period, while during the nineteenth century they pushed the boundaries and explored more distant harmonic realms.

Four facets of the Roman numerals deserve clarification.

1. The Roman numerals always relate back to the home key, not the preceding key. The interest is in how far the music has strayed from home, not the immediate relationship. If a piece modulates from C-major to G-major and then to A-minor, A-minor is identified as vi, not ii.

2. When modulating to the dominant in a minor key, composers move to the minor dominant. The only reason that the dominant *chord* is major is because the leading tone is needed. When modulating, the leading tone of an earlier key no longer matters. The minor dominant is closely related (one accidental changes); the major dominant is not (four accidentals change).

3. Although relative major and minor keys have identical closely related keys grids in terms of key names, the Roman numerals are different since the home key is different (see table 31.4).

4. Although Roman numerals are used, in this case they do not imply functionality. These are labels. Composers modulate to any key they want, and they can move through them in any order. No set progression must happen. Similarly, although ♭VII and v do not exist as functional chords, they do exist as closely related keys.

TABLE 31.4 | Generalized Closely Related Major and Minor Key Grids

Major		
IV	I	V
ii	vi	iii
Minor		
VI	III	♭VII
iv	i	v

Having said that there are no set progressions, conventions still exist. In a major key, composers almost always modulate first to the dominant. The submediant often follows the dominant. In minor, composers usually modulate first to the relative major. The minor dominant often follows this. Nothing outside of tradition, though, forces the composers to go in this order.

MODULATION VERSUS TONICIZATION

A vagueness exists about where a tonicization ends and modulation begins. If a passage has three applied chords, but then returns to the home key, what does that count as? Some textbooks state that any PD–D–T progression is a modulation, even if it immediately returns home. Although it is not a rigorous definition, I choose to go by ear. Do you hear a new key or not? A single chromatic chord is clearly a tonicization. Four measures of a new key is a modulation. Two measures of an implied key may depend upon the listener. And note that in my view, you could have an applied pre-dominant too, if the music then returned to the original key. Figure 31.11 shows an excerpt that some would say is a modulation. To me, it is a tonicization. This passage ends three measures before the final cadence of the movement. The music is clearly reinforcing the home key of G through repetitions of the cadential gesture. Having two single-measure modulations is possible but messy. The example also shows an alternate notation for tonicizations that last longer than one chord. A single line under all of the applied chords quickly gives the bigger picture: the passage hovers between a tonicization and a modulation.

SUMMARY

Terminology

Modulation. A change of key. Moving to a new tonal center.
Pivot chord. During a modulation, a chord that is diatonic in both the old and new key and that serves to smooth the transition between the two tonal centers.
Direct (chromatic) modulation. A modulation that results from the alteration of a chord or from abruptly shifting into the new key. A modulation that does not use a pivot chord.
Sectional modulation. A modulation in which a phrase or section ends in one key and the next phrase or section begins in a different key.
Closely related keys. Keys that differ by 0–1 accidentals from the original key. Contrasts with *distantly related keys*.
Distantly related keys. Keys that differ by two or more accidentals from the original key. Contrasts with *closely related keys*.

Figure 31.11 Mozart, Piano Sonata, K. 454, II, mm. 63–72

A modulation occurs when music moves to a new tonal center.

Cadences and chords that function uniquely in one key can help identify modulations and the new tonic.

A pivot chord is diatonic in the old and new key and can therefore segue between the two tonal centers.

Closely related keys can be represented by basic Roman numerals. Distantly related keys require alterations to the Roman numerals.

In minor, composers modulate to the minor dominant key, which is closely related to tonic.

WORKBOOK

1. Closely Related Keys Grid Drill: Complete a closely related keys grid for each key given.

Example:

Given:

	CM	

Answer:

FM	CM	GM
dm	am	em

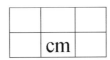

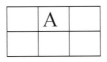

	bm	

	D	

	dm	

	E♭	

	cm	

	A♭	

	am	

	A	

	f#m	

	F	

	gm	

	G	

2. Analysis: Analyze the following excerpts. Be sure to include the following:

- Below each system, identify the key of the piece. Remember to identify modulations by both key name and Roman numeral relationship to the home key.

- Provide a functional Roman numeral analysis.

- Circle and label all nonchord tones.

- Bracket and label all cadences.

- Identify the method of modulation.

Some of these examples include secondary dominants.

A. Schubert, *Drei Klavierstücke*, II (*Three Piano Pieces*)

B. Beethoven, "Für Elise," mm. 15–41 ("For Elise")

C. Bach, Prelude 6, *Das Wohltemperirte Clavier I* (*The Well-Tempered Clavier Book I*)

D. Haydn, Sympony no. 104, III

3. Modulation versus Tonicization: Analyze Bach's arrangement of the hymn "Valet will ich geben" following the steps described in Workbook assignment 2 above. Does this piece modulate or is it a long tonicization? Use the notation appropriate to the way you hear it. What in the music makes you hear it that way?

Bach, "Valet will ich geben" ("I Bid You Farewell")

4. Figured Bass Realization: Realize the following figured basses in a four-voice chorale style (SATB), following common-practice conventions. You may add weak-beat dissonances if you like, but circle and label any that you use.

- Below the system, identify the key of the exercise.
- Perform a functional (Roman numeral) harmonic analysis.
- Bracket and label cadences.

A

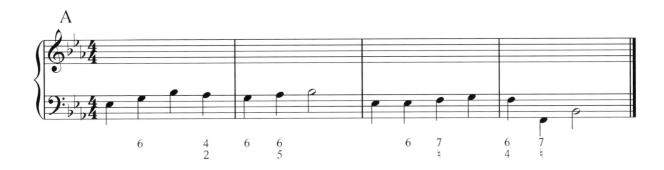

B

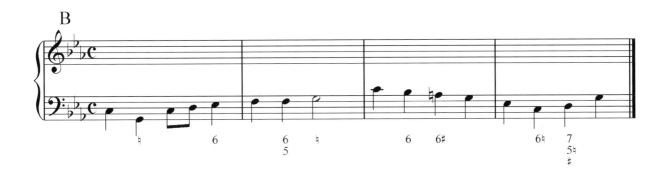

5. Outer Voices Given: You have the outer voices for a piece of music that begins in B-minor and ends in D-major. Determine the harmonies and complete the passage in a four-voice chorale style (SATB), following common-practice conventions.

- Below the system, identify the key of the exercise.
- Provide a functional (Roman numeral) analysis.
- Label cadences.
- Circle and label nonchord tones.

6. Your Own Modulation: In the system provided below, create a four-measure progression that modulates. Use a key other than C-major or A-minor. If you choose to work in major, modulate to the dominant; for minor, modulate to the relative major. For the most accurate representation of common-practice style, use the first two measures to solidify tonic, have a pivot chord in the third measure, and cadence in the new key in the fourth bar. Realize your progression in a four-voice chorale style (SATB). You may add common-practice dissonances if you like, weak or strong, but circle and label any that you add.

- Below the system, identify the key of the exercise.
- Provide a functional (Roman numeral) harmonic analysis.
- Bracket and label all cadences.

7. Harmonization: Harmonize the given melody in four voices, following the stylistic features of common-practice music. The melody begins in G-minor and ends in B♭-major.

- Below the harmonization, identify the key.
- Provide a Roman numeral analysis.
- Circle and label nonchord tones.
- Identify cadences.

Phrase-Level Analysis

CHAPTER LEARNING OBJECTIVES

This chapter:

- Briefly introduces Schenkerian harmonic reduction

When reading a book, not every word merits the same weight. The word "the" is extremely common but does not convey a lot of information. It is important for intelligibility, but other words convey the substance of the author's message.

Similarly, while it is important to understand how every chord connects to the preceding and following chords, we do not actually listen to music in that way. Not every harmony is equally important; some have more significant roles based on how they are used and where they fall in the phrase. For example, a phrase ending with a half cadence has a different feel from one ending on an authentic cadence. The choice of the final harmony has a huge impact on how we hear what is happening in that phrase. The choice of a ii or IV leading to the V at either of those cadences affects the sound, but not to the same extent that the cadence type, half or authentic, does.

This idea comes from the work of Heinrich Schenker (1868–1935). He felt that chord-by-chord harmonic analysis did not capture the long-range logic of a piece, and he attempted to compensate for that. A chord-by-chord analysis is still necessary, just like understanding a sentence is a prerequisite for understanding a paragraph. Schenker argued that, once every chord is analyzed, both the melodic line and the harmonic progression can be reduced to important pitches and chords. Reducing a passage to chorale style is the first step in this process.

In terms of the general definitions of the common musical forms, harmony is more important than melody. Since the next chapter of this book is on form, we will now focus on harmonic, rather than melodic, reduction. Certain harmonies provide important moments in the structure, while others are subordinate to those chords, functioning to connect or expand the structural ones.

Figure 32.1 shows some common patterns where one chord is subordinate to another. For example, a voice exchange (figure 32.1a) is really about revoicing the chord at the beginning and end. The vii°⁶ in the middle of the example serves to connect the two inversions. There is now smooth voice leading between the first and last chord, but our ears hear those three beats as being about tonic harmony. The vii°⁶ is said to prolong the tonic harmony. *Prolongation* is the idea that a chord embellishes and expands a structurally more important harmony. The subordinate chord is given a name analogous to our main contrapuntal dissonances. The vii°⁶ in figure 32.1a is a *passing chord*. Figure 32.1b shows a V⁶ serving as a *neighbor chord*. Figure 32.1c shows plagal motion, in which the IV serves as a neighbor chord to tonic. An example of this in music would be the Great Amen cadence, which embellishes the final tonic of a hymn. (The idea of prolongation was first introduced in Chapter 22 in the context of I–IV–I.) A short progression that prolongs a harmony (figure 32.1d) is called a *subordinate progression*.

Figure 32.1 Some common patterns for prolonging tonic harmony

A variety of ways exist to expand a harmony. Figure 32.1 shows four different ways to embellish tonic. Each one of those examples has other options too. The voice exchange in 32.1a could also have a passing six–four or a second-inversion V⁷ in the middle. Figure 32.1b could use vii°⁷ as the neighbor chord. In addition, any harmony, not just tonic, can be prolonged. Trying to catalogue every permutation is overwhelming. If the voice leading and the chord-to-chord progression works, then the metrical, durational, and rhythmic context will clarify the roles of the chords in the larger picture.

Every piece of functionally tonal music can be reduced to its structural harmonies. I refer to this as "phrase-level analysis."[1] Figure 32.2 shows a straightforward example. Measures 1 and 3 contain voice exchanges, so the central harmonies are passing chords. By considering these as subordinate to the harmonies on beats 1 and 3, the analysis becomes simplified (figure 32.3). This simplification also allows for a constant harmonic rhythm, so perhaps all of those pitches should be viewed as nonchord tones rather than as dominants anyway. In taking a step back and looking at the bigger picture, the changes in inversion also become less significant, and the chord function is what matters.

The process of reducing an analysis to important chords works on successive levels, referred to as the fore-ground (all of the notes), the middle ground (varying degrees of reduction), and the background (the point of ultimate reduction, in which an entire piece may be summarized by a few chords). Multiple middle-ground levels exist, and this is where musicians find the most insight. I will do one more reduction of the Schubert example (figure 32.4). At this level, an underlying progression from tonic through pre-dominant to dominant and back to tonic is clear.[2] Measure 6 is tonic harmony, but although tonic is the most important chord in the tonal hierarchy, in this context it is prolonging the dominant. At this point, the music is not about the release of tension but rather about building to the climax. Overall, the phrase structure defines tonic for one measure, then quickly moves on, spending most of its time prolonging dominant harmony.

Figure 32.2 Schubert, "Trauerwaltzer," op. 9, no. 2, D. 365 ("Mournful Waltz")

Figure 32.3 Schubert, "Trauerwaltzer," slightly reduced

Figure 32.4 Schubert, "Trauerwaltzer," two middle-ground reductions

Figure 32.5 provides a second example of a harmonic analysis and reduction. In this instance, the dominant and tonic chords on beat 2 of measures 1 and 3 are neighbor chords. At the middle level, it is easier to see subphrases, such as the repetition of the opening idea in the dominant. At the largest level, aspects such as the periodic (antecedent/consequent) structure of the music show through. While it is essential to understand the details of the chord-to-chord motion, these larger-level concepts help a musician understand and convey the overall narrative of a piece, guiding how to shape a phrase and how to perform multiple phrases in relation to one another.

Figure 32.5 Beethoven, Piano Sonata, op. 10, no. 1, II

Reductions are subjective, with no "right" answer. Different middle-ground analyses help explain how different performers hear and interpret a piece.

Spotlight On: MODULATIONS IN SCHENKERIAN ANALYSES

In Schenkerian analysis, modulations do not exist. Stepping back far enough, an entire piece becomes the prolongation of a single harmony—tonic. Modulations are considered very long tonicizations that expand I.

SUMMARY

Terminology

Schenkerian analysis. An approach to harmonic analysis that emphasizes structurally more important harmonies and ignores subordinate harmonies as a way to elucidate phrase-level and larger formal patterns.

Subordinate harmonies. A chord that serves to prolong a different, more structurally important, harmony.

Passing chord. A subordinate harmony in which the bass serves as a passing tone, connecting two inversions of the same chord or two harmonies with the same function.

Neighbor chord. A subordinate harmony in which the chord returns to the preceding chord.

Subordinate progression. A progression that serves to prolong a single, structurally significant harmony.

Phrase-level analysis. An analysis that identifies the structurally significant harmonies. Phrase-level analyses can be done on several levels, providing more details or more of the big picture.

Some harmonies in a phrase play a more important role than others in defining the structure of the music. Taking a step back and labeling these harmonies helps elucidate the bigger picture and guides performers in how to shape the music.

NOTES

1. This is my terminology and not in common use. Most people refer to it as reduction, but this term implies a complete process of reducing to chorale style, then further reducing both the melody and harmony to the structurally important components. My interest is looking at important structural harmonies to discuss form.
2. I have labeled the second harmony PD since it includes both a IV and a ii chord; ii also would have worked, since the IV can be viewed as part of a prolonged ii^7.

WORKBOOK

1. Reduction Analysis: Choose three of the following excerpts that were analyzed in earlier chapters. Perform two phrase-level analyses on them. The second should go one step further than the first.

From Chapter 22	Figure 22.7: Bach, "Minuet"
	Workbook: Schumann, "Erste Verlust"
	Workbook: Tchaikovsky, "Melodie antique francaise"
From Chapter 30	Workbook: Mozart, Piano Sonata, K. 457, III
	Workbook: Beethoven, Piano Sonata no. 8, op. 13 (*Pathetique*), II

Small Forms

CHAPTER LEARNING OBJECTIVES

This chapter:

- Explains the basic characteristics of contrasting forms and developmental forms

- Defines the general structures of ternary, binary, and rounded binary forms

- Differentiates ternary from rounded binary

We will now look at two small forms to see how the various elements we have been studying combine to form short pieces. To label a form, musicians use letters of the alphabet. Uppercase letters represent large sections, and lowercase letters stand for subsections of these larger sections. When a section returns, its letter is reused. If the music returns but is changed to any significant extent, a prime is added to the letter (e.g., A') to indicate this fact. Additional primes may be added to show multiple returns with variations.

Two factors determine a piece's subdivision into sections: melodic material and harmonic center. *Motives* are short, distinctive ideas contained within a melody. They may be rhythmic, in which a distinctive rhythmic pattern recurs while the pitch content freely changes, or they may preserve both rhythm and pitch contour. Either way, a motive should be identifiable as coming from the melody. The harmonic center is also an important determinant for form. Often the shift to a new key corresponds to a new formal section. For the first half of the common-practice era, tonal center took precedence over motivic content, although gradually both became equally important.

Often the two parameters work together, and sections are easy to identify. New motivic content plus a new key will create a new formal section. Sometimes, however, one changes and the other does not. Then you have to look at the scope of the piece and rely on musical common sense. Does the change in one parameter last for a long time or a short time relative to other sections of the form? What else is happening around it?

Once the sections of the form are identified, the form is categorized and named by how these sections relate to one another. Two broad categories exist: contrasting and developmental forms.

As implied by the name, in *contrasting forms*, sections differ from one another; the ensuing section provides a change from the preceding. In these forms, sections are usually *harmonically closed*, meaning they end on an authentic cadence in the same key in which they began. Forms that have harmonically closed parts are called *sectional* because, harmonically speaking, each part can stand on its own.

In *developmental forms*, melodic material from one section is used in later sections, usually broken into individual motives. The idea of exploring the motives by setting them in different ways is known as "developing" them, hence the name of this category. Developmental passages tend to be less harmonically stable (i.e., they modulate more) and also contain less regular phrases, as the composer plays with these small building blocks. Sections in developmental forms are usually *harmonically open*, meaning that they end in either a different key or on a half cadence in the home key. Since they do not close harmonically, these forms are called *continuous*; something else must follow since the music has not conclusively finished.

All of these terms and concepts will be clearer when applied to actual pieces. We will now look at a few simple examples of the forms to illustrate them.

TERNARY FORM

The simplest contrasting form is ternary. Although the name implies three sections, the third part of the form involves a return of the opening material since much of music is about a journey away and back again. The form is represented as ABA'. Figure 33.1 shows an example. III+ functions on the dominant level (see Chapter 25), so on the phrase-level analysis, its function appears as "V." (I would have used "D" for dominant, but I thought that might be confusing with the key.) The second-inversion subdominant chord in measures 11 and 15 is an accented six–four, meaning that it is an embellishment of the tonic that follows it. The change in the harmonic rhythm, in conjunction with the shortening of the melodic idea, merits giving that beat its own label.

The three-part structure and the contrast are easy to see; Schumann has been nice enough to mark sections with double bars. The key change is not drastic since it is only a change of mode, but within the scope of the piece, that is the most significant harmonic event. It therefore merits its own letter. (If the piece were larger and had other key changes, this may not be the case.) The B section is not harmonically closed, but the A sections are, and the sectional nature of the piece cannot be ignored. The rhythms (quarter notes in the A sections, sixteenth and thirty-second notes in the B section), the melodic contour (mostly scalar in the A sections, leaps in the B section), the mode (minor versus major), and even the tempo markings ("plaintively" and "happily") all emphasize that the role of the B section is to contrast with the A sections.

Some other aspects of interest: Each section is eight measures long, providing balance between the parts. The A sections each contain a single period. The B section contains two phrases, but they do not have an antecedent–consequent relationship. Since the piece is short, it is not necessary to label subsections; we would be labeling individual phrases, which in this case does not aid our understanding in any way.

The general definition of ternary form does not contain any particular key relationship between the A and B sections. The change of mode seen here is the most common, but any key relationship is possible.

BINARY FORM

The simplest developmental form is binary. As indicated by the name, it consists of two sections, A and B. Usually, each one of these sections repeats, emphasizing the two-part structure of the music. Since it is developmental, the motivic material does not change between sections, but its role within the music does. The A section is usually more "thematic," meaning more continuous and singable. The B section is more about fragmentation of the ideas. Figure 33.2 provides an example.

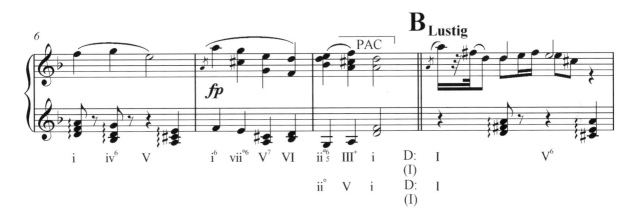

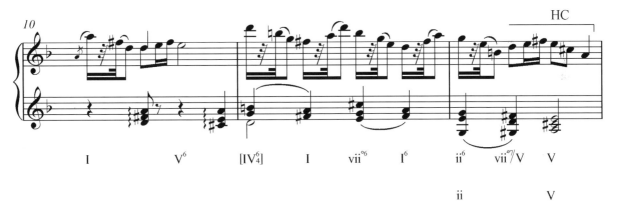

Figure 33.1a Schumann, "Volksliedchen" from *Album für die Jugend* ("Folksong" from *Album for the Young*)

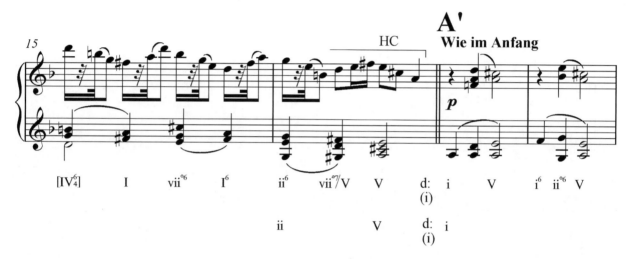

Figure 33.1b Schumann, continued

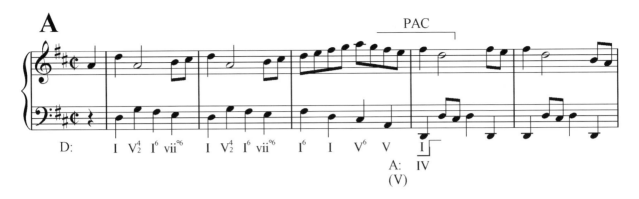

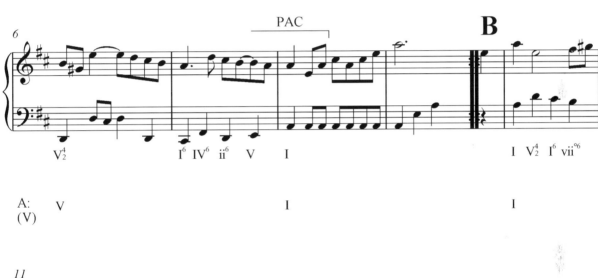

Figure 33.2a Bach, "March" from *Notenbüchlein für Anna Magdalena Bach*
(*The Notebook for Anna Magdalena Bach*)

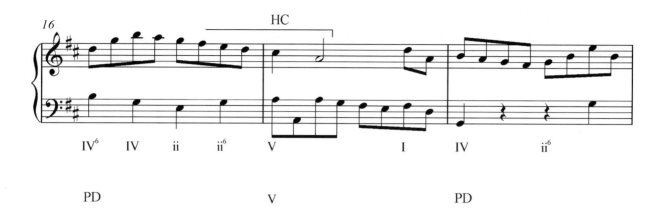

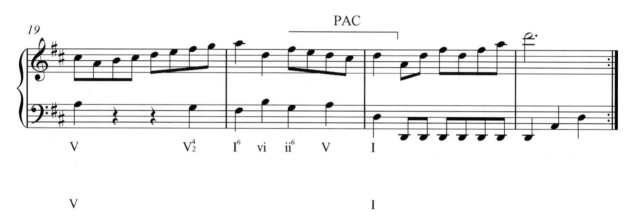

Figure 33.2b Bach, continued

The two-part structure is clearly seen from the repeat signs. The continuous nature of the form is also clear: The sections are harmonically open, the B section starts in the key that the A section ended in, and the same motives and rhythms are used throughout the piece. Not essential to the form but also worth noting is that all the modulations in this case use pivot chords, providing a smooth harmonic motion throughout. In the big picture, the A section presents the motives and travels away from tonic. The B section develops the motives and journeys home again.

In the Bach piece, the return is purely harmonic; we return to D and the piece ends. Often, especially during the Classical and Romantic eras, it was common to put a melodic return when the tonic key arrives in the B section of a binary form. In this way, composers emphasized the return and also ensured that listeners followed the structure. Bringing back earlier material as a summary is called "rounding" the form, and so the binary form with this return is known as *rounded binary*. Now it is worth using lowercase letters to label subsections; there is a significant moment contained within the B section.

Although figure 33.3 is not an entire piece, rather just the theme from a theme and variations, it is in rounded binary form. The A section is a period that modulates to the dominant. The B section consists of two phrases too. The first is developmental, maintaining the melodic ideas of the A section but moving harmonically. The second phrase of the B section is a return of A-section material, although it is an amalgam of the two phrases. The first two measures come from the antecedent, the second two from the consequent.

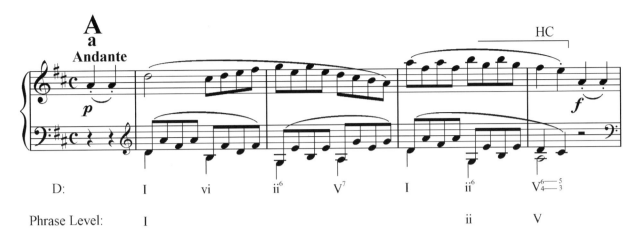

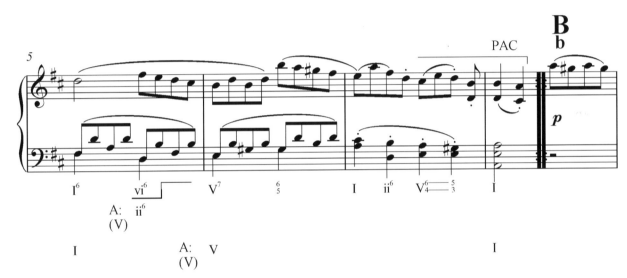

Figure 33.3a Mozart, Piano Sonata, K. 284, III, Theme

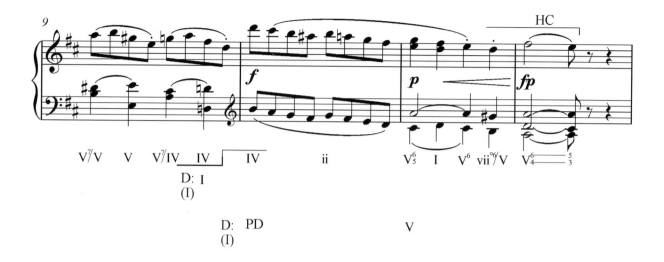

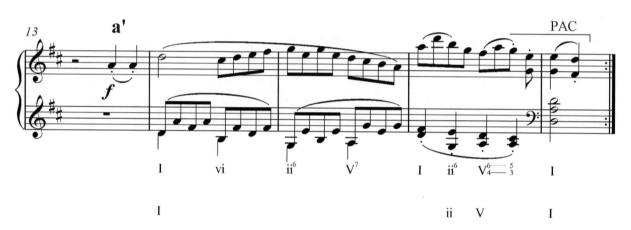

Figure 33.3b Mozart, continued

The A sections in both the Bach and the Mozart pieces modulate to the dominant. This relationship is by far the most common modulation, so much so that people include it as part of the form. In major pieces, the A section generally modulates to the dominant; in minor works, it usually moves to the relative major. Although the modulation is not essential to the form, it is common enough that it is included in the general "textbook" definition.

The diagram in figure 33.4 shows this standard definition for rounded binary form. The Roman numerals below the system indicate key areas not chords. The straight arrows indicate that the A sections move directly to the second key area. The squiggly arrows indicate that developmental sections are less harmonically stable and may move through other key areas. This modulatory nature was not part of the small examples used here but is true in general.

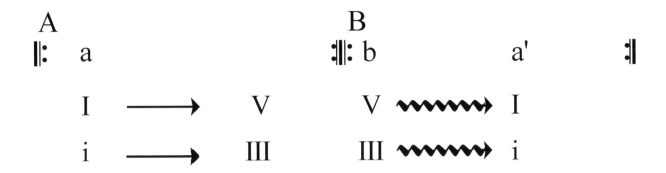

Figure 33.4 Diagram of the standard rounded binary form

TERNARY VERSUS ROUNDED BINARY

When looking at just the letters, the similarity of the ternary and rounded binary forms can be confusing since both contain an aba' structure. The difference between the uppercase and lowercase letters is significant, and the different names of the forms also indicate different compositional approaches.

Ternary—ABA'

- Three equally important large formal sections
  - o A' is approximately the same size as A; sections are balanced
- B section provides contrast to A sections
- Sectional form with harmonically closed parts

Rounded Binary—AB, aba'

- Two large formal sections, usually emphasized with repeats
  - o a' may be a complete or partial return of material, but either way, it fits within a larger section
- B section develops motives from A section
- Continuous form with harmonically open sections

These are guidelines, defining the most typical version of these forms. Not every A section of binary forms modulates. Sometimes ternary forms may have transitional material between sections. The important analytical skill is to look at the big picture—How many sections are there? Are they about contrast or development?—and determine the structure of the piece.

SUMMARY

Terminology

Motives. Short, distinctive melodic ideas that provide coherence to a melody and to an entire work. They may involve rhythm or rhythm and pitch.

Contrasting form. A form in which the sections of the piece provide variety and contrast from one another.

Developmental form. A form in which later sections develop motives from earlier sections.

Harmonically open. When a section of a piece ends with a half cadence in the same key as it began or with any cadence in a different key than it opened with.

Harmonically closed. When a section of a piece ends with an authentic cadence in the same key in which it began.

Sectional form. A form in which the sections are harmonically closed.

Continuous form. A form in which the sections are harmonically open.

Ternary form. A three-part contrasting form with the structure ABA'.

Binary form. A two-part developmental form with the structure AB.

Rounded binary form. A two-part developmental form with the structure AB in which the B section includes a repeat of material from the A section.

Formal sections are labeled with letters of the alphabet. Uppercase letters represent large sections, and lowercase letters indicate smaller subsections. Forms are named and categorized by how the sections relate to one another. The broadest division is between contrasting forms and developmental forms. Ternary is the smallest example of a contrasting form. Binary and rounded binary are the smallest examples of developmental forms.

WORKBOOK

1. Analysis: Analyze some full pieces in ternary, binary, or rounded binary forms. Do the following:

- Provide a complete harmonic analysis of the piece.
- Circle and label all nonchord tones.
- Bracket and label cadences.
- Provide a phrase-level analysis.
- Identify the form by name and label the sections of the form.

Rather than reproduce entire scores, here are a few suggested pieces. The student or teacher can get copies from the library or from imslp.org. Baroque suite movements and Classical minuets can provide additional options.

- Schubert, *Moments musicals*, op. 94, D. 780, III
- Bach, "Gavotte," French Suite no. 5
- Haydn, "Minuet," Piano Sonata in E♭, Hob. XVI/28

2. Composition: Compose a short work, approximately 20–32 measures, following the basic stylistic principles of the common-practice period. Choose a key other than C-major or A-minor. The piece will be in rounded binary form with the following proportions:

- A: The A section will consist of two phrases, either four or eight bars each. The first phrase should end in a half cadence. The second phrase should parallel the first but modulate to the dominant or the relative major. The modulation in this section is usually by pivot chord.

- B:
  - b: The b section will consist of eight bars. It will begin in the dominant or relative major and close on a half cadence in the home key. This section may contain sequences and may modulate in a variety of ways, including sequences or pivot chords.

  - a': The reprise will consist of a return of the opening material, usually the consequent phrase, and it will remain in the home key. It will be four or eight bars long, depending on the phrases in your A section.

Be musical with this. Include tempo, dynamics, and expression markings.

Include an analysis with your piece. Identify the key, chords (Roman numerals), nonchord tones, and cadences. Below the harmonic analysis, do a phrase-level analysis. Also identify the parts of the form.

COLOR CHORDS AND BOLD CHROMATICISM

The preceding chapters have presented the most common chords and their functions in classical music. What the book has covered so far explains the vast majority of tonal music. The next few chapters explain more advanced chromatic chords and techniques, which composers used for moments of special color or dramatic importance. While still important, especially in Romantic music, they are less common throughout the common-practice era.

I ——— PART

II ——— PART

III ——— PART

IV ——— PART

V ——— PART

Modal Mixture

CHAPTER LEARNING OBJECTIVES

This chapter:

- Defines modal mixture in terms of both scale degrees and harmonies

In *modal mixture*, also called *modal borrowing*, composers briefly "mix" the two modes of a key (e.g., parallel major/minor) or "borrow" from one mode into the other. The fact that the function of a chord does not change with mode makes this technique possible. The chords IV in C-major and iv in C-minor function identically, so one can be used in place of the other. Although "change of quality means change of function" is usually true, mixture is an exception. The chord will have the same function it normally does, but its quality will be that of the parallel mode.

The most common example of mixture, and one already encountered in this book (see Chapter 23) is the appearance of vii°7 in major. In order to create more tension, composers borrow L6̂ so that the leading-tone chord will be the fully diminished seventh that appears in minor. This borrowing appears frequently.

Mixture can be viewed as borrowing scale degrees or chords. Figure 34.1 compares the two across the parallel modes.[1] (In order to emphasize the change, the flat in front of the mediant and submediant in minor is included, even though it would not typically be included in an analysis in minor. It would be included, however, in an analysis in major.)

Scale Degrees

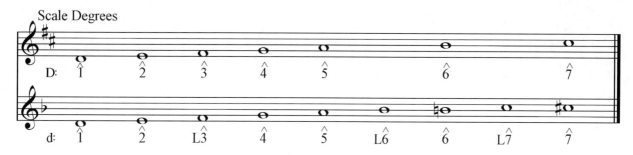

Chord Qualities

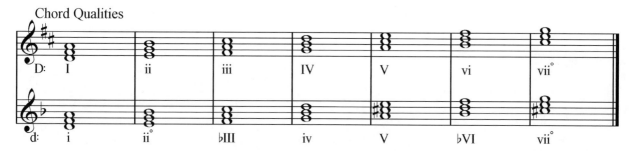

Figure 34.1 Comparison of scale degrees and chord qualities between parallel modes

In terms of scale degrees, the pitches that change are $\hat{3}$, $\hat{6}$, and $\hat{7}$. The major key can borrow all three, L$\hat{3}$, L$\hat{6}$, and L$\hat{7}$, from minor. Minor, however, already includes scale degrees R$\hat{6}$ and R$\hat{7}$. (The leading tone is essential to creating a functional key; it is necessary to create "minor" instead of a mode.) As a result, it is not an equal exchange; the minor key can only borrow R$\hat{3}$ from major.

In terms of harmony,[2] the dominant function chords do not change quality between the two modes, so these cannot be borrowed. The mediant does not have a clear function in major, so it, too, is not useful for borrowing. As such, mixture usually involves I, ii, IV, and vi.

IN MINOR

Borrowing in minor is rare. As just noted, $\hat{3}$ is the only scale degree that minor can borrow from major. Although ii and IV sometimes occur in minor, it is usually because of R$\hat{6}$ heading to the leading tone. These changes are not considered borrowing.

The only common borrowing in minor is the *Picardy third*. The Picardy third occurs when a minor piece ends on a major tonic triad. The effect appears most commonly in Baroque music. In order to be a Picardy third, the chord has to have a tonic function. Roman numerals reflect function. (See figures 34.2 and 34.3.)

In the first measure of the Bach chorale in figure 34.3, the E♮, and the resulting IV chord, is a linear effect, caused by the principal melody moving to F♯, the leading tone. The B♮ in the final measure is modal mixture, borrowing the major triad.

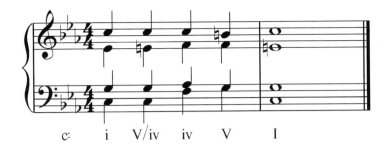

Figure 34.2 Same chord, different functions

Figure 34.3 Bach, "Ich hab' mein' Sach' Gott heimgestellt," ending (mm. 8–9)
("I Have Brought My Items Home to God")

IN MAJOR

Modal mixture occurs more frequently in major. Although it might seem easiest to mix the modes by borrowing the tonic chord, this is actually less common. Composers prefer to borrow pre-dominant chords. L$\hat{6}$ is an essential element of minor. It is a tendency tone, and its pull to $\hat{5}$ helps create the sad or yearning sound of the mode. Composers use the minor-key pre-dominants and then return to a major tonic chord, emphasizing the modal contrast. Musical motivations for mixture can be to color a particular moment, such as a dark word in a text (figure 34.4), or to write a chromatic line (figure 34.5).

(Translation: Here (in this graveyard) I will stop, I thought to myself.)

Figure 34.4 Schubert, "Das Wirtshaus" from *Winterreise*, mm. 8–9 ("The Inn" from *Winter Journey*)

Figure 34.5 Bach, "Herzliebster Jesu," mm. 5–7 ("Dearest Jesus")

While pre-dominants are the most typical chords to borrow in major, the minor tonic and lowered submediant are still usable. Composers sometimes use the minor tonic to enhance the tension while stretching out the dominant chord before the main theme of a piece returns. Figure 34.6 shows this; the B♭ pedal in the bass indicates that the structurally important chord is the dominant. The contrast between the minor mode in measures 92 and 93 and the major key of the main theme in measure 95 heightens the return of the opening melody. Figure 34.7 shows a borrowed lowered submediant chord. This harmony gives a wonderful effect in deceptive motion. Other borrowed chords, such as the minor dominant, are possible but rare. For a nonfunctional chord like that, there may be a better way to explain it, such as a modulation.

Figure 34.6 Schubert, *Drei Klavierstücke*, II, mm. 87–98 (*Three Piano Pieces*)

Figure 34.7 Beethoven, Piano Sonata, op. 2, no. 3, I, m,. 210–19

No clear boundary delineates mixture from a change of mode (i.e., actually moving to the parallel minor). The two techniques are conceptually the same; the difference is the duration and scale. Modal mixture implies a brief borrowing of one or two chords while the original mode is still heard, while a key change describes longer passages that sound consistent in the parallel mode.

Spotlight On: BORROWED KEY AREAS

Although the focus of this chapter is on borrowed chords, some theorists discuss certain key relationships as also resulting from mixture. For example, modulation from a major key to its lowered submediant (I → ♭VI) or lowered mediant (I → ♭III) can be described as borrowing the entire key area from the parallel minor since both new keys are closely related in that mode. While this idea does not change the fact that these tonal centers are remote relative to the original tonic, it has some usefulness in establishing a hierarchy among foreign keys. This model also does not necessarily explain how the modulation is achieved. Going through the parallel mode is not the only way to reach ♭VI or ♭III, yet they would still be called borrowed key areas, regardless of the approach.

SUMMARY

Terminology

Modal mixture (modal borrowing). Borrowing scale degrees or chords from the parallel major or minor mode. Can also be viewed as mixing the two modes together.

Modal mixture is the borrowing of a chord from the parallel key. The chord functions in its normal role. Mixture implies a short borrowing, lasting usually for one or two chords. It occurs more frequently and with more chords in major than in minor.

NOTES

1. A reminder of notation, repeated from Chapter 29: First, as discussed in the footnote in Chapter 3, many textbooks use a flat to represent the lowered form of scale degrees and chords. I prefer the more general L for scale degrees. When it comes to chords, however, I use the flat. *L* is the number 50 in Roman numerals, and it looks confusing to me to see a chord labeled 53 or 56. Second, a flat, natural, or sharp in front of a Roman numeral indicates that the root of the chord has been altered from what naturally occurs in the key. For example, in C-major, III is the E-major triad, while ♭III is the E♭-major triad.
2. Just as a reminder: figure 34.1 includes the functionally significant harmonies in the minor mode. As discussed in Chapter 20, although other combinations involving the two forms of $\hat{6}$ and $\hat{7}$ are possible, the important chords, the ones that composers used, are the ones that involve the tendency tones.

WORKBOOK

1. Analysis: Analyze the following excerpts by doing the following:
   - Identifying the key and providing a functional Roman numeral analysis
   - Circling and labeling nonchord tones
   - Bracketing and labeling cadences

In the Chopin, take a moment to think about what the bass note is in each chord before you begin analyzing. The excerpt is the very ending of the piece, so that should clarify any ambiguity as to the key. The Bach gives an example where a key area is "borrowed."

A. Chopin, Prelude in A♭, op. 28, no. 17, mm. 77 to the end

B. Bach, "Christus ist erstanden, hat überwunden" ("Christ Is Risen and Has Overcome")

C. Schubert, *Moments musicals*, op. 94, D. 780, II (*Musical Moments*)

2. Realization: Realize the following figured basses in a four-voice chorale style (SATB). You may add any weak-beat dissonances you like, but circle and label any that you use.

- Below each system, identify the key of the exercise.
- Perform a functional (Roman numeral) harmonic analysis.
- Bracket and label cadences.

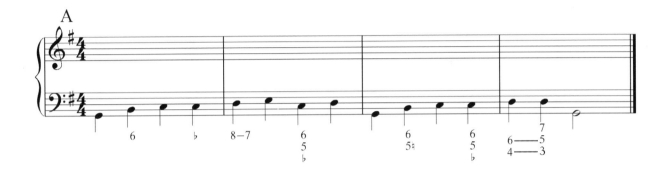

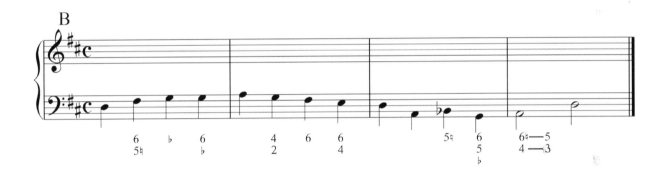

3. Harmonization: Harmonize the following melody in four-voice chorale style, following the functionality and voice leading of common-practice period music.

- Below the harmonization, identify the key.
- Provide a functional Roman numeral analysis.
- Circle and label nonchord tones.
- Identify cadences.

A

B

4. A Blast from the Past: Harmonize one of the first melodies in this book, "Twinkle, Twinkle." Follow the stylistic norms of common-practice music, and incorporate modal mixture. You may alter pitches in the melody to achieve the mixture, if necessary.

- Below the harmonization, identify the key.
- Provide a functional Roman numeral analysis.
- Circle and label nonchord tones.
- Identify cadences.

Neapolitan

**CHAPTER LEARNING
OBJECTIVES**

This chapter:

- Defines the Neapolitan chord
- Explains the idiomatic
  resolution of the Neapolitan
  sixth

In the Brahms example, the pitch G♭ appears twice, once on its own as
L$\hat{2}$ and once in a chord, specifically ♭II. In both cases it has a similar role,
adding darkness and intensity to the moment. The chromatic alteration
is striking because of both its unexpectedness and its push for resolution.

When L$\hat{2}$ appears in music, it is often part of the ♭II chord, which is also
known as the Neapolitan. This name comes from a group of opera composers in Naples in the early 1600s. They were not the only composers who used
the chord, but it became associated with them and was named after their city.

The *Neapolitan* is the major chord built on scale degree L$\hat{2}$. It is always
major. It appears more frequently in minor keys for two reasons: (1) it
requires only one accidental instead of two, so it does not sound as abrupt
in minor as it does in major; and (2) the striking sound of it better suits the
darker minor keys. The Neapolitan also usually appears in first inversion,
so much so that it is often called the Neapolitan sixth.

The Neapolitan is an altered ii° chord, and as such it functions and
behaves like a pre-dominant. It usually leads to the dominant, although it
occasionally can return to tonic harmony. (Remember, ii° more commonly
leads to V, while iv more commonly returns to i, but they belong to the
same functional level and can substitute for one another.) Also, since ii°
often appears in first inversion, so does the Neapolitan. Composers choose
the Neapolitan over the supertonic when they want a bold sonority—major
instead of the expected diminished and with the extra tension of the L$\hat{2}$. It
provides a darker sound and can highlight a particular moment in the music
or text. Figure 35.2 compares a ii° chord with the Neapolitan. The use of
either ♭II or N is acceptable for the notation of the Neapolitan chord.

Figure 35.1 Brahms, Clarinet Sonata, op. 120, no. 1, I (clarinet in concert pitch)

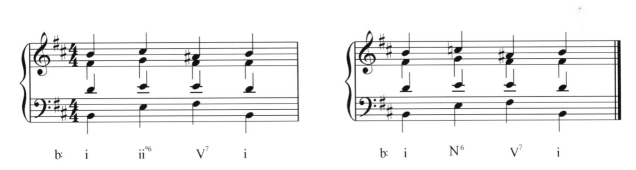

Figure 35.2 Comparison of supertonic and Neapolitan chords

The approach to the Neapolitan chord is the same as approaching the ii°. Many ways exist, but some common ones include coming from VI, which moves by fifth down to the Neapolitan, moving from iv or ii°, which involve changing only one note, or approaching from tonic.

As for the voice leading, the basic rule of chromatic pitches still applies: pitches that are chromatically lowered resolve downward. This pull and resolution is clear in the Brahms example, especially at the beginning, when the music is a single line. The G♭ pulls down to the tonic. Because of this alteration, the Neapolitan has the unusual voicing of a doubled third. The general rule is to double the most stable pitch. L$\hat{6}$ is a tendency tone that pulls to $\hat{5}$, and L$\hat{2}$ pulls to tonic. The third, $\hat{4}$, is the only stable pitch in the chord, so it is doubled.

In addition to its idiosyncratic doubling, the Neapolitan also has a particular and distinctive resolution. Melodically, the lowered supertonic pulls to tonic. Harmonically, the Neapolitan chord pulls to dominant. No tonic pitch exists in the dominant chord. Somehow the voice leading needs to satisfy both tendencies (figure 35.3).

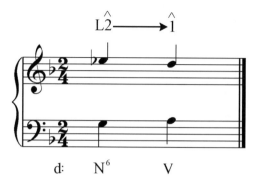

Figure 35.3 Melodic and harmonic resolutions are in conflict

The solution to satisfying both pulls is to delay the resolution of the altered pitch. The harmony moves to dominant as expected, but scale degree L$\hat{2}$ moves to the leading tone. When the leading tone resolves, the melodic line ends on tonic, resolving the tension of the altered scale degree. By moving through the leading tone, the tension created by the chromaticism is sustained. Do not move L$\hat{2}$ up to diatonic $\hat{2}$. That motion thwarts the resolution of the pitch and undermines the tension, which just disappears rather than sustaining and resolving. Also, an awkward melodic tritone appears in the tenor (or an A2 could appear in the alto) when the Neapolitan resolves incorrectly. The cross-relation that appears with the correct resolution is not a problem since an inner voice is involved. (See figure 35.4.)

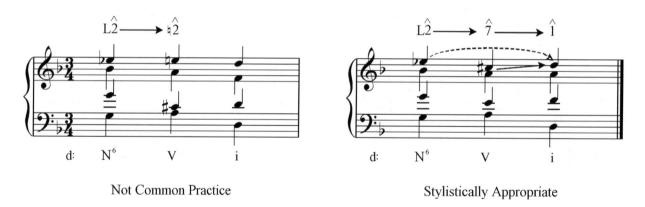

Figure 35.4 The resolution of the Neapolitan

This particular melodic gesture, $\hat{2}$ → $\hat{7}$ → $\hat{1}$, is characteristic of the Neapolitan and often occurs in the soprano line. Some people refer to this as a "double leading-tone gesture" because both notes, a half step above and below the tonic, pull toward home. In the Brahms example, this resolution is in the alto of the right hand of the piano in measures 8 and 9. (In the rolled left-hand chords, he does move L$\hat{2}$ up to the supertonic, but he has no other choice because of the thick chords with many doublings in them. If you were to simplify the texture, you would keep the bass note and leave off the roll.)

Other solutions are possible. Two common ones are to move through the cadential six–four or the vii°⁷/V (figure 35.5). Both chords allow the L$\hat{2}$ to resolve to tonic while intensifying the motion to dominant, honoring both the melodic and the harmonic pulls. Both chords lead to the exact same voice leading as when the Neapolitan moves directly to V; the extra chords are like an insertion in the middle of the progression. Note that when using the cadential six–four, if the L2̂ appears below L6̂, parallel fifths result, so one of the other resolutions will be necessary.

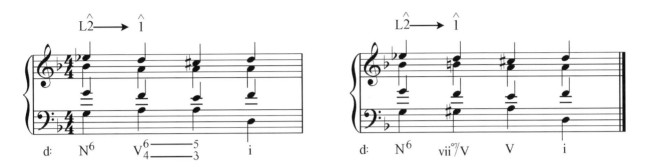

Figure 35.5 Two other ways to resolve the Neapolitan to the dominant

A few examples follow. Figure 35.6 shows a typical Neapolitan moving directly to the dominant.

Figure 35.6 Beethoven, Piano Sonata, no. 14, op. 27, no. 2 (Moonlight), I

Figure 35.7 shows the Neapolitan moving through a cadential six–four. Like Brahms, Corbin has thick chords and doubles L2̂, although the rhythmic activity softens the effect. Despite the leaps in the melody, the L2̂ in the soprano, the more prominent one, resolves in the expected way. This example also provides a nice contrast between ii° and the Neapolitan in an actual piece.

Figure 35.8 shows a Neapolitan both in a major key and moving to tonic instead of dominant. Brahms revoices the Neapolitan chord while sustaining it, but he correctly resolves the L2̂ in the voice it last appears.

Figure 35.7 Corbin, "Santiago"

Figure 35.8 Brahms, "Wie Melodien zieht es mir," op. 105, no. 1 ("Like Melodies, It Moves through My Mind")

In the Romantic era, composers used the Neapolitan more frequently and a little more freely. Sometimes composers put the Neapolitan in root position, tonicized it, or even modulated to it. To tonicize the Neapolitan, composers add a seventh to the VI, making it into a secondary dominant—V^7/N. Figure 35.9 shows a famous example in which Chopin tonicizes the Neapolitan and then puts it in root position. Melodically, he uses a passing tone to connect $L\hat{2}$ to the leading tone.

Figure 35.9 Chopin, Prelude in B-Minor, op. 28, no. 6, mm. 9–15

SUMMARY

Terminology

Neapolitan. ♭II. Functions as a pre-dominant.

The Neapolitan is the major chord built on $L\hat{2}$. It can be notated as ♭II or N. It usually occurs in minor keys and in first inversion. Since the third is the only stable pitch, it is doubled. The Neapolitan is an altered ii° chord, and it functions as a pre-dominant, usually resolving to dominant.

$L\hat{2}$, being a chromatically lowered supertonic, must resolve to tonic. When the chord moves directly to dominant, $L\hat{2}$ should move to $\hat{7}$ and then $\hat{1}$. This allows the pitch to resolve without sacrificing the tension. The pitch can be resolved more immediately by moving through a cadential six–four or vii°⁷/V before continuing onto V.

WORKBOOK

1. Analysis: Four musical excerpts follow.
   - Identify the key of each excerpt.
   - Provide functional (Roman numeral) harmonic analyses.
   - Circle and label nonchord tones.
   - Identify all cadences.
   - When you encounter a Neapolitan chord, circle the pitch L$\hat{2}$ and show its resolution to tonic.

Don't let the busyness of the Chopin passage deceive you. Reduce it and you will see that it is fairly straightforward.

A. Bach, "Ach Gott, von Himmel sieh darein" ("Oh God, Look Down from Heaven")

B. Schubert, "Der Müller und das Bach" from *Die schöne Müllerin*
("The Miller and the Brook" from *The Beautiful Miller Woman*)

C. Chopin, Etude in A-Minor, op. 25, no. 4

D. Schubert, "Erlkönig" ("The Elf-King")

2. Practice resolving the Neapolitan chord. Assume the key signature corresponds to the minor key. In a four-voice chorale style, write the Neapolitan and resolve it to V (or V7), and then resolve that dominant to tonic. Each key should have a three-chord progression.

3. Realization: Realize the specified progression in a four-voice chorale style. You may add sevenths to the dominant chords if you want.

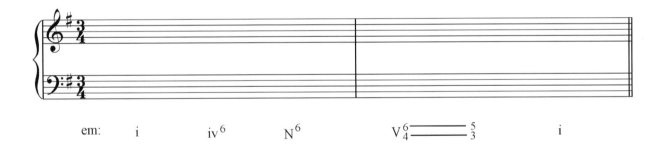

em: i   iv⁶   N⁶   V$^6_4$ —— $^5_3$ i

B♭M: I   N⁶   vii°⁷/V   V   I

4. Realization: Realize the following figured bass in a four-voice chorale style (SATB). You may add any weak-beat dissonances you like, but circle and label any that you use.

- Below the system, identify the key of the exercise.
- Perform a functional (Roman numeral) harmonic analysis.
- Bracket and label cadences.

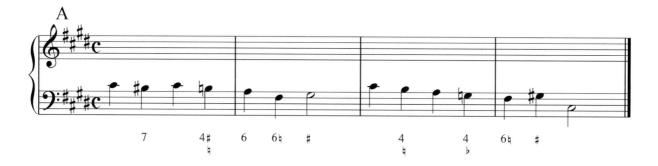

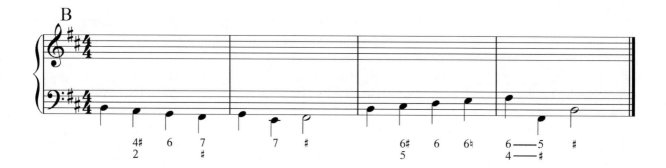

5. You have the outer voices for a piece of music. Determine the harmonies and complete the passage in a four-voice chorale style. The first place an accidental appears can be harmonized by a Neapolitan or with modal mixture.

- Below the system, identify the key of the exercise.
- Provide a functional (Roman numeral) analysis.
- Label cadences.
- Circle and label nonchord tones.

Augmented Sixth (Nationality) Chords

CHAPTER LEARNING OBJECTIVES

This chapter:

- Defines augmented sixth chords
- Defines the three variants of augmented sixth chords
- Explains the idiomatic resolution of all three augmented sixth chords

In the Mozart excerpt in figure 36.1, the three marked chords are called augmented sixth chords because they contain the interval of an augmented sixth. These are not augmented triads, which contain an augmented fifth. The interval is an augmented sixth, between scale degrees $L\hat{6}$ and $R\hat{4}$. $L\hat{6}$ almost always appears in the bass, so the interval is an augmented sixth and not a diminished third.

The Mozart example demonstrates the most popular approach to augmented sixth chords; the chromatic pitches are passing tones as a IV^6 moves to V. Other chords can also lead to an A6 chord, such as vi and ii^7 in second inversion (and their analogs in minor). In minor, tonic can also effectively connect to an A6 chord.

The resolution of the augmented sixth interval is exactly as implied by the notation. It resolves out to an octave on $\hat{5}$. (See figure 36.2.) There are two ways to think of this: (1) Augmented intervals resolve by both voices moving outward by a half step. (Think of a tritone when written as an A4.) (2) Tendency tones and chromatic pitches want to resolve. When in minor, $L\hat{6}$, which naturally occurs there, is a tendency tone that pulls to $\hat{5}$. In major, it is a chromatically lowered pitch, which wants to continue moving down, so it will resolve down to $\hat{5}$. In both modes, $R\hat{4}$ is a chromatically raised pitch, so it resolves up to $\hat{5}$.

Figure 36.1 Mozart, Sonata in D, K. 284, III, Variation VII

Understanding the resolution also makes writing the A6 easier. Rather than figuring out what is L6̂ and R4̂, it is easier to think about the dominant and then find the pitch a half step above and below it.

As might be expected, since they resolve to octaves on the dominant pitch (and in light of their role as a bridge between IV⁶ and V), augmented sixth chords lead to the dominant. They are much like a V/V, intensifying the motion and putting more emphasis on the arrival on the dominant.

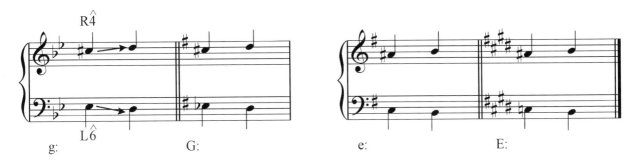

Figure 36.2 Resolution of the augmented sixth

NATIONALITY CHORDS

Augmented sixth chords come in three flavors, which differ from each other by one pitch. To differentiate between the three, each has been named after a different nationality—Italian, French, and German—and they are sometimes called the nationality chords.

Italian Sixth

The Italian sixth (It^6) is the most basic augmented sixth chord. The other two chords consist of an Italian sixth plus an additional note. The Italian sixth consists of three pitches: L$\hat{6}$, R$\hat{4}$, and $\hat{1}$. Since the pitches in the augmented sixth are unstable, the tonic is doubled.

The resolution of the Italian sixth is that the A6 resolves out to the octave on the dominant, one tonic moves down to the leading tone, and the other moves up to the supertonic.

Figure 36.3 The Italian sixth and its resolution

French Sixth

The French sixth (Fr^6) consists of the Italian sixth plus the supertonic, so its pitches are L$\hat{6}$, R$\hat{4}$, $\hat{1}$, and $\hat{2}$. It contains two tritones (L$\hat{6}$/$\hat{2}$ and $\hat{1}$/R$\hat{4}$), so it has a pungent sound. The voice leading of its resolution is very smooth; the A6 resolves by half steps to the octave on dominant, the tonic moves by half step to the leading tone, and the supertonic stays as a common tone.

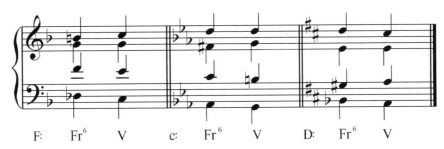

Figure 36.4 The French sixth and its resolution

German Sixth

The German sixth (Ger⁶) is the Italian sixth plus the minor mediant (which occurs diatonically in minor). Its pitches are L6̂, R4̂, 1̂, and L3̂. The pitches resolve as expected, with the A6 resolving to the octave on dominant, the tonic moving to the leading tone, and the mediant moving to the supertonic. The one issue is that L6̂ → 5̂ and L3̂ → 2̂ produce parallel fifths. The most common way around this is to pass through a cadential six–four (i.e., resolve the tonic and mediant after the A6), or to pass through a Fr⁶ (i.e., move the mediant down before the other voices).

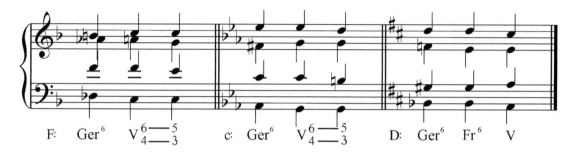

Figure 36.5 The German sixth and its resolution

Although the chords have slightly different members and sounds, they are all variations on the same function and sonority (figure 36.6). Composers often move freely between them.

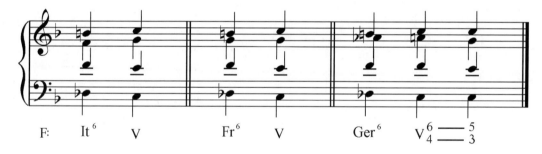

Figure 36.6 Comparison of the three nationality chords

Sometimes people talk about a fourth flavor to the nationality chords, one whose pitch members are L6̂, R4̂, 1̂, and R2̂. Several theorists have suggested names for this chord, including the "Swiss" (being between the French and the German) and the "doubly augmented sixth" (for the presence of the augmented fourth). A new name is not necessary; it is a German sixth with the L3̂ written enharmonically as R2̂. The motivation for the respelling is so that the accidentals in the melodic lines look correct. In major, moving from the German sixth to the cadential six–four leads to a line with L3̂ → ♮3̂, which violates the function of a chromatically lowered pitch. R2̂ → 3̂ looks much better. Not all composers bother with this more proper voice leading, but it appears occasionally (figure 36.7).

The following figures provide several examples. The first 50 measures of the third movement of Beethoven's *Pathetique* sonata contain an appearance of each nationality chord.

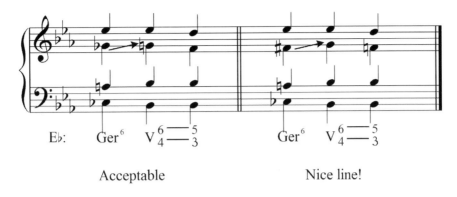

Figure 36.7 Enharmonic spelling of the German sixth

Beginning

Figure 36.8a Beethoven, Piano Sonata no. 8, op. 13 (*Pathetique*), III

Measure 25

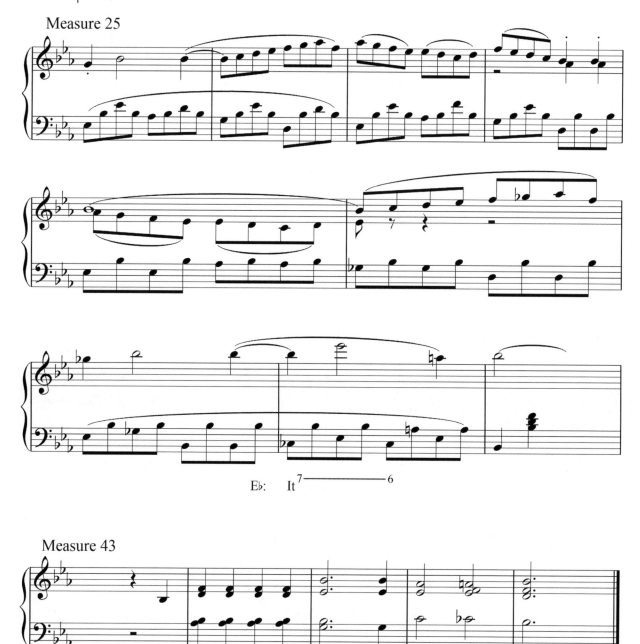

Figure 36.8b Beethoven, continued

Figure 36.9 shows how composers can freely move between the three different nationality chords. Since the principal melody moves between scale degrees $\hat{1}$, $\hat{2}$, and L$\hat{3}$, it is difficult to assign a particular name to these augmented sixth chords. The last one may work best as a German sixth, since the melody leaps from a L$\hat{3}$, implying that it is a chord tone. Given the thin texture and melodic motion, however, it moves directly to the dominant.

In figure 36.10, Chopin does something striking. He prolongs the German sixth chord for seven measures. He voices it with an open fifth drone in the bass and with a melodic augmented second,[1] creating, to Western ears, an exotic folk sound. The chord still resolves as it should. When moving through a cadential six–four, Chopin keeps the lowered mediant, creating a moment of modal mixture, rather than moving it up.

Figure 36.9 Mozart, Sonata in B♭, K. 333, I, mm. 79–85

Figure 36.10 Chopin, Mazurka in B♭, op. 7, no. 1, mm. 45–52

Figure 36.11 shows the enharmonic spelling of the German sixth.

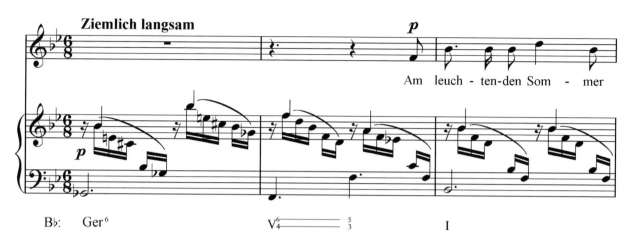

Figure 36.11 Schumann, "Am leuchtenden Sommer morgen" from *Dichterliebe* ("On a Bright Summer Morning" from *A Poet's Love*)

LESS COMMON ROLES OF AUGMENTED SIXTH CHORDS

Occasionally, an augmented sixth chord will behave in an unexpected way. The following instances are very rare. They are unusual behavior for an uncommon chord. For completeness, though, they are included.

Sometimes, when the bass is an ascending line, and the pre-dominant chord is IV or ii⁶, the A6 chord is inverted, and the R4̂ appears in the bass. The chord functions and resolves in the typical way. The one advantage/ change is that the Ger°3 (not an official name for this chord) may resolve directly to V without passing through another chord. As mentioned, this is rare; composers prefer using a V/V or a vii°⁷/V in this context.

A common-tone augmented sixth is a linear chord that is analogous to the common-tone diminished seventh. It is actually a collection of nonchord tones, only one of which belongs to the functioning chord. That chord-member pitch remains as a common tone while the others resolve. The best label for this is to identify the functioning chord and the dissonances. An example of a CTA6 appears in figure 37.3.

An apparent augmented sixth chord may resolve to a harmony other than dominant. Theorists are divided on what to call this function. Some argue that it is an "applied A6," although then it would resolve to the dominant of the applied chord. Others argue that it is a dominant with a passing tone; this interpretation is explained further in Chapter 38. Still others say it is a linear chord with passing tones in two voices. Given the lack of consensus, no decent notation exists for it. In the example in figure 36.12, the first German sixth is one of these undefined ones. The second is a standard German sixth that resolves to dominant.

Figure 36.12 Tchaikovsky, "Valse des fleurs" from *Casse-Noisette*, mm. 45–53
("Waltz of the Flowers," from *The Nutcracker*)

Spotlight On: AUGMENTED SIXTH CHORDS AS LINEAR CHORDS

Because of their origin as chromatic passing tones, some people argue that A6 chords are not chords in their own right—that they are truly linear chords. While this argument is sound, people have discussed these sonorities as chords for several hundred years, so, practically speaking, we call them chords.

SUMMARY

Terminology

Augmented sixth chords. A family of chords—Italian, French, and German—containing an augmented sixth between L$\hat{6}$ (in the bass) and R$\hat{4}$ (which appears in any of the upper voices). Leads to V.

Italian sixth. The augmented sixth chord containing scale degrees L$\hat{6}$, R$\hat{4}$, and $\hat{1}$.

French sixth. The augmented sixth chord containing scale degrees L$\hat{6}$, R$\hat{4}$, $\hat{1}$, and $\hat{2}$.

German sixth. The augmented sixth chord containing scale degrees L$\hat{6}$, R$\hat{4}$, $\hat{1}$, and L$\hat{3}$.

Augmented sixth chords contain an augmented sixth between L$\hat{6}$, which appears in the bass, and R$\hat{4}$, which can appear in any of the three upper voices. The two pitches resolve outward to an octave on $\hat{5}$. Harmonically, the chord moves to the V chord.

Three flavors of augmented sixth chords exist, defined by the pitches in them.

- Italian—L$\hat{6}$, R$\hat{4}$, and $\hat{1}$
- French—L$\hat{6}$, R$\hat{4}$, $\hat{1}$, and $\hat{2}$
- German—L$\hat{6}$, R$\hat{4}$, $\hat{1}$, and L$\hat{3}$

The German has to move through a cadential six–four in order to avoid parallel fifths.

NOTE

1. Technically, it is acceptable to write a melodic A2 if a chord that contains the interval is being arpeggiated. For example, arpeggiating a vii°7 can produce a melodic A2. The harmonic support justifies the atypical melodic line. Augmented seconds are not stylistically appropriate when moving from one chord to another.

WORKBOOK

1. Analysis: Analyze the following excerpts.

- Identify the key and provide functional (Roman numeral) harmonic analyses.
- Circle and label nonchord tones.
- Identify all cadences.
- When you encounter a nationality chord, use arrows to show the resolution of the augmented sixth.

Before beginning the Tchaikovsky analysis, think about the harmonic rhythm and which pitch is the bass note. Reduce it accordingly. The Chopin example contains a regular augmented sixth chord as well as an inverted one.

A. Tchaikovsky, "Mazurka" from *Album pour la jeunesse* (*Album for the Young*)

B. Beethoven, String Quartet, op. 18, no. 2, III

C. Haydn, String Quartet, op. 74, no. 3, II

D. Chopin, Nocturne in C#-Minor, op. posthumous

2. Realization: Realize the following figured basses in a four-voice chorale style (SATB). You may add any weak-beat dissonances you like, but circle and label any that you use.

- Bracket and label cadences.
- Below each system, identify the key of the exercise.
- Perform a functional (Roman numeral) harmonic analysis.

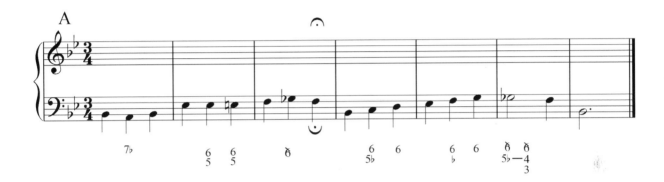

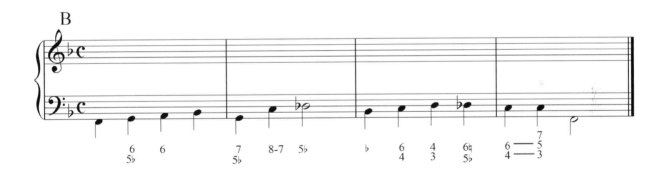

3. You have the outer voices for a piece of music. Determine the harmonies and complete the passage in a four-voice chorale style (SATB), following common-practice conventions.

- Below the system, identify the key of the exercise.
- Provide a functional (Roman numeral) analysis.
- Label cadences.
- Circle and label nonchord tones.

4. Harmonization: Harmonize the following melody in four-voice chorale style, following the functionality and voice leading of common-practice music. For notes with an asterisk (*), use an augmented sixth chord.

- Below the harmonization, identify the key.
- Provide a functional Roman numeral analysis.
- Circle and label nonchord tones.
- Identify any cadences.

Altered Dominants

CHAPTER LEARNING OBJECTIVES

This chapter:

- Examines the relationship between many chromatic harmonies and diatonic pre-dominant chords

- Explains the way composers sometimes alter the fifth of a dominant chord

In theory classes, we study each chromatic harmony as its own entity. Each color chord is distinct from the others, having its own particular resolution. Sometimes this sectionalizing of the harmonies sacrifices the larger musical picture.

Although it has not been readily apparent, since each chromatic chord has its own chapter, most of these harmonies are variants of the predominant chords. In the same way that the three augmented sixth chords differ from one another by the pitches Do–Re–Me, the chromatic chords are all basically a ii chord with one or two pitches chromatically altered. (See figure 37.1. If a IV6/5 began the progression, or if the chart started in minor, the order of the chords would change, but the basic structure would remain.)

This tie between chromatic harmony and pre-dominant chords makes sense. The tonic–dominant relationship is the most important connection in tonal music. Changing the pitches in either of these chords could undermine that relationship and destroy the functional hierarchy. On the other hand, pre-dominants are common chords, but the functionality is not dependent on them. Alteration of them can intensify the motion to the dominant while maintaining tonal integrity.

Taking a step back and looking at the bigger picture, that is, at the phrase level, counterpoint drives many of the chromatic chords. The basic progression is T–P–D–T. The composer usually aims for the D or the D–T at the cadence. A few well-placed chromatic passing or neighbor tones on the predominant chords provide a myriad of chromatic harmonies, increasing the tension and pushing the music forward. Figure 37.2 shows a basic progression with possible chromatic pitches between the pre-dominant and dominant chords, followed by one option of how those different pitches could be incorporated.[1] (The German sixth occasionally appears in this inversion, although it is rare.)

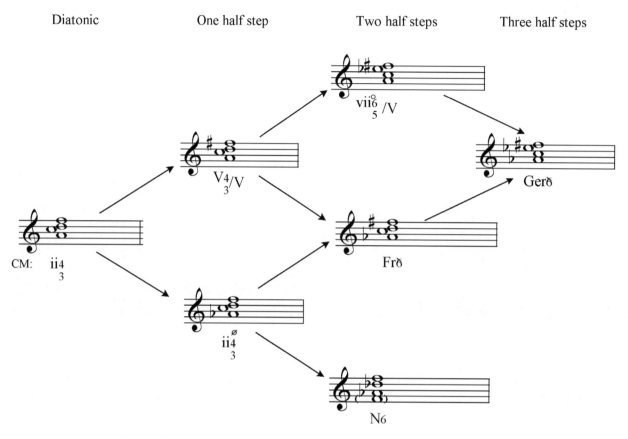

Figure 37.1 Many chromatic chords are variants of pre-dominant chords

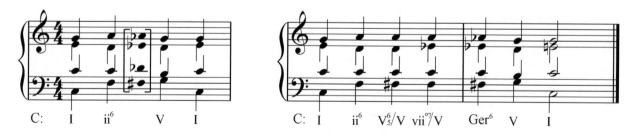

Figure 37.2 The contrapuntal underpinning of chromatic harmonies

ALTERED DOMINANTS

Having said that, there are occasions when the dominant is altered. These instances are rare, primarily happening in the very late Romantic era.

As mentioned, chromatically altering the dominant could affect the dominant–tonic relationship, so composers handle it carefully. The root cannot be changed, or else it will no longer be a V chord. The leading tone cannot be changed, since that is what provides the tension. The only pitch that can be altered without affecting the function of the chord is the fifth. The alterations to the fifth usually result from a chromatic passing or neighbor tone gesture, much like one can view the aforementioned changes to the pre-dominants.

Augmented Triads

The only augmented triad we have seen so far is III+, which functions as a dominant (see chapter 25). It is an uncommon chord, although it appears throughout the common-practice period. When the fifth of the V is raised a half step, the chord becomes augmented. A raised pitch will keep ascending, so the R$\hat{2}$ resolves into $\hat{3}$ in the tonic chord. V+ is characteristic of the late Romantic era, most notably late Liszt, Mahler, and Strauss. In figure 37.3, the V is a functional label. The D♯ is a chromatic neighbor tone that alters the quality without affecting the function or voice leading.

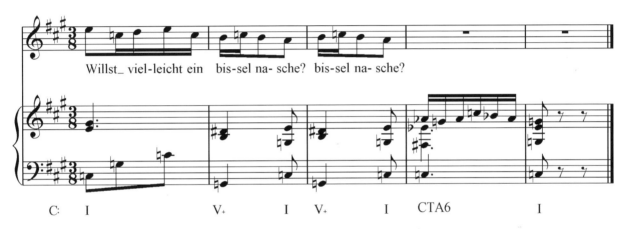

Figure 37.3 Mahler, "Verlor'ne Müh'" from *Das Knaben Wunderhorn*, mm. 44–48
("Labor Lost" from *The Boy's Magic Horn*)

As mentioned in Chapter 36, the chord in the penultimate measure is a common-tone augmented sixth chord. This harmony is a linear chord, not really a German sixth, and is analogous to the common-tone diminished seventh. (A CT°7 would have an A♮ instead of A♭. The two common-tone chords are also variants of one another, differing by a half step.) The C is a chord tone and the other notes are all chromatic neighbors. The C holds as common tone while the other pitches resolve appropriately. Regarding the notation of the CTA6 chord, D♯ would be better than E♭.

The Beatles' song "Oh! Darling" opens with V+ → I in A-major. Augmented triads may appear on applied dominants too.

Throughout much of the common-practice era, treating the R$\hat{2}$ as a passing or neighbor tone makes as much as or more sense than calling the V chord augmented.

Five with Flat Fifth

When the fifth of the dominant chord is lowered a half step, the chord becomes a V$^{♭5}$. This chord has no common name, other than "five with a flat fifth," because it is so rare. It is most characteristic of Strauss and other late Romantic composers of the early twentieth century. The flatted fifth resolves down, so L$\hat{2}$ leads to $\hat{1}$. On the phrase level, it often appears as a chromatic passing tone.

Figure 37.4 Elgar, "Ave verum corpus," mm. 36–39

The V$^{♭5}$ in measure 38 of figure 37.4 is inverted. Out of context, the chord appears to be a French sixth. As mentioned in Chapter 36, progressions sometimes contain an augmented sixth chord built on atypical scale degrees and resolving to the "wrong" chord. Here is a second such case. (The first was the Tchaikovsky excerpt in figure 36.12.) As stated previously, theorists disagree on the function in these situations. Given the context in this particular case, and in general too, I think that the V$^{♭5}$ makes more sense than the Fr^6. The chord does not resolve to dominant harmony, as augmented sixth chords usually do, and I hear a dominant–tonic pull, especially considering the downbeat of the measure. Having said that, the harmony is ambiguous. The passage is driven by counterpoint, with smooth lines moving by chromatic half steps. Composers think about that when writing such music.

SUMMARY

Terminology

Altered dominants. Dominant chords with either a raised or lowered fifth.

Most local (nonmodulating) chromatic chords are variants of the pre-dominants; the chromaticism can be viewed, on the phrase level, as chromatic passing tones and neighbor tones embellishing the pre-dominant harmony.

Dominant chords can be altered, but the only pitch that can change without affecting function is the fifth. The chromatic pitches are usually chromatic passing or neighbor tones. A raised fifth leads to an augmented dominant, in which the R$\hat{2}$ leads to $\hat{3}$ in the tonic chord, while a lowered fifth creates a "five with a flat fifth" in which L$\hat{2}$ leads to $\hat{1}$ in the tonic chord.

NOTE

1. Just to clarify: This passage does not say that *all* chromatic harmonies are variants of the pre-dominants. It says that all of the color chords and the most common secondary dominants, V/V and vii°/V, are. This category covers much of the chromatic harmony in common-practice music. Still, applied dominants to chords other than the dominant exist. Linear chords that involve the same basic idea of half-step motion also appear periodically.

WORKBOOK

1. Analysis: Analyze the following excerpts.
   - Identify the key and provide functional (Roman numeral) harmonic analyses.
   - Circle and label nonchord tones.
   - Identify all cadences.
   - Is it better to treat the augmented chord as a harmonic entity or as containing passing tones?

A. Schubert, Ten Variations, Theme

B. Strauss, Till Eulenspiegel's Merry Pranks, Op. 28

2. Figured Bass: Realize the following figured bass in a four-voice chorale style (SATB). You may add any weak-beat dissonances you like, but circle and label any that you use.

- Bracket and label cadences.
- Below the system, identify the key of the exercise.
- Perform a functional (Roman numeral) harmonic analysis.

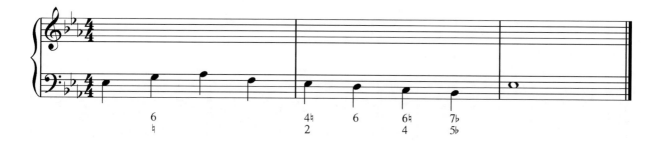

Enharmonic Reinterpretation

This chapter:

- Defines enharmonic reinterpretation
- Explains the pitch respellings and resolutions for the three common enharmonically reinterpreted harmonies

Q: What do you get when you drop a piano down a mineshaft?
A: A flat miner.

(Explaining a joke ruins it. Apologies.) Homonyms make great puns. "A flat miner" can be heard as "A♭-minor." The words are spelled differently and have different meanings, but when spoken aloud sound the same. The humor comes from being able to understand the words both ways simultaneously.

Musically, notation and function go together. Although F♯ and G♭ sound the same, in context they function differently. But what if a composer creates a musical pun, changing from one form to another midthought? That is the point of *enharmonic reinterpretation*.

Enharmonic reinterpretation is the first of two techniques for bold modulations. (The second is in the next chapter.) In this method, a composer changes between two enharmonic spellings of a chord, thereby causing an abrupt modulation to a distantly related key. The *sound* makes sense in both keys, much like a pivot chord. The *chord*, however, does not make sense in both keys (respelling makes it a different chord), so unlike a pivot chord, instead of smoothing the transition, it creates a surprising effect.

For the technique to work, a functional chord has to turn into another functional chord when respelled. It works best with symmetric chords, meaning fully diminished sevenths and augmented triads. German sixths, while not symmetric, happen to work too, being enharmonic with a dominant seventh.

FULLY DIMINISHED SEVENTHS

Fully diminished seventh chords are completely symmetric. Every pitch is a minor third from its neighbors. Even moving from the seventh back to the root, the interval is an augmented second, which is enharmonic with a minor third. Any chord member can be the root, and the sonority, out of context, will sound the same. In context, however, the function and the resolution become clear (figure 38.1).

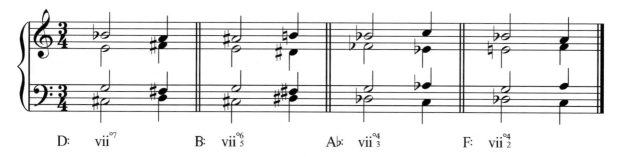

Figure 38.1 Enharmonic diminished chords and their resolutions

Because of this structure, the chord is easily reinterpreted. Figure 38.1 shows the four ways a vii°⁷ can be written. The chord is always a vii°⁷, but the tonal center changes with the spelling. Each chord member gets a turn as the root of the chord, which means it is the leading tone in the functioning key. Since the chord tones are each a minor third apart, the connected keys are also a minor third from each other. On top of that, the parallel minors are also accessible. Counting the major and minor modes as separate keys, composers can easily move between eight keys with enharmonic reinterpretation.

In the example in figure 38.2, Beethoven explicitly writes out the enharmonic spelling. In passages where the chord happens only once, composers choose the key in which to write it. It often leads to a moment of odd-looking voice leading, which is, when considered enharmonically, completely appropriate.

Figure 38.2 Beethoven, Piano Sonata no. 8, op. 13 (*Pathetique*), I, mm. 133–36

The diminished seventh can also function as an applied dominant, leading to additional remote key areas. By enharmonically reinterpreting the vii°⁷/V, eight more key areas become available. By treating the chord of resolution as a V/V, one can modulate to eight more keys. Practically any two key areas can be connected through enharmonic reinterpretation of the diminished seventh chord. (See the first workbook assignment.)

AUGMENTED TRIADS

Augmented triads are also symmetric, with each chord member a major third from its neighbors. Reinterpreting these chords results in modulation by major third. As discussed in chapter 37, augmented triads usually function as dominants.

In figure 38.3, Mahler chose to use the spelling of the augmented triad in the approaching key, not the starting key. This choice is probably from a preference for the more common C♮ than the less common B♯. It leads to incorrect notation the first time it appears.

Figure 38.3 Mahler, "Verlor'ne Müh'" from *Das Knaben Wunderhorn*, mm. 74–80 ("Labor Lost" from *The Boy's Magic Horn*)

Although it is possible to reinterpret augmented triads, it almost never occurs. Augmented triads are rare on their own, let alone one that undergoes enharmonic reinterpretation.

GER⁶ AND V⁷

Although it is not symmetric, the Ger⁶ happens to be enharmonic with V⁷. Reinterpretation of this type leads to modulation by half step (figure 38.4).

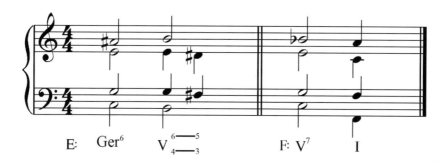

Figure 38.4 Enharmonic spellings and resolutions of a Ger⁶ and a V⁷

In figure 38.5, Schubert moves deceptively to a cadential six–four in the key of the Neapolitan. He then reinterprets the C♭ in the V⁷ as B♮, turning it into a German sixth in F-minor, the home key.

SUMMARY

Terminology

Enharmonic reinterpretation. An abrupt modulation achieved by using enharmonic spellings of pitches in a chord, thereby changing the key in which it is functioning.

Enharmonic reinterpretation creates an abrupt modulation by respelling a chord so that it functions in a distant key. Diminished seventh chords, the most common chords for this technique, connect keys a minor third apart. Augmented triads connect keys a major third apart. German sixth chords can be respelled as dominant sevenths, connecting keys a half step apart.

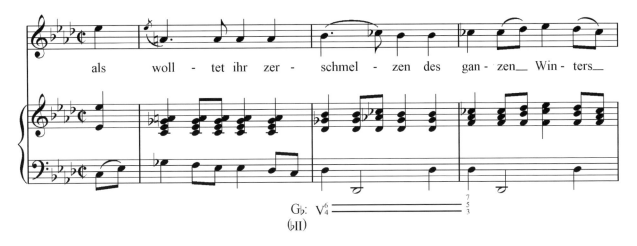

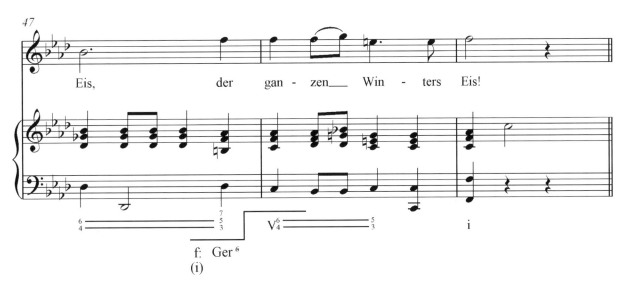

Figure 38.5 Schubert, "Gefrorene Tränen" from *Winterreise*, mm. 44–49 ("Frozen Tears" from *Winter Journey*)

WORKBOOK

1. Connecting Keys: In the first system, the first measure gives you the vii°⁷ in C-major and resolves it. In the following three measures, correctly write and resolve that chord in the three other keys in which it functions enharmonically. Identify the keys and label the chords with Roman numerals.

    In the second system, write the same chord and again resolve it, but this time assume the second chord is a dominant. Resolve that dominant to tonic in the new key. Identify the keys and label the chords with Roman numerals. The first measure is again done for you.

Chord of Resolution is Tonic

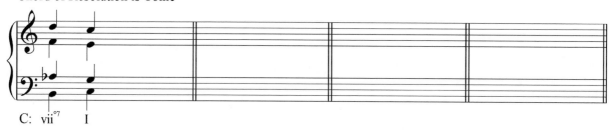

C: vii°⁷   I

Chord of Resolution is Dominant

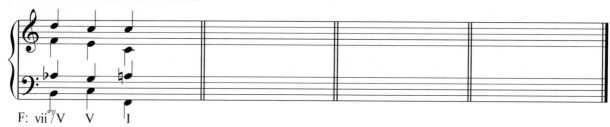

F: vii°⁷/V   V   I

2. Reinterpretation Drill: Modulate from the given key to the specified key by enharmonically reinterpreting the chord. First, respell the given chord, and then properly resolve it. Note that the initial key signature (for each exercise) remains in effect. Label the chords with Roman numerals. The first one is done as an example. Sometimes you may have to use an intermediate dominant chord (i.e., you are resolving to V in the new key) to get to the goal key; if so, continue to the tonic chord.

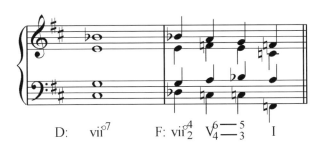

D: vii°⁷   F: vii°⁴₂ V⁶₄—⁵₃ I

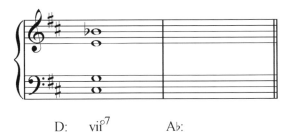

D: vii°⁷   A♭:

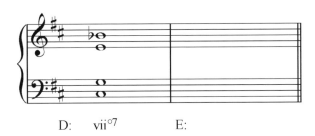

D: vii°⁷   E:

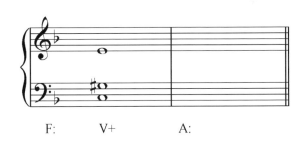

F: V+   A:

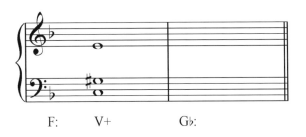

F: V+   G♭:

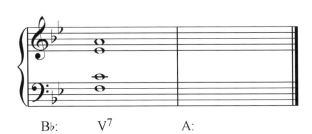

B♭: V⁷   A:

3. Analysis: Analyze the following two excerpts, both by Schumann.
   - Identify the keys, using both name and Roman numeral relation to tonic.
   - Provide functional (Roman numeral) harmonic analyses.
   - Circle and label nonchord tones.
   - Identify all cadences.
   - Label enharmonically reinterpreted chords in both keys.

A. Schumann, "Glückes genug" from *Kinderszenen*, op. 15, mm. 13–24
("Perfect Happiness" from *Scenes from Childhood*)

B. Schumann, Symphony no. 2, II

4. Figured Bass: Realize the figured bass in a four-voice chorale style (SATB), following the conventions of common-practice music. You may add any weak-beat dissonances you like, but circle and label any that you use.

- Bracket and label cadences.
- Below the system, identify the key of the exercise
- Perform a functional (Roman numeral) harmonic analysis.

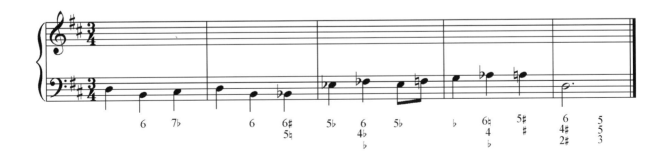

Third Relations

CHAPTER LEARNING OBJECTIVES

This chapter:

- Defines third relations
- Explains the voice leading in a third relation

In the prelude in figure 39.1, Chopin moves abruptly between distantly related keys, moving down a major third to the key of the lowered submediant. Although this modulation is sectional and no connection between chords is necessary, a logical relationship exists. It is known as a *third relation*, *mediant relation*, or *common-tone modulation*.

A third relation involves an abrupt key change in which, as implied by the name, the adjacent chords are related by a third. The harmony can move by major or minor third, up or down, so, assuming that the first chord is tonic, the second chord can be ♭VI, VI, ♭III, or III. (The term is reserved for chromatic relationships; motion between the tonic and the diatonic submediant fits within the norms of diatonic harmony.)

No functional connection exists in a mediant relationship; the tonal center suddenly changes. There is, however, a logic that sounds correct to our ears: smooth voice leading. One voice keeps a common tone throughout the key change, hence the name common-tone modulation. Two other voices move by step or half step. The bass usually moves by third, emphasizing the tonal shift. Figure 39.2 shows the four possible chord progressions. The tie shows the common tone. Note the smooth voice leading in the three upper voices.

The first is the most common. It works nicely, with the two voices moving by half steps in contrary motion. All of the progressions connect two major chords. Connecting a major and minor chord through a mediant relation causes the loss of the common tone or the creation of

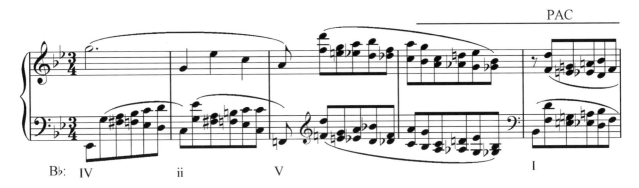

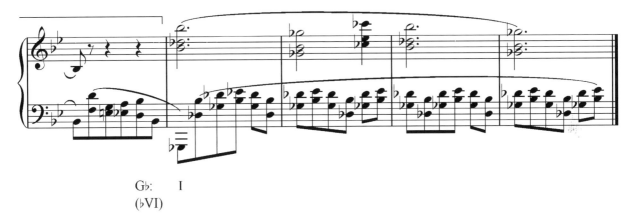

Figure 39.1 Chopin, Prelude in B♭, op. 28, no. 21, mm. 11–20

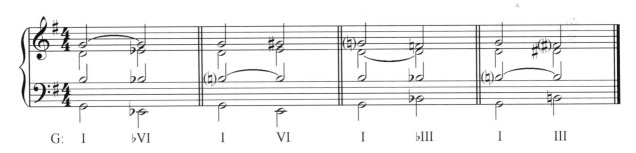

Figure 39.2 Possible common-tone progressions

a diatonic passage. It is possible to connect two minor harmonies through chromatic thirds (e.g., g-minor with e-minor), but these occur less frequently than with major triads. (See figure 39.4 for an example.)

While it is common for third relations to occur as a sectional modulation between tonic harmonies, as in the Chopin B♭ Prelude, they also can occur midphrase and between chords that are not tonic, as seen in figure 39.3, also by Chopin. The piece consists of three four-measure phrases. The second phrase, the one given here, is harmonically turbulent. The first key change, from E to C, involves a common-tone modulation. The second modulation, C to A♭, is a two-step process;[1] first Chopin writes a third relation to get to the A-major chord, and then he enharmonically reinterprets a fully diminished seventh. The last two chords of the excerpt, A♭ and B, which modulate back to E, also employ a common tone. (The C♭ and G♯ create the appearance of additional common tones, but they are nonchord tones. Removing these and reducing the passage leads to the typical voice leading.) A final observation: the three key areas evenly divide the octave into major thirds—E, C, and A♭. The two bold modulation techniques of enharmonic reinterpretation and third relations make any key available, so composers began exploring unusual harmonic structures, such as this one, in their forms.

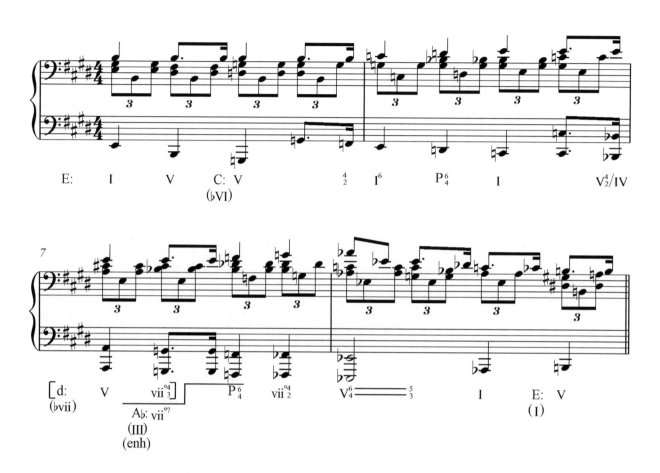

Figure 39.3 Chopin, Prelude in E, op. 28, no. 9, mm. 5–8

Mediant relations occur throughout the common-practice period, but they are rare until the Romantic era. By the end of the nineteenth century, however, composers used them extensively.

Strauss, one of the last Romantic composers, typifies the end of the common-practice era. The harmonic pattern in figure 39.4, which serves as the introduction to the song and continues throughout the first line, consists of alternating third relations. The passage is striking because it is not tonal. It is triadic, but not tonal. No dominant exists to point the way home. The submediant returns to tonic, which is not common-practice functionality. Harmonic function is gone; what is left is chords joined by smooth counterpoint.

Figure 39.4 Strauss, "Frühling" from *Vier letzte Lieder*, op. posthumous
("Spring" from *Four Last Songs*)

SUMMARY

Terminology

Mediant relation. An abrupt harmonic shift by a chromatic third. Synonymous with *third relation* and *common-tone modulation*.

Third relation. An abrupt harmonic shift by chromatic third. Synonymous with *mediant relation* and *common-tone modulation*.

Common-tone modulation. An abrupt modulation by chromatic third, in which one voice keeps a common tone and two others move by step or half step. Synonymous with *mediant relation* and *third relation*.

Mediant relations, third relations, and common-tone modulations are all names for the same pattern. In it, a key change occurs between two chromatic chords related by a third. The sound is an abrupt modulation to a remote key. The progression is not tonal; the aural logic comes from the smooth voice leading, which involves one common tone and two other voices moving by half step or step.

NOTE

1. The key of D-minor is a linear effect, which is why it appears in brackets. The two-step process described here is how the harmony moves, but there is no functional way to notate that with Roman numerals since it is between keys. The linear nature of the A-major chord is also evident from the fact that it is the middle chord in a voice exchange. The bass and the tenor swap the pitches G and B♭ from the last beat of measure 6 to the second beat of measure 7. This contrapuntal technique helps propel the progression while also providing coherence.

WORKBOOK

1. Analysis: Analyze the following excerpts.

   - Identify the key and provide functional (Roman numeral) harmonic analyses.
   - Circle and label nonchord tones.
   - Identify all cadences.
   - When you encounter the third relation, circle and identify the common tone, and use arrows to show the half-step motion in the other voices.

Falsely attributed to Beethoven, "Farewell to the Piano"

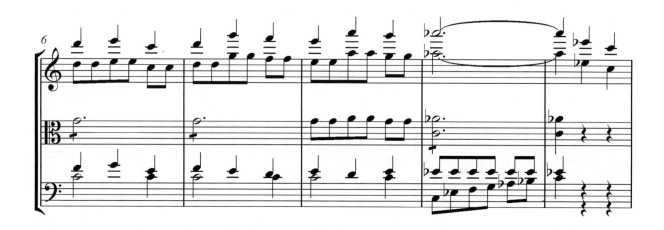

Schubert, String Quintet, D. 956, III, mm. 21–34

2. Third Relation Drill: Practice moving to all four keys accessible through common-tone modulations. For each exercise, move to the tonic in the new key using proper voice leading. Identify the key, including both name and Roman numeral relationship with the original key of D, and label the chord with a Roman numeral.

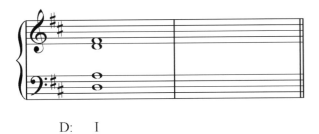

D: I

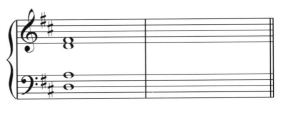

D: I

D: I

D: I

3. Figured Bass: Realize the following figured basses in a four-voice chorale style (SATB). You may add any weak-beat dissonances you like, but circle and label any that you use.

- Below the system, identify the key of the exercise.
- Perform a functional (Roman numeral) harmonic analysis.
- Bracket and label cadences.

A

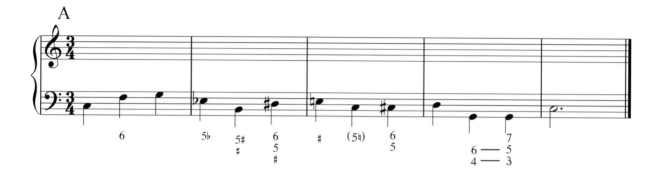

B

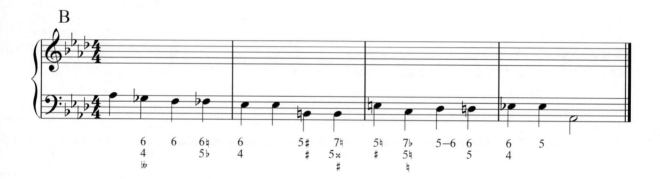

4. Composition: Compose a short work, approximately 24–32 measures, following the basic stylistic principles of the common-practice period. Choose a key other than C-major or A-minor. The piece should be in ternary form and incorporate chromatic color chords (mixture, Neapolitan, A6 chords, or altered dominants). The two keys should be distantly related (a chromatic third is convenient but is not required). One modulation may be a sectional modulation, but the other must be contained in a transitional passage.

Be musical with this. Include tempo, dynamics, and expression markings. Include an analysis with your piece. Identify the key, chords (Roman numerals), nonchord tones, and cadences. Below the harmonic analysis, do a phrase-level analysis. Also identify the parts of the form.

POPULAR MUSIC

This book will now drastically change focus. While the preceding chapters have all focused on common-practice music, the following chapters discuss popular music. This change is driven by several issues, but the most noteworthy are:

1. It will clarify and emphasize that music theory changes with the genre under discussion. Conventions are idiomatic to a specific style.

2. Many students are more familiar with popular music than with classical. The expansion into pop makes sense for their interests and to clarify how the common-practice material fits into this style.

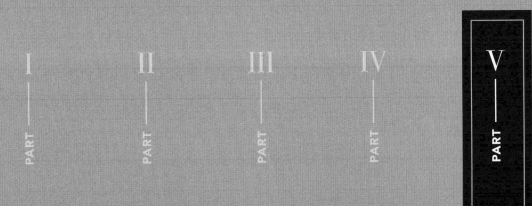

Introduction to Popular Music

CHAPTER LEARNING OBJECTIVES

This chapter:

- Delineates the upcoming chapters from the preceding ones
- Defines the common parts and sections of popular songs

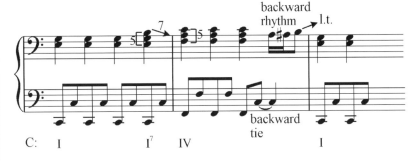

Figure 40.1 John Lennon, "Imagine"

Figure 40.1 shows the opening of John Lennon's "Imagine." In it, Lennon violates many of the stylistic traits that we have studied so far. In just two measures, he uses a I^7, resolves that seventh up instead of down, leaves a leading tone in an outer voice unresolved, writes parallel fifths, and uses both a backward rhythm and a backward tie. Can we conclude this is bad music?

Of course not. This song is one of the masterpieces of the rock era. In addition to being one of Lennon's most popular works, and in addition to the bumper stickers, T-shirts, and poster that follow such success, the song has become an important part of our contemporary culture. "Imagine" is sung every year at the Time Square New Year's festivities, immediately preceding the ball drop. After the 2015 Paris terrorist attacks, a German pianist chose to play this song in the street outside the theater where the main attack occurred. Clearly, it has struck a chord and resonates with many people.

In the "Student's Introduction," I emphasized that this book would discuss common-practice music, that is, music written by European composers during a 300-year time period. The focus will now switch to popular music. Several impetuses motivate this. First, many people today are more familiar with pop than they are with classical music; it is worth discussing such a common genre. Second, it clarifies the context of everything in the first 39 chapters. Acknowledging that there are other genres is one thing, but to discuss another one, even briefly, solidifies that the "rules" of music are not absolute. These generalizations characterize a particular style, and different types of music have different "rules." Third, the comparison of two different genres reinforces the stylistic traits of both.

Popular music is a broad term that sometimes includes jazz, show tunes, rock, disco, punk, rap, and more. This book will focus on songs that have received mainstream radio play over the last seventy years, appearing, for example, on Billboard's Top 40. Jazz will be mentioned briefly, but that style has its own well-established set of "rules" that can fill entire books; most schools offer a multisemester sequence of courses in jazz theory. Blues will be touched upon as a precursor to rock. The music under study here begins with Chuck Berry, Buddy Holly, and Elvis Presley and continues up to today.

In order to discuss pop songs, we need to define the terms that will indicate particular parts of a song. *Verses* are the sections where the melodic and harmonic material returns, but with different lyrics. The *chorus* is a section that returns with the same melody, harmony, and lyrics. It is usually the most ingratiating part of the song, and it usually contains the title in its lyrics. A *refrain* is a particular line that recurs throughout a song. It is like a chorus but is only a single line rather than a section. An example of a song containing a refrain is Simon and Garfunkel's "The Sound of Silence," in which each verse ends with a line with lyrics containing the title. Finally, a *bridge* is a section that provides contrast from the other parts of the song. Whereas the verses and chorus may use similar progressions, chords, or texture, a bridge will contrast in some way, such as by focusing on a new harmony or by changing the accompaniment. Bridges usually appear only once in a song.

Furthermore, since this book has focused on harmonic progressions and voice leading, it will continue in this vein. As a result, the popular music under investigation here is further restricted to songs that are constructed around a melody with a harmonic accompaniment. Hip-hop music that is built from looping a sample, rather than through a harmonic progression, is not discussed. Again, this is not a value judgment. The decision is based on being able to have a narrow enough category that generalizations can be made. In order to keep the overall book coherent, those generalizations revolve around harmony.

Having said that, rock music is about much more than harmony. A huge component is *timbre*, that is, the distinctive sound of the voices and instruments. Folk uses acoustic guitar while heavy metal uses a distorted electric. When discussing the Beatles' "Norwegian Wood," people usually comment on the inclusion of the sitar. In the 1970s, synthesizers became mainstream and changed the typical sound of pop. Another crucial element of popular music is lyrics. Many of the current analyses of pop focus on the words. Bob Dylan won the Nobel Prize for Literature for his lyrics, not his chords. Other components are rhythm and form. All of these elements can and should be discussed in examining popular music. Doing justice to all of them, however, would require additional books, not chapters.

Despite the lines that are drawn between hard rock, soft rock, R&B, and other pop subgenres (achieved through changes in instruments, effects, lyrics, and rhythm), the basic chord patterns underneath remain fairly consistent. This is what allows songwriters to work in different genres. The heavy metal band Kiss can incorporate disco in "I Was Made for Lovin' You" by the use of a different drum pattern, singing style, and a few other conventions. Taylor Swift can switch from country to pop fairly easily. Garth Brooks can cover Billy Joel's "Shameless."

Throughout the following study of popular music, the basic argument is that this genre employs a broad harmonic palette, created by pulling from and combining earlier styles. Musicians internalize all of the idioms that they frequently hear. Popular song composers have heard classical music and understand, at least intuitively if not intellectually, its conventions. They can pull on these gestures when they want. They can also utilize elements from jazz, blues, and any other genres that they know. In addition to these options, there are still other progressions that are exclusively idiomatic to pop.

Basically said, the classical harmonic progressions that we have studied (specifically those in use up to 1900) will still work in pop songs. Many textbooks use the occasional song to illustrate a classical function. To understand harmony in popular music, however, more gestures and different functions need to be understood. We will now look at these.

SUMMARY
Terminology

Verse. The section of a song that returns several times with the same music but different lyrics.

Chorus. The section of a song that returns several times with the same music and lyrics.

Refrain. In a song, a single line that recurs with the same music and lyrics.

Bridge. In popular songs, a sections that contrasts with the verses and chorus and that usually appears only once.

Timbre. The characteristic and distinctive sound of a particular instrument.

General Stylistic Elements

CHAPTER LEARNING OBJECTIVES

This chapter:

- Defines stylistic changes in parameters other than harmony, including

  o Rhythm

  o Harmonic rhythm

  o Counterpoint

  o Melody

Although the first section of this book emphasizes harmony and voice leading, understanding the common-practice style requires an appreciation of other facets of the music, such as common melodic and rhythmic gestures. The same is true for popular music. Although most of the chapters in this second section discuss harmony, presenting these other stylistic elements will help develop a deeper appreciation of the genre.

Also, although these traits will be described in terms of popular song, similar changes happened in all genres of Western music. Over the course of the common-practice era, composers gradually treated dissonances more freely, emphasized harmony over counterpoint, and loosened their rhythms relative to the meter. By the start of the twentieth century, the traits discussed in this chapter were appearing in classical and popular music.

RHYTHM

Rhythm in popular music is about syncopation. The standard backbeat in rock and roll clearly displays this trait, accenting beats 2 and 4 over the metrically strong beats 1 and 3 (figure 41.1).

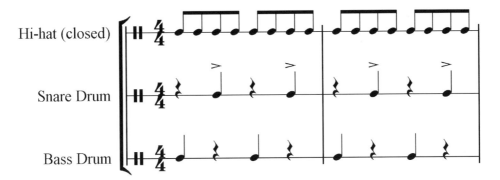

Figure 41.1 The standard backbeat

Although early rock and roll used syncopation in the drums to give energy to the music, by the late 1960s, musicians expanded rhythmic play to many components, not just the backbeat. Vocal lines became particularly fluid. Figure 41.2 shows the melody to Elton John's "Levon." It is rife with backward rhythms and backward ties. Subphrases do not end on the downbeat of a measure; rather, the vocal line arrives a sixteenth note before the next downbeat or continues moving until shortly after it. This melody does not reinforce the meter; it floats over and against it, keeping the music flowing and avoiding the squareness of excessive downbeats.

Figure 41.2 Elton John, "Levon"

Figure 41.3 shows the rhythm of the guitar in the opening of the Stone Temple Pilots' "Vasoline." This riff, which alternates F and G, implies a different meter than that of the song. The sixteenth–eighth note figure fits in 3/8, not 4/4. The pattern moves at a different rate than the other instruments, matching up every three beats, and not landing on beat 1 again for three measures, thereby creating tension and contributing to the uneasy feeling of the song.

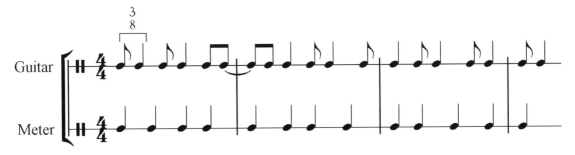

Figure 41.3 Rythmic interaction in Stone Temple Pilots, "Vasoline"

Songwriters also play with the harmonic rhythm. Figure 41.4 shows the basic accompaniment for Michael Jackson's "Billie Jean." The G#-minor chord arrives on the second half of beat 2, on a weak offbeat, and continues through the rest of the measure, contradicting common practice and the meter. The metrical accentuation is not completely destroyed, however. The downbeat of every measure has a harmonic change that lands directly on it, confirming the meter in the bigger picture. This constant emphasis on beat 1 enables the syncopation of the second harmony in each measure.

Figure 41.4 Michael Jackson, "Billie Jean"

The rhythm in "Billie Jean" is common in contemporary popular music, both for melodic gestures and for harmonic rhythm. Figure 41.5 shows three common rhythmic patterns. The first is called the "Bo Diddley Beat," named after Bo Diddley, who popularized it. It has been used numerous times throughout the rock/pop era, such as in the Who's "Magic Bus," George Michael's "Faith," and KT Tunstall's "Black Horse and Cherry Tree." It is usually a guitar rhythm played with a single chord. The other two rhythms are clearly related and are used both for the surface rhythm and for harmonic rhythm. The last is the rhythm used for the harmonic changes in "Billie Jean," although the chords are staccato rather than sustained.

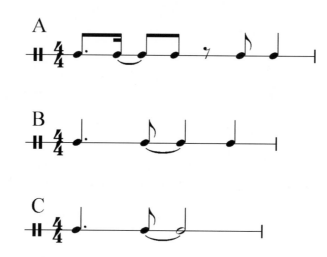

Figure 41.5 Common rhythmic patterns in rock and pop

All three patterns group smaller durations, either sixteenth or eighth notes, into sets of three, thereby creating the syncopation against the quarter-note pulse. All three also return to landing on the down beat in the next measure.

In "Beautiful Day," U2 creates an even more complicated harmonic rhythmic pattern (figure 41.6). It is based on the second pattern in figure 41.5, but it syncopates across the next bar line. It moves almost independently of the meter, but only for two measures. Every second measure has an arrival on the downbeat, and every fourth measure repeats the entire pattern. These two landings solidify the harmonic rhythm's relationship to the meter, allowing the other chord changes to syncopate against it.

Figure 41.6 U2, "Beautiful Day"

Although syncopation in the surface and harmonic rhythm are characteristic of contemporary popular music, not all pieces use it in the same way. The Beatles' "Let It Be" and Rhianna's "Stay" are the more effective for the straightforward quarter-note rhythms in the piano. The choice to use such techniques depends on the desired mood.

COUNTERPOINT

Texturally, most popular music is homophonic; the focus is a vocal melody with instrumental accompaniment. It is common, however, for musicians to add voices at important structural positions, such as in the chorus of a song.

Figure 41.7 shows two different levels of counterpoint in popular music. Both extract the vocal lines from the surrounding accompaniment. The first, Extreme's "More Than Words," displays the most typical pop vocal arrangement; the two voices move primarily in thirds. This texture is not about independent melodies. The goal of the additional voice is to increase the fullness of the sound. This additional voice comes in only at the chorus; the verses are sung solo. The second, the Beatles' "If I Fell," shows more intervallic contrast between the voices but no rhythmic differentiation. This song is also different in that the two voices sing together throughout the majority of the song. This is not the standard technique. In the mid-1960s, thick vocal textures were briefly popular, characterized by such bands as the Mamas and the Papas, the Seekers, the Association, the Beach Boys, and Free Design. True rhythmic and intervallic freedom between equal voices, such as in the final chorus of Paul McCartney's "Silly Love Songs," rarely occurs in pop. When it does occur, it is usually at the end, when two lines repeat and overlay with each other as the song fades out.

Extreme, "More than Words"

The Beatles, "If I Fell"

Figure 41.7 Different levels of counterpoint in rock and pop

Although popular music is not about counterpoint in the common-practice sense, pop composers focus a great deal on *layers* or, when recording, *tracks*. The accompaniment is usually realized with short *riffs* (short melodic ideas that repeat) and rhythmic patterns to give the song additional linear motion. Figure 41.8 shows the basic accompaniment patterns from Kelly Clarkson's "Miss Independent." The main *hook* (the most ingratiating riff in a song) in the guitar defines the main harmony as B while providing melodic interest. The percussion provides the syncopation within the measure, typical of the style. The bass is regular, defining the downbeats. This rhythmic pattern continues throughout the verses, with the bass and guitar transposing to E when the harmony changes.

Figure 41.8 Kelly Clarkson, "Miss Independent"

"Billie Jean" (figure 41.4) shows a similar layering of ideas to flesh out the accompaniment. The layers to this are the walking bassline and the first-inversion chords in the middle voice. The drums play a basic backbeat. This pattern continues as the voice sings the main melody over it.

The layers are stratified, usually being separated widely in register and timbre. "Miss Independent" has layers made of percussion, guitar, and voice. "Billie Jean" uses bass (albeit a synthesized bass), a midregister synthesizer, and voice. In addition, they usually have rhythmic independence that helps further separate them. Of course, they combine into a gratifying whole, the same way counterpoint does, but there is less blend than when writing for a choir, string quartet, or brass band.

In popular music, the harmony drives the lines. Often composers write the melody, lyrics, and chords, and then the accompaniment is realized in production. The goal is to write several riffs or rhythms that complement each other. Background vocals may be added. The only melody that typically spins out in a longer fashion is the main tune. Given the different focus, harmony over counterpoint, the common-practice rules of voice leading are not relevant in this style. But the general principle of creating a rich texture that contains both melodic and harmonic components still holds true.

As a reminder, popular music is a broad category that includes many styles. Not all songs are driven by riffs. Still, it is a common technique.

MELODY AND SCALES

Even though they are harmonically driven, pop melodies follow many common-practice conventions. Melodies are still mostly scalar. Stepwise motion is still most comfortable for the human voice. It also provides direction to the tune, and it can make a song more idiomatic to and playable on an instrument. Melodies use interesting rhythms, even if those rhythmic patterns are different from common practice. They often repeat motives, especially the hooks in the accompaniment.

Scale degree function and the scale in use, however, has not yet solidified. Tonic and the idea of a key is still relevant. Common chromatic pitches, however, lead to a question of if they are truly chromatic or if another scale is in play. For example, $\flat\hat{7}$ appears frequently in rock songs. If the subtonic replaces the leading tone throughout a song, is the music actually in the mixolydian mode rather than in major? (See Appendix C for information on the church modes.) A common argument about this is the song "Sweet Home Alabama" (figure 41.9). Most people hear it in D-mixolydian. Some, however, hear the song in G-major, with a progression that contains a retrogression. In *What to Listen for in Rock*, Ken Stephenson has an excellent example of the ambiguity in this progression.[1] The exact same progression is used at the same tempo in Lynyrd Skynyrd's "Sweet Home Alabama" and Warren Zevon's "Werewolves of London." (Kid Rock exploited this relationship nicely in "All Summer Long.") Due to the vocal emphasis on the pitch D in "Sweet Home Alabama" and on G in "Werewolves of London," Stephenson hears the exact same progression implying different tonal centers in the two songs.

Figure 41.9 Lynyrd Skynyrd, "Sweet Home Alabama"

As a result of this phenomenon, the definition of the scales in popular music is still open to debate. Some theorist argue that they are in the conventional major and minor scales, with chromatic pitches. Some argue that all pop is in mixolydian. Others argue that popular music employs a variety of scales, including major, minor, mixolydian, major pentatonic, minor pentatonic, blues, and more.

This book treats most pop songs as using the common-practice major and minor scales. While it is true that composers sometimes limit the pitches in a melody, the harmony almost always completes the full scale. For example, the melody of "Amazing Grace" uses only the pitches of the major pentatonic scale ($\hat{1}$, $\hat{2}$, $\hat{3}$, $\hat{5}$, and $\hat{6}$). The harmony, however, gives the missing two notes (figure 41.10). An analogous situation exists for the blues. Blue notes will be treated as chromatic embellishments of the major scale since both variants of those particular pitches (the lowered and diatonic forms) are often used together in the same piece. In Chapter 50, we will look at modal pop songs—songs that function in one of the church modes.

Figure 41.10 "Amazing Grace"

The popular music convention for Roman numerals is always to refer to the major key. In minor, the mediant and submediant chords are referred to as ♭III and ♭VI. This book will now switch to this convention.

SUMMARY

Terminology

Layers. In popular music, several melodic ideas used simultaneously to embellish a harmony, providing energy and some contrapuntal interest.

Tracks. In popular music, analogous to layers, but refers more to the recording process.

Riff. In popular music, a short melodic idea that repeats. A riff is usually instrumental.

Hook. In popular music, the most ingratiating riff in a song.

Rhythm in popular music emphasizes syncopation. It employs backward rhythms and groupings of three eighth or sixteenth notes to syncopate against the meter.

Both the surface rhythm and the harmonic rhythm are frequently syncopated.

Popular music still employs a sense counterpoint, but not in the common-practice sense. A harmonic progression is often realized by layering short, repeating melodic ideas. The harmony drives the layers.

Scales in popular music are still open to debate. This textbook will continue to refer to the major and minor scales.

Roman numerals will now indicate all harmonies relative to the major mode.

NOTE

1. Ken Stephenson, *What to Listen for in Rock: A Stylistic Analysis* (New Haven, CT: Yale University Press, 2002), 45.

WORKBOOK

1. Analysis: The openings of three pop songs follow. Discuss the surface and harmonic rhythms. Also examine the sense of melodic line, voice leading, and counterpoint contained in each example.

A. Coldplay, "Clocks"

B. Simon and Garfunkel, "Sound of Silence," vocal parts

C. Van Halen, "Jump"

Sonorities from Jazz
Stable Sevenths, Extended Tertian, and Added-Note Harmonies

CHAPTER LEARNING OBJECTIVES

This chapter:

- Defines sevenths as part of a stable chord
- Defines extended tertian harmonies
- Defines added-note and suspended-note chords

The basic harmonic sonority in the common-practice period was the triad, frequently destabilized through the addition of a seventh. Over the course of the era, composers treated dissonances more and more freely. By the early twentieth century, musicians began viewing the seventh as a consonant chord member. The seventh no longer requires a downward resolution; it requires no resolution at all. A melody can leap to or from a seventh. I^7 now exists, and jazz musicians frequently use it, even to end a piece.

The stability of the seventh happened as part of a larger change. Jazz and classical (specifically impressionist) composers added more notes to the basic triad. These additions were not intended to destabilize but rather to create a fuller, richer sound. Depending on the notes present, theorists categorize the chords as either extended tertian or added-note harmonies.

EXTENDED TERTIAN HARMONIES

By stacking additional thirds on top of a seventh chord, composers can create *extended tertian harmonies*. In order to qualify as extended tertian, the chords must include a seventh; the term implies an extension of the process of adding thirds. These sonorities are named after the overall interval between the root and the top note when the chord is stacked in thirds. Possible sonorities are the ninth, eleventh, and thirteenth.

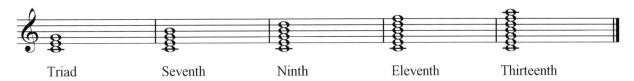

Figure 42.1 Extended tertian chords

Although these appear in common-practice music, they are rare. Appendix D has more information on extended tertian harmonies in that style. Most people associate the sound with jazz or show tunes. Simply turning a triad into a ninth chord evokes a stereotypical "jazz" sound. Play a C-major triad and then a Cmaj⁹ (as shown in figure 42.1) to hear the difference.

Identifying the quality of an extended tertian chord is analogous to that of seventh chords: it is a listing of the quality of the triad followed by those of the successive intervals. A dominant chord with a major ninth is a MmM9 chord. A tonic chord with a ninth is a MMM9. (See figure 42.2.) A huge variety of qualities exists. Considering there are four possible triad qualities (diminished, minor, major, augmented), three qualities for the seventh (diminished, minor, major), and three for the ninth (minor, major, augmented), 36 different ninth chords are possible. Eleventh and thirteenth chords have even more combinations. Only a handful are typically used though. Figure 42.2 shows the common diatonic qualities for ninth chords.

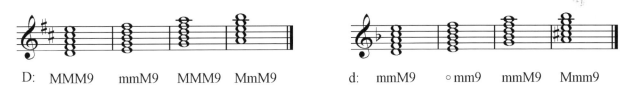

Figure 42.2 Common qualities for ninth chords

As mentioned in regard to chordal sevenths, jazz musicians view the entire extended tertian chord as a stable harmony. The desire was for a lush sound. There is no pull for a downward resolution to any of the notes stacked on top of the basic triad. All of the pitches can lead anywhere.

Extended tertian harmonies almost always appear in root position. With so many notes sounding, and with the availability of added notes (discussed presently), the root becomes ambiguous. When the chord is in an inversion, the ear can hear the new bass as the root. As a result, composers generally place these harmonies in root position. Or perhaps we hear them as being in root position.

Specifics on the different extended tertian chords follow.

Ninth Chords

Ninth chords are usually complete (see figure 42.2). Given the prominent use of piano and guitars in jazz, it is possible to have all five notes sounding simultaneously. When a chord member is omitted, it is the fifth. The root is necessary to identify the chord, the third clarifies the quality, the seventh allows for the extended tertian designation, and the ninth is required to make it a ninth chord.

Eleventh Chords

Eleventh chords, on the other hand, frequently omit the third. On a dominant or tonic chord in major, the eleventh forms a minor ninth (second) with the third, which creates a stark clash. (See figure 42.3.) When using an eleventh chord where this minor second would result, the third is often omitted. Another solution is to raise the eleventh by a half step. This change moves the clash, which now occurs between the fifth and the eleventh, but it also changes it from a minor ninth into a major seventh. The major seventh, while still a half step, is less pungent than the minor ninth. When using a raised eleventh, the fifth is sometimes omitted and sometimes retained. For harmonies in which the third and eleventh form a major second, it is possible to have a complete chord. (See figure 42.3.)

Common Eleventh Chords

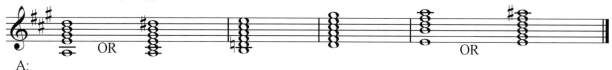

Figure 42.3 Eleventh chords

The minor ninth can appear in ninth chords in minor (figure 42.2). The harsh sound is more appropriate in this darker mode.

Thirteenth Chords

The thirteenth chord is the final extended tertian harmony since it includes all seven diatonic pitches. Given that there are so many pitches in the chord, composers frequently leave out some of them. The root, seventh, and thirteenth are essential to calling the chord a thirteenth chord. The third is also necessary, clarifying the quality of the chord. As a result, the eleventh is usually omitted to avoid the minor-second clash. The fifth, as always, is optional. The presence of the ninth depends on the voicing and the instruments involved. (See figure 42.4.)

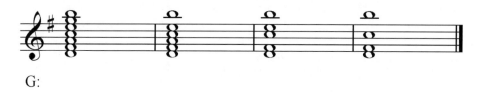

Figure 42.4 Thirteenth chords

ADDED NOTES

If the seventh of the chord is not present, pitches that are part of the harmony but not a part of the triad are called "added notes." Only three options are possible for added notes—the sixth, ninth, and fourth.

The most common added note is the sixth. The sound is typical of big bands (e.g., Glenn Miller and Count Basie) and of show tunes, especially ending a song on a tonic chord with an added sixth. The Beatles' song "She Loves You" concludes this way, but by the early 1960s the sound was dated. "'George Martin [their producer] laughed when we first played it to him like that,' said Paul [McCartney]. 'He thought we were joking. But it didn't work without it so we kept it in and eventually George was convinced.'"[1] It periodically appears in other positions in popular music. The Beatles use it with a less stereotypical sound in "The Fool on the Hill" (figure 42.5).

Figure 42.5 The Beatles, "The Fool on the Hill"

The added ninth, also referred to as the added second, is another jazz sonority that occasionally appears in pop music. The added fourth is uncommon, due to the half-step clash between the third and fourth in a major chord. The situation is analogous to the clash in an eleventh chord, and once again, the third is omitted. As a result, rather than calling this an added note, musicians call it a suspension. Suspensions omit the note of resolution while the suspension is sounding, so this label confirms that the third has been omitted. It is also possible to have a suspended second, in which the third is omitted, although this harmony is rare. (See figure 42.6.) Figure 42.7 shows a sus4 chord from the classic rock literature.

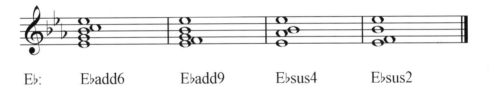

Figure 42.6 Added and suspended notes

Figure 42.7 The Who, "Pinball Wizard"

In jazz, the additional pitches from extended tertian harmony and from added notes do not affect function. Much of the harmony still follows a descending-fifth pattern, especially ii–V–I. Figure 42.8 shows the harmonic progression for Duke Ellington's signature piece "Take the 'A' Train," composed by Billy Strayhorn. Most of the piece follows standard common-practice harmonic function. The motion from D-major to D-minor is the reverse of the common-practice style, but other than that, function is as expected. The use of added notes and extended tertian chords, however, places the harmony clearly in the jazz idiom.

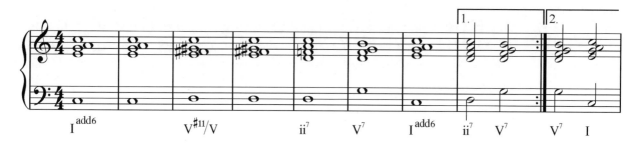

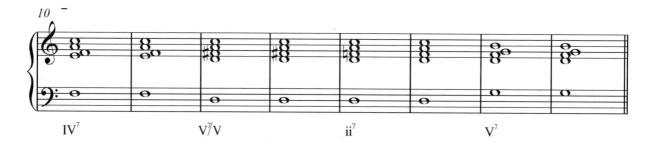

Figure 42.8 Duke Ellington, "Take the 'A' Train"

SUMMARY

Terminology

Extended tertian harmony. Chords that stack additional thirds on top of the seventh chord. Extended tertian harmonies include ninth, eleventh, and thirteenth chords.

Ninth chord. A harmony containing a seventh chord plus the pitch a ninth above the root.

Eleventh chord. A harmony containing a seventh chord plus the pitch a fourth above the root.

Thirteenth chord. A harmony containing a seventh chord plus the pitch a sixth above the root.

Added-note harmony. A pitch, usually a sixth or ninth above the root, added to a basic triad.

Sus chord. A harmony in popular music that includes an added fourth while omitting the third.

Extended tertian harmony results by stacking additional thirds on a seventh chord. The seventh must be present for the sonority to be considered extended tertian.

In popular music, the entire sonority is considered stable. No particular resolution is necessary.

Added notes result when a harmony contains a triad plus extra notes but the seventh is not present.

NOTE

1. Steve Turner, *A Hard Day's Write: The Stories behind Every Beatles Song* (New York: MJF Books, 2009), 48.

WORKBOOK

1. Analysis: Analyze the following excerpts from the musical theater genre. Identify the key and then provide common-practice functional (Roman numeral) labels. The keys correspond to the Ella Fitzgerald recordings of "Bewitched, Bothered, and Bewildered" and "It's All Right with Me" and the Shirley Bassey recording of "As Long as He Needs Me." Notice the prominence of harmonic motion by descending fifth in these excerpts.

A. Rodgers, *Pal Joey*, "Bewitched, Bothered, and Bewildered" - Second Phrase of Opening

B. Bart, *Oliver*, "As Long as He Needs Me" - Opening

C. Porter, *Can-Can*, "It's All Right With Me" - Ending

2. Progression Realization: Each staff has a progression written above it. On the staff, realize the progression, incorporating stable sevenths, extended tertian harmonies, and added notes. Voice the chords for piano. Although not required, feel free to craft a melody and to embellish the melody and harmony with nonchord tones. Remember that common-practice voice leading rules no longer apply, although smooth lines often make the music idiomatic and playable.

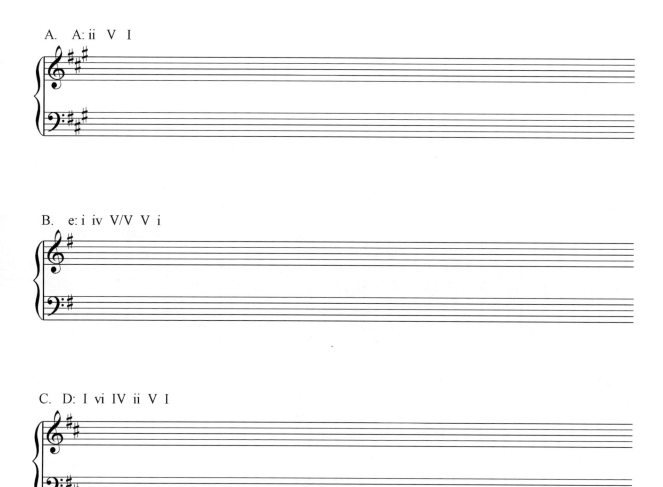

A. A: ii V I

B. e: i iv V/V V i

C. D: I vi IV ii V I

Lead Sheet Notation

CHAPTER LEARNING OBJECTIVES

This chapter:

- Defines lead sheet and chart notations
- Explains the notation for chords in this pop music shorthand

As discussed at the start of Chapter 17, musicians have shorthand notations for indicating music, especially the harmony. Baroque composers used figured bass. In the twentieth century, composers of popular music began using lead sheet or chord chart (also known as just "chart") notation.

Lead sheet notation gives a single staff with the main melody on it. Above that staff, the chords are written (e.g., F). *Chart* notation does not include the melody. It usually gives the lyrics with the chord names above them, requiring no music notation. (See figure 43.1.) (Sometimes chart will use a single staff to indicate the rhythm of a chord.) Although different, the two indicate chords the same way, which is the focus of this chapter.

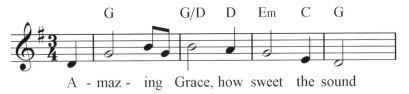

Lead Sheet

     G   G/D   D   Em   C   G

A - maz - ing Grace, how sweet the sound

Chord Chart

    G   G/D   D   Em   C   G
Amazing Grace, how sweet the sound

Figure 43.1 Lead sheet versus chart notation

As shown in figure 43.1, chords are indicated by their name, which corresponds to their root. Capital letters are used for all chords. The name alone indicates a major chord. For minor, the capital letter is followed by a lowercase *m* or "min." For diminished chords, "dim" is appended. For augmented chords, a + is added. (See figure 43.2a.)

There are some less common variants too. Minor can be indicated with a minus sign. This one is more common in jazz than in Top 40 pop songs. The classical notation of a small superscript circle can indicate diminished; "aug" may be used for augmented.

Chords are assumed to be in root position. If a note other than the root is in the bass, the bass note is indicated after a slash. F/A indicates an F-major chord in first inversion, while F/C indicates second inversion. Dissonances in the bass can also be indicated in this way. (See figure 43.2b.) Realize the harmonies in figure 43.1. The answer is in Chapter 41, figure 41.10.

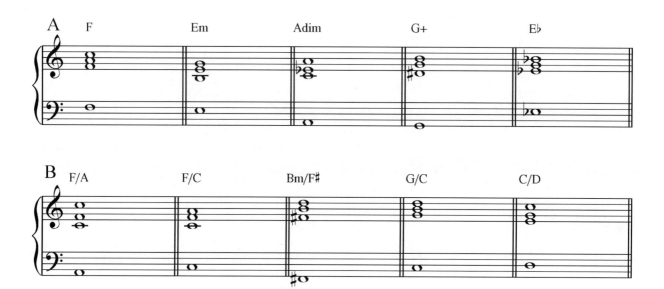

Figure 43.2 Triads in lead sheet notation

For seventh chords, the number 7 follows the chord name. The number may be the same size as the chord name, or it can be in superscript. The default quality for the seventh is a minor seventh. When attached to a major chord, it produces a dominant (major–minor) seventh harmony. On minor chords, the result is a minor–minor seventh sonority.

Other qualities need to be indicated. For major–major sevenths, "maj7" is added. A triangle is also sometimes used. Fully diminished sevenths are usually indicated with just "dim." Popular musicians are freer than classical ones with the distinction between the diminished triad and the fully diminished seventh chord. As a result, for half-diminished chords, the term "dim" no longer works. Instead, the half-diminished is notated as an altered minor triad. The quality of the seventh is correct, but the quality of the triad needs to be changed. Alterations to individual pitches can be achieved much like in figured bass, where the chord member is indicated with an alteration. Actual accidentals can be used, or more generally, a minus can be used to indicate a half-step lower while a plus indicates a half-step higher. A half-diminished seventh chord can be indicated with a 7–5. An augmented dominant seventh chord can either be indicated with a + and a 7, or with a 7+5. (The first option works if superscripts are used for the seventh. If the 7 is the same size as the chord name, the second method is clearer.) Figure 43.3 contains a variety of seventh chords.

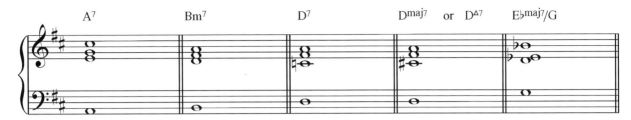

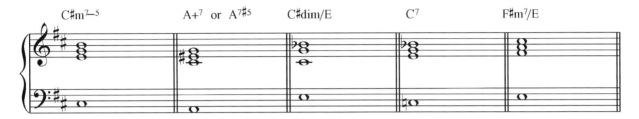

Figure 43.3 Seventh chords in lead sheet notation

Moving forward in this book, this convention for sevenths will hold for Roman numerals too. Any Roman numeral followed by a 7 will indicate a minor seventh. For example, I⁷–IV⁷–V⁷ contains chords that are all the same quality, major–minor sevenths. Deviations will have to be indicated with terms such as I^{maj7}.

As with seventh chords, extended tertian harmonies assume a minor seventh. The additional pitches (the ninth, eleventh, and thirteenth) are assumed to be diatonic in the key of the root. Any changes from these qualities are indicated by altering the individual chord members with minuses, pluses, or accidentals. Figure 43.4 shows a variety of extended tertian harmonies.

Figure 43.4 Extended tertian chords in lead sheet notation

Sometimes lead sheet notation will indicate a chord with a bass note that is a step above its root, for example F/G. While this could result from melodic motion in the bass, it frequently indicates an eleventh chord in which the third and fifth have been omitted. If the chord has a seventh on it, then the actual composite harmony is a thirteenth chord. The last example in figure 43.4 shows this situation.

For added notes, "add 6" or "add 9" is appended to the chord name. Often, the added sixth is shortened to just 6. In classical notation, this would indicate a first-inversion chord; in lead sheet, it indicates a root-position triad with an added sixth. For the added ninth, the "add" must be included to distinguish it from an extended tertian ninth chord.

For the suspended note, where the third is omitted, the term "sus" and the interval are appended after the root of the chord. The fourth is by far the most commonly suspended interval, so the number is sometimes left off and is just indicated by "sus." The suspended second requires the interval. Figure 43.5 shows examples of added notes and suspensions.

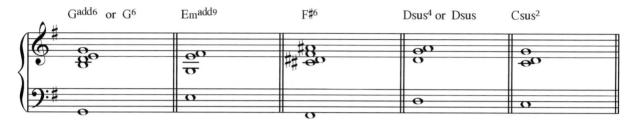

Figure 43.5 Added and suspended notes in lead sheet notation

Finally, idiomatic to hard rock, heavy metal, and punk is the power chord (figure 43.6). This is an open fifth played on the lower end of the guitar. Sometimes the upper octave is included. The notation for this is the number five after the chord name. Although open fifths sound hollow, power chords commonly use a lot of distortion. The distortion adds in overtones and extra frequencies, thereby producing a full and aggressive sound.

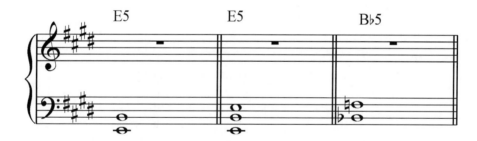

Figure 43.6 Power chords in lead sheet notation

SUMMARY

Terminology

Lead sheet notation. A notational system in popular music that uses a single staff for the melody with the chord names written above it.

(Chord) chart notation. A popular music notational system in which chord names are written above the song lyrics. Also called "chord chart."

Power chords. Guitar chords, common in hard rock, that use open fifths on the low strings of the guitar.

Lead sheet notation includes a staff with the melody and chords written above.
Chords are indicated by their name, corresponding to their root.
Capitals are always used for chords. The default quality is major. Other qualities are indicated by writing "min," "dim," or "+" after the chord name.

Root position is assumed. If a note other than the root is in the bass, it is indicated by writing the chord name, a slash, and that particular pitch.

For seventh chords, a seven is written after the note name. The default seventh is a minor seventh. Other qualities must be indicated by including the alterations.

Extended tertian chords work similarly to seventh chords.

Added notes and suspensions are also indicated by appending the terms to the chord names.

Power chords are written as the root note followed by a 5.

WORKBOOK

1. Lead Sheet Notation: In the first half of the exercise, you are given a chord voiced in notes on the staff. Above the system, identify the name of the chord in lead sheet notation. In the second half of the exercise, you are given the chord in lead sheet notation. Write the chord on the system below it.

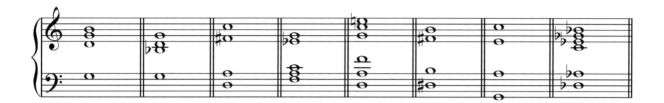

| E | C♯m/E | A^7 | Am^9 | A^5 | Gm^{maj7} | Bdim/D | E♭+/G |

| A♭^{11} | Dm$^{7♭5}$ | C^{13} | C^{13maj7} | E^{Δ7} | B♭sus^2 | B♭add2 | A♭^{7}/B♭ |

2. Realize Lead Sheet: The following excerpts, all from the beginnings of the songs, are written in lead sheet notation. On the grand staff below the lead sheet, write out the chords. Below the system, identify the key and provide a functional Roman numeral analysis.

A. The Beatles, "I Will"

B. Elton John, "Blue Eyes"

C. Elvis Costello, "Veronica"

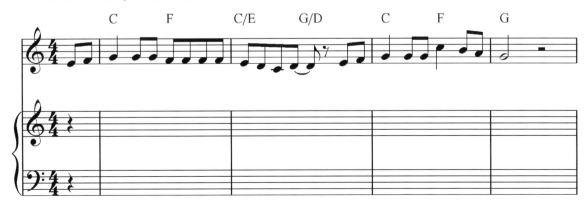

Pop Progressions Following Classical Diatonic Functions

CHAPTER LEARNING OBJECTIVES

This chapter:

• Examines several pop song progressions that follow common-practice harmonic function

As discussed in chapter 40, the introduction to this section, popular music pulls from a number of earlier genres and styles. Pop theory is more about plurality than one single harmonic hierarchy.

Common-practice music is one of those earlier styles with which pop musicians are familiar. As a result, many pop songs follow classically functional patterns. As a reminder, the root determines function; sevenths, extended tertian pitches, added notes, suspensions, and power chords do not. All of the songs in this chapter use either basic triads or seventh chords, which is typical of pop. The use of extended tertian harmonies with these progressions happens frequently but is more characteristic of jazz.

T → PD → D → T

Everyone has heard that rock songs consist of only three chords—I, IV, and V. While this is patently not true, many songs do limit themselves, or at least a subsection of the song, to these three chords. Of these, a number even use the common-practice functions for the chords—T, PD, and D (table 44.1)

Table 44.1 does not contain any metrical or phrase-level information. For example, "Heartbreak Hotel" has one iteration of its progression over the course of the verse and refrain. The verse is all tonic harmony, and the refrain moves IV–V–I. "My Life" contains the exact same progression, but it happens twice in each verse. The first phrase moves I–IV and the second moves V–I. This then repeats for the third and fourth phrases.

TABLE 44.1	Pop Songs Using Common-Practice Harmonic Functions	
Song	**Performer(s)**	**Progression**
"Heartbreak Hotel"	Elvis Presley	I⁷–IV⁷–V⁷–I
"My Life" (verses)	Billy Joel	I–IV–V–I
"Save the Last Dance for Me" (verses and refrain)	The Drifters	I–V–I–IV–I–V–I
"Act Naturally" (verses)	The Beatles	I–IV–I–V–I–IV–V–I
"I Wanna Be Sedated"	The Ramones	I–IV–I–IV–I–V–I–V–I–V–I–IV–V
"Tubthumping" (verses)	Chumbawamba	I–IV–I–IV–I–IV–V
"Istanbul, Not Constantinople" (verses)	Four Lads They Might Be Giants	i–V⁷–i–iv–i–V⁷–i–V⁷–i
"Istanbul, Not Constantinople" (chorus)	Four Lads They Might Be Giants	i–ii⁷–V–i–V⁷–i–V⁷–i

For the time being, the focus is on functionality—which chord leads to which. From that angle, the chart is clear that all of these songs use common-practice patterns. The pre-dominant chords either lead to dominant or return to tonic. All of the songs end with authentic cadences, except for "I Wanna Be Sedated" and "Tubthumping," which end with half cadences. In both of those songs, the dominant chord resolves into tonic at the beginning of the next phrase. All of these songs follow the basic pattern of moving to V and then resolving to tonic.

The chart reveals two changes from common practice though. First, pop songs use IV as the main pre-dominant chord, whereas in classical music the ii is more common. Since popular music does not involve the same voice-leading ideals—specifically, no prohibition against parallel fifths—IV can move to V as easily as ii can. IV became the default pre-dominant in the pop genre. In the same way, since parallel fifths are now usable, ii can return to and prolong tonic harmony. Although using the supertonic as a neighbor chord to tonic is not as common as using the subdominant, it happens with more frequency in pop songs than in classical music.

Second, vii° rarely substitutes for V. In general, pop does not use diminished chords. They appear sporadically, much like the iii chord in classical music. It is not that they never appear, but they are so infrequent that it is hard to make any broad statement about them. Musicians use V instead of vii° and, in minor, iv instead of ii°.

Both of the preceding differences are about pop songs—Top 40 hits. Jazz still relies on ii as the principal pre-dominant, and it employs diminished chords more frequently.

I–VI–IV–V

Figure 44.1 shows a progression that enjoyed immense popularity for a decade and which still appears periodically. This specific pattern became associated with doo-wop music in the late 1950s and was the basis of a number

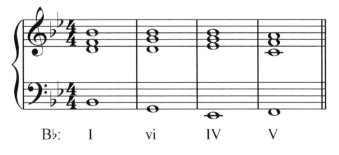

Figure 44.1 Typical doo-wop progression

of hits until the mid-1960s. (In *The Foundations of Rock*, Walter Everett has an excellent graph showing the spike in the use of the progression at this time.)[1] In doo-wop, the pattern repeats throughout much of the song, with one cycle corresponding to each phrase. A phrase opens on tonic and ends on dominant; the dominant resolves with the beginning of the next line.

In terms of common-practice use, one of the submediant's most common functions is leading to pre-dominant harmonies. This is an embellishment of the basic T–PD–D pattern by inserting the submediant between the tonic and subdominant. The chord smoothly connects the two harmonies because of the common tones it shares with each. (See Chapter 24 for more information on this use of the submediant chord, and see figure 26.1 for an example of it from the classical literature, although in that instance vi connects to the classically more common ii.)

Table 44.2 includes a number of songs, both doo-wop and more recent, that use this progression. Substitutions of ii in place of IV are included since this happens in both the classical and popular genres.

TABLE 44.2	Songs Using the Doo-Wop Progression	
Song	**Performer(s)**	**Progression**
"You Send Me"	Sam Cooke	I–vi^7–ii^7–V
"Stand By Me"	Ben E. King	I–vi–IV–V
"Sherry" (chorus)	The Four Seasons	I–vi–ii–V
"I Will" (opening line only)	The Beatles	I–vi^7–ii^7–V^7
"Crocodile Rock" (fade out)	Elton John	I–vi–IV–V
"Baby"	Justin Bieber	I–vi–IV–V
"Dear Future Husband"	Meghan Trainor	I–vi–IV–V

Some of the later songs, such as "Crocodile Rock" and "Dear Future Husband," intentionally imitate the doo-wop sound, but "Baby" uses the progression without any reference to earlier styles. "I Will" also does not reference doo-wop, but the pattern is just the first few chords of a much longer phrase with other harmonies.

Some songs use this progression with small adjustments. For example, the Police's "Every Breath You Take" uses the pattern I–vi–IV–V–vi–V. In this song, one statement of the progression lasts for the entire verse. Sting resolves the dominant at the end of the phrase instead of at the start of the next line; the harmony moves deceptively to avoid closure. Although not used with the same phrase structure as a doo-wop song, the progression is almost identical. The chorus of R. City's "Locked Away" (Adam Levine's part) uses the basic pattern with a tonic chord inserted between the subdominant and dominant: I–vi–IV–I–V. While it is not identical to the doo-wop progression, it clearly is related to it.

Weezer's "Island in the Sun" also uses this cycle but shifts the starting and ending points to create a different progression. Instead of beginning on I and ending on V, they begin on vi and cadence on the tonic: vi–ii–V–I. This pattern brings the motion by fifth to the fore rather than the motion by descending third. Although it uses the same chords, it is not the doo-wop pattern. And this statement returns us to the basic point of the chapter: Although R. City varies the pattern and Weezer creates a new progression with the chords, all of these songs employ common-practice functionality.

PACHELBEL'S CANON AND I–V–VI–IV

Most musicians have probably seen Rob Paravonian's "Pachelbel Rant" and Axis of Awesome's "Four Chords." If you have not, go watch them on YouTube now.

Pachelbel

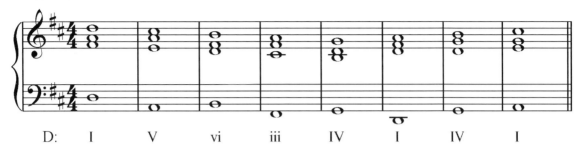

Axis of Awesome

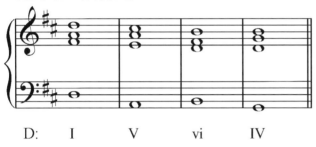

Figure 44.2 Pachelbel, Canon in D, and Axis of Awesome, "Four Chords"

These skits contain some truth and some slights of hand. First, the Pachelbel progression, a sequence by descending third, is not common but does occasionally happen in pop music. Examples from "Pachelbel Rant" are Vitamin C's "Graduation" (which quotes Pachelbel in order to evoke a graduation), the Original Caste's (or Coven's) "One Tin Soldier" (verses), and Blues Traveler's "Hook." In addition, Green Day's "Basket Case" and Aerosmith's "Cryin'" shorten the progression by one chord.

Pachelbel's Canon, "Graduation," "One Tin Soldier," "Hook"	I–V–vi–iii–IV–I–IV–V
"Basket Case," "Cryin'"	I–V–vi–iii–IV–I–V

For most of the other songs in Paravonian's skit, however, he usually breaks off from the pop song and begins singing Pachelbel again by the time the music would reach the iii chord. Most of the songs move to IV at that point. Axis of Awesome uses this pattern:

Awesome   I–V–vi–IV

Although the two skits do not use identical progressions, significant overlaps exist. I–V–vi–IV is a common pop pattern. Some of the songs that the routines reference use those chords as part of a larger progression that moves somewhere else after sounding the pattern. For example, the Beatles' "Let It Be" opens with this progression but continues to other chords over the phrase. Others repeat the pattern during the verses (Train's "Hey Soul Sister") or the chorus (Men at Work's "Land Down Under"). And some use the progression throughout the song, such as U2's "With or Without You" and Green Day's "When I Come Around." Other examples abound.

BIG PICTURE

The specific progressions in this chapter are not the only pop progressions that follow classical conventions. They are some common ones, presented to illustrate that common-practice functionality is not irrelevant in pop. The first section, on T → PD → D → T, has more of the intended tone, which is not that I, IV, and V have to appear in a certain order but rather that everything already discussed in this book is still relevant. In pop, however, these stylistic conventions do not hold ultimate authority like they do in the common-practice era. Common-practice music is one of several genres that have influenced pop. All common-practice functional progressions make sense in pop music. The reverse is not true; not all pop music progressions make sense in terms of common-practice conventions.

SUMMARY

Common-practice harmonic functionality still makes sense in current pop music. Chords *may* still proceed in typical classical music progressions. Due to the influence of other genres, however, they are not required to do so. Here are the conventional functions:

- Tonic is the point of rest.
- Dominant contains the most tension.
- Pre-dominants either move to dominant or return to (prolong) tonic harmony.
- Submediant usually connects I to IV or ii, and although not discussed here, it also can still move to V or be used deceptively.

But unlike classical roles, in pop music

- IV is more common than ii.
- Diminished chords are rarely used.
- V is the only dominant-function chord, practically speaking.

NOTE

1. Walter Everett, *The Foundations of Rock* (New York: Oxford University Press, 2009), 220.

WORKBOOK

1. Lead Sheet Analysis: The following two excerpts are from the openings of their respective songs. Analyze each. Beneath the staff, identify the key and provide Roman numerals to show how the harmonies follow common-practice roles.

A. The Beatles, "Golden Slumbers"

B. Imagine Dragons, "Demons"

2. Score Analysis: The following two excerpts show the openings of two songs. Analyze each. Beneath each system, identify the key and provide Roman numerals to show how the harmonies follow common-practice functions.

A. Toby Keith, "I Wanna Talk About Me"

B. Coldplay, "Viva la Vida"

Blues and the Retrogression

The genre of music that most influenced early rock and roll was the blues. This style emerged circa 1900 in the American South. It grew from and contains elements of African music and American spirituals. Like jazz, it has a rich history and is still popular today, with numerous books written about it. This chapter will give a brief introduction to its harmony and its influence on rock and roll and later popular songs.

MELODIC INFLUENCE: BLUE NOTES AND THE BLUES SCALE

The important melodic influence from blues is the use of blue notes. *Blue notes* are pitches that have been flatted relative to the major scale, used as an expressive coloration to a melody. They do not replace the diatonic scale degree in the major key; rather, they appear occasionally to contrast with it, as in figure 45.1. The verse of "All That Jazz" uses E♮ throughout until the cadence, which employs the blue note E♭. Their use as melodic ornamentation sometimes leads to a clash between the diatonic pitch in the accompaniment and the blue note in the voice (as in figure 45.2). This harmonic clash occurs between the third of the chord and is called a *split third*. It can occur within a single instrument, such as a piano chord, but the flatted note usually appears on top, given its melodic origins. This also voices the split third as a major seventh and not a minor ninth.

Figure 45.1 Kander, *Chicago*, "All That Jazz," end of verse

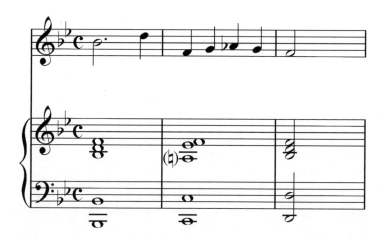

Figure 45.2 Gershwin, *Porgy and Bess*, "Bess, You Is My Woman Now"

Blue notes appear on scale degrees $\hat{3}$, $\hat{7}$, and occasionally $\hat{5}$. Some theorists use them to create the *blues scale*. Several different blues scales have been suggested. One option includes the blue notes and omits the diatonic analogs $\hat{3}$, $\hat{5}$, and $\hat{7}$. My preference is for the model that incorporates both forms (see figure 45.3) since both occur in the music. Also, I use only the two frequently occurring blue notes on $\hat{3}$ and $\hat{7}$.

Figure 45.3 Blues scale

HARMONIC INFLUENCE: TWELVE-BAR BLUES, SEVENTH CHORDS, AND RETROGRESSIONS

The most famous standard progression, definitely for the blues and perhaps in general, is the twelve-bar blues, shown written for the guitar in figure 45.4. Other blues progressions exist, as do variations of the twelve-bar blues, but the one shown is the most common. Examples of blues songs that use this progression are Robert Johnson's "Sweet Home Chicago" and "Cross Road Blues." (Both of these songs use a variation of the progression in which the second measure is the subdominant. The basic pattern is still clear.) Some rock and pop songs that use it are Little Richard's "Tutti Frutti," Elvis Presley's "Hound Dog," Chuck Berry's "Maybellene" (chorus), the Beach Boys' "Barbara Ann," the Beatles' "Birthday," and Tracy Chapman's "Give Me One Reason." It has appeared on the charts as recently as summer/fall 2015 in 5 Seconds of Summer's "She's Kinda Hot."

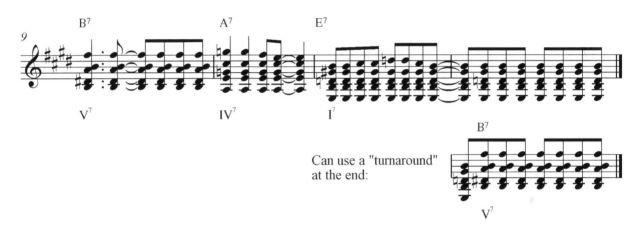

Figure 45.4 Twelve-bar blues progression on guitar

The first noteworthy aspect of this progression is the role of the major–minor seventh chord. All of the major chords have minor sevenths on them. In common-practice music, all of these harmonies would function as dominants and resolve accordingly. Here, however, they are seen as stable sonorities, functioning according to their root. Many rock songs end on a I⁷, for example, Pat Benatar's "Hit Me with Your Best Shot." In classical music, seventh chords on different scale degrees would have different qualities. The Roman numeral of a chord implies its quality; a IV⁷ is understood to be a major–major chord. Jazz also employs a wider variety of seventh-chord sonorities, although the major–minor seventh is the most common. In blues and rock, however, every harmony can be, and often is, a major–minor seventh chord. In these genres, I⁷, IV⁷, and V⁷ all imply major–minor chords. The presence of these minor sevenths on the I and IV chord also reinforce the choice of including L3̂ and L7̂ in the blues scale in figure 45.3.

The second significant characteristic of the blues is that it contains a retrogression. Rather than resolving to tonic, the dominant chord returns to the subdominant, which then cadences to tonic. The larger ramification of this is that the basic structures of classical music and blues differ. On the phrase level, classical music is about the motion I–V–I, while blues songs are about I–IV–I. Classical music usually uses half and authentic cadences. The blues uses plagal cadences. As a result, the subdominant and dominant chords change roles. In classical music, the IV functions as a pre-dominant, leading to V. In the blues, and many pop songs, the V functions as a "pre-subdominant," leading to IV. ("Pre-subdominant" is not standard terminology.)

This situation does not imply that in some genres IV contains more tension than V. The tension of the leading tone and the dominant chord's pull to tonic still exist. When the turnaround is included in the twelve-bar blues, it clearly points back to tonic (see figure 45.1). The significance has more to do with the feeling of the music. The classical structure is more goal oriented, while the blues progression is more an alternation of two harmonic levels; it emphasizes the neighboring motion of IV.

The important contribution of the blues in contemporary pop songs is that IV can now be the structural goal harmony; this, in turn, permits retrogressions. The following songs do not follow a blues progression, but they feature a prominent V → IV motion: the Young Rascals' "Good Lovin'," the Who's "Baba O'Reilly," Michael Jackson's "Man in the Mirror," and Bruno Mars's "The Lazy Song." The retrogressions in them show their indebtedness to the blues.

Although the common pop progression of I–V–vi–IV follows common-practice function on a chord-by-chord level, the phrase level belies its pop context. In the big picture, the phrase moves I → IV and then uses plagal motion to return to the start of the pattern. While this could occur in classical music, it is uncommon. A common-practice composer would probably attach a V to the end, giving I–V–vi–IV–V, providing the goal harmony in that genre.

The reverse is true too: a progression that contains a retrogression can still have a structural dominant chord. Some chord patterns are ambiguous. Compare the two progressions in figure 45.5. In terms of harmonies, the two progressions are identical, but considering the rhythm, they emphasize different chords on the phrase level. In "I Need a Lover," the retrogression moves to a neighbor chord that then returns to the V. The structural harmony here is the dominant. In "Let My Love Open the Door," however, the shorter durations of the V chords place the emphasis on the IV. Here, the structural harmony is the subdominant. The second dominant chord feels like an ornament on the basic pattern that Townshend had previously used in "Baba O'Reilly."

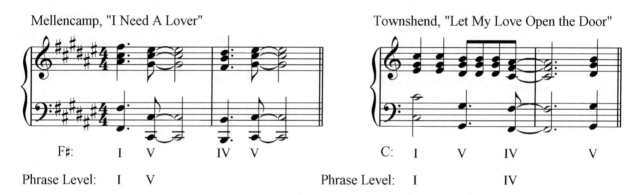

Figure 45.5 Same progression, different structural harmonies

The two influences, classical and blues, have mixed so that songs can freely borrow chord functions from either genre. IV can lead to V, or V can lead to IV. The verse of a song can have one phrase-level focus while the chorus has another. Popular music is not a binary system, where the progressions follow either classical norms or the twelve-bar blues. Harmonic functions have broadened to include both of the earlier styles.

SUMMARY

Terminology

Blue note. A melodic ornament, common in blues, where a pitch is flatted relative to the diatonic pitch. Blue notes usually fall on scale degrees $\hat{3}$ or $\hat{7}$ and occasionally on $\hat{5}$.

Split third. A sonority in jazz and the blues in which a harmony contains two thirds, both the diatonic pitch as well as its flatted blue note analogue.

Blues scale. The scale created by combining the pitches that frequently occur in blues songs; the major scale plus the blues notes $L\hat{3}$ and $L\hat{7}$.

The blues influenced later popular music in three ways:

1. Major–minor seventh chords are now the most common nontriadic harmony. They do not function as dominants; they are stable sonorities that can appear on any scale degree.

2. IV can be the phrase-level harmonic goal. I–IV–I can be the structural underpinning for a song.

3. Retrogressions, with V leading to IV, are possible.

Harmonies in popular music have broader, less defined functions.

WORKBOOK

1. Lead Sheet Analysis: The following two excerpts, notated in lead sheet, are from the first lines of their respective songs. Analyze each. Beneath the staff, identify the key and provide Roman numerals to show how the harmonies use retrogressions.

A. Tommy James and The Shondells, "Crimson and Clover"

B. The Ramones, "My Head is Hanging Upside Down (Bonzo Goes to Bitburg)"

2. Score Analysis: The following excerpts, notated on the grand staff, show the openings of two songs. The guitar accompaniment to the verses of "Soak Up the Sun" is also given. (Although "Soak Up the Sun" is played on guitar, it is notated here on the grand staff at pitch.) Analyze each. Beneath each system, identify the key and provide Roman numerals to show how the harmonies use retrogressions.

A. The Beatles, "Let It Be"

B. Sheryl Crow, "Soak Up the Sun," Intro

Verses

Mediant and Ascending Thirds

CHAPTER LEARNING OBJECTIVES

This chapter:

- Explains the three common functions of the mediant
- Examines motion by ascending third

Figure 46.1 compares the original harmonization of the melody "Plaisir l'amour" (Martini, 1784) with that of Elvis Presley's "Can't Help Falling in Love" (Weiss/Peretti/Creatore, 1961). (Despite the differences in the first three notes, they are the same melody. After this point, the two continue almost identically. Also, the Elvis version has been transposed for ease of comparison.) The first one follows common-practice expectations, with I–V–I. While the same harmonies could have been used in the second arrangement, they are not. Instead, a iii chord appears in the second measure, belying the pop music context.

In popular music, the iii chord occurs with some frequency. The mediant is not nearly as common as tonic, subdominant, or dominant. It is slightly less common than vi, but it is more common than vii°. It occurs enough that, unlike in a classical context where it rarely occurs (see Chapter 25), theorists can ascribe three characteristic functions to it.

"Can't Help Falling in Love" displays one of the two most common functions: moving to vi. The motion by fifth down, of course, sounds good. Some pop songs employing motion from iii to vi include the Beatles' "Can't Buy Me Love" and "Day Tripper," Tommy James and the Shondells' "I Think We're Alone Now," and Cat Stevens's arrangement of "Morning Has Broken."

When the iii appears in second inversion, it functions as a passing chord, with the bass moving stepwise from $\hat{1}$ to $\hat{6}$. Figure 46.2 gives the pop analysis of figure 28.3, which illustrated the passing nature of the harmony. In this context, the chord can serve as a variant for the common

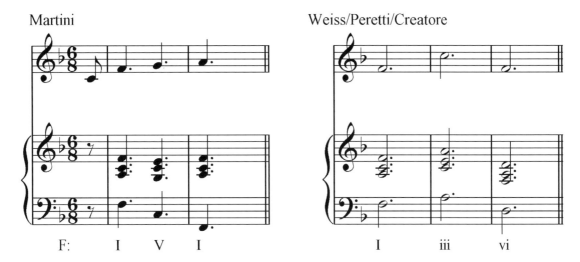

Figure 46.1 Comparison of "Plaisir l'amour"

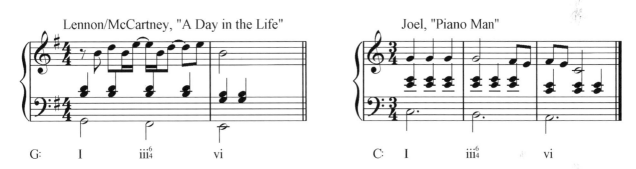

Figure 46.2 Passing second-inversion iii chords

I–V–vi pattern (used in the "Pachelbel Rant" and "Four Chords" routines) with the iii substituting for the V. For example, "Piano Man" could have been harmonized with a V for the second chord. The use of the passing iii gives a nicer sense of traditional counterpoint than a root-position V, although a first-inversion V would work equally well.

Another common use of the mediant is to move by step up to IV. Just as V can serve as a "pre-subdominant," so can the iii. Figure 46.3 shows an example. Elton John is particularly fond of this use of the mediant, using the progression I–iii–IV in the songs "Crocodile Rock," "Sorry Seems to Be the Hardest Word" (in minor—i–III–iv), "I Guess That's Why They Call It the Blues," and "Nikita." It also appears in the the Seekers' "Georgy Girl" and the chorus of Kelly Clarkson's "Since U Been Gone."

Figure 46.3 Peter, Paul and Mary, "Puff, the Magic Dragon"

As we saw in classical music, it is common for chords a third apart to substitute for each other. In both of these cases, iii serves a similar function as V. I–V–vi becomes I–iii–vi, and I–V–IV becomes I–iii–IV.

The third function of the submediant chord is connecting to the dominant. This is not as common as the first two functions, but it happens. An example is given in figure 46.4. Here the ♭III replaces the tonic harmony that is expected at the end of the phrase. It then moves to dominant, which leads to the i that begins the next phrase.

Figure 46.4 The Beatles, "Girl"

MOTION BY ASCENDING THIRD

Figures 46.1, 46.2, and 46.3 also show the most common approach to the iii chord: from tonic. The mediant can be approached by almost any chord; sometimes IV leads to it, sometimes ii, and sometimes V. But I is the typical choice.

As discussed in Chapter 25, in common-practice music, motion by third down is strong (I–vi–IV–ii–vii°–V) but motion by ascending third is not. This limitation does not hold in popular music. Motion by ascending third has become an option and, although not ubiquitous, happens with regularity. For example, the entirety of the Isley Brothers' "Shout" alternates between I and vi. The motion iii → V discussed in the last section is motion by ascending third. Figure 46.5 shows examples of chords moving up by third. Tonic to mediant appeared in the three previous examples. V → vii° and vii° → ii are ignored since vii° is a rare chord. In common-practice music, all of this motion would be treated as a change from a root-position triad to a first-inversion seventh chord; ii moving to IV would be a ii⁷. Pop musicians view it as a change in harmony.

SUMMARY

The mediant chord occurs with some regularity in popular music.
It is frequently approached from tonic.
It usually leads to IV or vi.
It also moves to V.
Motion by ascending third, while not the most common motion, occurs in popular music. Any chord can move to the harmony a third above it.

ii - IV: Elton John, "Your Song" (end of verse)

iii - V: The Beatles, "She Loves You" (verses)

IV - vi: The Killers, "Mr. Brightside" (chorus)

vi - I (and IV-vi): Dave Mathews Band, "Ants Marching" (chorus - second and third time)

Figure 46.5 Motion by ascending third

WORKBOOK

1. **Lead Sheet Analysis:** The following three excerpts, notated in lead sheet, are from the first lines of their respective songs. Analyze each. Beneath the staff, identify the key and provide Roman numerals to show the role of the iii chord and motion by ascending third.

A. The Pretenders, "I'll Stand By You"

B. Dexys Midnight Runners, "Come On Eileen"

C. Billy Joel, "A Matter of Trust"

Supertonic, Linear Harmonic Motion, and Diatonic Summary

CHAPTER LEARNING OBJECTIVES

This chapter:

- Reviews the three pop music functions of the supertonic chord
- Examines harmonic motion along the scale
- Summarizes harmonic function in popular music

Several chapters in this book serve to fill in gaps or to provide a summary of the material so far. This is one of those chapters. First, it will restate the functions of the supertonic chord. These roles have already been defined in other chapters, but always in relation to some other chord (e.g., the ii can substitute for the subdominant in the doo-wop progression). Here they will be defined explicitly for the ii chord. Then it will introduce harmonic motion along the scale. And finally, it will summarize diatonic functions in popular music.

SUPERTONIC

The supertonic chord appears with a regularity similar to the iii chord. In minor, since it is diminished, it almost never occurs. It is not as common as the I, IV, V, or vi, but it is frequent enough that it has a few characteristic functions. Its principle functions are the following:

1. Move to V
2. Move to IV
3. Move to I

First, common-practice functions still work. The ii can move to V. In popular music, the IV and the ii have switched priority from that in classical music. In the common-practice style, the ii was stronger and more common, and occasionally the subdominant would substitute for it. In rock and pop, the IV is the more prevalent harmony; the ii may substitute for it. Examples of ii serving its traditional pre-dominant function are in Chapter 44 on common-practice functions.

This swapping of the relevance of the two pre-dominants explains the second function of the supertonic—moving up by third to the subdominant. As discussed in Chapter 46, motion by ascending third is acceptable in the popular music style. IV is more common than ii. As a result, motion from ii to IV sounds fine. A progression such as I–ii–IV–V makes perfect sense in pop songs, the same way the reverse, I–IV–ii–V, makes sense in classical pieces. Figure 47.1 shows an example in which ii moves to IV. Another example appears in figure 46.5, which illustrates motion by ascending third.

Figure 47.1 U2, "Beautiful Day"

A third function of the ii chord also stems from common-practice functions. Pre-dominants can move to tonic. In classical music, the prohibition against parallel fifths complicates the voice leading from ii to I, so IV almost always serves in plagal motion. In popular music, IV still usually fulfills this role, but ii will, on occasion, substitute. Figure 47.2, which illustrates this role, shows the ending of the chorus of ABBA's "Dancing Queen." The song opens with the second half of the chorus, so this will be the first big arrival in the song.

Figure 47.2 ABBA, "Dancing Queen," end of chorus

The supertonic can also move to the mediant. This role will be discussed in the next section.

LINEAR HARMONIC MOTION

Sometimes harmonic progressions move directly along the scale—for example, I–ii–iii–IV. On some level, this fact is not surprising; it does not violate any harmonic principles. Tonic can move to supertonic. Mediant often moves to subdominant. In this context, however, more than being about function, the motion seems to be about the scalar ascent in the bass. This motion displays linear chord functions.

A clear example of this is the opening of Bill Withers's "Lean on Me" (figure 47.3). Considering the durations and metrical placement, the tonic and subdominant are the important harmonies. The ii and iii pass quickly. They do not seem to merit any weight as chords; the listener hears the scale, while the sonorities follow it.

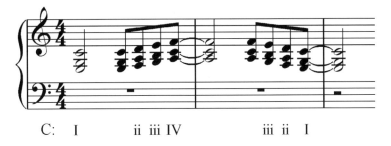

Figure 47.3 Bill Withers, "Lean on Me"

When the chords all move at the same rate, they sound more equal. Still, what seems to propel the music is the ascending scalar bassline, rather than the motion from one chord to the next. (See figure 47.4.)

Figure 47.4 The Beatles, "Here, There, and Everywhere"

Another common scalar motion occurs in minor, descending from tonic to dominant. The Stray Cats' "Stray Cat Strut" is an example of this (figure 47.5). Once again, the first and last chords, i and V, are the important chords. The ♭VII and ♭VI follow the descending bassline rather than functioning as significant harmonies. ("Hit the Road Jack" is sometimes played this way, but Ray Charles's version uses a L7 passing tone in the bass on the second harmony rather than changing to the ♭VII chord.)

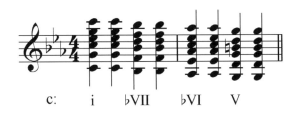

Figure 47.5 Stray Cats, "Stray Cat Strut"

SUMMARIZING DIATONIC FUNCTION IN POPULAR SONGS

The last three chapters have shown the expansion of diatonic harmonic function in twentieth-century popular music. Common-practice functions, with motion to a V that resolves to tonic, are still possible. The blues elevated the role of the plagal cadence, making IV a different, equally important cadential goal. This structural role of the IV chord permits retrogressions. In addition, the ascending third has been added into possible harmonic motions. Table 47.1 shows some common progressions, organized by their structural harmony.

TABLE 47.1	Some Common Progressions in Popular Music		
		Standard	**Substitution**
V–centric			
Basic Progression		I–IV–V	I–ii–V
Embellished Progression		I–vi–IV–V	I–vi–ii–V
IV–centric			
Basic Progression		I–V–IV	I–iii–IV
Embellished Progression		I–V–vi–IV	I–iii–vi–IV

In these general chord patterns, if the goal harmony is V, IV serves as pre-dominant, moving to the dominant. If IV is the goal harmony, the reverse is true, with V moving to IV. In both cases, it is possible for the chord a third down to substitute for the pre-dominant or "pre-subdominant." The ii chord can replace IV and move to V, while iii can replace V in moving to IV. In both categories, vi may embellish the progression by appearing before the IV chord. If ii is substituting for IV, vi leads to ii.

From these progressions, we can see the common functions of each chord (table 47.2). These functions have broadened considerably since the common-practice style. Instead of having one main function and one secondary motion, pop chords have three common options and two less common options. Combining the "common" motion with the "also" motion shows that every chord can lead to five others; essentially, a chord can move to any other diatonic harmony. In *What to Listen for in Rock*, Ken Stephenson refers to pop songs as having harmonic successions rather than progressions, in direct contrast to Schoenberg's statement paraphrased at the end of Chapter 20. This is why most music theory books and classes start with common-practice conventions. They are more narrowly defined, which allows for broader generalizations.

TABLE 47.2	Common-Practice versus Popular Music Harmonic Functions	
COMMON PRACTICE		
Chord	**Commonly Leads To**	**Can Also Lead To**
I	Anywhere	
ii	V	I
iii	Rare	
IV	I	V
V	I	vi
vi	IV, ii	V
vii°	I	vi
POPULAR MUSIC		
Chord	**Commonly Leads To**	**Can Also Lead To**
I	Anywhere	
ii	V, IV, I	iii, vi
iii	IV, vi, V	ii, I
IV	I, V, ii	iii, vi
V	I, IV, vi	ii, iii
vi	IV, ii, V	I, iii
vii°	Rare	

SUMMARY

The supertonic has three main functions. It may move to V, IV, or I.

Harmonic motion can move up and down the scale. The ascending or descending scale in the bass drives the motion as much if not more than the harmonic function.

In popular music, harmonies have more typical and less typical functions. Combining these two categories, however, shows that any diatonic chord can move to any other diatonic chord.

WORKBOOK

1. Analysis: Three excerpts, notated in lead sheet, follow. The first and last are from the first lines of their respective songs. The second one is from the end of the verse, immediately preceding the arrival of the chorus. Analyze each excerpt. Beneath the staff, identify the key and provide Roman numerals to show the role of the ii chord.

A. Louis Armstrong, "What a Wonderful World"

B. Righteous Brothers, "You've Lost That Lovin' Feelin'"

C. The Beatles, "The Fool on the Hill"

2. Harmonization: The melodies to two children's songs follow. Harmonize them in a popular music idiom. Although common-practice functions would work, write a uniquely pop progression. Add lead sheet notation above the given melody and write an accompaniment on the grand staff. You may include the melody on the grand staff. Beneath the staff, identify the key and provide Roman numerals.

A. "Mary had a Little Lamb"

B. "Twinkle, Twinkle"

Chromaticism from Classical Music

As with diatonic functions, the common-practice chromatic harmonies still make sense in popular music. None happen with the same regularity as in classical music. Pop has its own stylistic use of chromaticism that happens more frequently. Still, secondary dominants, modulation, and modal mixture have relevance. Augmented dominants are uncommon but occasionally happen, more frequently in jazz and show tunes. Augmented sixth chords and third relations are rare. Neapolitan chords and enharmonic reinterpretation almost never happen.

SECONDARY DOMINANTS

Secondary dominants, so prevalent in classical music, appear periodically in pop. Figure 48.1 shows two examples. In "She's Got a Way," the secondary dominant embellishes the very common I–V–vi–IV pattern. Inserting the chromatic chord enables a stepwise descent in the bass. This addition also moves the IV chord to the start of the next subphrase rather than the ending of the first, the normal phrasing for the I–V–vi–IV pattern. The Four Seasons' "Sherry" uses secondary dominants in a sequence by descending fifth.

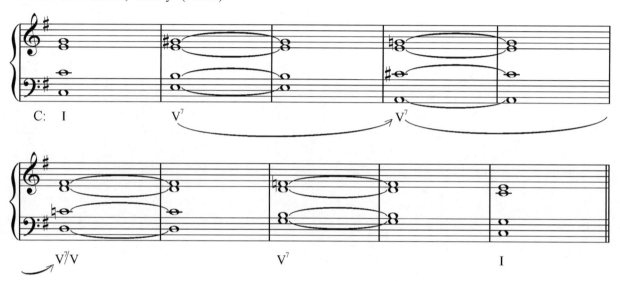

Figure 48.1 Secondary dominants in pop songs

MODULATION

Generally, pop music stays in one key. Occasionally, however, songs will emphasize their sections through modulations. For example, in the Beatles' "For No One," the verses are in C-major and the chorus is in D-minor. The introduction to Madonna's "Like a Prayer" is in D-minor, while the song proper is in F-major. "Let It Go" from *Frozen* also opens in the relative minor (F-minor) with the arrival of the relative major (A♭-major) at the chorus, which corresponds to Elsa's acceptance of her abilities. Some modulations are even more pronounced. The Beatles' "Lucy in the Sky with Diamonds" has verses in A-major, a pre-chorus that begins in B♭-major and ends in G-major, and a chorus in G. The piano introduction to Cat Stevens's "Morning Has Broken" (figure 48.2) begins in D-major and modulates to C-major. The song proper begins in C, then returns to D with the next piano interlude.

A relatively common use of modulation in popular music is the abrupt shift up a half step at the end of a song. It creates a dramatic moment, although some consider it meretricious. Examples of songs that use this device are Tommy James and the Shondells' "Crystal Blue Persuasion," the Beatles' "And I Love Her," and Michael Jackson's "Man in the Mirror."

MODAL MIXTURE

Modal mixture also appears in popular music. Figure 48.3 shows the opening of "If I Were a Rich Man" from *Fiddler on the Roof*, which modally borrows L3̂ and the minor tonic chord.

Figure 48.2 Cat Stevens, "Morning Has Broken"

Figure 48.3 Bock, "If I Were a Rich Man" from *Fiddler on the Roof*

In classical music, modal borrowing usually affects the pre-dominant chords and occasionally the tonic. In popular music, since the iii chord is now fairly common, it is possible to borrow the ♭III as well (figure 48.4).

Figure 48.4 The Beatles, "Back in the U.S.S.R."

The Beatles' song "I'll Be Back" (figure 48.5) spends significant time in both modes. Phrases 1, 2, and 4 are all the same and correspond to the first line of the figure, the material in the repeats. These three phrases are in A-minor, using the linear descending scale pattern, I–♭VII–♭VI–V. (The second-inversion ♭III chord is basically a delay/embellishment of the G chord. Notice the harmonic rhythm change in that one measure.) All of them, though, cadence on A-major, a Picardy third. The third phrase, the second two lines after the second ending, does the reverse. It begins in A-major and all the chords have typical major-key qualities and functions. At the end of the phrase, however, it returns to A-minor. It is hard to say which mode is the actual key of the piece. The two coexist, flipping back and forth.

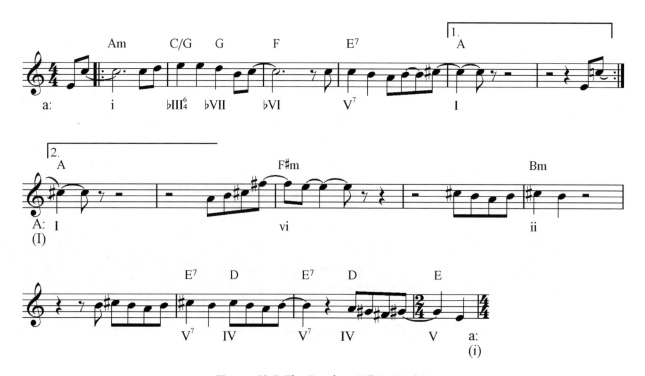

Figure 48.5 The Beatles, "I'll Be Back"

ALTERED DOMINANTS

Pop musicians sometimes use augmented dominant chords. They are more characteristic in show tunes and jazz than in pop songs, and they tend to be brief colorations. Figure 48.6 shows two examples. (In the Elton John song, the VII is a linear chord in a descending bassline pattern.)

THIRD RELATIONS AND AUGMENTED SIXTH CHORDS

Third relations are abrupt chromatic modulations, and pop songs do not usually modulate. Although local (non-modulating) motion by chromatic third happens, it usually is better explained with another chromatic technique, such as a secondary dominant. For example, in "Sherry" (figure 48.1), the motion from C to E is a third relation, but it is easier to identify the E triad as the start of a sequence by descending fifth with secondary dominants. For these two reasons, third relations are uncommon in popular songs. Figure 48.7 shows an example with three successive third relations—IV → II → ♭VII → V. Here the music does not modulate but rather cycles through a pattern of descending thirds. The ending motion from I to ♭VI⁷ also appears as a chromatic third, but it can be better understood as a German augmented sixth chord. (German augmented sixths are enharmonic with major–minor seventh chords. See Chapter 36.) Another way to view the ♭VI⁷ is as a tritone substitution, a jazz chromaticism discussed in the next chapter.

Figure 48.6 Augmented dominants in pop songs

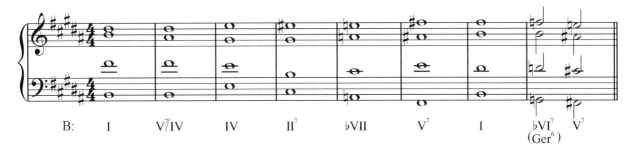

Figure 48.7 The Turtles, "She'd Rather Be with Me," chorus

OTHER COMMON-PRACTICE CHROMATICISM

Neapolitans and dominants with a flatted fifth almost never occur. Like augmented sixth chords, they overlap with the tritone substitution, explained in the next chapter. Given the infrequency of modulation and of diminished chords, enharmonic reinterpretation is not a stylistic technique.

SUMMARY

Most classical chromaticism still functions in popular music. Secondary dominants are common. Modulation and modal mixture happen periodically but less so. V+, third relations, and augmented sixths are uncommon. Neapolitans, dominants with a flatted fifth, and enharmonic reinterpretation are not typical of the pop style.

WORKBOOK

1. Analysis: Three excerpts, notated in lead sheet, follow. The first is from the chorus, the other two are from the first lines of their respective songs. Analyze each excerpt. Beneath the staff, identify the key and provide Roman numerals. How do the musicians use common-practice chromaticism?

A. Elvis Presley, "Love Me Tender" Chorus

B. Rodgers, *The Sound of Music*, "Climb Ev'ry Mountain"

C. The Beatles, "The Continuing Story of Bungalow Bill"

CHAPTER

Chromaticism from Jazz
Tritone Substitution

CHAPTER LEARNING OBJECTIVES

This chapter:

- Defines the tritone substitution
- Explains the resolution of the tritone substitution
- Explains the relationship between the tritone resolution and the German sixth chord

As stated in Chapter 40, this book will not delve deeply into jazz theory. The topic merits and has entire books dedicated to it. It is, however, a form of popular music, and it has influenced pop songs, so the more salient features need to be discussed.

In many ways, jazz music follows classical principles more closely than pop. The primary motion is still by descending fifth, as opposed to the descending fourth; ii–V–I is the common cadential gesture. One of the main differences in the sound is the use of extended tertian harmonies, not the specific harmonic functions.

The same is true about chromaticism in jazz. Secondary dominants appear frequently. Modal mixture is not unusual. A common form of chromaticism in jazz that does not appear in classical music, however, is the tritone substitution.

The *tritone substitution* is exactly what it sounds like; a harmony is replaced by the chord a tritone away. This substitution most frequently happens on the V^7 chord, with a $\flat II^7$ appearing in its stead. Classically, this would be labeled as a Neapolitan chord, but it does not function in the same way. While it is possible to for the N^6 to move to tonic, it primarily functions as a pre-dominant. In jazz, this harmony moves down by half step to tonic. When inserted into the typical ii–V–I progression, it gives a satisfying, chromatically descending bassline: $\hat{2}$–L$\hat{2}$–$\hat{1}$ (figure 49.1). The main melody can either stay the same (the soprano and alto in figure 49.1), or it can become embellished with a chromatic passing tone (the tenor in figure 49.1).

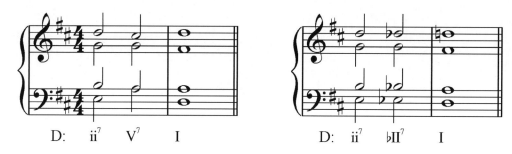

Figure 49.1 The tritone substitution

The musical logic behind the substitution is that the two chords share the pitches $\hat{4}$ and $\hat{7}$, the key-defining tritone. This tritone still resolves the same way it does in the V^7. (In figure 49.1, this corresponds to the treble clef. Although this voice leading is not required in the popular idiom, the tension in the tritone and the satisfaction of its resolution are not irrelevant.) The other two pitches, A and E in this example, are replaced with pitches a half step away, B♭ and E♭, allowing for the chromatic bass and tenor lines.

Although the substituted chord appears to be the Neapolitan, it actually has a closer analogue in common-practice theory: augmented sixth chords. This harmony corresponds to the "irregularly resolving" A6, as discussed in Chapter 36. The top note of the augmented sixth is written enharmonically to be a minor seventh, but it still has the same voice leading (figure 49.2).

Anywhere the harmony moves by fifth, a tritone substitution produces this half-step motion. Although less common, substituting for the ii chord in the basic progression results in a traditional Ger⁶ (also shown in figure 49.2). It may be better to continue to call this harmony an augmented sixth chord.

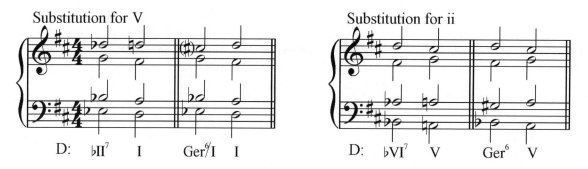

Figure 49.2 The tritone substitution and the German sixth

The song "Luck Be a Lady" from *Guys and Dolls* makes extensive use of tritone substitution (figure 49.3). (Frank Sinatra actually begins this song in D♭, but that just seemed cruel, so I transposed it to C.) What would be the straightforward diatonic alternation of I and V^7 becomes the more colorful alternation of I and ♭II⁷. The melodic line in the measures with the ♭II⁷ would make perfect sense (more sense in terms of common-practice conventions) with a V^7 harmonizing it. The second measure would have a split third, but that is not an unusual vocal coloring. All of the other measures emphasize F and G, which fit neatly in a G⁷ chord.

Although tritone substitutions are common in jazz and show tunes, they occur only sporadically in pop and rock songs. A pop example appears in the previous chapter in figure 48.7. In "She'd Rather Be with Me," the Turtles use a tritone substitution on the ii chord in the ii–V turnaround at the end of the chorus, which results in a ♭VI⁷–V⁷. Again, this progression is analogous to the German sixth in common-practice music, minus the voice-leading restrictions.

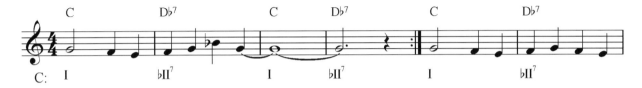

Figure 49.3 Loesser, "Luck Be a Lady" from *Guys and Dolls*

Spotlight On: TRITONE SUBSTITUTIONS IN CLASSICAL MUSIC

Tritone substitutions are a staple of jazz theory, but they do not appear in traditional common-practice music theory. As described in this chapter, the classical perspective is that they function as an altered dominant, an augmented sixth chord, or a linear chord.

Some theorists argue that this situation should change. As mentioned in Chapter 36, sometimes "apparent" augmented sixth chords appear, which resolve to harmonies other than dominant. By using tritone substitutions, some of these chords can be better classified.

The A6 chords and tritone substitution can be distinguished by function (pre-dominant or dominant) and voice leading (whether the A6 resolves or not). A brief paper that draws this distinction and contains examples is "Augmented Sixth Chords versus Tritone Substitutes" by Nicole Biamonte (*Music Theory Online* 14, no. 2 [2008], http://www.mtosmt.org/issues/mto.08.14.2/mto.08.14.2.biamonte.html).

SUMMARY

Terminology

Tritone substitution. A jazz chromatic technique in which a chord is replaced with the harmony a tritone away. Most typically, the V^7 is replaced with $\flat II^7$.

A tritone substitution involves replacing a chord in a diatonic progression with the harmony a tritone away. It occurs most frequently on the V^7.

WORKBOOK

1. Analysis: The harmonic progressions for three pop songs follow. Analyze each excerpt. Beneath the staff, identify the key and provide Roman numerals. Which chord is the tritone substitution replacing? In "The Girl from Ipanema," the E-major chord is the result of linear motion in an inner voice.

A. Astrud Gilberto, "Girl from Ipanema," Verses

B. Louis Armstrong, "What a Wonderful World," Verses

C. The Beatles, "Things We Said Today," Bridge

2. Part Writing: You are given a key and a progression. Write out each progression on the grand staff two times, using two different tritone substitutions. Write in four or five voices. You may embellish the harmonies with sevenths, extended tertian pitches, or added notes, if desired. Provide an analysis, including the key and Roman numerals, beneath the system.

A. G: I - vi - ii - V - I

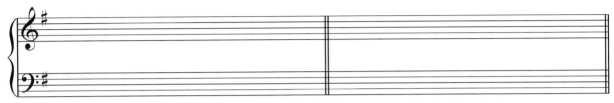

B. E: I - IV - V/V - V - I

Pop Chromaticism 1
L$\hat{7}$ and ♭VII

CHAPTER LEARNING OBJECTIVES

This chapter:

- Examines the influence of L$\hat{7}$ and the uniquely pop harmonies of ♭VII and v

- Explains ♭VII functioning as IV/IV

- Explains ♭VII and v as resulting from the use of a mode

Popular music often has IV as the goal chord of a phrase. As discussed in Chapter 45, this does not mean that the subdominant now has more tension than the dominant. The leading tone still pulls toward home; it remains the scale degree with the most tension.

A number of popular melodies avoid using a prominent leading tone, with its clear directionality. Some place it in weak positions or keep it short. Some leap over the leading tone, moving between $\hat{1}$ and $\hat{6}$. A common melodic pattern that does this is $\hat{5}$–$\hat{6}$–$\hat{1}$; examples are the pickup notes to "She'll Be Coming 'Round the Mountain" and John Mellencamp's "I Need a Lover." Sometimes the entire melody avoids the leading tone. Many hymns and folk songs use the pentatonic scale, which is like major but omits scale degrees $\hat{4}$ and $\hat{7}$ (see figure 41.10). Removing the key-defining tritone frees the melody a bit with regard to the key and pointing toward home.

Some songs use L$\hat{7}$ instead. Melodically, the presence of this note is not overly striking. It is a common blue note, and the pitch often appears as coloration on I^7. Using it in these ways feels organic in the popular music style.

When the pitch chromatically alters a basic triad (i.e., when the Roman numeral itself is affected), however, the sound grabs the attention more. The most common chord that supports L$\hat{7}$ is ♭VII, followed by v. The functions of these harmonies can be explained in several ways:

1. The ♭VII functions as a IV/IV.

2. The song is modal, employing one of the traditional church modes.

3. The song briefly borrows from a parallel church mode, analogous to common-practice modal mixture.

IV/IV

Paul Simon's "Me and Julio Down by the Schoolyard" (figure 50.1) shows the most common use of the ♭VII chord: moving to IV. The entire song is solidly in A-major, using almost all diatonic chords. (One V/V appears early in the chorus; other than these two chords, everything is a I, IV, or V.) In the last line of the chorus, a ♭VII sounds, providing the most harmonically colorful moment in the song. It then moves to IV and returns to a clear A-major.

Figure 50.1 Paul Simon, "Me and Julio Down by the Schoolyard"

This motion serves as a tonicization of the subdominant in the IV-centric worldview. In classical music, tonicization exploits the role of the dominant, chromatically altering the third of the ii chord to change it into the V/V. Applying that principle to the reverse relationship found in blues, we would move back from IV by an ascending fourth, arriving at ♭VII, the IV/IV.

Another way to think about it is that pop music has three central diatonic chords: I, IV, and V. The keys of IV and V, the closely related major keys, both share two of the three chords with tonic. For example, the keys of C-major and F-major share the chords C and F; they differ only by their third chord (see figure 50.2). The same is true for C-major and G-major, which share the chords C and G. By adding in a single chord, the other key can

Figure 50.2 I, IV, and V in C-, G-, and F-major

be briefly implied (i.e., tonicized) through its I, IV, and V. If we want to emphasize G, we can use D, the V/V. If we want to imply F, we can use B♭, the IV/IV. In "Me and Julio Down by the Schoolyard," the entire pattern A–G–D can be viewed as V–IV–I, the standard blues retrogression pattern, in D. It should not be analyzed in this way, but it explains why the IV/IV works as it does.

Many pop songs exploit this relationship. For example, the basic harmonic pattern in Lynyrd Skynyrd's "Sweet Home Alabama" is I–♭VII–IV, perhaps better thought of as I–IV/IV–IV. The vamp at the end of the Beatles' "Hey Jude" is the same pattern, except it returns to tonic at the end of the phrase before repeating: I–IV/IV–IV–I.

In classical music, the idea of motion by descending fifths can be extended; we often see motion around the circle of fifths in the descending direction, whether it be a sequence or the basic functions of vi–ii–V–I. The reverse rarely happens in that genre. In popular music, though, motion by repeating descending fourths can happen (see figure 50.3)

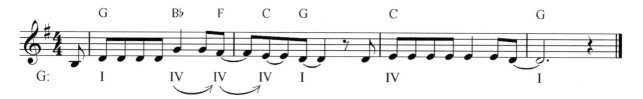

Figure 50.3 The Beatles, "Sgt. Pepper's Lonely Hearts Club Band"

Tonicization through descending fourths has a more striking sound than that through secondary dominants. The root of the chord is altered, which emphasizes the chromaticism more than when the third or fifth is changed.

MODALITY

In the twentieth century, both classical and popular music expanded the scales in use. They explored a variety of pitch collections, but the most common (non-major or -minor) scales in rock and pop songs were three church modes: Mixolydian, Aeolian, and Dorian. (See figure 50.4.) Although often referred to as "church modes," these scales are also characteristic of the folk music of many European cultures.

The Mixolydian scale is basically the major scale but with the subtonic instead of the leading tone. The harmonies that distinguish this from major are ♭VII and v. In a similar fashion, the Aeolian scale is basically the natural minor scale. The important pitches parallel those in minor except that L$\hat{7}$ replaces the leading tone, again making the distinguishing chords ♭VII and v. The Dorian is slightly further from minor, containing R$\hat{6}$ and L$\hat{7}$. It removes the L$\hat{6}$ tendency tone, thereby brightening the sound relative to minor or Aeolian. In terms of harmony, instead of i, iv, and v all being minor, the subdominant is major. ♭VII is also characteristic of this mode.

Table 50.1 lists songs that are in modes rather than major or minor. In the Police's "Wrapped around Your Finger," the chorus pulls toward C-major, alternating G and F^{maj7}. The chorus is not included in the chart, but it does not destroy the primarily Aeolian feeling of the song. Similarly, the bridge of "La Isla Bonita" ends on a major V chord, using the leading tone to return to tonic at the beginning of the next section. Other than that moment, however, the music is completely in the Aeolian mode. Finally, "Scarborough Fair" is a Dorian medieval folk melody, not an original rock tune; it is harmonized accordingly.

The Beatles' "Eleanor Rigby" is modal, but it wavers between E Dorian and E Aeolian (figure 50.5). Throughout the entire song, the harmony alternates between E-minor and C-major (I → ♭VI), placing the majority of the music in E Aeolian. Melodically, though, a C♯ occasionally occurs. The song provides a nice example of the contrast between the two minor-sounding modes. Midphrase the melody employs the brighter C♯ (R$\hat{6}$); at the end of the phrase, C♮ (L$\hat{6}$) appears, functioning as a tendency tone, pulling down to B ($\hat{5}$), and darkening the sound.

Figure 50.4 Common modes in rock and pop

TABLE 50.1	Songs in a Mode Rather Than Major or Minor		
Song	**Performer**	**Mode**	**Progression**
"Tomorrow Never Knows"	The Beatles	C Mixolydian	I–v⁷
"Louie, Louie"	The Kingsmen	A Mixolydian	I–IV–v
"Wrapped around Your Finger"	The Police	A Aeolian	Instrumental v–iv⁷–i–v⁷–i Verses i–♭VII–v–i–v⁷
"La Isla Bonita"	Madonna	C♯ Aeolian	Verses i–♭VII–i–♭VI–♭III–♭VII Chorus i–v–iv–♭III–♭VII–iv–v–i
"Poker Face"	Lady Gaga	G♯ Aeolian	Verses i–♭VI–♭VII Chorus i–♭VI–♭III–♭VII
"Scarborough Fair/Canticle"	Simon and Garfunkel	E Dorian	i–♭VII–i–♭III–i–IV–i i–♭III–♭VII–i–♭VII–i

Figure 50.5 The Beatles, "Eleanor Rigby"

MODAL MIXTURE

More common than songs that are entirely in a mode are ones that borrow briefly from a parallel mode. This is the same as mixture between major and minor, but now a chord comes from the parallel Mixolydian, Aeolian, or other scale. Pop music most commonly borrows ♭VII or v. The typical pattern is either to return directly to tonic (♭VII → I or v → I) or to move ♭VII → V, giving a modal color but then restoring the tonal dominant–tonic relationship. In the Beatles' "I'm a Loser," the verses repeat the progression I–V–♭VII–I four times. The slow introduction uses the reverse pattern, ii–♭VII–V–I.

Another common gesture involving modal borrowing is when a major-key song deceptively moves to ♭VI. Although this could be from the parallel minor, it is common to resolve the lowered submediant chord through the modal progression V–♭VI–♭VII–I (figure 50.6). Examples of this are at the end of the choruses of the Beatles' "P.S. I Love You" and Sixpence None the Richer's "Breathe Your Name."

Figure 50.6 The lowered submediant and its resolution through the subtonic

SUMMARY

A common chromatic pitch in popular harmony is L$\hat{7}$. It is usually harmonized by ♭VII and sometimes by v.

The most common function for ♭VII is IV/IV, which tonicizes the subdominant by exploiting the blues' IV-centricity.

♭VII and v also appear in modal songs and songs that borrow from the modes. In this context, ♭VII usually moves to either I or V; v usually moves to I.

WORKBOOK

1. Lead Sheet Analysis: Three excerpts, notated in lead sheet, follow. Analyze each excerpt. Beneath the staff, identify the key and provide Roman numerals. If the song is modal, what mode is it in?

A. Jimmy Buffett, "Come Monday," Ending

B. Billy Joel, "She's Got a Way," End of Verses

C. Imagine Dragons, "Radioactive," Chorus

2. Grand Staff Analysis: Two excerpts, notated on the grand staff, follow. Both repeat throughout their songs. Analyze each excerpt. Beneath the staff, identify the key and provide Roman numerals. If in a mode, which modes could it be, and which mode is most likely.

A. U2, "Beautiful Day"

B. Alicia Keys, "Fallin'"

Pop Chromaticism 2
Quality Change

CHAPTER LEARNING OBJECTIVES

This chapter:

- Examines the pop chromatic technique of replacing a diatonic minor chord with a major chord built on the same diatonic scale degree

In "Dancing Queen" (figure 51.1), ABBA uses a major II chord, but it does not function as a V/V. Instead, it leads to IV. The ascending third motion, ii → IV, is common in pop music, but in this case the quality of the ii chord has been altered

Popular music composers sometimes change the quality of a diatonic chord, usually from minor to major. Unlike in classical music, where a change in quality generally indicates a change in function, here the alteration is purely for color. Popular music relies on the root to clarify function more. For example, sevenths can be added to a triad for coloration without affecting its role. An analogous situation applies to this type of quality change. Since the root is the same, the listener hears the same harmonic function; the chord just has a brighter sound to it. In this instance, the motion by ascending third, ii → IV, has been embellished and turned into II → IV. Play the progression using a B-minor chord. It sounds darker, but does its role in the passage seem any different?

Another example of this same progression is at the end of the verses in the Beatles' "Yesterday." At "I believe in yesterday" and all subsequent appearances of that material, the music moves vi–II–IV–I. In terms of harmonic function, a ii chord would work equally well in that passage.

The supertonic chord can also return to tonic (for example, the last two chords in figure 51.1). Chromatically altering the ii triad in this context also happens. (See figure 51.2.)

Figure 51.1 ABBA, "Dancing Queen"

Figure 51.2 Barenaked Ladies, "Pinch Me," chorus

The iii chord may also be altered in this way. The most common function for iii is to move to IV. KT Tunstall's "Suddenly I See" (figure 51.3) serves as an example of this progression. Here the III could be viewed as a V/vi that resolves deceptively. Although that is possible, in the pop idiom, motion from iii to IV is common enough that I do not hear a pull to vi when on a III. Motion to IV sounds appropriate, not surprising.

Figure 51.3 KT Tunstall, "Suddenly I See," chorus

The other common function for the mediant chord is to fall by fifth to vi. In this case, the III chord can be analyzed as a secondary dominant, V/vi. The C#^{7} chord in "Dancing Queen" (figure 51.1) functions in this way. That statement makes no claims as to what the composer was thinking. It only says that the harmony functions in a traditional secondary-dominant role.

Songwriters less frequently change the quality of the vi chord, but it does happen. The end of the chorus in the Rivieras' "California Sun" (figure 51.4) contains a doo-wop pattern embellished with a major submediant. This pattern is not used throughout the piece, only at the end of the chorus, "Where they're out there having fun . . ."

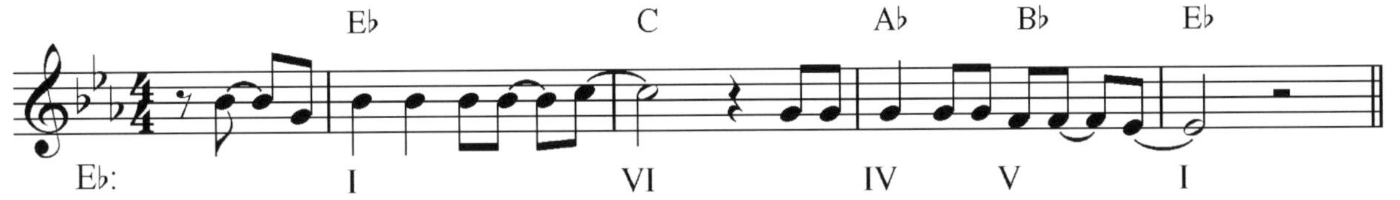

Figure 51.4 The Rivieras, "California Sun"

The reverse quality change, turning a major chord into minor, is less common. Practically speaking, such passages can often be viewed in terms of a different chromatic technique. For example, "Louie, Louie" uses the progression I–IV–v. Perhaps the dominant is changed for color, but the alteration also places the music in the Mixolydian mode. At the end of the chorus of "Suddenly I See," Tunstall uses iv instead of IV (figure 51.5). Theorists would classify this change as modal mixture. Again, this statement says nothing about how the composer herself views what she did; it is a statement about the parlance of music theory.

Figure 51.5 KT Tunstall, "Suddenly I See," chorus, ending

Figure 51.5 shows a variety of pop chromaticism techniques. The III chord is the change of quality discussed in this chapter. The iv fits in this category, too, but it would be labeled as modal mixture, as noted in Chapter 48. The ♭VII is borrowing from the Mixolydian mode, as presented in Chapter 50.

SUMMARY

In popular music, songwriters sometimes change the quality of diatonic minor chords into major, brightening the sound of the harmony. The alteration has no effect on the role of the chord.

The technique is more common on the ii and iii chords and less common on the vi chord.

Changing major chords to minor is also possible, but theorists usually think of this alteration as modal borrowing, either from minor or from a mode.

WORKBOOK

1. Analysis: The openings of fours songs, notated on the grand staff, follow. (I have clarified the harmony on "Our House.") Analyze each excerpt. Beneath the staff, identify the key and provide Roman numerals. For "Our House," what other techniques could explain the qualities of the harmonies? For "The Trouble with Love Is," what factors contribute to the soulful jazz sound?

A. Phil Phillips, "Sea of Love"

B. Madness, "Our House"

C. Kelly Clarkson, "The Trouble with Love Is"

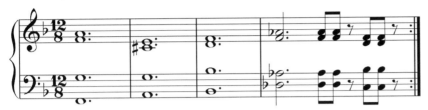

D. Cee Lo Green, "Forget You"

2. Harmonization: The melodies to two children's songs follow. Harmonize them in a popular music idiom, using the chromatic techniques presented in the last four chapters. Although common-practice functions are allowed, use them sparingly and write a more uniquely pop progression. Add lead sheet notation above the given melody and write an accompaniment on the grand staff. You may include the melody on the grand staff. Beneath the system, identify the key and provide Roman numerals. If you harmonized these melodies in the Workbook section in Chapter 47, you may use that diatonic pattern as a starting point for this assignment.

A. "Mary had a Little Lamb"

B. "Twinkle, Twinkle"

Three Analyses

CHAPTER LEARNING OBJECTIVES

This chapter:

- Analyzes three pop songs to show harmonic functions derived from different sources

In order to review the different stylistic traits influencing contemporary popular music, we will conclude with analyses of three pop songs. The first will be a song that employs common-practice conventions. The second makes sense only in the pop style. The last shows a hybridization of the classical and contemporary techniques. I am not including a song that was heavily influenced by jazz, using extended tertian harmonies or tritone substitutions, but the same basic observations would apply to those pieces too.

THE BEATLES, "SOMETHING"

George Harrison's masterpiece "Something" follows the conventions of common-practice music in almost every element. It is highly chromatic, but this chromaticism follows the classical concept of a half-step inflection with resolution in the same direction of the alteration (i.e., raised notes resolve up, lowered notes resolve down). Basically, conventional voice leading still holds.

For example, the introduction begins on a IV and moves to a V, but in between a ♭III appears (figure 52.1a). While this harmony could be viewed as modally borrowed, I hear it as a linear effect, analogous to a German sixth that is missing the upper part of the augmented sixth (see figure 52.1b and c). Notating the B♭ as an A♯ shows its proper voice-leading structure. Removing the C♯ from a German sixth (figure 52.1c) leaves a linear chord that is enharmonic with an E♭-major triad (figure 52.1b). It is not a conventional augmented sixth chord, but it has the same underlying pattern. Common-practice composers hearing this song would understand the contrapuntal origins of this progression.

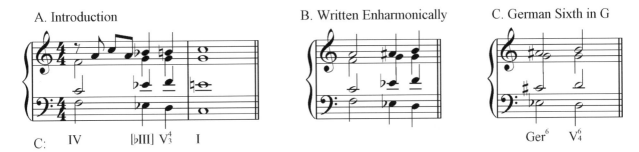

Figure 52.1 The Beatles, "Something"

The verses all center on dominant resolutions (figure 52.2). Phrases lead to either dominant or tonic harmonies, and most of the other chromatic moments are secondary dominants. The tonic at the beginning turns into a V⁷/IV, which resolves appropriately. (The I^{maj7} in the second measure is I with a passing tone in the melody.) This subdominant then moves to a V/V that also resolves as expected. The common-practice voice leading shows clearly through the chromatic descent that creates the song. Over the first phrase, the melodic line drops chromatically from $\hat{1}$ to $\hat{6}$. In the second phrase, the bassline continues this descent, moving from $\hat{6}$ to $\hat{4}$, which then moves to a cadential dominant.

Figure 52.2 The Beatles, "Something," verses

Another classical element is that Harrison maintains the tension over the entire verse. This song does not repeat a riff or harmonic pattern; it contains a longer progression with a variety of chords. The chromatic lines and secondary dominants impart a goal-oriented sense to the music. The half cadence in measure 6 clearly pulls to tonic. In measure 7, this dominant resolves deceptively, avoiding a sense of closure. Harrison does not provide an authentic cadence until the very end, including the instrumental lick that opened the song.

The harmonic rhythm also follows common-practice conventions. For the first half of the verse, the song has one chord per measure. (There are a couple chords, such as the I⁶ in measure 4, which smooth the bassline, but the larger pattern is one chord.) In the second half of the verse, the harmonic rhythm increases to two chords per measure, driving the music forward faster, and pushing to the final cadence. All of the chords change on strong beats, either the downbeat of the measure or the downbeat and beat 3.

A few elements in this excerpt might be better analyzed as pop traits. If measure 4 is seen as a "half plagal cadence on IV," this would make sense in the pop idiom. Of course, it moves onto V at a larger structural pause two measures later, downplaying this moment. Although not shown, the melody includes a number of backward rhythms. This is not unheard of in classical music, but it is common in pop. Finally, in measure 8 of the verses, the motion II → IV is a pop progression. Given the prominent descending line in the bass, the harmony could make sense as a linear chord in classical music, but a basic pop analysis works fine.

The bridge, not given here, also contains one moment of a pop idiom. It is in A-major, and the first phrase ends with a ♭VII → I, borrowed from the Mixolydian mode. (On the repetition, this G-major chord creates a direct modulation back to C-major.) Other than this, the bridge also follows common-practice conventions.

OTIS REDDING, "(SITTIN' ON) THE DOCK OF THE BAY"

Otis Redding's "(Sittin' on) The Dock of the Bay" epitomizes popular music. Figure 52.3 shows the harmonic progressions in the verses and the chorus.

Figure 52.3 Otis Redding, "(Sittin' on) The Dock of the Bay"

Although this song also has a harmonic rhythm of one chord per measure, the changes violate common-practice conventions. In most measures, the chord begins an eighth note "early," starting on a weak beat and continuing through a strong one. This pattern syncopates the harmonic rhythm against the meter, providing a pop energy to the music.

The progression itself is distinctly pop too. On the local level, it contains motion by ascending third, moving both from the tonic to the mediant (I–iii, ignoring the chromaticism for a moment) and from the submediant to the tonic (vi–I). The presence of the iii chord is more likely in pop than in classical, and in the verses it is being used in its most typical role—connecting to IV. The motion by step down from ii to I is also much more typical in this genre than in common-practice compositions.

The chromaticism on these chords, a change to major without affecting function, is also unique to popular music. The verses and chorus use a lot of II's, III's, and VI's, behaving as their diatonic variants would.

In terms of structural harmony, the verses move between I and IV. The chorus is atypical, even for pop: it features neither a structural IV nor V; rather, the structural motion is between I and VI. A dominant chord does not appear at all in the verses or the chorus.

The dominant finally appears in the bridge (figure 52.4), but it is in the blues role as a "pre-subdominant." The first three appearances (counting the repeat of the first two bars) move by a retrogression to IV; all three have IV as the structural harmony of their progressions. In contrast to the verses and chorus, almost all of the chords in the bridge are diatonic. The one moment of chromaticism is a ♭VII, borrowed from the parallel Mixolydian, a uniquely pop technique.

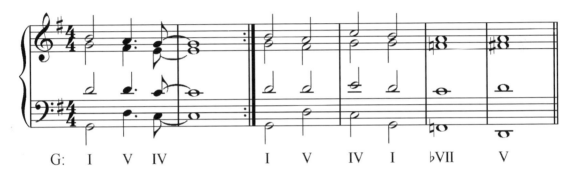

Figure 52.4 Otis Redding, "(Sittin' on) The Dock of the Bay," bridge

The only point in the song that follows common-practice harmonic conventions is the end of the bridge. The bridge lands on a prominent V chord, setting up the return of the last verse.

RIHANNA, "STAY"

As mentioned several times before, songs do not follow only classical rules or only popular idioms. The previous two examples were chosen because they fall primarily into one camp or the other. Over time, harmonies broadened in function, and most can now serve in multiple ways, pulling from different historical sources within a single song. Rihanna's "Stay" displays a good mix of influences.

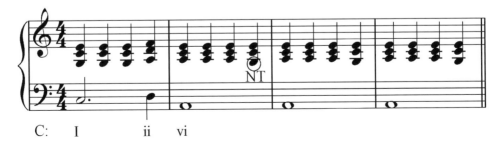

Figure 52.5 Rihanna, "Stay," verses

The verses in "Stay" (figure 52.5) have ambiguity about the tonal center. Each phrase begins on a C-major triad but then spends three of the four measures on an A-minor chord. There is no structural IV or V to indicate the tonic. The harmonies use no accidentals, and the melody is pentatonic, using only the notes C, D, E, G, and A. At the start, it is unclear whether the piece is in C-major or A Aeolian.

In actuality, the piece is in C-major; each phrase begins on that chord, and later sections of the song clarify C as home. But this constant pull toward the relative minor and the initial uncertainty whether the song is in major or Aeolian impacts the sound immensely. Rather than hearing the brightness of major or the darkness of minor, the mood is somewhere in between, creating melancholy or uncertainty, which fits with the content of the lyrics.

The chorus consists of two parts, a pre-chorus ("Round and around . . .") and the chorus proper ("Not really sure . . ."). For the first two statements, the two parts appear together. The third and final time, the bridge leads directly to the chorus, skipping over the pre-chorus.

In the pre-chorus (figure 52.6), the ascent from ii to vi is distinctly pop, but the other local harmonic motion is by descending third or fifth, which makes sense in both the pop and classical styles. The first phrase ends on the ii–vi motion, out of the common-practice idiom, but the passage ends with a traditional ii–V half cadence.

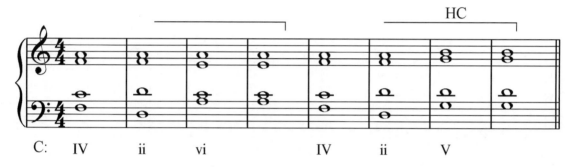

Figure 52.6 Rihanna, "Stay," pre-chorus

That half cadence resolves with the arrival of tonic in the chorus, which repeats the progression shown in figure 52.7. In here, the harmony evenly blends stylistic influences. The motion from ii–vi is unique to pop, while the vi–IV that follows was used in the common-practice era. Structurally, the music moves to a IV at the end of each phrase. The first time, this subdominant connects to the tonic when the pattern repeats. After the second statement, it connects to the tonic that begins the verse. The pre-chorus confirms the key through a common-practice cadential V, and the chorus confirms it through the blues cadential IV.

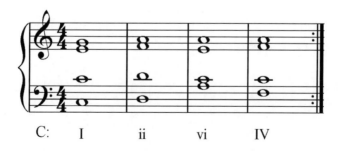

Figure 52.7 Rihanna, "Stay," chorus

The only other section in the song is the bridge (figure 52.8). In here, the local progression veers toward the pop idiom; much of the motion is by ascending third. Also, the first two phrases end on ii chords, and the third phrase ends on a vi chord. The entire section, however, ends on a half cadence, with a clear dominant setting up the return of the chorus.

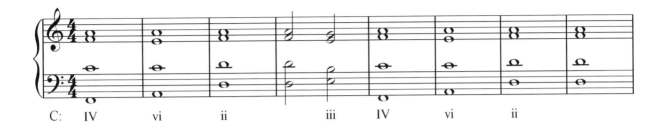

C: IV   vi   ii   iii   IV   vi   ii

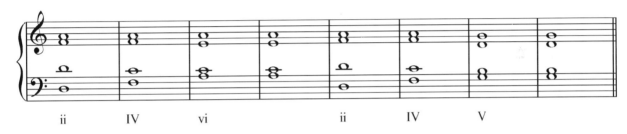

ii   IV   vi   ii   IV   V

Figure 52.8 Rihanna, "Stay," bridge

The ambiguity created at the beginning does not resolve completely. The song ends on a IV chord, never returning to tonic or releasing its tension. Perhaps this corresponds to the lack of resolution to the singer's dilemma.

"Stay" demonstrates harmonic function in contemporary popular music. Locally, pop harmonies may move analogously to common-practice function, or they may move in ways idiomatic only to pop. Structurally, a phrase may lead to a cadential IV or V. The functions and traits of previous genres coexist, allowing composers to use any of them at any time.

SUMMARY

Popular music may use idioms from any of the earlier styles that have influenced it as well as gestures that are unique to it. Some songs may lean toward one genre or another. Most freely combine the harmonic functions and structures from multiple sources.

WORKBOOK

1. Analysis: Choose a pop song you like. Notate it on staff paper, either in lead sheet or in a piano arrangement. Analyze it.

   - Identify the key and provide a Roman numeral harmonic analysis.
   - Bracket and label cadences
   - Examine the melody. Does it include all pitches of the scale? How does it handle rhythm?
   - What nondiatonic pitches does the song include? How do these chromatic pitches function?
   - What elements identify this as popular music?

2. Composition: Compose a pop song in any key besides C-major or A-minor. Do not use a time signature with 2 as the top number. You may use a riff that repeats. Once you are finished, analyze your song as in question 1.

3. Analysis: Choose a song you like from any genre of tonal music. Notate it on staff paper, either in lead sheet or in a piano arrangement. Analyze it.

   - Identify the key and provide a Roman numeral harmonic analysis.
   - Bracket and label cadences.
   - Does the piece have a climax? If so, identify it.
   - Examine the melody. Does it include all pitches of the scale? How does it handle rhythm?
   - What nondiatonic pitches does the song include? How do these chromatic pitches function?
   - What traits identify the song as belonging to its genre?

APPENDIXES

Melodies for Study

This appendix offers melodies for study. Some are excerpts, and some are complete. They are taken from a variety of styles, but all are vocal melodies since that is the focus of the first part of this book. (The melody from "The Moldau" is instrumental in that piece, but the tune is based on a Czech folk song.) On several, I have added breath marks to clarify the phrasing.

MAJOR KEYS

Figure A.1 illustrates major diatonic keys. Figure A.2 shows major-key melodies that include a chromatic pitch.

"Là ci darem la mano" from *Don Giovanni*

Clementine

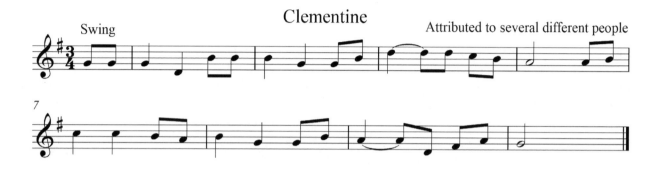

Long, Long Ago

Figure A.1

Figure A.2

MINOR KEYS

Figure A.3 is an example of minor diatonic keys, and figure A.4 illustrates minor-key melodies containing a chromatic note.

"The Moldau" from Mà Vlast

Sevivon

Llangloffan

Figure A.3

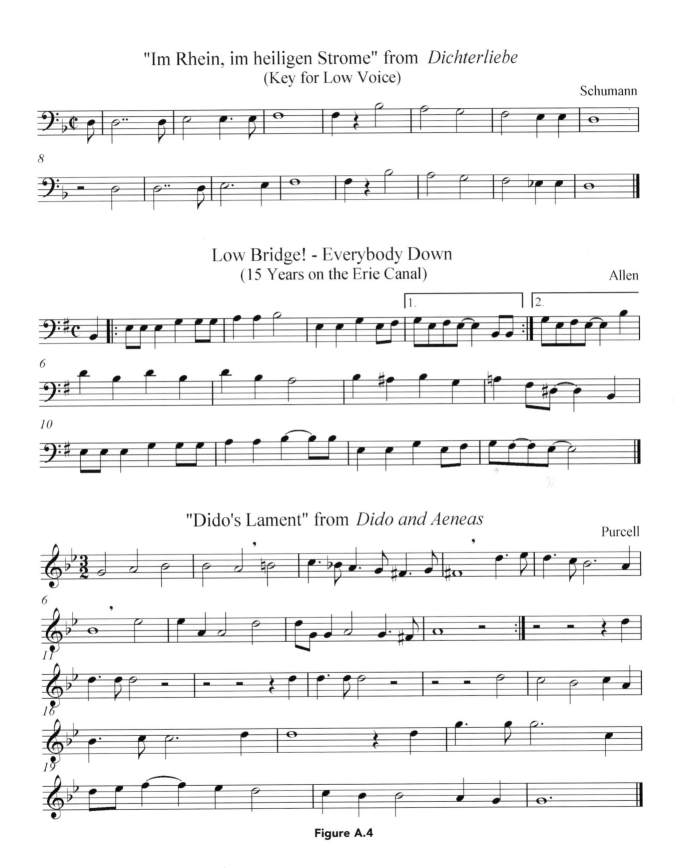

Figure A.4

Cantus Firmi and Figured Basses

This appendix offers cantus firmi for use in species counterpoint Workbook assignments. They should be transposed into different keys, registers, and rhythmic durations to provide a variety of exercises. Most are newly written, but some come from other books and are so credited.

Some teachers prefer to have functional progressions, even when focusing on counterpoint. This book may be used for teaching figured bass notation first and then employing species counterpoint with figured basses. This approach prohibits the students' exploration of chord choices but ensures the tonal function of harmonies. Figured basses appear after the cantus firmi in this list. They too are written in C-major or A-minor and should be transposed into different keys for the Workbook exercises.

CANTUS FIRMI

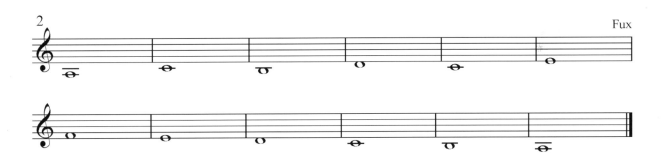

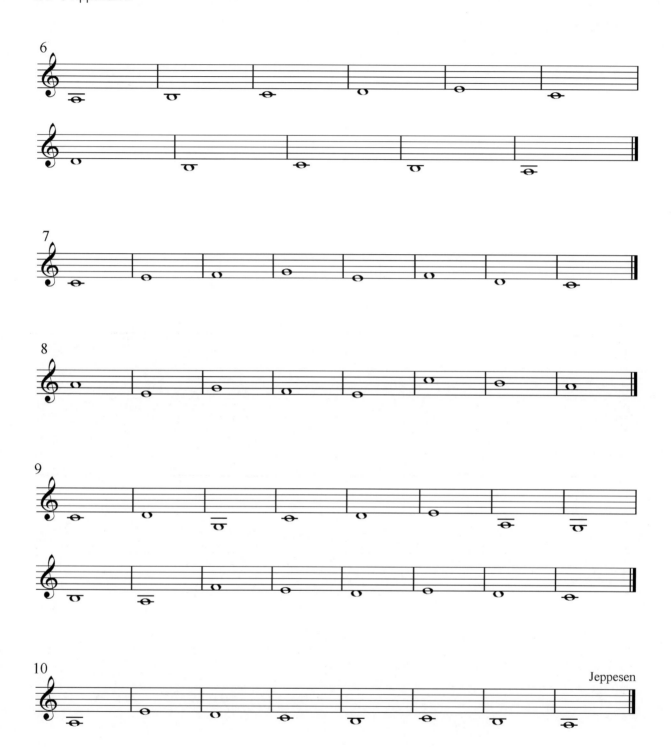

Jeppesen

11
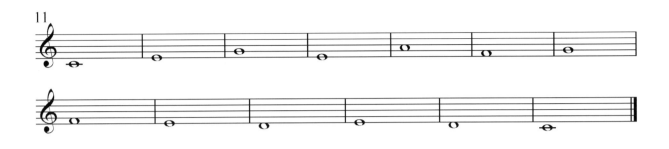

12
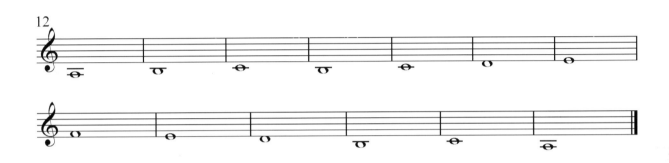

13

14
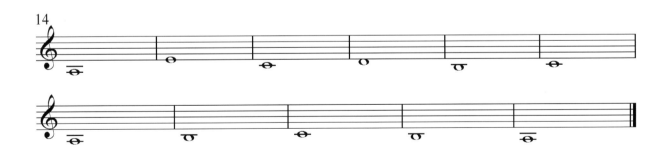

FIGURED BASSES

In transposing the following figures, do not forget to adjust chromatic alterations appropriately. When the bass moves in eighth notes, the offbeats are nonchord tones.

Church Modes

The major and minor scales that we use are not musical absolutes; in fact, they are characteristic only of the common-practice period and popular music in the twentieth and twenty-first centuries. Many other scales exist. Throughout the Middle Ages and the Renaissance, other scales, now commonly called the *church modes* because of their use in sacred music from Gregorian chants through Renaissance masses, were standard in the Western world.

Four principal modes existed, each containing a different pattern of half and whole steps. They are typically represented by the white keys on the piano, with each mode beginning on a different starting pitch. This corresponds to their actual use; accidentals did not appear until after the modes developed. The starting pitch of the mode, the note to which the music resolves, is called the *final*. Early theorists named the scales after the ancient Greek modes, which in turn were named after Greek ethnic groups. The medieval names and the Greek names do not match for the modes; the medieval names are standard today.

Church modes

Three other modes are theoretically possible, but they were not used. In 1547, Heinrich Glarean identified and named them. The Aeolian and Ionian appear occasionally in the late Renaissance. The Locrian was not practical due to the prominent tritone between the final and the fifth of the mode.

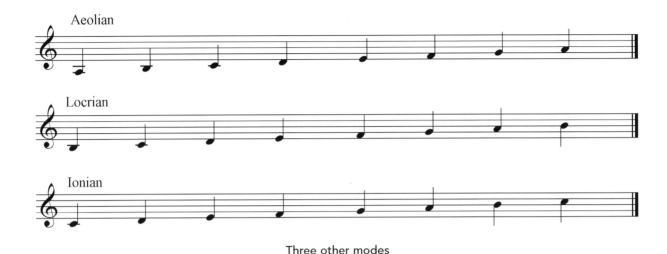

Three other modes

Renaissance theory and the role of the modes is more nuanced and sophisticated than this brief introduction implies, but is also out of the scope of this text. Modes are mentioned enough in music that it is important to be familiar with the basic names. More important for our purposes, however, is that the major and minor scales and the functional chord progressions of the common-practice era are a defining trait of that time period.

TERMINOLOGY

Aeolian mode. The church mode that corresponds to the white piano keys starting on A and has A as its final. Analogous to the natural minor scale.

Church modes. The scales in frequent use prior to the common-practice period, mostly associated with the Middle Ages and Renaissance.

Dorian mode. The church mode that corresponds to the white piano keys starting on D and has D as its final.

Final. The goal pitch and point of rest in a church mode. Analogous to tonic, but a different term is used since modes are different from functional common-practice harmony.

Ionian mode. The church mode that corresponds to the white piano keys starting on C and has C as its final. Analogous to the C-major scale; used infrequently before the common-practice era.

Lydian mode. The church mode that corresponds to the white piano keys starting on F and has F as its final.

Mixolydian mode. The church mode that corresponds to the white piano keys starting on G and has G as its final.

Phrygian mode. The church mode that corresponds to the white piano keys starting on E and has E as its final.

Locrian mode. The church mode that corresponds to the white piano keys starting on B and has B as its final. Practically speaking, it was not used in the Middle Ages or Renaissance, being more theoretical.

Extended Tertian Harmony in Classical Music

As seen in Chapter 23, stacking a third on top of a triad creates a seventh chord. The addition of the dissonant seventh intensifies the drive of the harmonic progression. As with all prominent dissonances, the seventh resolves down by step as it moves into the next chord.

Continuing to stack thirds beyond the seventh chord creates *extended tertian harmonies*. Like seventh chords, these are named after the interval between the root and the topmost note. Various qualities are possible. Figure D.1 features the dominant chord because it is the most common.

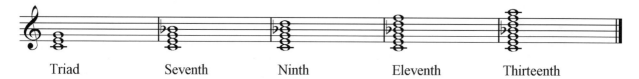

| Triad | Seventh | Ninth | Eleventh | Thirteenth |

Figure D.1 Extended tertian harmonies

These chords appear in this appendix and not in the main book because, while common in rock and twentieth-century classical music and pervasive in jazz and show tunes, they rarely happen in common-practice music. This lack depends somewhat on my definition of them. If a dissonance resolves while the harmony sustains, I analyze it as a nonchord tone. If the dissonance remains for the entire duration and resolves into the next chord, I consider it extended tertian. Refer back to figure 23.2 for an example with seventh chords versus suspensions. Some argue that if the dissonance is present longer than its resolution, even if the harmony does not change, then it should be counted as a chord member. I obviously disagree. If a simpler explanation exists using common dissonances, I prefer this analysis to the invocation of extended tertian harmonies.

Having said that, here are guidelines and a few examples for using these harmonies. When they do appear in the common-practice era, they are on root-position chords, usually dominants. The reason for the root-position requirement is that, with so many notes present, the root becomes ambiguous, and the ear hears the bass as the root. Theorists also require that a seventh be present to hear the extended tertian harmony; otherwise, the ear hears the addition as an "added note," a distinctly jazz and show tune gesture. As with sevenths, the dissonances in extended tertian harmonies are all prominent and therefore resolve down by step into the next chord.

NINTH CHORDS

Five or more voices are necessary to have a complete ninth chord. In four voices, composers omit the fifth, as they do with most incomplete harmonies. Figures D.2 and D.3 show examples of an apparent and a real V^9 chord. In the Beethoven passage, the harmony briefly looks like a V^9, but in the context, the A in the bass serves as a pedal point, and the harmony is a vii^{o7} above this pedal. Chopin uses a true V^9 in the excerpt from his prelude. Although the resolution of the dissonance switches hands, it still occurs in the same voice. The seventh also resolves down by step as it should, although it is suspended briefly. (Look closely and you will see parallel fifths in the example too.) Another excellent example of a V^9 is at the climax of Wagner's "Prelude" from *Tristan und Isolde*.

Figure D.2 Beethoven, Piano Sonata, op. 28, II, mm. 9–17

Figure D.3 Chopin, Prelude, op. 28, no. 7

ELEVENTH CHORDS

In figure D.4, Brahms uses an eleventh chord on a pre-dominant harmony. While the dissonance in the melody functions as an accented passing tone, it works as an eleventh too since it holds for the entire chord and resolves into the next harmony. The omission of the third of the chord is typical, although more relevant in a major harmony, where the third and eleventh form a minor ninth. Many composers find that interval too pungent for their tastes.

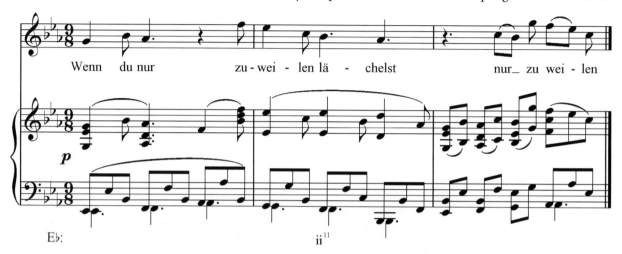

Figure D.4 Brahms, "Wenn du nur zuweilen lächelst" from *Lieder und Gesänge*, op. 57, no. 2 ("If Only You Would Smile Sometimes" from *Songs*)

THIRTEENTH CHORDS

The four essential pitches to a thirteenth chord are the root, third, seventh, and thirteenth. If more voices are available, more pitches can be added in. They are infrequent enough that I do not have a good example of a thirteenth chord from the common-practice literature. Figure D.5 shows an excerpt from Tchaikovsky. Given that the D ornaments a C, and because the V^7 is in inversion (the tenor and bass cross voices), I would consider the D an escape tone instead of a V^{13}. The V^9 is a true V^9.

Figure D.5 Tchaikovsky, Overture, *Casse-Noisette* (*The Nutcracker*)

TERMINOLOGY

Extended tertian harmony. Chords that stack additional thirds on top of the seventh chord. Extended tertian harmonies include ninth, eleventh, and thirteenth chords.

Ninth chord. A harmony containing a seventh chord plus the pitch a ninth above the root.

Eleventh chord. A harmony containing a seventh chord plus the pitch a fourth above the root.

Thirteenth chord. A harmony containing a seventh chord plus the pitch a sixth above the root.

Extended tertian harmony results by stacking thirds on top of a chord beyond the standard seventh. Ninth, eleventh, and thirteenth chords are possible. While they occur frequently in jazz and popular music, they rarely occur in the common-practice era. More typical of the time is a suspension or appoggiatura that resolves while the chord still sustains, rather than a chordal dissonance that resolves into the next harmony.

WORKBOOK

Analyze the given excerpt from "Mein schöner Stern!" by Schumann. Are the extended tertian harmonies real or are they apparent, caused by standard dissonances?

Schumann, "Mein schöner Stern!" from *Minnespiel* ("My Beautiful Star!" from *Love Game*)

GLOSSARY

A

Accented neighbor tone. A strong dissonance approached by step and left by step in the opposite direction.

Accented passing tone. A strong dissonance approached by step and left by step in the same direction.

Accented six–four. A linear chord that falls in a strong metrical position and appears as a second-inversion triad. The functioning harmony is revealed when the dissonances creating the apparent six–four resolve.

Accidental. A symbol that changes a pitch, moving it up or down a half step (sharps, flats, and naturals) or a whole step (double flats and sharps).

Added note. A pitch, usually a sixth or ninth above the root, added to a basic triad.

Aeolian mode. The church mode that corresponds to the white piano keys starting on A and having A as its final. Analogous to the natural minor scale.

Alberti bass. An accompaniment pattern that involves a repeating arpeggiation of a chord in order to provide rhythmic energy and motion.

Altered dominants. Dominant chords with either a raised or lowered fifth.

Anacrusis. Also called a pick-up. An incomplete measure at the start of a piece, usually consisting of just the upbeat, that leads into the first full measure.

Antecedent. The first phrase of a period, which ends in a weaker cadence, thereby creating a sense of incompletion. See also *period*.

Anticipation. A weak dissonance, approached by step and resolved by common tone.

Applied dominant. A chromatic chord that has a dominant function in a key other than the main one that is functioning. An applied dominant places emphasis on the following harmony by exploiting the dominant–tonic relationship in that key. Synonymous with *secondary dominant*. See also *tonicization*.

Appoggiatura. A strong dissonance approached by leap and left by step in the opposite direction. Usually approached by leap up and resolved by step down.

Arpeggio. A melodic presentation of a chord. The melody skips through the pitches of the harmony.

Augmented sixth chords. A family of chords—Italian, French, and German—containing an augmented sixth between L$\hat{6}$ (in the bass) and R$\hat{4}$ (which appears in any of the upper voices). Leads to V.

Augmented triad. A chord with two consecutive major thirds. It contains an augmented fifth.

Authentic cadence. A cadence in which dominant moves to tonic, providing closure.

B

Backward rhythm. A rhythmic pattern in which the shorter durations land in stronger positions, leading to a syncopated effect.

Backward tie. A tie in which a shorter duration is tied to a longer one.

Beat. The underlying pulse of a piece of music.

Binary form. A two-part developmental form with the structure AB.

Blue note. A melodic ornament, common in blues, in which a pitch is flatted relative to the diatonic pitch. Blue notes usually fall on scale degrees $\hat{3}$ and $\hat{7}$ and occasionally $\hat{5}$.

Blues scale. The scale created by combining the pitches that frequently occur in blues songs; the major scale plus the blues notes L$\hat{3}$ and L$\hat{7}$.

Bridge. In popular songs, a section that contrasts from the verses and chorus and that usually appears only once.

C

Cadence. An arrival in music, indicating the completion of a thought. Cadences can end a phrase, a section, or an entire piece. Cadences of varying strengths are used for different effects.

Cadential six–four. A dissonant harmony in which the dominant chord at a cadence is embellished by what appears to be a second-inversion tonic chord but is actually a collection of nonchord tones.

Cantus firmus. Meaning "fixed song." The given melody in a species counterpoint exercise, to which a newly composed melody is added.

Chain of suspensions. A pattern in which the resolution of one suspension serves as the preparation for the next.

Chart. Also called chord chart. A popular music notational system in which chord names are written above the song lyrics.

Chorale style. An arrangement emulating church hymns, with four voices moving in a relatively homorhythmic pattern.

Chord. A harmonic sonority in which three or more notes sound simultaneously.

Chorus. The section of a song that returns several times with the same music and lyrics.

Chromatic. A description of music that contains pitches from outside the scale of the functioning key.

Chromatic neighbor tone. A weak nondiatonic dissonance approached by half step and left by half step in the opposite direction.

Chromatic passing tone. A weak nondiatonic dissonance approached by half step and left by half step in the same direction.

Church modes. The scales in frequent use prior to the common-practice period, mostly associated with the Middle Ages and Renaissance.

Circle of fifths. An organizing of the keys and key signatures by ascending/descending perfect fifths around a circle, to show the gradual addition of accidentals to the key signatures. It also shows how closely related keys are to one another.

Clef. A symbol used at the beginning of a staff to indicate the staff's location in pitch space. The clef indicates where a particular pitch is located on that staff.

Close spacing. A chord voicing in which the upper three voices are placed as closely together as possible. The three voices contain adjacent chord members. Contrasts with *open spacing*.

Closely related keys. Keys that differ by 0–1 accidentals from the original key. Contrasts with *distantly related keys*.

Coherence. A melody or piece contains an internal consistency, resulting from the reuse of a limited set of ideas, rhythms, motives, or patterns.

Common-tone modulation. An abrupt modulation by chromatic third in which one voice keeps a common tone and two others move by step or half step. Synonymous with *mediant relation* and *third relation*.

Compound interval. An interval that is larger than an octave.

Compound time. A meter in which the beat subdivides into three or six smaller units.

Conjunct. Melodic motion by step, whole or half.

Consequent. The second phrase in a period, ending in a stronger cadence, thereby providing a sense of closure. See also *period*.

Consonance. Two pitches that sound pleasant and stable together

Consonant six–four. A second-inversion chord that expands a more stable inversion through melodic motion or an arpeggio in the bass.

Continuous form. A form in which the sections are harmonically open.

Contrary motion. When two voices move in opposite directions.

Contrasting form. A form in which the sections of the piece provide variety and contrast from one another.

Counterpoint. Combining two or more independent melodies in a way to make a satisfying whole.

Cross-relation. Two forms of the same pitch, such as D♮ and D♭, appearing on adjacent chords in different voices.

D

Deceptive cadence. A cadence in which the dominant resolves to a chord other than tonic, usually the submediant, creating a surprising effect and an increase in tension.

Deceptive motion. Motion from a dominant-function chord to a harmony other than tonic, usually the submediant.

Developmental form. A form in which later sections develop motives from earlier sections.

Diatonic. When all pitches in the music fit within the scale of a single key.

Diminished seventh chord. A seventh chord containing a diminished triad and a diminished seventh. Also called a *fully diminished seventh chord*.

Diminished triad. A chord with two consecutive minor thirds. It contains a diminished fifth.

Direct (chromatic) modulation. A modulation that results from the alteration of a chord or from abruptly shifting into the new key. A modulation that does not use a pivot chord.

Direct perfect consonances. When two voices move to a perfect consonance by similar motion.

Disjunct. Melodic motion by an interval greater than a second. Motion by leap.

Dissonance. Two pitches that clash with each other, sounding unstable and pulling toward a resolution. Any intervals not listed in the consonances are dissonances.

Distantly related keys. Keys that differ by two or more accidentals from the original key. Contrasts with *closely related keys*.

Dominant. (1) Scale degree $\hat{5}$ or (2) the chord built upon this scale degree, V, or (3) the second most important harmonic functional level in a key, consisting of the V and vii° chords. The role of these chords is to provide the most tension of any harmonies and to pull back to tonic.

Dorian mode. The church mode that corresponds to the white piano keys starting on D and having D as its final.

Dotted note. A note with an additional 50 percent durational value. A dotted note sustains 1.5 times the duration of the undotted note.

Double neighbor tone. A dissonance in which both the upper and lower neighbor tones are given in succession with a leap of a third between them.

Downbeat. The first and strongest beat of a measure.

Duple time. A meter that contains two beats in every measure. It has an accentuation pattern of Strong–Weak.

E

Eleventh chord. A harmony containing a seventh chord plus the pitch a fourth above the root.

Enharmonic. Describes two notes that sound the same but have different spellings, such as C♯ and D♭.

Enharmonic reinterpretation. An abrupt modulation achieved by using enharmonic spellings of pitches in a chord, thereby changing the key in which it is functioning.

Escape tone. A weak dissonance approached by step and left by leap in the opposite direction.

Extended tertian harmony. Chords that stack additional thirds on top of the seventh chord. Extended tertian harmonies include ninth, eleventh, and thirteenth chords.

F

Fifth. The chord member that is a fifth above the root when the triad is in root position.

Figure. In figured bass, the number below the bass note, indicating the intervals present above that pitch.

Figured bass. A Baroque shorthand for harmony, in which chords are represented by a bass notes with numbers below them. See also *figure*.

Final. The goal pitch and point of rest in a church mode. Analogous to tonic, but a different term is used since modes are different from functional common-practice harmony.

First inversion. A chord with its third in the bass.

Forward rhythm. A rhythmic pattern in which the shorter durations fall in weaker positions, driving into the next strong beat.

Forward tie. A tie in which a longer duration is tied to an equal or shorter one.

French sixth. The augmented sixth chord containing scale degrees L$\hat{6}$, R$\hat{4}$, $\hat{1}$, and $\hat{2}$.

Fully diminished seventh chord. A seventh chord containing a diminished triad and a diminished seventh. Also called a *diminished seventh chord.*

Functionality. A system in which a musical element has a particular role. In common-practice tonality, the scale degrees and chords within a key serve characteristic functions.

G

Generic interval. Also called size. The distance between two pitches ignoring accidentals and counting only letter names.

German sixth. The augmented sixth chord containing scale degrees L$\hat{6}$, R$\hat{4}$, $\hat{1}$, and L$\hat{3}$.

Grand staff. A treble staff and bass staff joined together.

H

Half cadence. A cadence ending on V, containing tension and requiring the music to continue.

Half-diminished seventh chord. A seventh chord with a diminished triad and a minor seventh.

Half step. The smallest distance between two notes in common-practice music.

Harmonically closed. When a section of a piece ends with an authentic cadence in the same key it began in.

Harmonically open. When a section of a piece ends with a half cadence in the same key it began in or with any cadence in a different key than it opened in.

Harmonic interval. The distance between two intervals sounding simultaneously. Contrasts with *melodic interval.*

Harmonic minor scale. The minor scale that uses the two tendency tones, L$\hat{6}$ and R$\hat{7}$; the pitches most frequently used in chords in minor.

Harmonic rhythm. The rate of change of the harmony.

Homophony. A style of music characterized by melody with an accompaniment.

Homorhythmic. When all voices move together, with no rhythmic diversity between them.

Hook. In popular music, the most ingratiating riff in a song.

I

Imperfect authentic cadence. A cadence ending with dominant moving to tonic, in which the soprano ends on $\hat{1}$ or $\hat{3}$, the V is in inversion, or a vii° appears instead of a V.

Imperfect consonance. A consonance in which the two pitches are less stable and have a fuller sound than the perfect consonances. Intervals in this category are the m3, M3, m6, and M6.

Incomplete neighbor tone. A dissonance that is approached or left by leap.

Interval. The distance between two pitches.

Ionian mode. The church mode that corresponds to the white piano keys starting on C and having C as its final. Analogous to the C-major scale; not used much before the common-practice era.

Italian sixth. The augmented sixth chord containing scale degrees L$\hat{6}$, R$\hat{4}$, and $\hat{1}$.

K

Key signature. A listing of the accidentals in a key, placed at the start of the staff, to set the accidentals for the duration of the music.

L

Layer. In popular music, one of several melodic ideas used simultaneously to embellish a harmony, providing energy and some contrapuntal interest.

Lead sheet. A notational system in popular music that uses a single staff for the melody with the chord names written above it.

Ledger lines. Lines drawn through, above, or below notes that are above or below a staff. They extend the staff's range past the five lines.

Linear chord. A harmony that is created and driven by melodic issues rather than harmonic function.

Local chromaticism. A chromatic note that has implications only for itself and the next note. Contrasts with *long-range chromaticism.*

Locrian mode. The church mode that corresponds to the white piano keys starting on B and having B as its final. Practically speaking, it was not used in the Middle Ages or Renaissance; more theoretical.

Long-range chromaticism. A chromatic note that indicates a larger effect on the overall structure of the music, such as a modulation. Contrasts with *local chromaticism.*

Lydian mode. The church mode that corresponds to the white piano keys starting on F and having F as its final.

M

Major–minor seventh chord. A seventh chord consisting of a major triad and a minor seventh. In classical music, a major–minor seventh chord will function as a dominant. In popular music, the major–minor seventh is one of the most common sonorities and can appear on any scale degree.

Major seventh chord. A seventh chord containing a major triad and a major seventh.

Major triad. A chord with a minor third on top of a major third. It contains a perfect fifth, and the third of the chord is a major third above the root.

Measure. A section of music that contains one unit of the recurring accentuation pattern of the meter. Every measure starts with the strongest beat of the pattern.

Mediant. Scale degree $\hat{3}$ or the chord built upon this scale degree, iii (or III in minor).

Mediant relation. An abrupt harmonic shift by a chromatic third. Synonymous with *third relation* and *common-tone modulation.*

Melodic interval. The distance between two adjacent notes in a melody, one heard immediately after the other. Contrasts with *harmonic interval.*

Melodic minor scale. The minor scale that incorporates the tendency tones in a melodic context, when they must appear adjacent to each other. R$\hat{6}$ and R$\hat{7}$ are used when ascending, where the leading tone is necessary to return to tonic. L$\hat{6}$ and L$\hat{7}$ are used when descending, where the tendency tone to $\hat{5}$ is desired.

Meter. The recurring accentuation pattern in the beats of a piece of music.

Minor seventh chord. A seventh chord with a minor triad and a minor seventh.

Minor triad. A chord with a major third on top of a minor third. It contains a perfect fifth, and the third of the chord is a minor third above the root.

Mixolydian mode. The church mode that corresponds to the white piano keys starting on G and having G as its final.

Modal mixture (modal borrowing). Borrowing scale degrees or chords from the parallel major or minor mode. Can also be viewed as mixing the two modes together.

Mode. In its broadest sense, any collection of pitches in a scale. In this book, it usually means the difference between a major and a minor key.

Modulation. A change of key. Moving to a new tonal center.

Motives. Short, distinctive melodic ideas that provide coherence to a melody and to an entire work. They may involve rhythm or rhythm and pitch.

Musical alphabet. The letters used as note names. Runs from A to G and then repeats.

N

Natural minor scale. The minor scale that includes the pitches corresponding to the key signature.

Neapolitan. ♭II. Functions as a pre-dominant.

Neighbor chord. A subordinate harmony in which the chord returns to the preceding chord.

Neighbor six–four. A linear second-inversion chord that results from neighbor tones in the upper voices.

Neighbor tone. A weak dissonance approached by step and left by step in the opposite direction.

Ninth chord. A harmony containing a seventh chord plus the pitch a ninth above the root.

Nonchord tone. Another term for a dissonance in the context of chords. Synonymous with *nonharmonic tone*.

Nonharmonic tone. Another term for a dissonance in the context of chords. Synonymous with *nonchord tone*.

O

Oblique motion. When one voice moves while the other remains on the same pitch

Octave equivalence. Pitches an octave apart sound similar and behave the same way in tonal music.

Open spacing. A chord voicing in which the upper three voices are placed so that at least one chord member is missing between two adjacent voices. Contrasts with *close spacing*.

P

Parallel keys. The major and minor scales that share a tonic pitch.

Parallel motion. When two voices move in the same direction, starting and ending on the same generic interval

Parallel perfect consonances. When two of the same perfect consonance occur in the same two voices on adjacent harmonies. The voices must move to constitute parallel perfect consonances; repeated notes do not count.

Passing chord. A subordinate harmony in which the bass serves as a passing tone, connecting two inversions of the same chord or two harmonies with the same function.

Passing six–four. A linear second-inversion chord built on a passing tone in the bass. Frequently occurs in conjunction with a voice exchange.

Passing tone. A weak dissonance approached by step and left by step in the same direction.

Pedal point. A nonchord tone approached and left by common tone. The pedal point sustains while the harmony changes.

Pedal six–four. A linear second-inversion chord that results from a pedal point in the bass.

Perfect authentic cadence. A cadence ending with V → I, in which the soprano line ends on tonic. Since there is both harmonic and melodic closure, it is the most final sounding cadence.

Perfect consonance. A consonance in which the two pitches are so complementary that they sound extremely stable and somewhat "hollow." Intervals in this category are the P1, P8, and P5

Period. A frequent thematic structure in common-practice music, consisting of two phrases, the antecedent and consequent. The antecedent ends with a weaker cadence, while the consequent ends with a stronger one, creating an effect of a question and an answer.

Phrase-level analysis. An analysis that identifies the structurally significant harmonies. Phrase-level analyses can be done on several levels, providing more details or more of the big picture.

Phrygian cadence. A half cadence in minor, in which iv^6 moves to V.

Phrygian mode. The church mode that corresponds to the white piano keys starting on E and having E as its final.

Pitch. A tone with a distinct frequency.

Pitch class. The group of pitches that are the same when using octave equivalence. All pitches with the same note name, regardless of octave.

Pivot chord. During a modulation, a chord that is diatonic in both the old and new key and that serves to smooth the transition between the two tonal centers.

Plagal cadence. A cadence ending with a pre-dominant, usually IV, moving to I.

Power chords. Guitar chords, common in hard rock, that use open fifths on the low strings of the guitar.

Pre-dominant. The third most important functional level, consisting of the ii and IV (ii° and iv) chords. These chords serve two functions, either leading to dominant or returning to tonic.

Prolongation. The expansion and elaboration of a main harmony or functional level through other chords.

Q

Quadruple time. A meter that contains four beats in every measure. It has a recurring accentuation pattern of Strong–Weak–Semistrong–Weak.

Quality. The difference in sound between ambiguous sonorities, such as intervals with the same generic size but different accidentals or chords with the same root but a different third or fifth.

R

Realization. In figured bass, the writing/completion of all voices.

Refrain. In a song, a single line that recurs with the same music and lyrics.

Relative keys. The major and minor keys that share a key signature. The relative minor is located a minor third below its relative major.

Retrogression. Harmonic motion from dominant to pre-dominant, which is not appropriate in the common-practice style.

Riff. In popular music, a short melodic idea that repeats. A riff is usually instrumental.

Root. The bottom note in a chord stacked in thirds.

Root position. Describes a chord with its root in the bass.

Rounded binary form. A two-part developmental form with the structure AB in which the B section includes a repeat of material from the A section.

S

SATB. Indicates a chorale-style setting using soprano, alto, tenor, and bass.

Scale. A collection of pitches, presented as a stepwise succession of notes. Used to organize the pitches present in a key or section of music.

Scale degree. The identification of a pitch and its melodic role through its position in the scale of the functioning key. Each scale degree has its own name and can be represented by an Arabic numeral with a caret above it.

Schenkerian analysis. An approach to harmonic analysis that emphasizes structurally more important harmonies and ignores subordinate harmonies as a way to elucidate phrase-level and larger formal patterns.

Second inversion. Describes a chord with its fifth in the bass.

Secondary dominant. A chromatic chord that has a dominant function in a key other than the main one that is functioning. A secondary dominant places emphasis on the following harmony by exploiting the dominant–tonic relationship in that key. Synonymous with *applied dominant*. See also *tonicization*.

Sectional form. A form in which the sections are harmonically closed.

Sectional modulation. A modulation in which a phrase or section ends in one key and the next phrase or section begins in a different key.

Sequence. The repetition of a musical pattern at successively higher or lower pitches, each time moving by the same interval.

Seventh chord. A dissonant harmony is which a seventh has been added to the basic triad. Another third has been stacked on top of the fifth in the chord.

Similar motion. When two voices move in the same direction, starting and ending on different generic intervals

Simple interval. An interval between and including a unison and an octave.

Simple time. A meter in which the beat subdivides into two or four smaller units.

Species counterpoint. A pedagogical tool for teaching the basics of composition, specifically focusing on voice leading and dissonance control.

Split third. A sonority in jazz and the blues in which a harmony contains two thirds, both the diatonic pitch as well as its flatted blue note analogue.

Staff. Five parallel lines used to indicate pitch.

Submediant. Either scale degree $\hat{6}$ or the chord built upon this scale degree, vi (or VI in minor).

Subordinate harmonies. A chord that serves to prolong a different, more structurally important, harmony.

Subordinate progression. A progression that serves to prolong a single, structurally significant harmony.

Sus chord. A harmony in popular music that includes an added fourth while omitting the third.

Suspension. A strong dissonance, approached by common tone and resolved by step down.

T

Tempo. The rate of the beats in a piece of music. Measured in beats per minute (bpm).

Tendency tones. Scale degrees that contain tension and pull to a particular resolution. They result when an unstable pitch is a half step away from a significantly more stable one.

Ternary form. A three-part contrasting form with the structure ABA'.

Tertian. A harmony built from consecutive thirds.

Third. The chord member that is a third above the root when the triad is in root position.

Third inversion. Describes a seventh chord with its seventh in the bass.

Third relation. An abrupt harmonic shift by chromatic third. Synonymous with *mediant relation* and *common-tone modulation*.

Thirteenth chord. A harmony containing a seventh chord plus the pitch a sixth above the root.

Tie. A symbol that stretches between two notes, indicating that their durations are combined.

Timbre. The characteristic and distinctive sound of a particular instrument.

Time signature. A symbol that indicates the meter of a piece of music.

Tonality. The functional system of common-practice music, that is, music written in the time period 1600–1900 and employing major and minor scales.

Tonic. The most important scale degree and chord in a key, being the point of rest and ultimate stability.

Tonicization. Briefly implying a different key, other than the main one that is functioning. See also *secondary dominant*.

Track. In popular music, analogous to a layer, but refers more to the recording process.

Triad. A three-note, tertian chord.

Trichord. Any three-note chord.

Triple time. A meter that contains three beats in every measure. It has an accentuation pattern of Strong–Weak–Weak.

Tritone substitution. A jazz chromatic technique in which a chord is replaced with the harmony a tritone away. Most typically, the V^7 is replaced with $\flat II^7$.

Types of motion. The possible ways two voices can move relative to each other.

U

Upbeat. The last beat in a measure. Will be a weak beat that leads into the next measure.

V

Verse. The section of a song that returns several times with the same music but different lyrics.

Voice crossing. When a lower voice sounds above a higher voice and vice-versa.

Voice exchange. A contrapuntal pattern in which two voices swap pitches, frequently through scalar melodies in contrary motion.

Voice leading. The relationship between voices as they move in music. Topics such as types of motion, voice crossings, voice overlaps, parallel perfect consonances, and direct perfect consonances are all voice-leading issues.

Voice overlap. When a higher voice moves below the position of a lower voice on the preceding beat or vice-versa.

W

Whole step. Made of two half steps. The second smallest interval in common-practice music, and pitches separated by a whole step may still be perceived as adjacent.

Page locators in italics refer to figures and tables. Scale degrees are referred to by carets, such as tonic (1̂), supertonic (2̂), etc. Specific chords are referred to by Roman numerals, such as tonic chord (I), supertonic chord (ii), etc. Specific intervals are referred to by their name and (interval) following the name.

ABOUT THE AUTHOR

Stephen C. Stone was born and raised in Pittsburgh, Pennsylvania. He studied at Oberlin College (B.A., music and chemistry), Cornell University (M.S. and Ph.D., physical chemistry), and the Peabody Conservatory (M.M. and D.M.A., music composition). His numerous commissions have ranged from pieces for solo guitar to works for full orchestra, and his compositions have been performed internationally. He previously taught music theory at Towson University. He currently teaches music theory at the Peabody Conservatory and is the former director of the music program at Johns Hopkins' Krieger School of Arts and Sciences.